CHAPTER 32: "THE YUKI-ONNA'S DILEMMA PART 3"

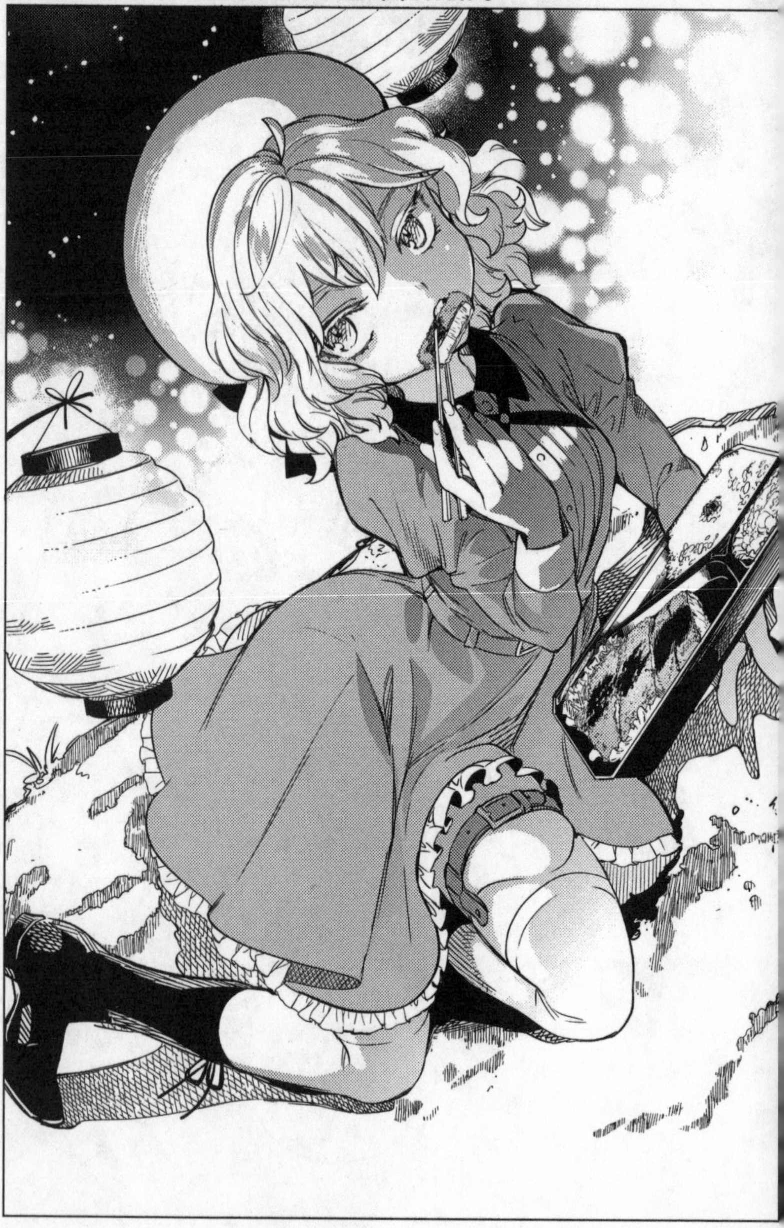

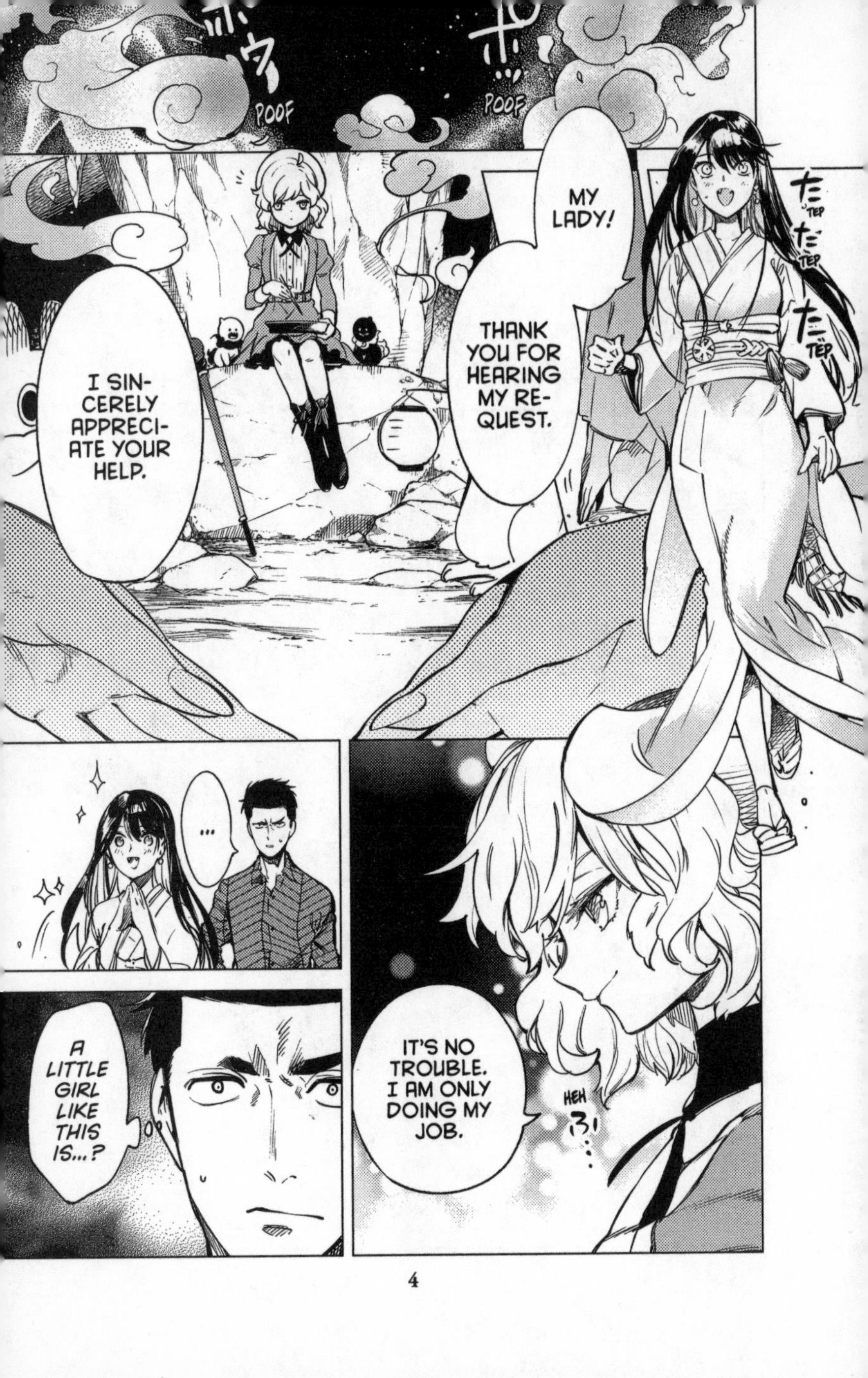
POOF
POOF
MY LADY!
TEP TEP TEP
THANK YOU FOR HEARING MY RE-QUEST.
I SIN-CERELY APPRECI-ATE YOUR HELP.
IT'S NO TROUBLE. I AM ONLY DOING MY JOB.
HEH
...
A LITTLE GIRL LIKE THIS IS...?

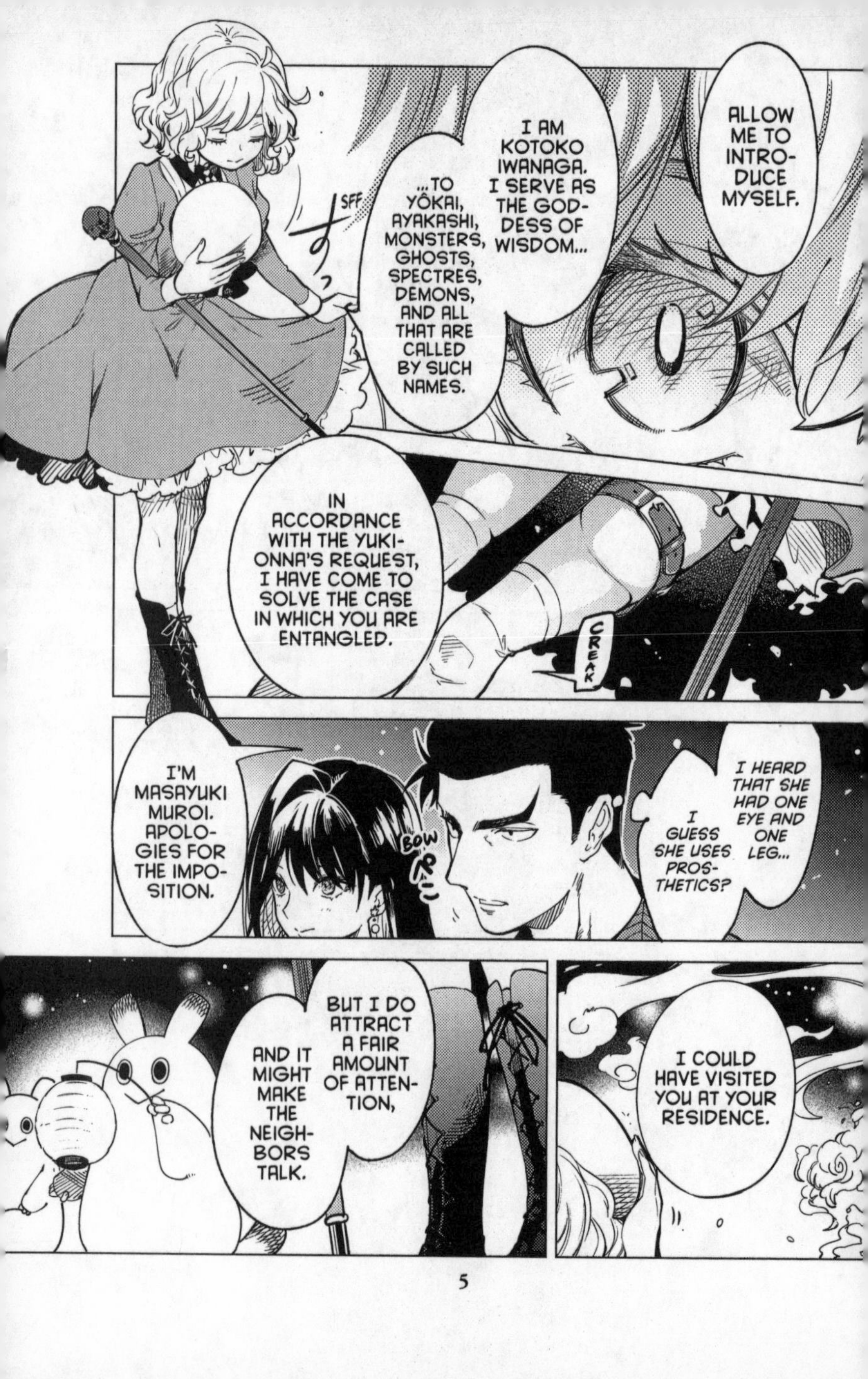

ALLOW ME TO INTRODUCE MYSELF.
I AM KOTOKO IWANAGA. I SERVE AS THE GODDESS OF WISDOM...
...TO YŌKAI, AYAKASHI, MONSTERS, GHOSTS, SPECTRES, DEMONS, AND ALL THAT ARE CALLED BY SUCH NAMES.
SFF
IN ACCORDANCE WITH THE YUKI-ONNA'S REQUEST, I HAVE COME TO SOLVE THE CASE IN WHICH YOU ARE ENTANGLED.
CREAK
I HEARD THAT SHE HAD ONE EYE AND ONE LEG...
I GUESS SHE USES PROSTHETICS?
BOW
I'M MASAYUKI MUROI. APOLOGIES FOR THE IMPOSITION.
I COULD HAVE VISITED YOU AT YOUR RESIDENCE.
BUT I DO ATTRACT A FAIR AMOUNT OF ATTENTION,
AND IT MIGHT MAKE THE NEIGHBORS TALK.

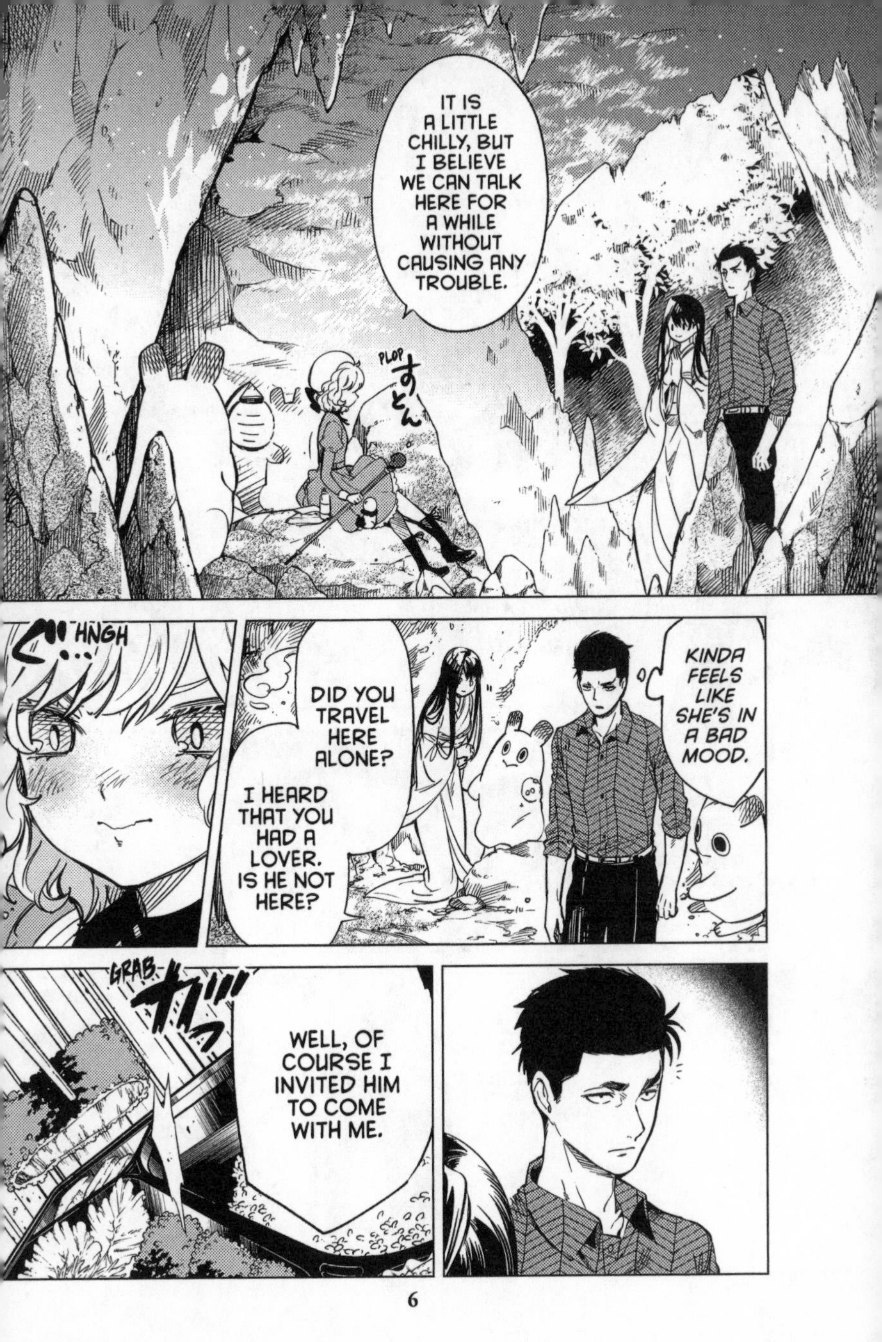
IT IS A LITTLE CHILLY, BUT I BELIEVE WE CAN TALK HERE FOR A WHILE WITHOUT CAUSING ANY TROUBLE.
PLOP
すとん
KINDA FEELS LIKE SHE'S IN A BAD MOOD.
DID YOU TRAVEL HERE ALONE?
I HEARD THAT YOU HAD A LOVER. IS HE NOT HERE?
HNGH
GRAB
WELL, OF COURSE I INVITED HIM TO COME WITH ME.

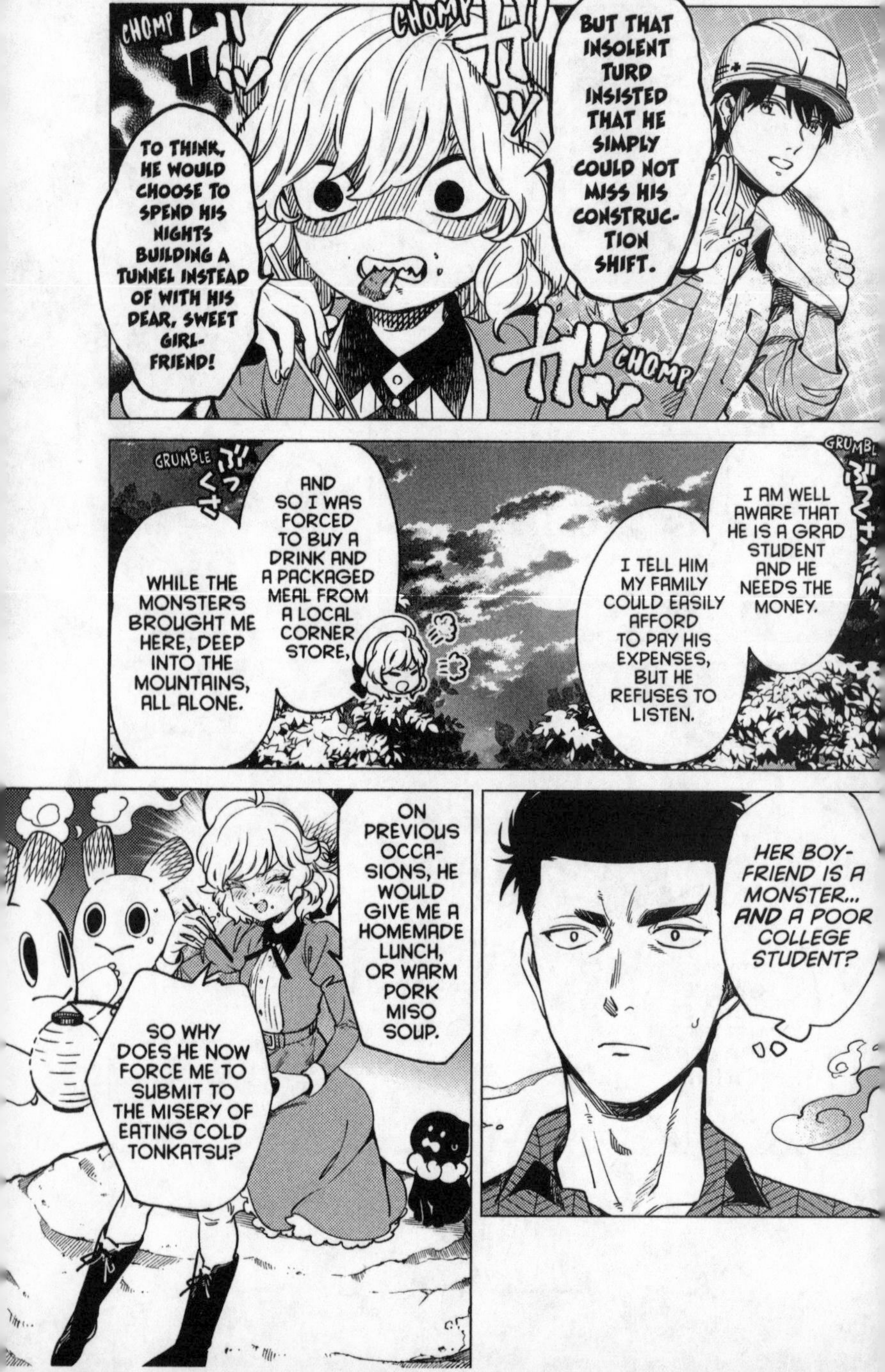
CHOMP
BUT THAT INSOLENT TURD INSISTED THAT HE SIMPLY COULD NOT MISS HIS CONSTRUCTION SHIFT.
CHOMP
TO THINK, HE WOULD CHOOSE TO SPEND HIS NIGHTS BUILDING A TUNNEL INSTEAD OF WITH HIS DEAR, SWEET GIRLFRIEND!
CHOMP
GRUMBL
I AM WELL AWARE THAT HE IS A GRAD STUDENT AND HE NEEDS THE MONEY.
I TELL HIM MY FAMILY COULD EASILY AFFORD TO PAY HIS EXPENSES, BUT HE REFUSES TO LISTEN.
GRUMBLE
AND SO I WAS FORCED TO BUY A DRINK AND A PACKAGED MEAL FROM A LOCAL CORNER STORE,
WHILE THE MONSTERS BROUGHT ME HERE, DEEP INTO THE MOUNTAINS, ALL ALONE.
HER BOYFRIEND IS A MONSTER... AND A POOR COLLEGE STUDENT?
ON PREVIOUS OCCASIONS, HE WOULD GIVE ME A HOMEMADE LUNCH, OR WARM PORK MISO SOUP.
SO WHY DOES HE NOW FORCE ME TO SUBMIT TO THE MISERY OF EATING COLD TONKATSU?

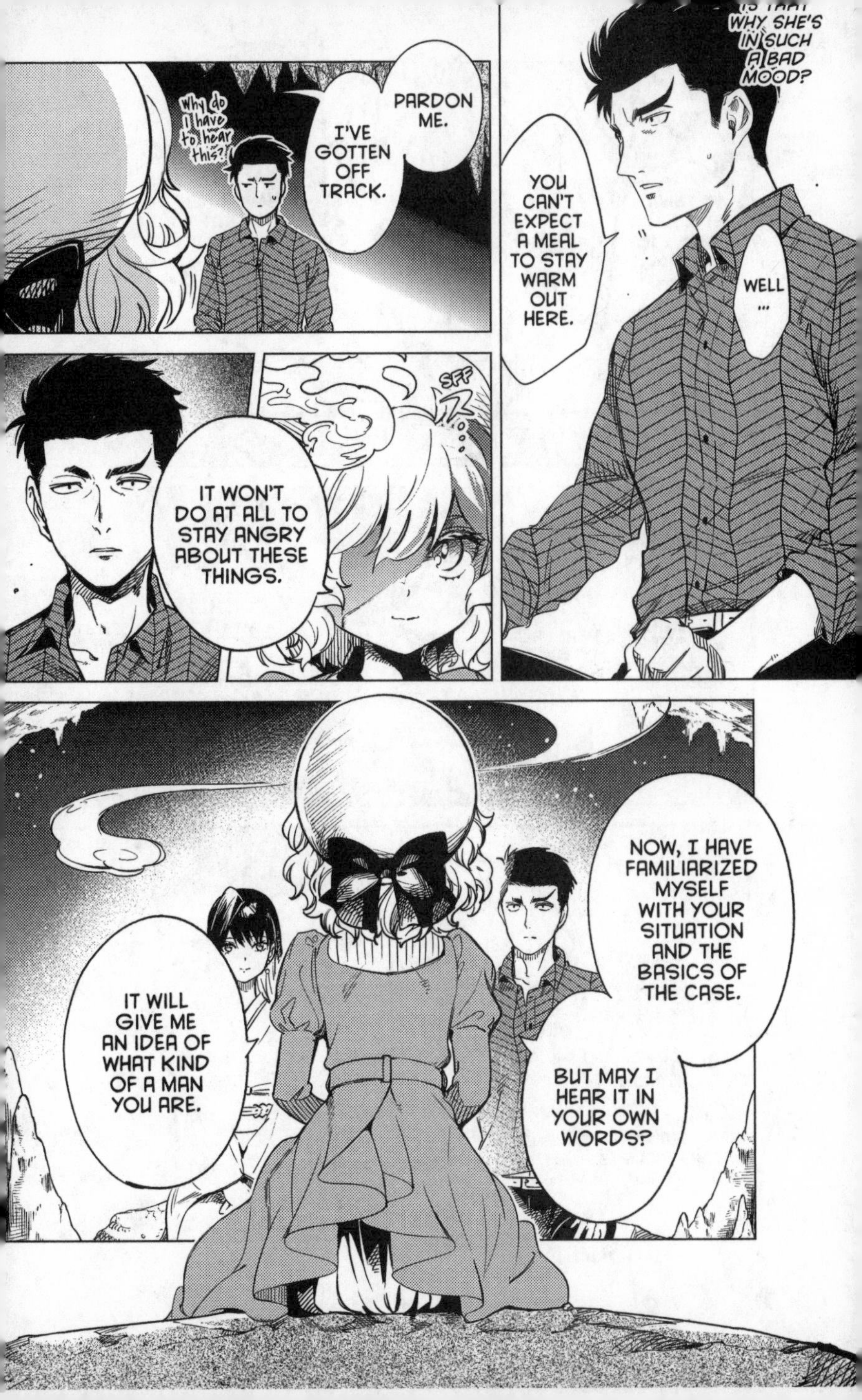
IS THAT WHY SHE'S IN SUCH A BAD MOOD?
WELL ...
YOU CAN'T EXPECT A MEAL TO STAY WARM OUT HERE.
PARDON ME.
I'VE GOTTEN OFF TRACK.
Why do I have to hear this?
SFF
IT WON'T DO AT ALL TO STAY ANGRY ABOUT THESE THINGS.
NOW, I HAVE FAMILIARIZED MYSELF WITH YOUR SITUATION AND THE BASICS OF THE CASE.
BUT MAY I HEAR IT IN YOUR OWN WORDS?
IT WILL GIVE ME AN IDEA OF WHAT KIND OF A MAN YOU ARE.

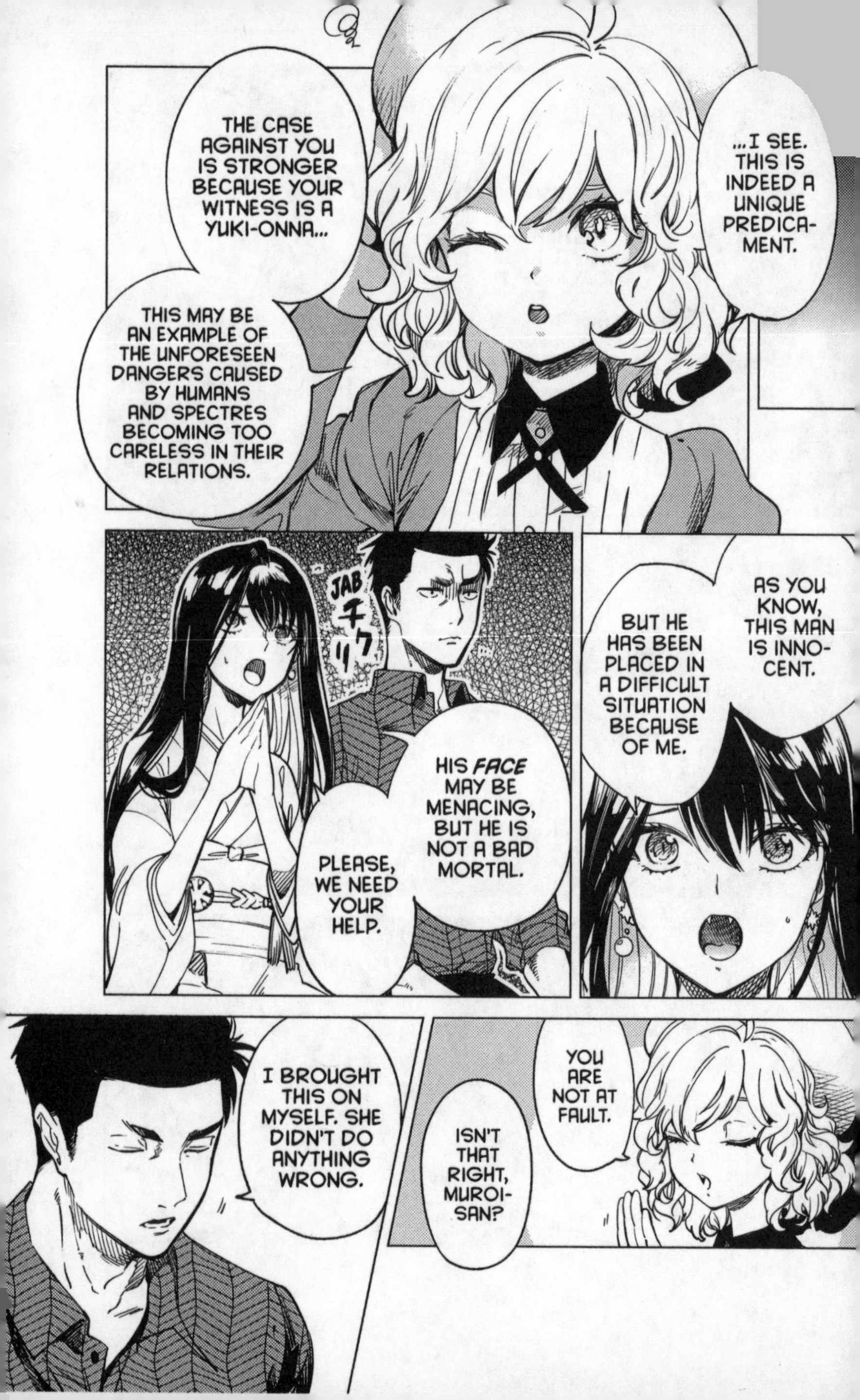
...I SEE. THIS IS INDEED A UNIQUE PREDICAMENT.
THE CASE AGAINST YOU IS STRONGER BECAUSE YOUR WITNESS IS A YUKI-ONNA...
THIS MAY BE AN EXAMPLE OF THE UNFORESEEN DANGERS CAUSED BY HUMANS AND SPECTRES BECOMING TOO CARELESS IN THEIR RELATIONS.
AS YOU KNOW, THIS MAN IS INNOCENT.
BUT HE HAS BEEN PLACED IN A DIFFICULT SITUATION BECAUSE OF ME.
JAB チクリ
HIS *FACE* MAY BE MENACING, BUT HE IS NOT A BAD MORTAL.
PLEASE, WE NEED YOUR HELP.
YOU ARE NOT AT FAULT.
ISN'T THAT RIGHT, MUROI-SAN?
I BROUGHT THIS ON MYSELF. SHE DIDN'T DO ANYTHING WRONG.

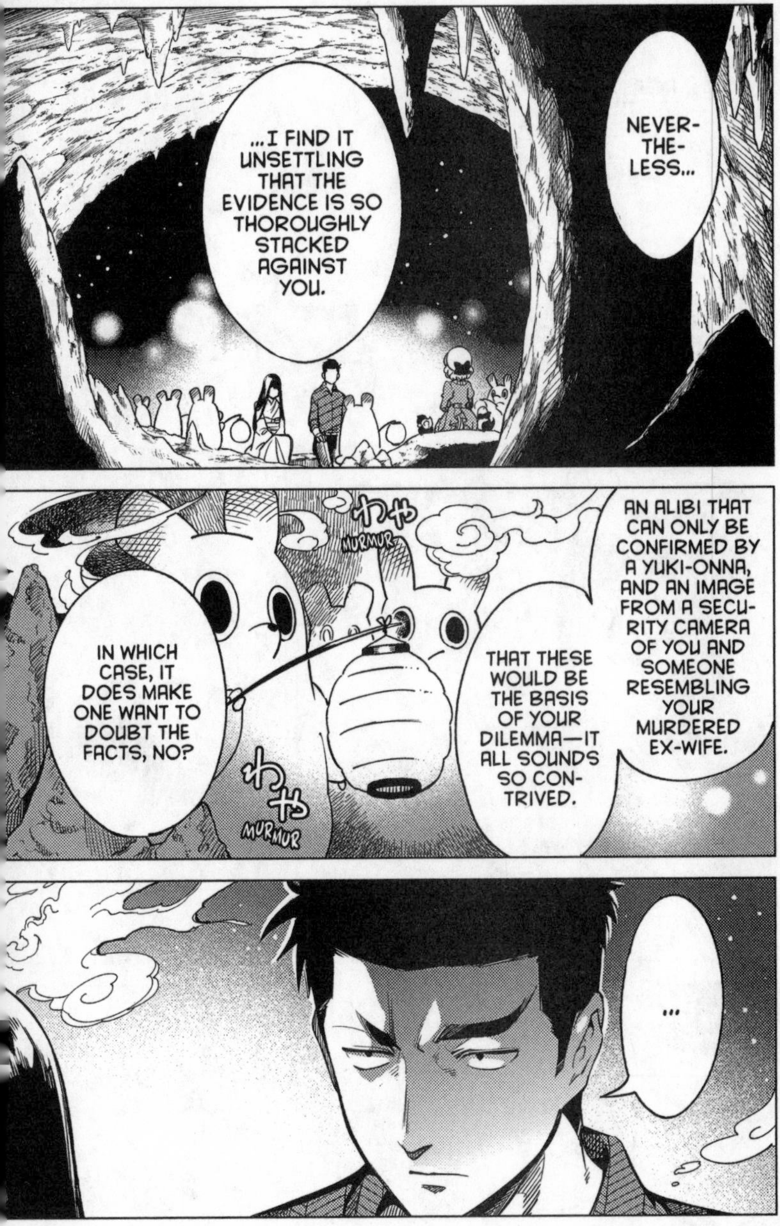
NEVER-THE-LESS...
...I FIND IT UNSETTLING THAT THE EVIDENCE IS SO THOROUGHLY STACKED AGAINST YOU.
AN ALIBI THAT CAN ONLY BE CONFIRMED BY A YUKI-ONNA, AND AN IMAGE FROM A SECURITY CAMERA OF YOU AND SOMEONE RESEMBLING YOUR MURDERED EX-WIFE.
わや
MURMUR
THAT THESE WOULD BE THE BASIS OF YOUR DILEMMA—IT ALL SOUNDS SO CONTRIVED.
IN WHICH CASE, IT DOES MAKE ONE WANT TO DOUBT THE FACTS, NO?
わや
MURMUR
...

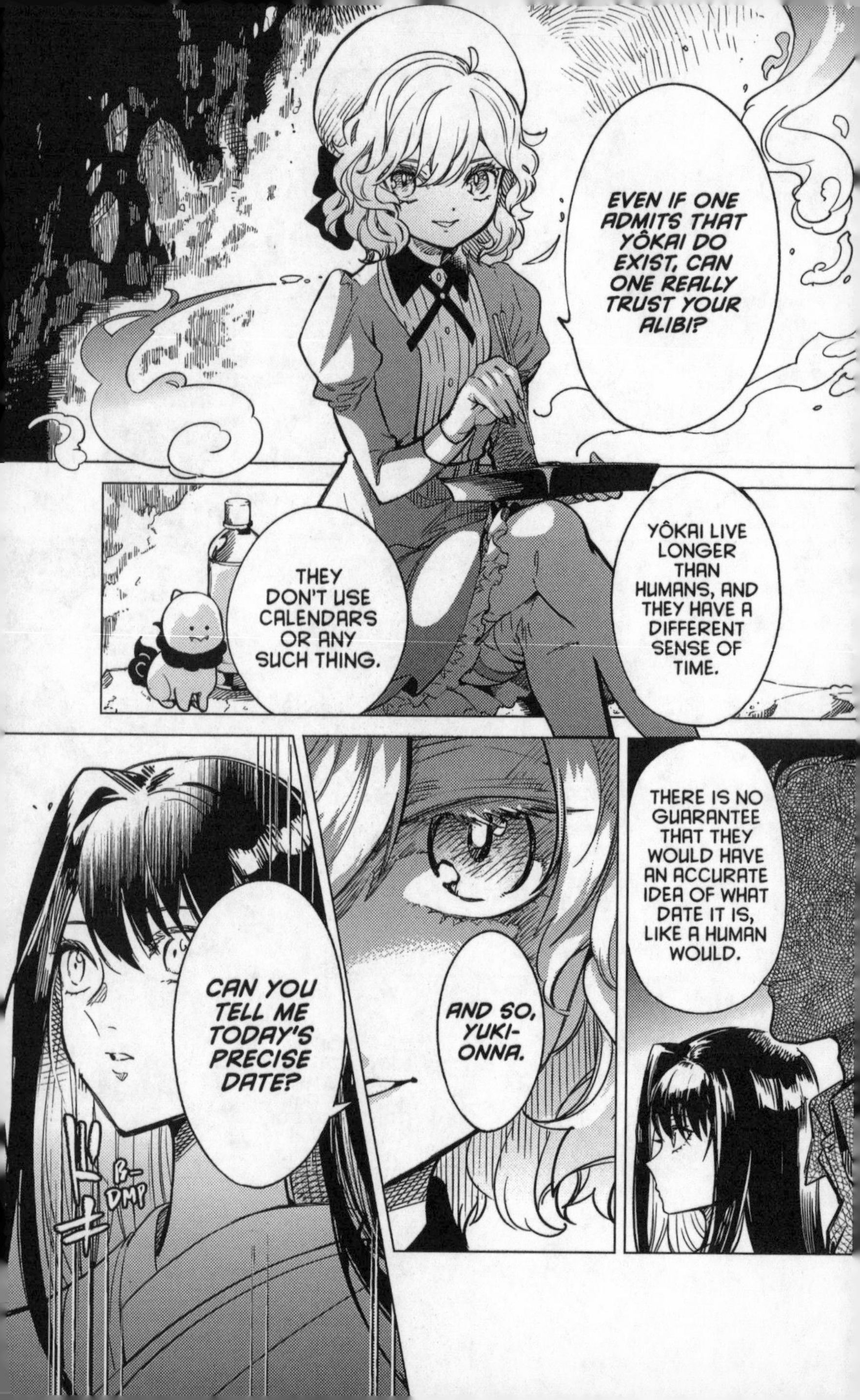
EVEN IF ONE ADMITS THAT YÔKAI DO EXIST, CAN ONE REALLY TRUST YOUR ALIBI?
YÔKAI LIVE LONGER THAN HUMANS, AND THEY HAVE A DIFFERENT SENSE OF TIME.
THEY DON'T USE CALENDARS OR ANY SUCH THING.
THERE IS NO GUARANTEE THAT THEY WOULD HAVE AN ACCURATE IDEA OF WHAT DATE IT IS, LIKE A HUMAN WOULD.
AND SO, YUKI-ONNA.
CAN YOU TELL ME TODAY'S PRECISE DATE?
B-DMP

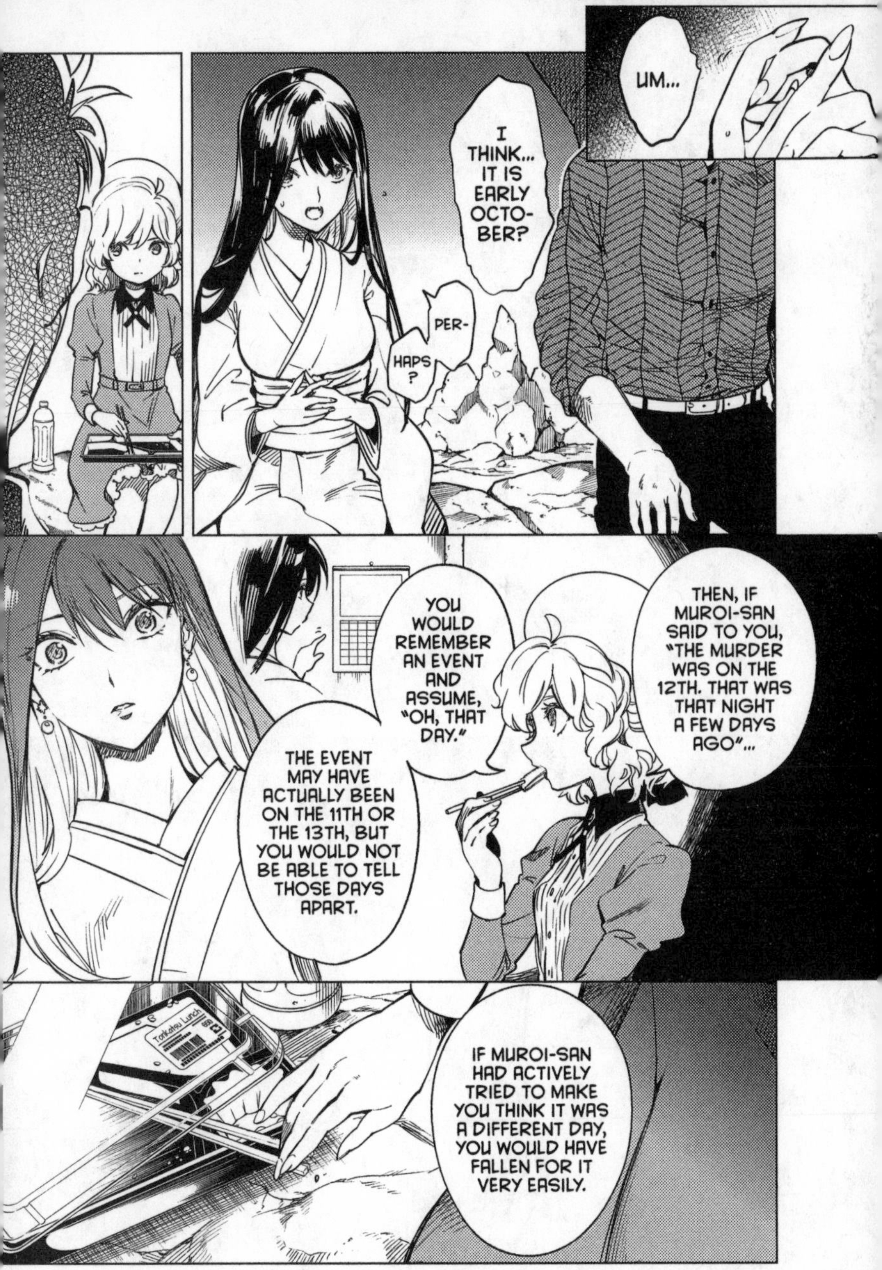
UM...
I THINK... IT IS EARLY OCTOBER?
PER-HAPS?
THEN, IF MUROI-SAN SAID TO YOU, "THE MURDER WAS ON THE 12TH. THAT WAS THAT NIGHT A FEW DAYS AGO"...
YOU WOULD REMEMBER AN EVENT AND ASSUME, "OH, THAT DAY."
THE EVENT MAY HAVE ACTUALLY BEEN ON THE 11TH OR THE 13TH, BUT YOU WOULD NOT BE ABLE TO TELL THOSE DAYS APART.
IF MUROI-SAN HAD ACTIVELY TRIED TO MAKE YOU THINK IT WAS A DIFFERENT DAY, YOU WOULD HAVE FALLEN FOR IT VERY EASILY.
Tonkatsu Lunch

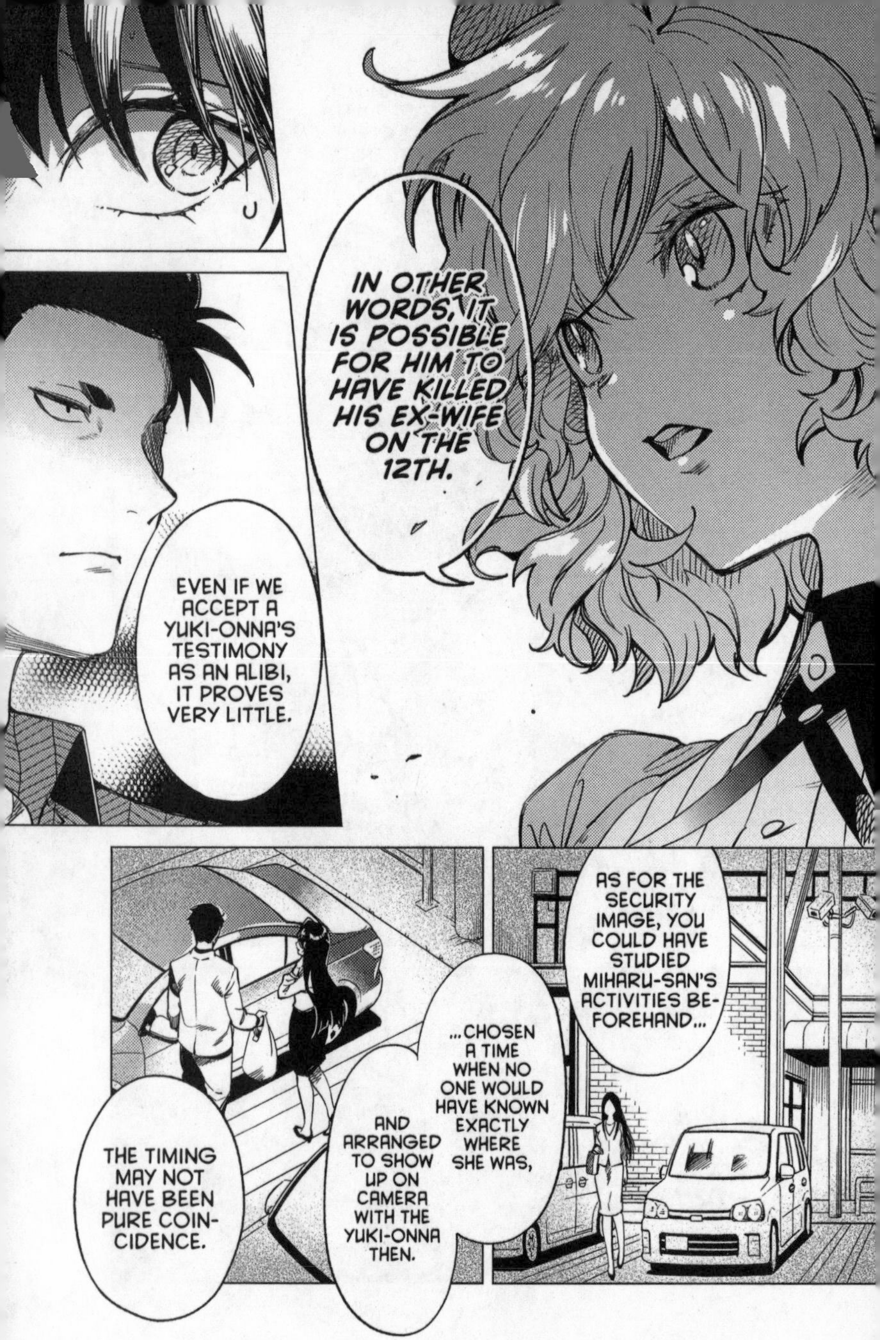
IN OTHER WORDS, IT IS POSSIBLE FOR HIM TO HAVE KILLED HIS EX-WIFE ON THE 12TH.
EVEN IF WE ACCEPT A YUKI-ONNA'S TESTIMONY AS AN ALIBI, IT PROVES VERY LITTLE.
AS FOR THE SECURITY IMAGE, YOU COULD HAVE STUDIED MIHARU-SAN'S ACTIVITIES BE-FOREHAND...
...CHOSEN A TIME WHEN NO ONE WOULD HAVE KNOWN EXACTLY WHERE SHE WAS,
AND ARRANGED TO SHOW UP ON CAMERA WITH THE YUKI-ONNA THEN.
THE TIMING MAY NOT HAVE BEEN PURE COIN-CIDENCE.

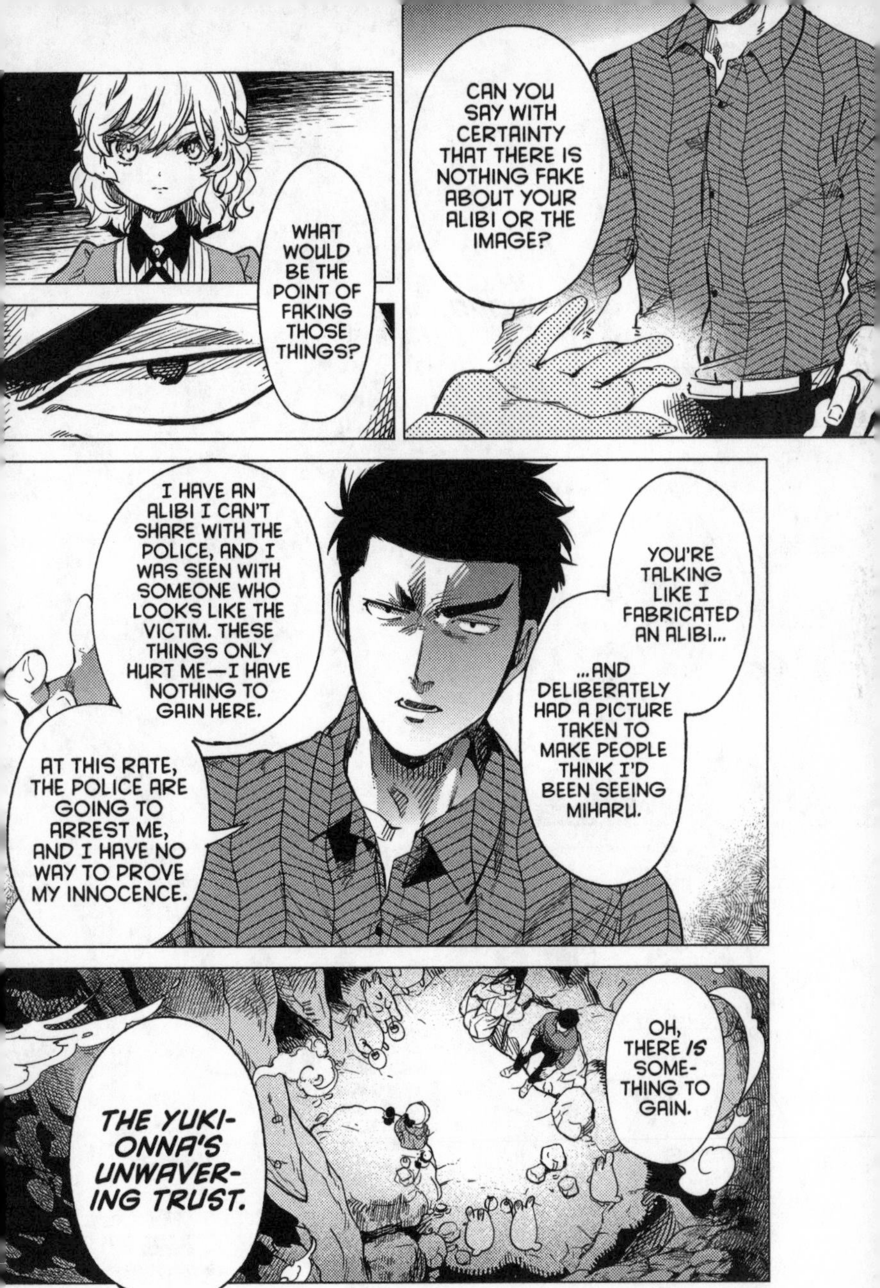
CAN YOU SAY WITH CERTAINTY THAT THERE IS NOTHING FAKE ABOUT YOUR ALIBI OR THE IMAGE?
WHAT WOULD BE THE POINT OF FAKING THOSE THINGS?
YOU'RE TALKING LIKE I FABRICATED AN ALIBI...
...AND DELIBERATELY HAD A PICTURE TAKEN TO MAKE PEOPLE THINK I'D BEEN SEEING MIHARU.
I HAVE AN ALIBI I CAN'T SHARE WITH THE POLICE, AND I WAS SEEN WITH SOMEONE WHO LOOKS LIKE THE VICTIM. THESE THINGS ONLY HURT ME—I HAVE NOTHING TO GAIN HERE.
AT THIS RATE, THE POLICE ARE GOING TO ARREST ME, AND I HAVE NO WAY TO PROVE MY INNOCENCE.
OH, THERE *IS* SOMETHING TO GAIN.
THE YUKI-ONNA'S UNWAVERING TRUST.

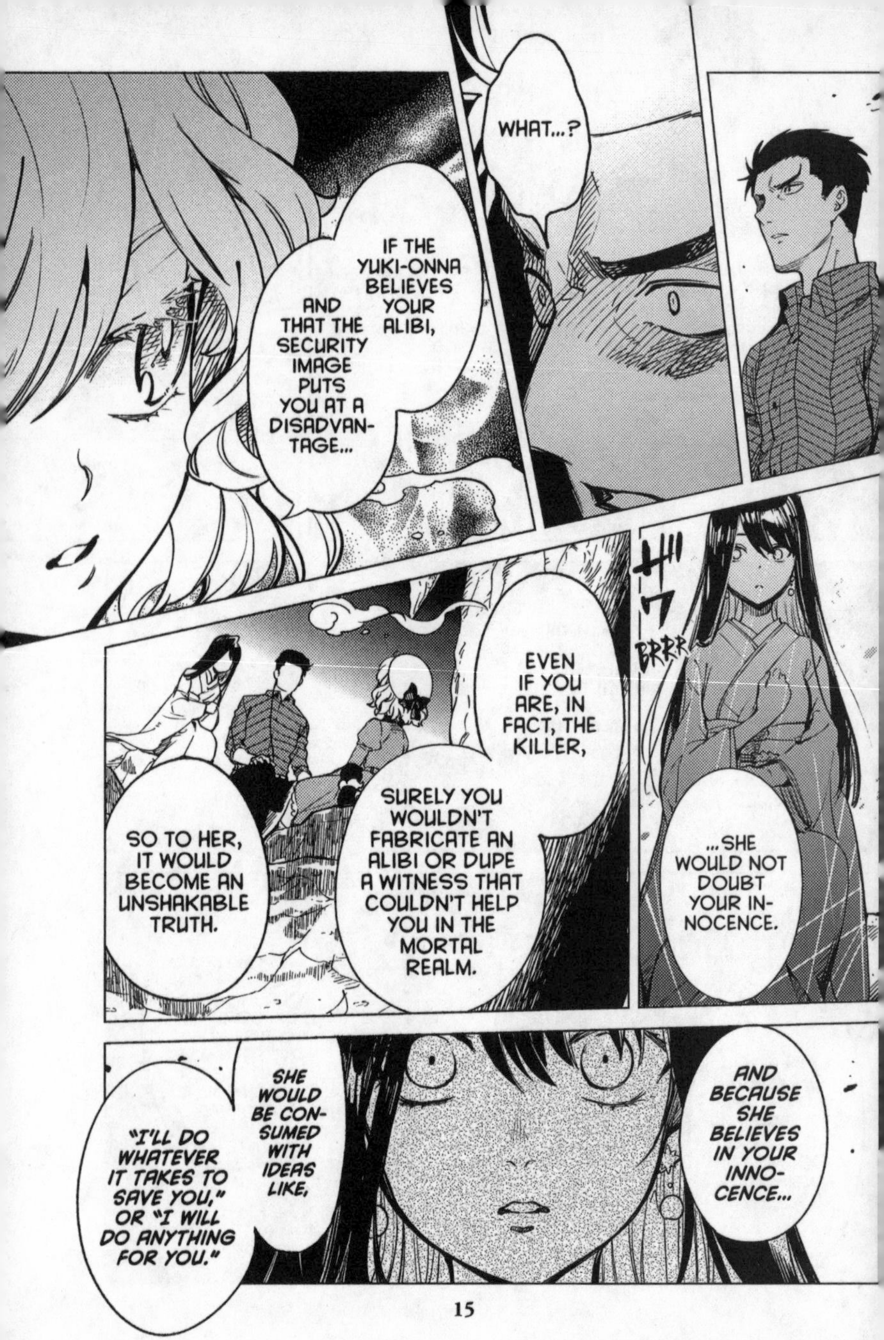
WHAT...?
IF THE YUKI-ONNA BELIEVES YOUR ALIBI, AND THAT THE SECURITY IMAGE PUTS YOU AT A DISADVANTAGE...
ザワ BRRR
...SHE WOULD NOT DOUBT YOUR INNOCENCE.
EVEN IF YOU ARE, IN FACT, THE KILLER,
SURELY YOU WOULDN'T FABRICATE AN ALIBI OR DUPE A WITNESS THAT COULDN'T HELP YOU IN THE MORTAL REALM.
SO TO HER, IT WOULD BECOME AN UNSHAKABLE TRUTH.
AND BECAUSE SHE BELIEVES IN YOUR INNOCENCE...
SHE WOULD BE CONSUMED WITH IDEAS LIKE,
"I'LL DO WHATEVER IT TAKES TO SAVE YOU," OR "I WILL DO ANYTHING FOR YOU."

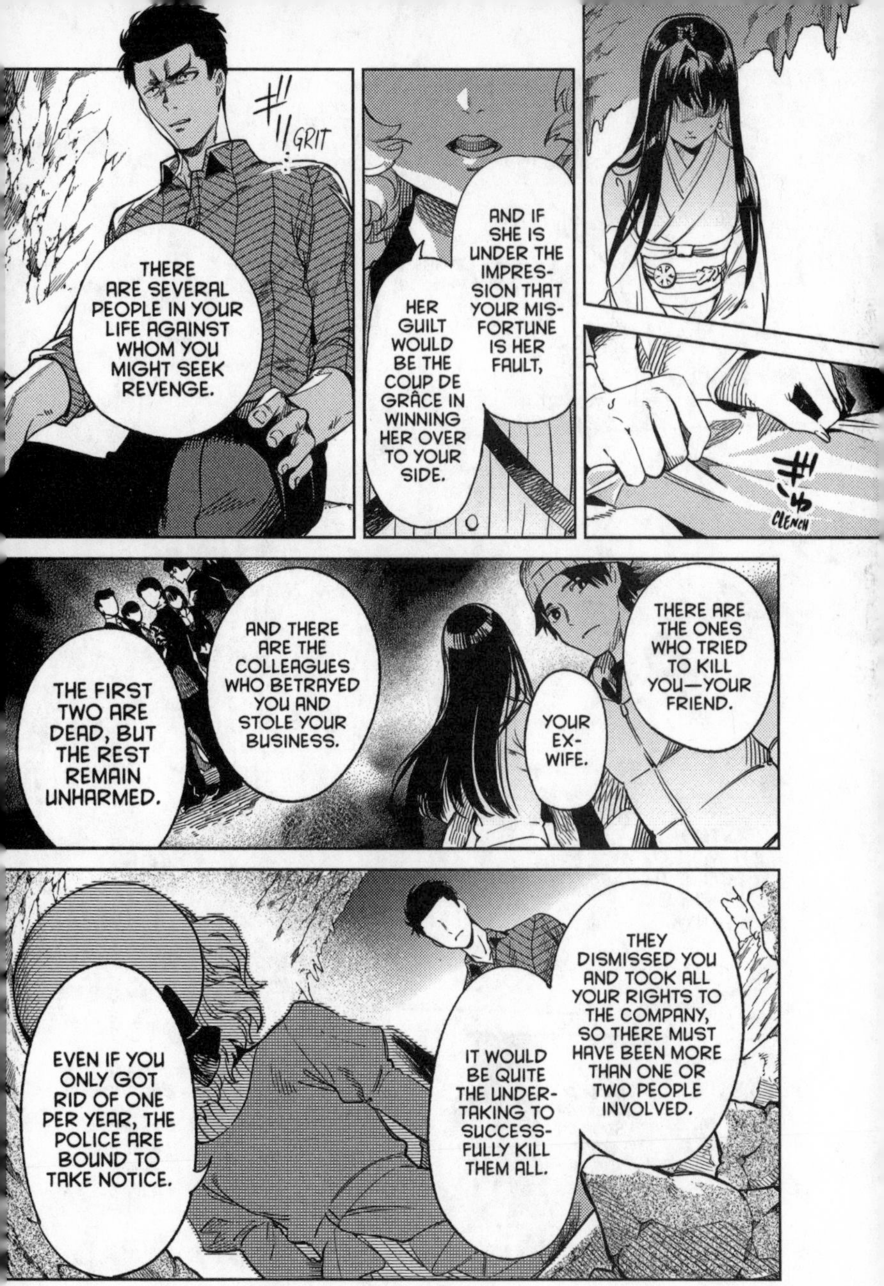
CLENCH
AND IF SHE IS UNDER THE IMPRESSION THAT YOUR MISFORTUNE IS HER FAULT,
HER GUILT WOULD BE THE COUP DE GRÂCE IN WINNING HER OVER TO YOUR SIDE.
GRIT
THERE ARE SEVERAL PEOPLE IN YOUR LIFE AGAINST WHOM YOU MIGHT SEEK REVENGE.
THERE ARE THE ONES WHO TRIED TO KILL YOU—YOUR FRIEND.
YOUR EX-WIFE.
AND THERE ARE THE COLLEAGUES WHO BETRAYED YOU AND STOLE YOUR BUSINESS.
THE FIRST TWO ARE DEAD, BUT THE REST REMAIN UNHARMED.
THEY DISMISSED YOU AND TOOK ALL YOUR RIGHTS TO THE COMPANY, SO THERE MUST HAVE BEEN MORE THAN ONE OR TWO PEOPLE INVOLVED.
IT WOULD BE QUITE THE UNDERTAKING TO SUCCESSFULLY KILL THEM ALL.
EVEN IF YOU ONLY GOT RID OF ONE PER YEAR, THE POLICE ARE BOUND TO TAKE NOTICE.

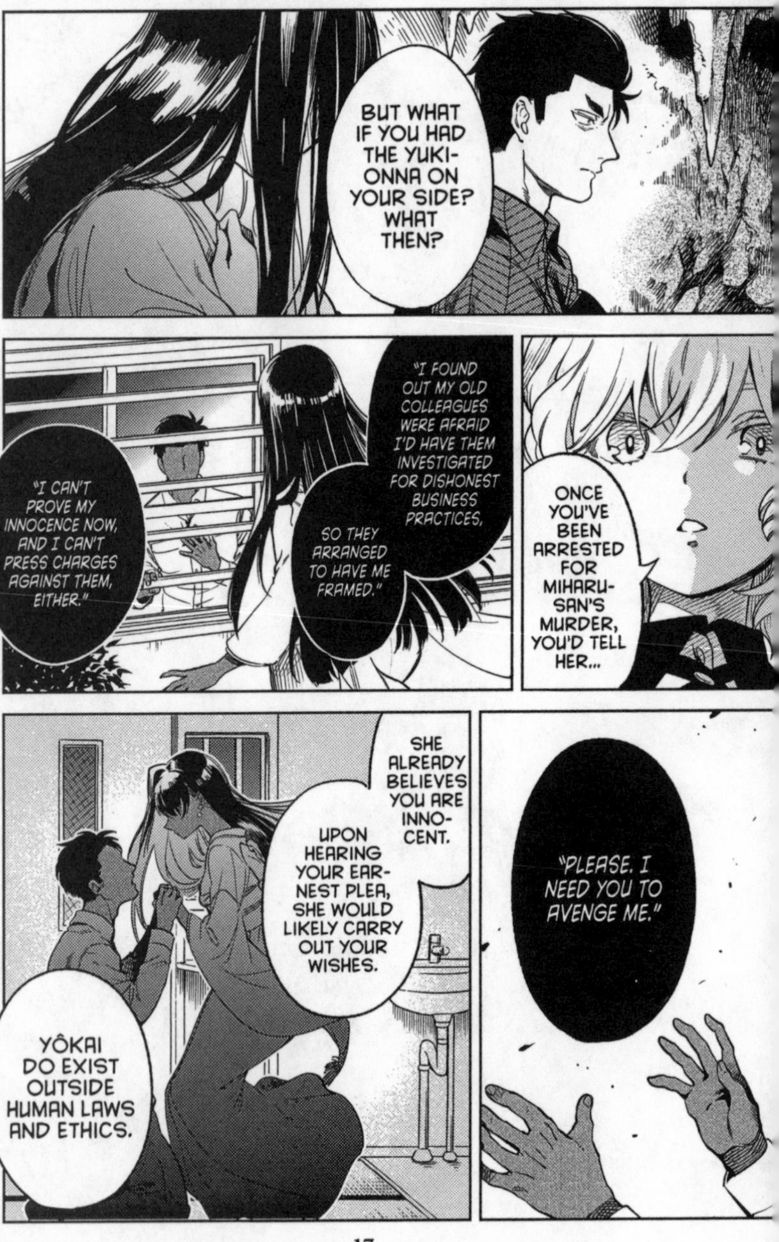
BUT WHAT IF YOU HAD THE YUKI-ONNA ON YOUR SIDE? WHAT THEN?
ONCE YOU'VE BEEN ARRESTED FOR MIHARU-SAN'S MURDER, YOU'D TELL HER...
"I FOUND OUT MY OLD COLLEAGUES WERE AFRAID I'D HAVE THEM INVESTIGATED FOR DISHONEST BUSINESS PRACTICES,
SO THEY ARRANGED TO HAVE ME FRAMED."
"I CAN'T PROVE MY INNOCENCE NOW, AND I CAN'T PRESS CHARGES AGAINST THEM, EITHER."
"PLEASE. I NEED YOU TO AVENGE ME."
SHE ALREADY BELIEVES YOU ARE INNO-CENT.
UPON HEARING YOUR EAR-NEST PLEA, SHE WOULD LIKELY CARRY OUT YOUR WISHES.
YÔKAI DO EXIST OUTSIDE HUMAN LAWS AND ETHICS.

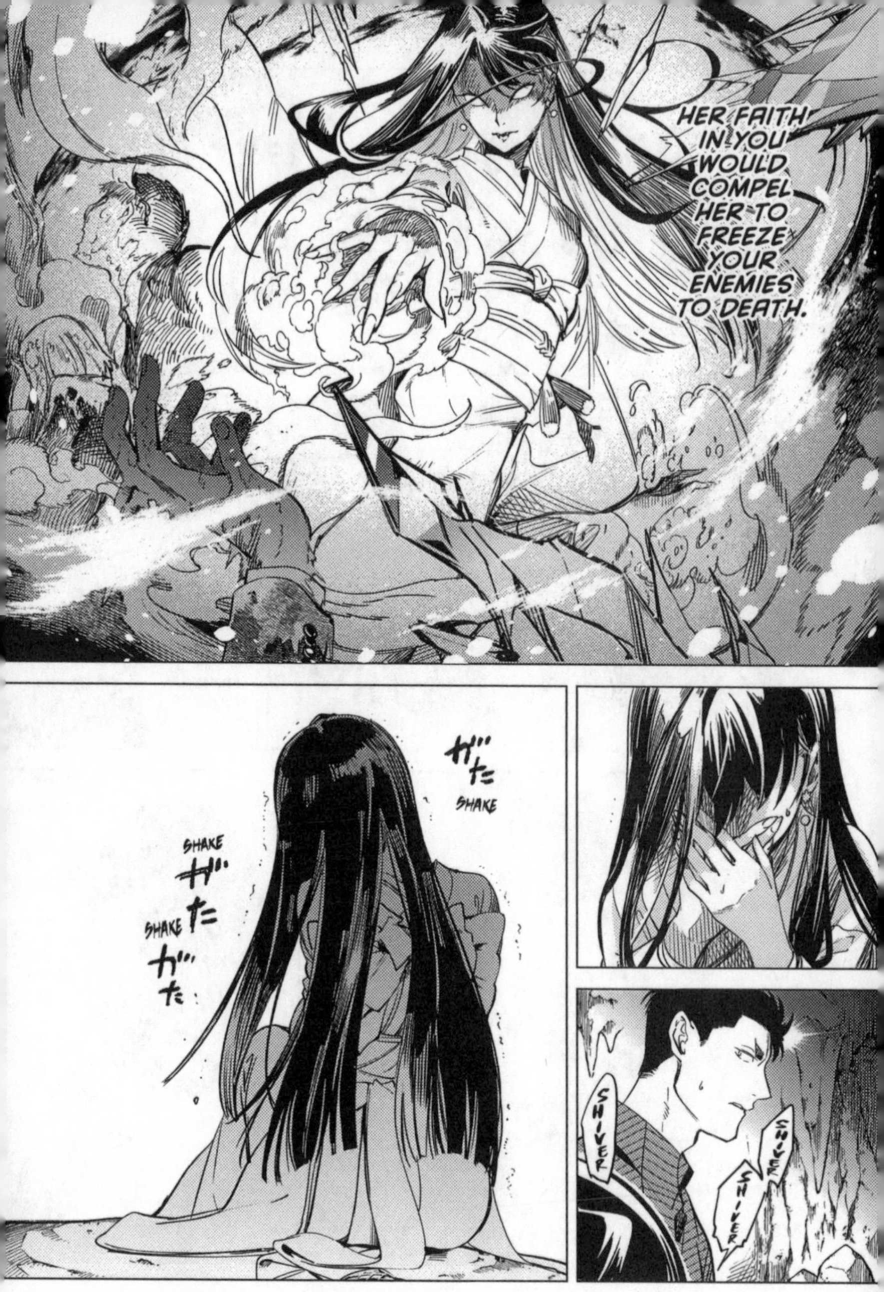
HER FAITH IN YOU WOULD COMPEL HER TO FREEZE YOUR ENEMIES TO DEATH.
SHIVER
SHIVER
SHIVER
ガた
SHAKE
SHAKE
ガた
SHAKE
ガた

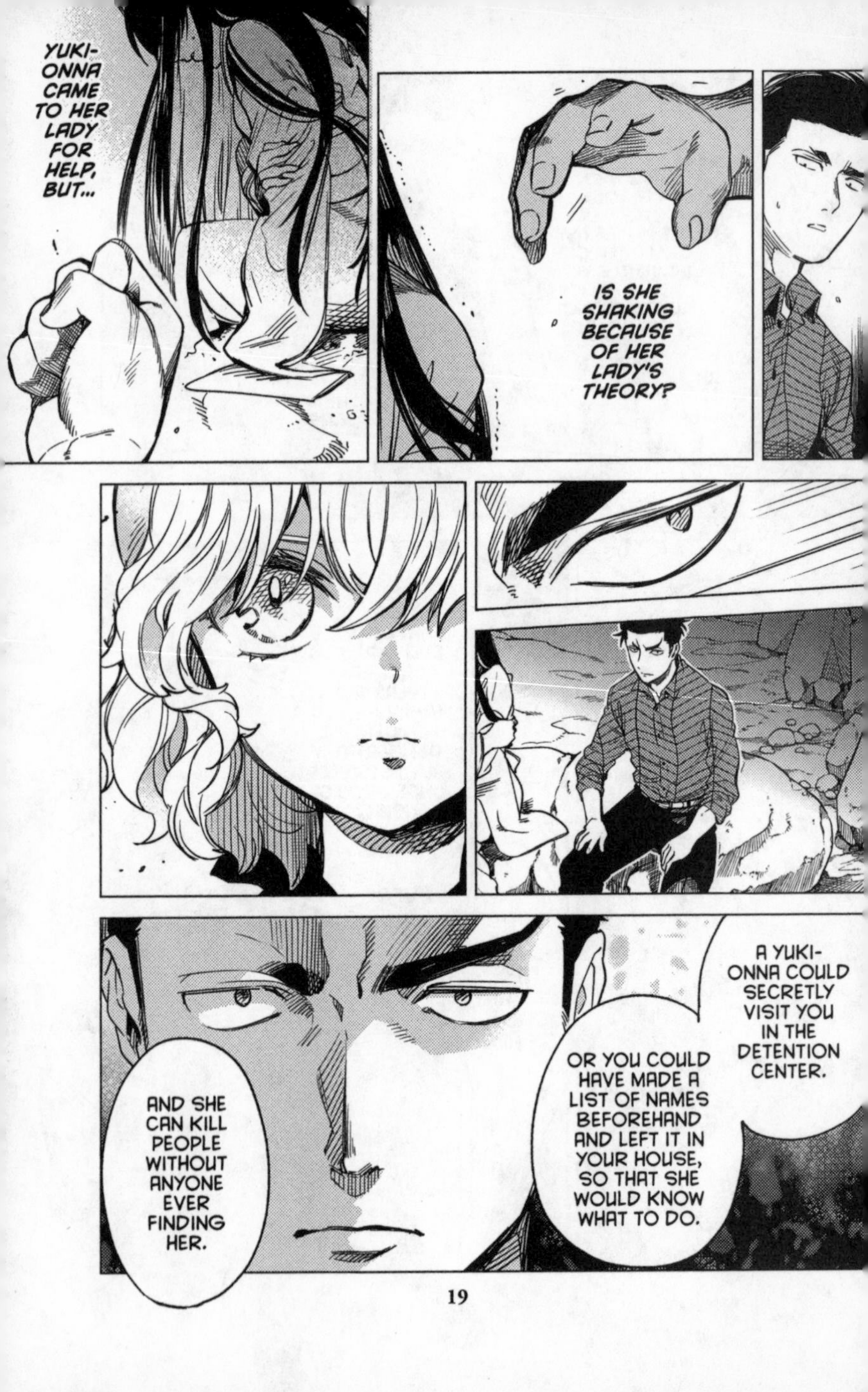
IS SHE SHAKING BECAUSE OF HER LADY'S THEORY?
YUKI-ONNA CAME TO HER LADY FOR HELP, BUT...
A YUKI-ONNA COULD SECRETLY VISIT YOU IN THE DETENTION CENTER.
OR YOU COULD HAVE MADE A LIST OF NAMES BEFOREHAND AND LEFT IT IN YOUR HOUSE, SO THAT SHE WOULD KNOW WHAT TO DO.
AND SHE CAN KILL PEOPLE WITHOUT ANYONE EVER FINDING HER.

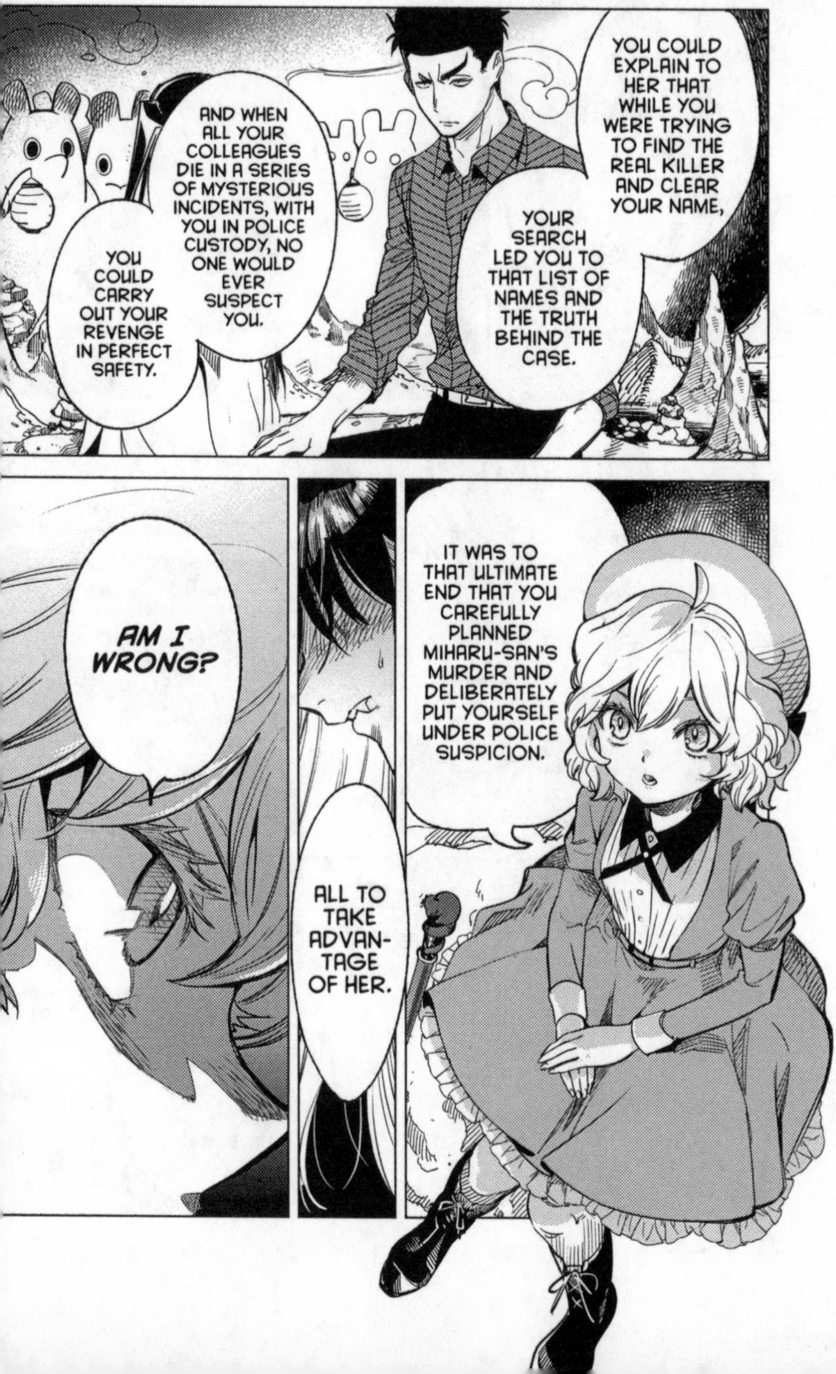
YOU COULD EXPLAIN TO HER THAT WHILE YOU WERE TRYING TO FIND THE REAL KILLER AND CLEAR YOUR NAME,
YOUR SEARCH LED YOU TO THAT LIST OF NAMES AND THE TRUTH BEHIND THE CASE.
AND WHEN ALL YOUR COLLEAGUES DIE IN A SERIES OF MYSTERIOUS INCIDENTS, WITH YOU IN POLICE CUSTODY, NO ONE WOULD EVER SUSPECT YOU.
YOU COULD CARRY OUT YOUR REVENGE IN PERFECT SAFETY.
IT WAS TO THAT ULTIMATE END THAT YOU CAREFULLY PLANNED MIHARU-SAN'S MURDER AND DELIBERATELY PUT YOURSELF UNDER POLICE SUSPICION.
ALL TO TAKE ADVAN-TAGE OF HER.
AM I WRONG?

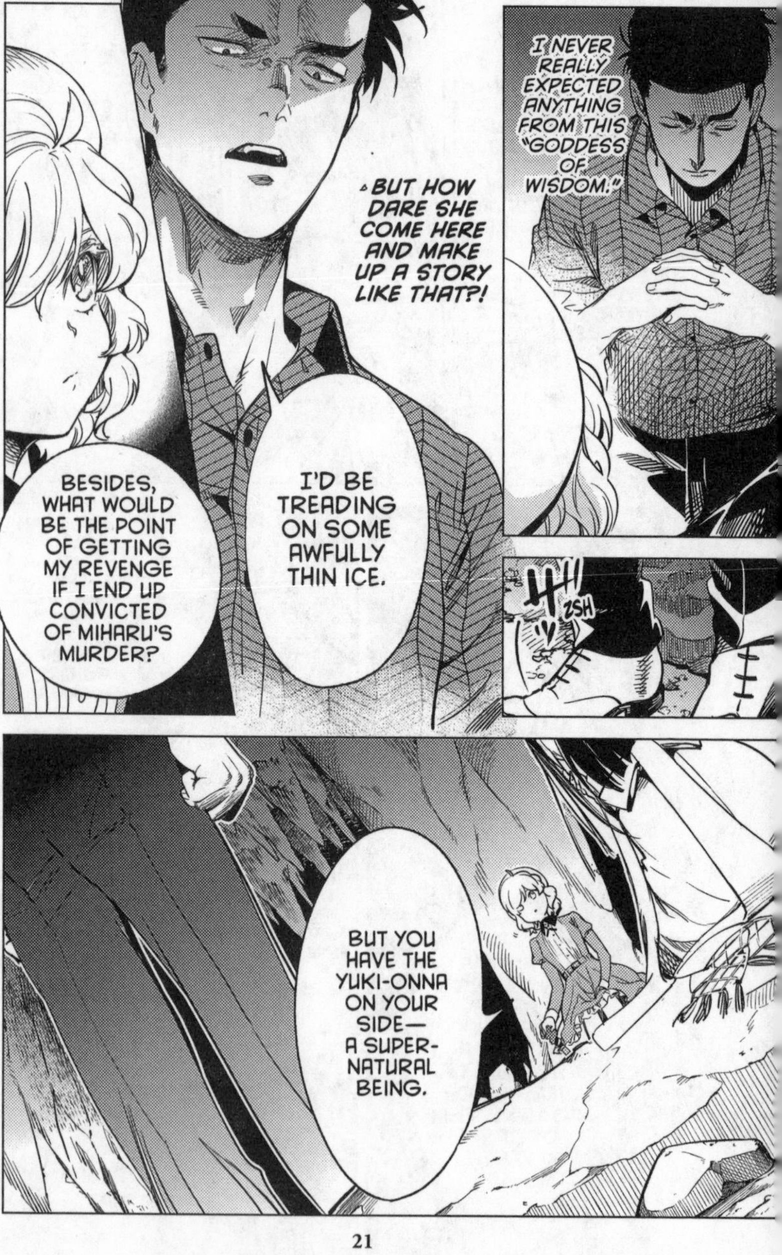
I NEVER REALLY EXPECTED ANYTHING FROM THIS "GODDESS OF WISDOM."
ZSH
BUT HOW DARE SHE COME HERE AND MAKE UP A STORY LIKE THAT?!
I'D BE TREADING ON SOME AWFULLY THIN ICE.
BESIDES, WHAT WOULD BE THE POINT OF GETTING MY REVENGE IF I END UP CONVICTED OF MIHARU'S MURDER?
BUT YOU HAVE THE YUKI-ONNA ON YOUR SIDE—A SUPER-NATURAL BEING.

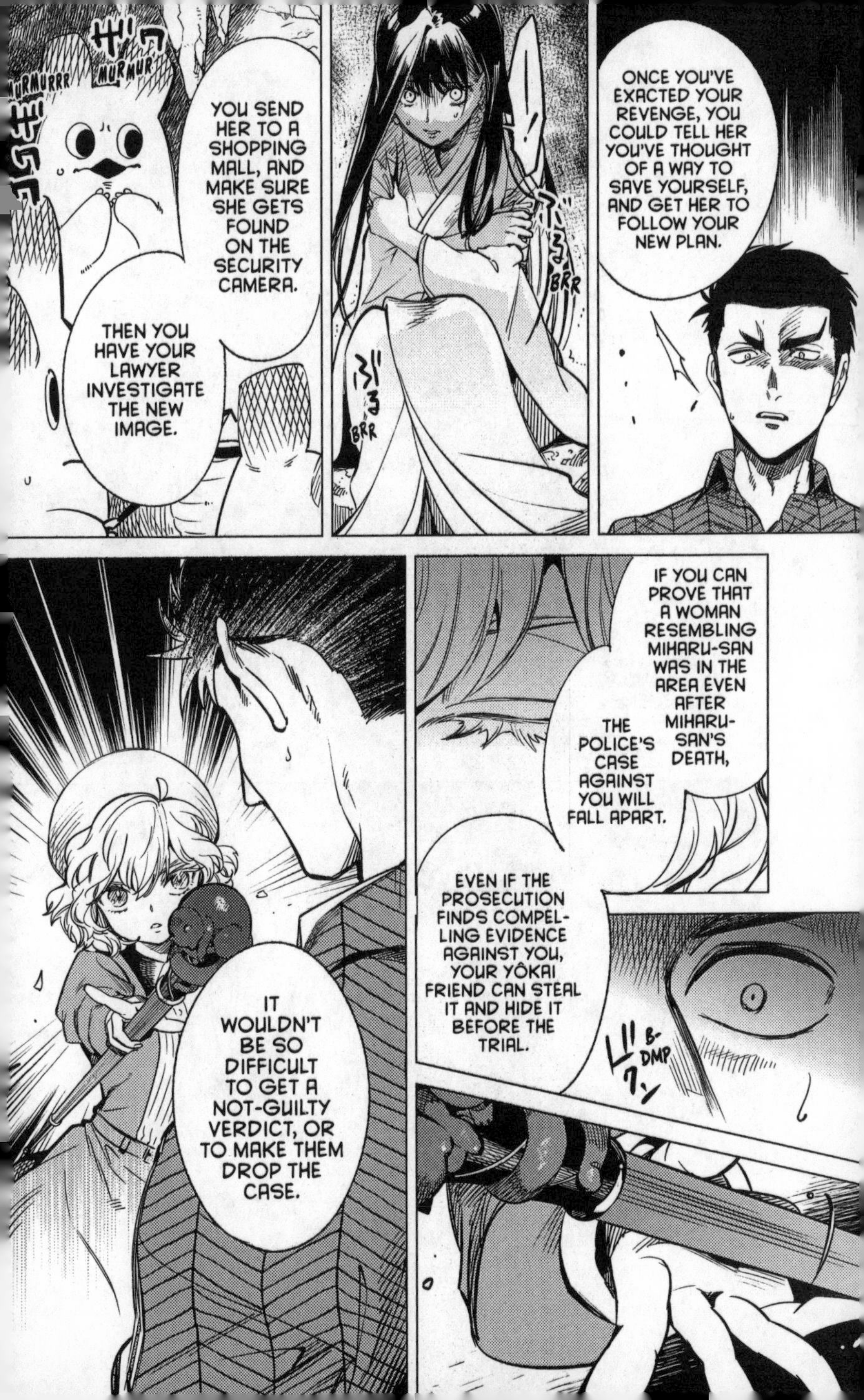
ONCE YOU'VE EXACTED YOUR REVENGE, YOU COULD TELL HER YOU'VE THOUGHT OF A WAY TO SAVE YOURSELF, AND GET HER TO FOLLOW YOUR NEW PLAN.
BRR
BRR
YOU SEND HER TO A SHOPPING MALL, AND MAKE SURE SHE GETS FOUND ON THE SECURITY CAMERA.
THEN YOU HAVE YOUR LAWYER INVESTIGATE THE NEW IMAGE.
MURMUR
MURMURRR
IF YOU CAN PROVE THAT A WOMAN RESEMBLING MIHARU-SAN WAS IN THE AREA EVEN AFTER MIHARU-SAN'S DEATH,
THE POLICE'S CASE AGAINST YOU WILL FALL APART.
EVEN IF THE PROSECUTION FINDS COMPEL-LING EVIDENCE AGAINST YOU, YOUR YÔKAI FRIEND CAN STEAL IT AND HIDE IT BEFORE THE TRIAL.
B-DMP
IT WOULDN'T BE SO DIFFICULT TO GET A NOT-GUILTY VERDICT, OR TO MAKE THEM DROP THE CASE.

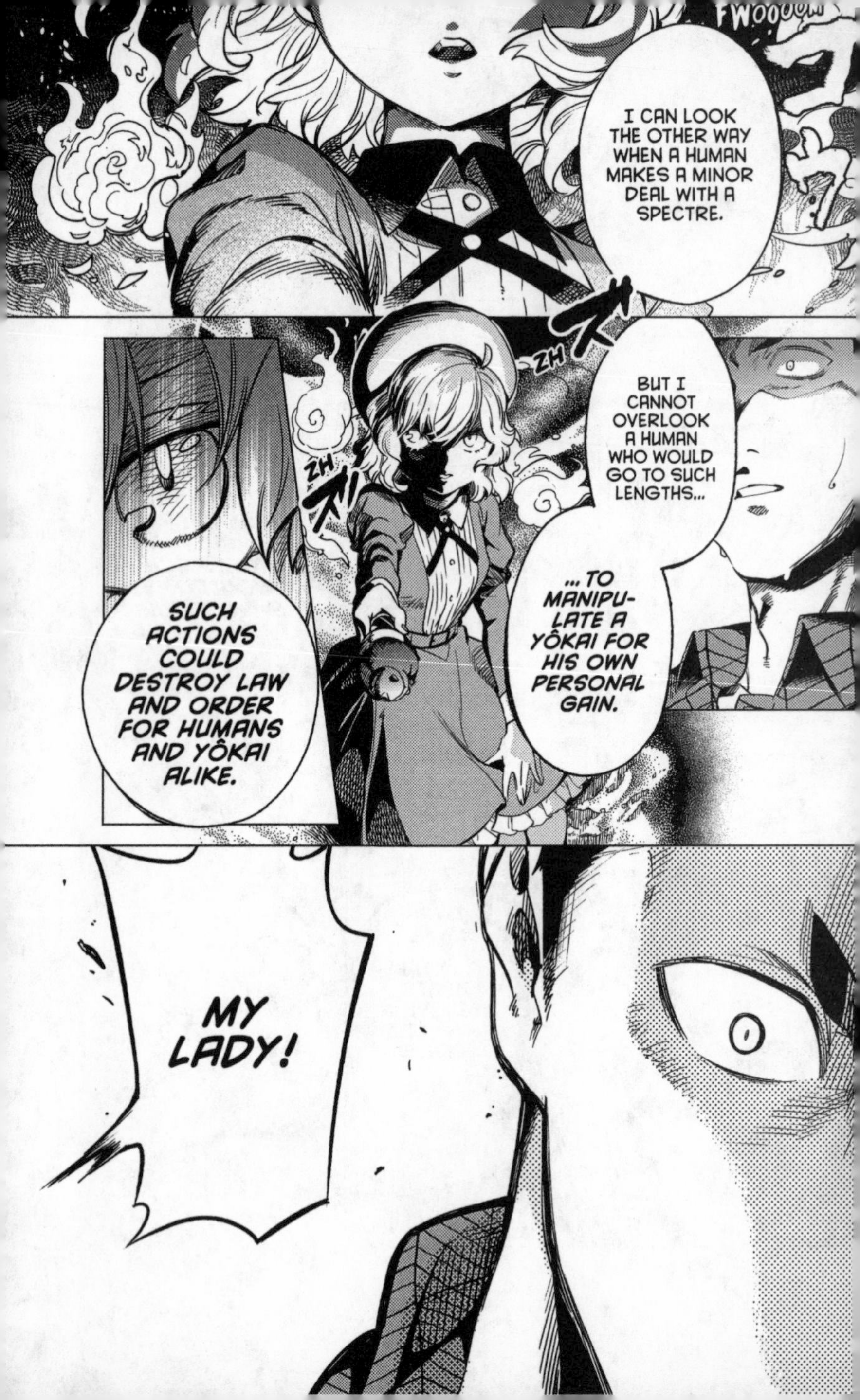
FWOOOM
I CAN LOOK THE OTHER WAY WHEN A HUMAN MAKES A MINOR DEAL WITH A SPECTRE.
ZH
BUT I CANNOT OVERLOOK A HUMAN WHO WOULD GO TO SUCH LENGTHS...
...TO MANIPU-LATE A YÔKAI FOR HIS OWN PERSONAL GAIN.
ZH
SUCH ACTIONS COULD DESTROY LAW AND ORDER FOR HUMANS AND YÔKAI ALIKE.
MY LADY!

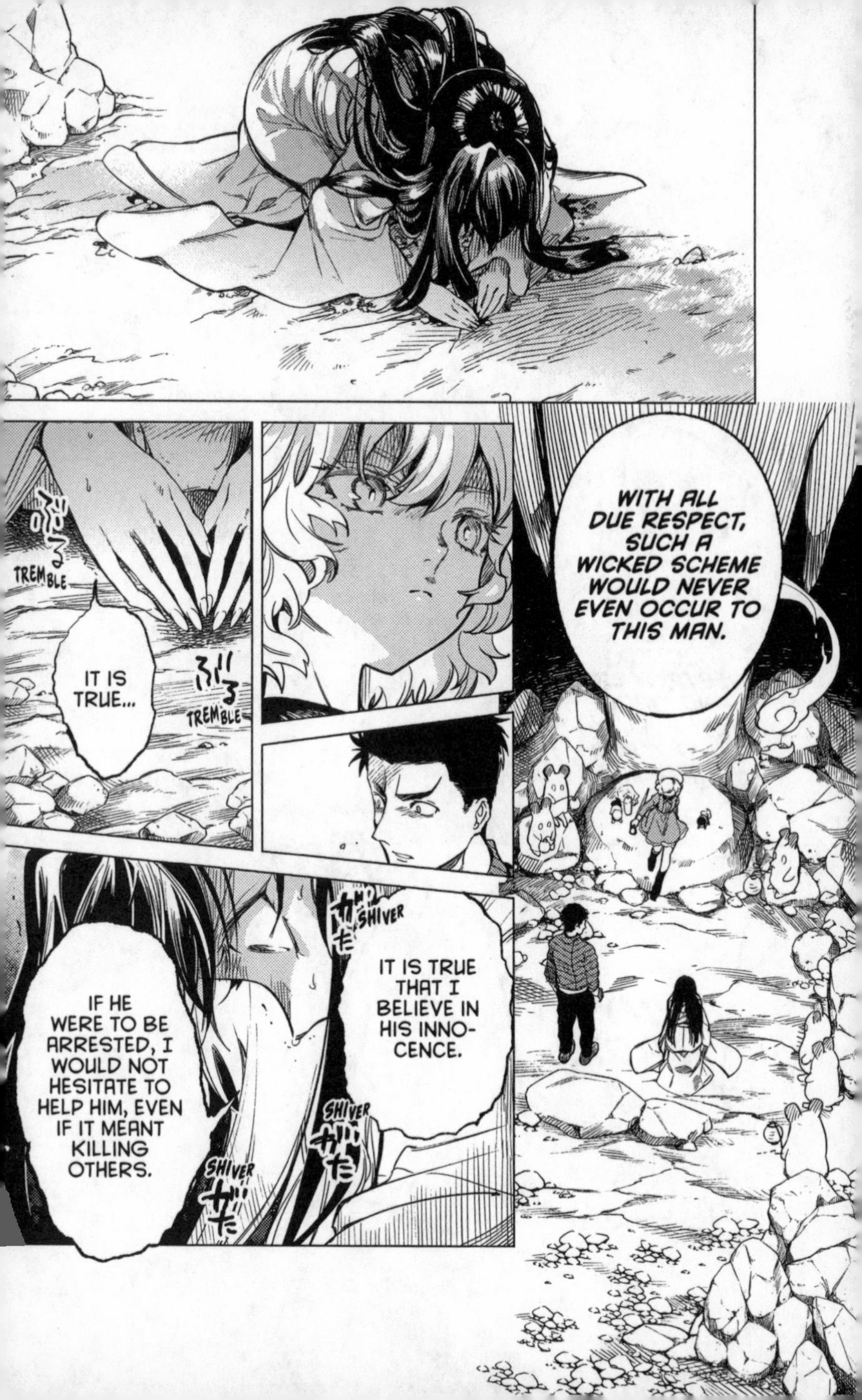
WITH ALL DUE RESPECT, SUCH A WICKED SCHEME WOULD NEVER EVEN OCCUR TO THIS MAN.
TREMBLE
IT IS TRUE...
TREMBLE
SHIVER
IT IS TRUE THAT I BELIEVE IN HIS INNO-CENCE.
IF HE WERE TO BE ARRESTED, I WOULD NOT HESITATE TO HELP HIM, EVEN IF IT MEANT KILLING OTHERS.
SHIVER
SHIVER

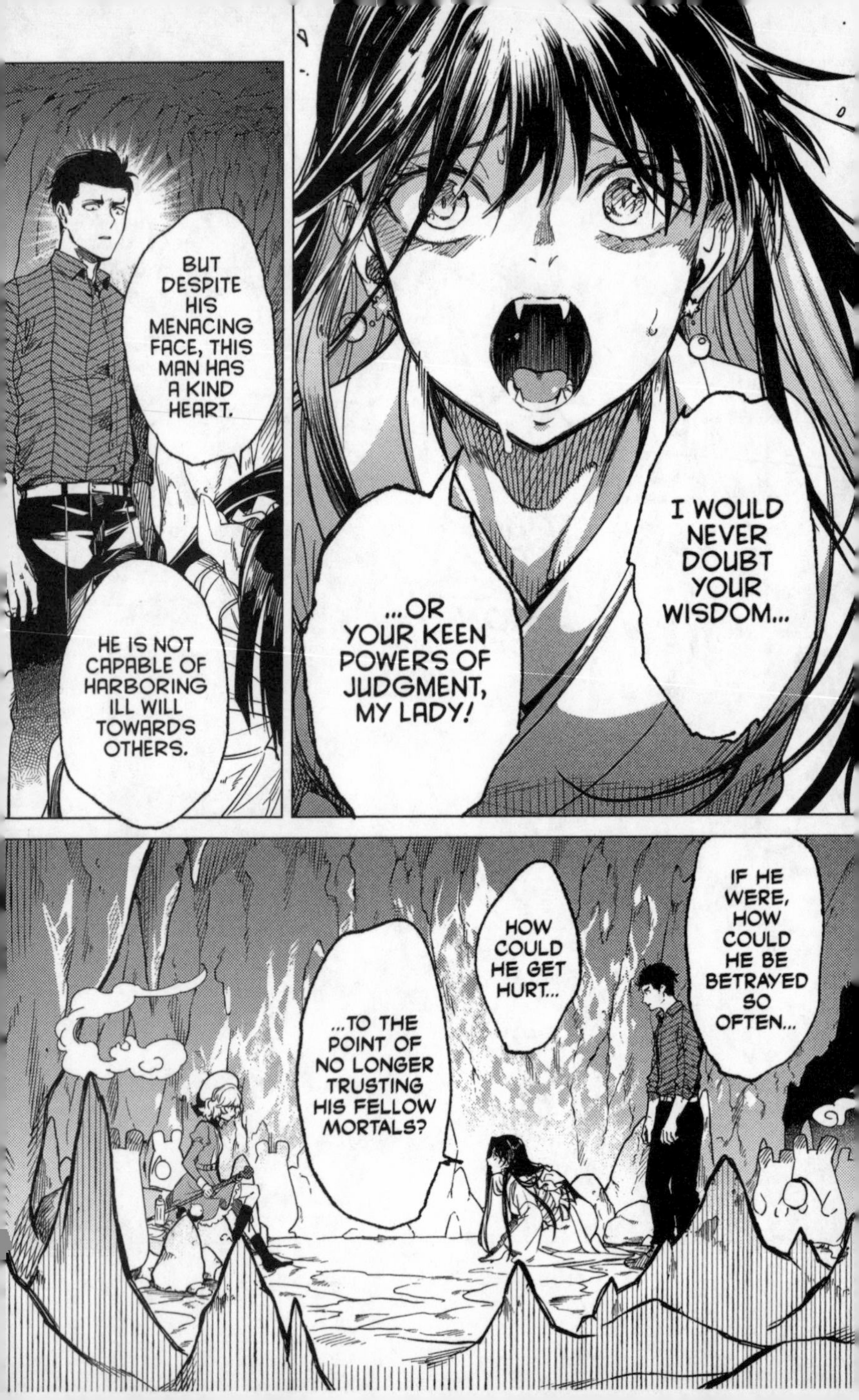
I WOULD NEVER DOUBT YOUR WISDOM...
...OR YOUR KEEN POWERS OF JUDGMENT, MY LADY!
BUT DESPITE HIS MENACING FACE, THIS MAN HAS A KIND HEART.
HE IS NOT CAPABLE OF HARBORING ILL WILL TOWARDS OTHERS.
IF HE WERE, HOW COULD HE BE BETRAYED SO OFTEN...
HOW COULD HE GET HURT...
...TO THE POINT OF NO LONGER TRUSTING HIS FELLOW MORTALS?

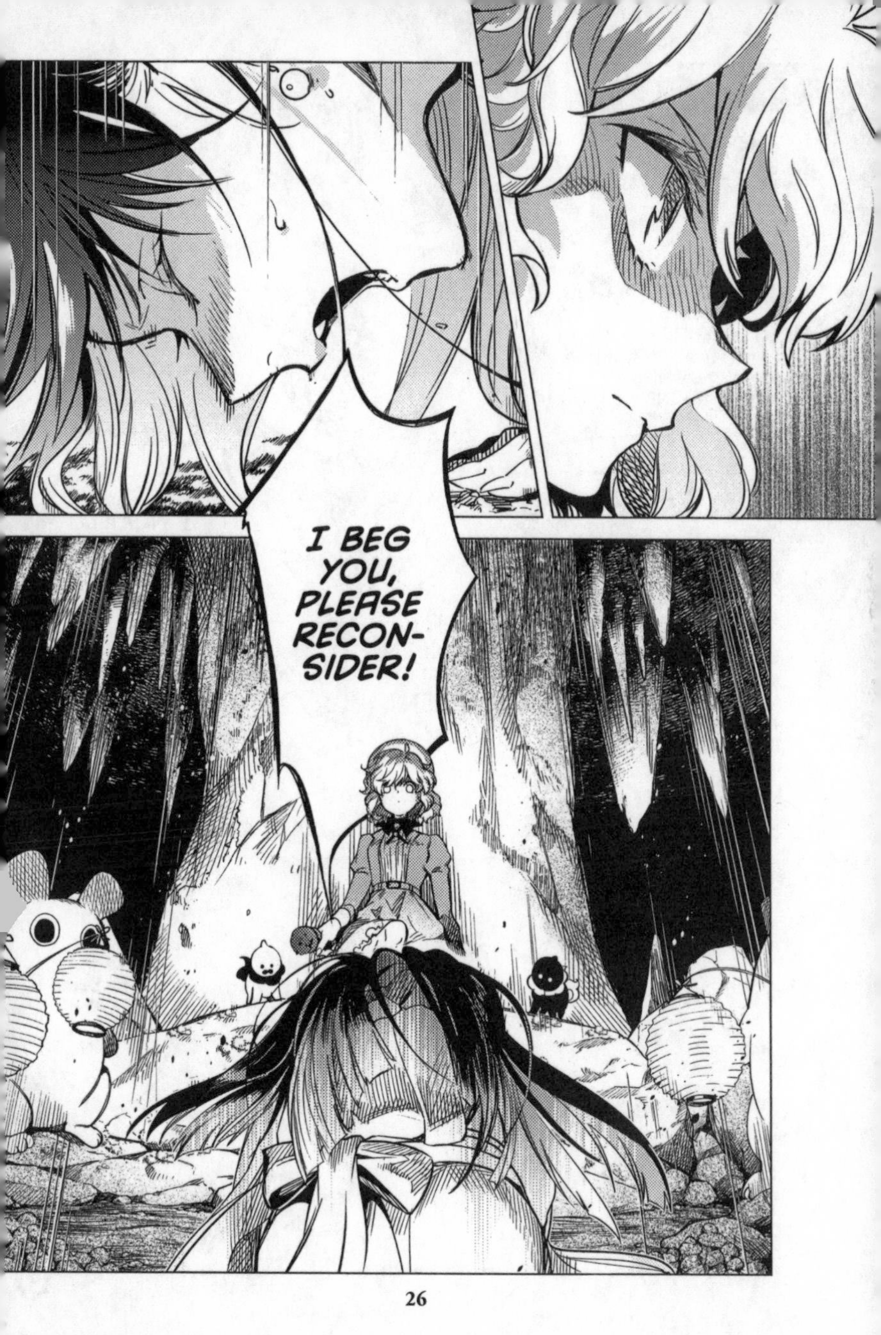
I BEG YOU, PLEASE RECON- SIDER!

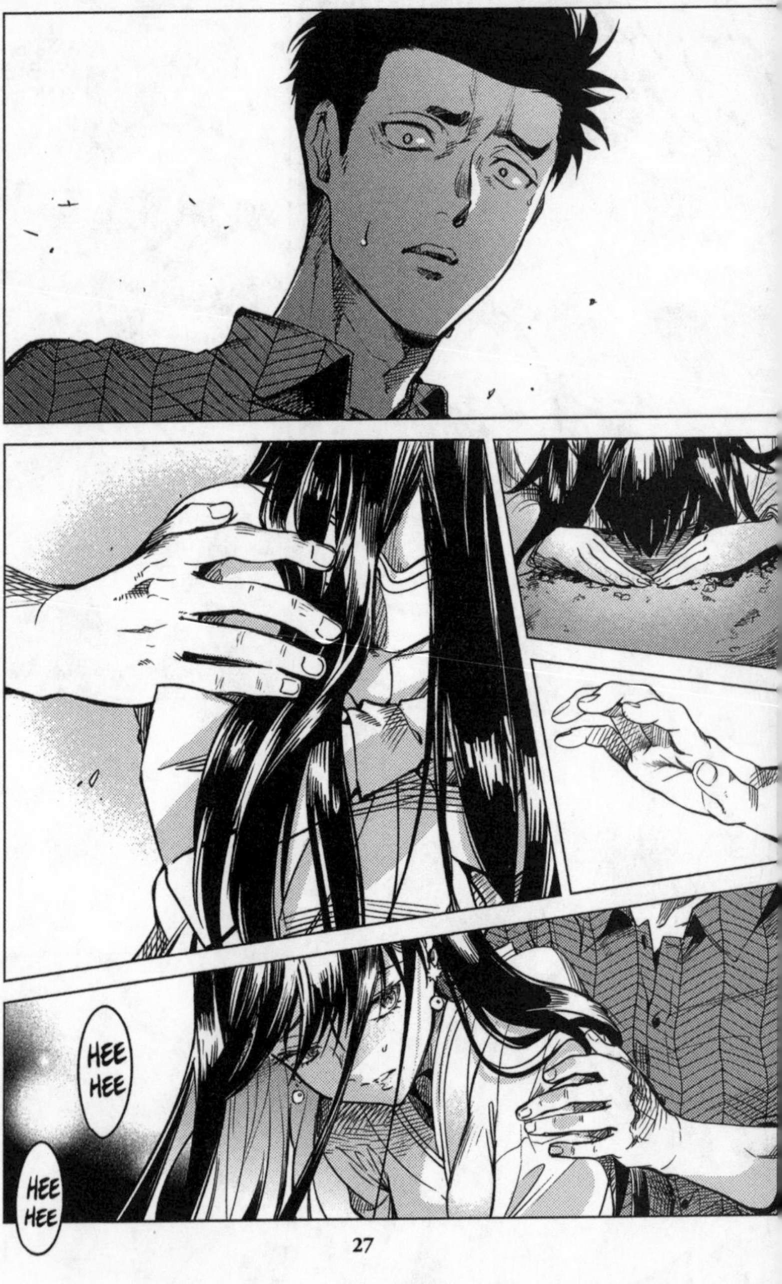
HEE HEE
HEE HEE

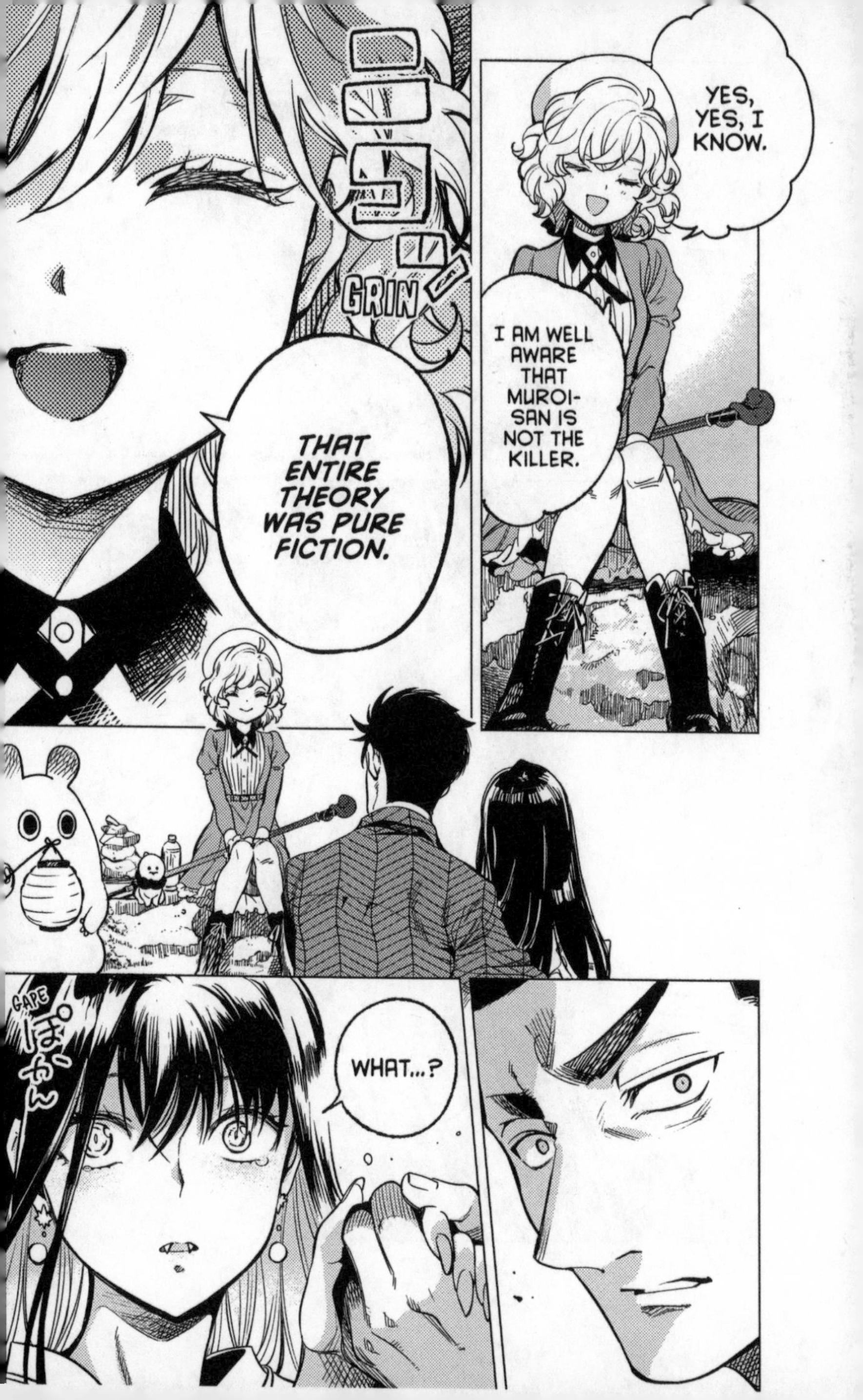

YES, YES, I KNOW.
I AM WELL AWARE THAT MUROI-SAN IS NOT THE KILLER.
GRIN
THAT ENTIRE THEORY WAS PURE FICTION.
GAPE
ぽかん
WHAT...?

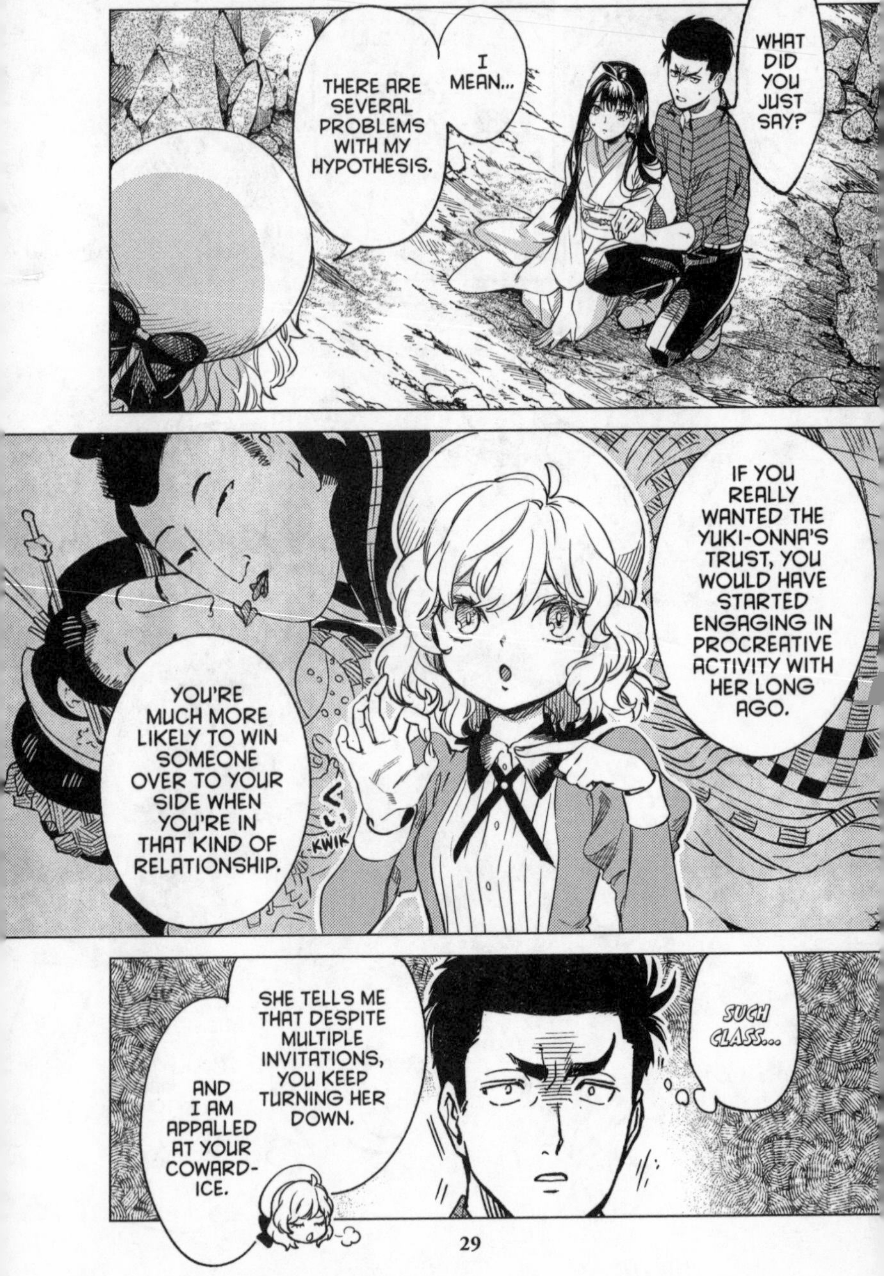
WHAT DID YOU JUST SAY?
I MEAN...
THERE ARE SEVERAL PROBLEMS WITH MY HYPOTHESIS.
IF YOU REALLY WANTED THE YUKI-ONNA'S TRUST, YOU WOULD HAVE STARTED ENGAGING IN PROCREATIVE ACTIVITY WITH HER LONG AGO.
KWIK
YOU'RE MUCH MORE LIKELY TO WIN SOMEONE OVER TO YOUR SIDE WHEN YOU'RE IN THAT KIND OF RELATIONSHIP.
SUCH CLASS...
SHE TELLS ME THAT DESPITE MULTIPLE INVITATIONS, YOU KEEP TURNING HER DOWN.
AND I AM APPALLED AT YOUR COWARD-ICE.

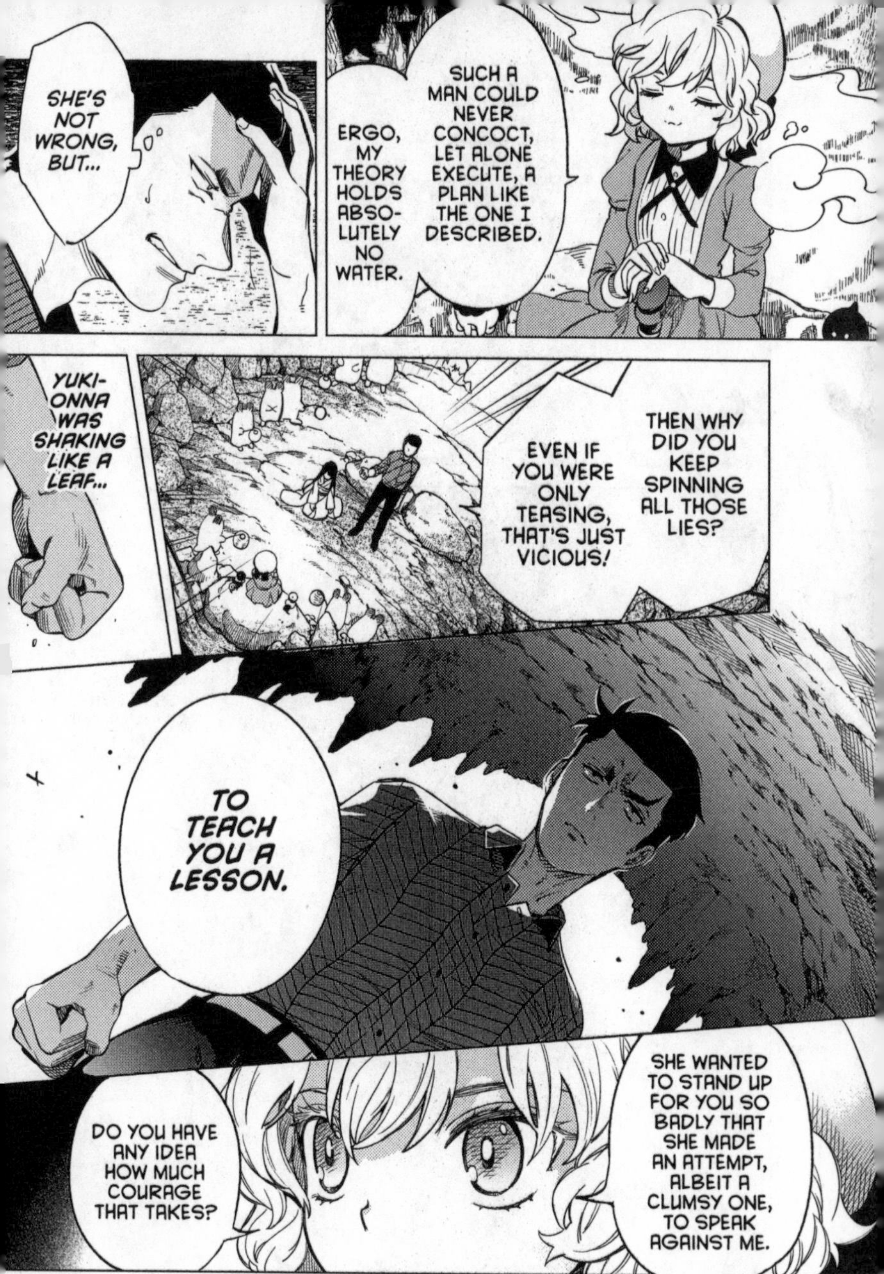
SUCH A MAN COULD NEVER CONCOCT, LET ALONE EXECUTE, A PLAN LIKE THE ONE I DESCRIBED.
ERGO, MY THEORY HOLDS ABSO-LUTELY NO WATER.
SHE'S NOT WRONG, BUT...
THEN WHY DID YOU KEEP SPINNING ALL THOSE LIES?
EVEN IF YOU WERE ONLY TEASING, THAT'S JUST VICIOUS!
YUKI-ONNA WAS SHAKING LIKE A LEAF...
TO TEACH YOU A LESSON.
SHE WANTED TO STAND UP FOR YOU SO BADLY THAT SHE MADE AN ATTEMPT, ALBEIT A CLUMSY ONE, TO SPEAK AGAINST ME.
DO YOU HAVE ANY IDEA HOW MUCH COURAGE THAT TAKES?

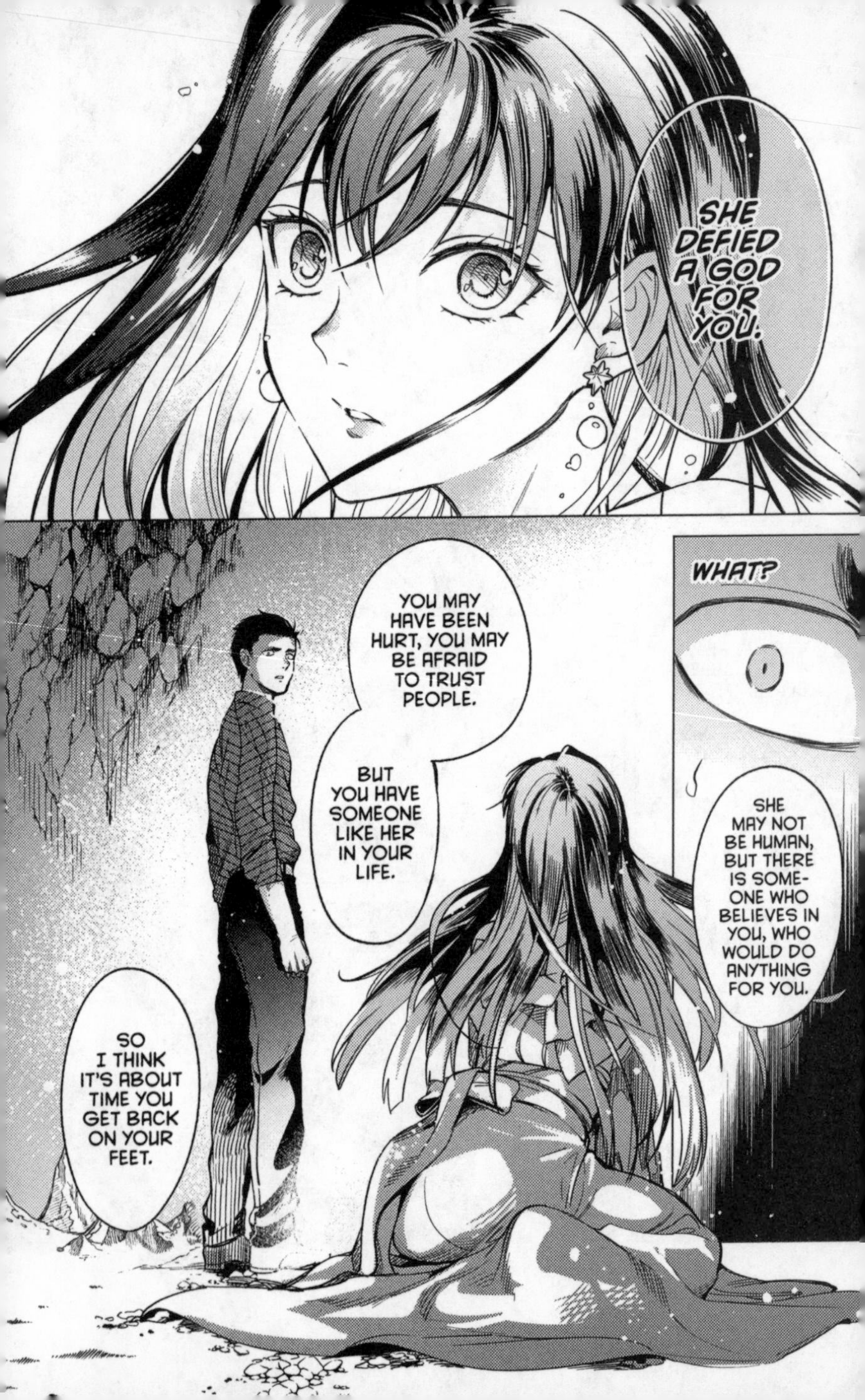
SHE DEFIED A GOD FOR YOU.
WHAT?
YOU MAY HAVE BEEN HURT, YOU MAY BE AFRAID TO TRUST PEOPLE.
BUT YOU HAVE SOMEONE LIKE HER IN YOUR LIFE.
SHE MAY NOT BE HUMAN, BUT THERE IS SOME-ONE WHO BELIEVES IN YOU, WHO WOULD DO ANYTHING FOR YOU.
SO I THINK IT'S ABOUT TIME YOU GET BACK ON YOUR FEET.

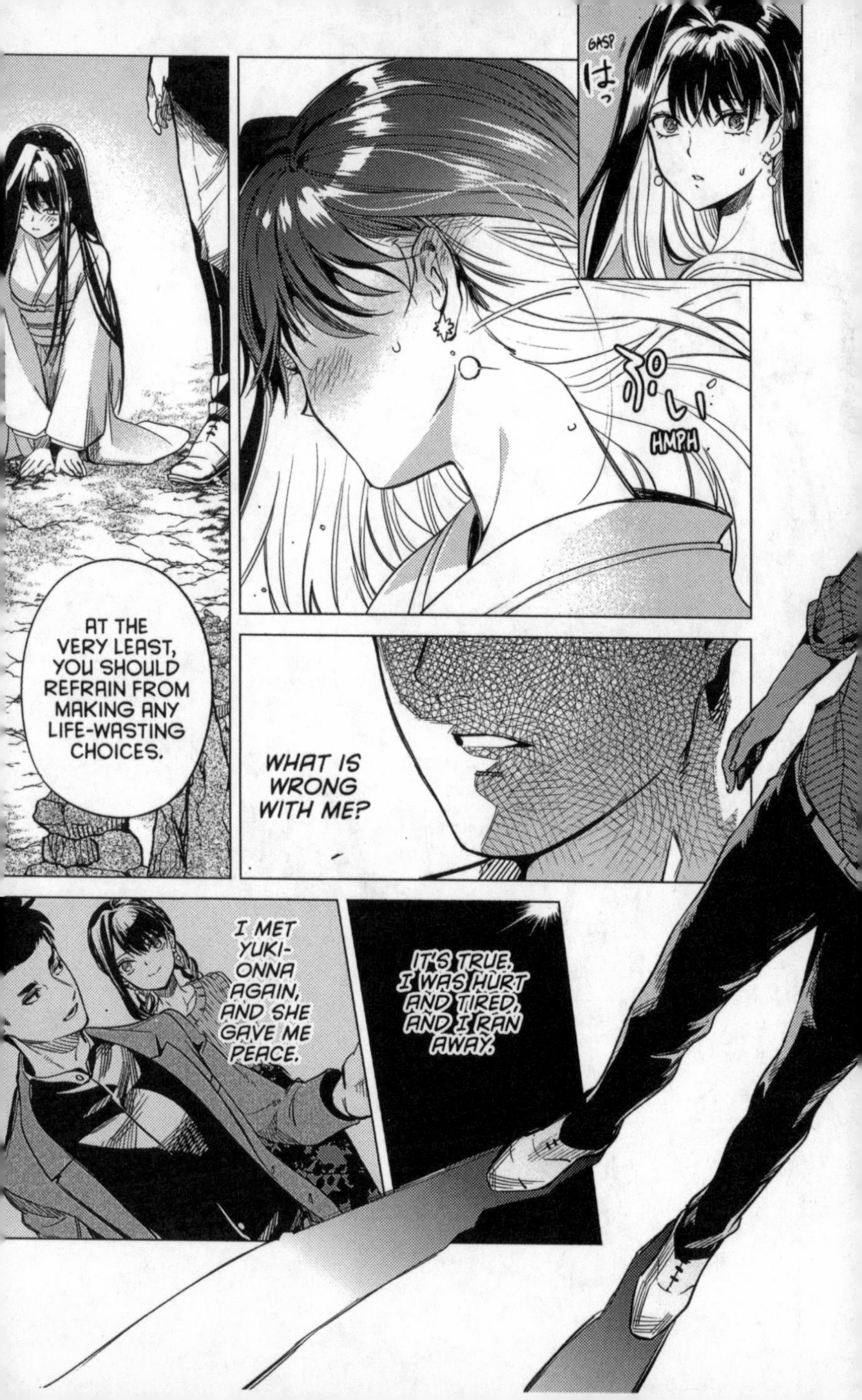
GASP
はっ
ぷい
HMPH
WHAT IS WRONG WITH ME?
AT THE VERY LEAST, YOU SHOULD REFRAIN FROM MAKING ANY LIFE-WASTING CHOICES.
IT'S TRUE. I WAS HURT AND TIRED, AND I RAN AWAY.
I MET YUKI-ONNA AGAIN, AND SHE GAVE ME PEACE.

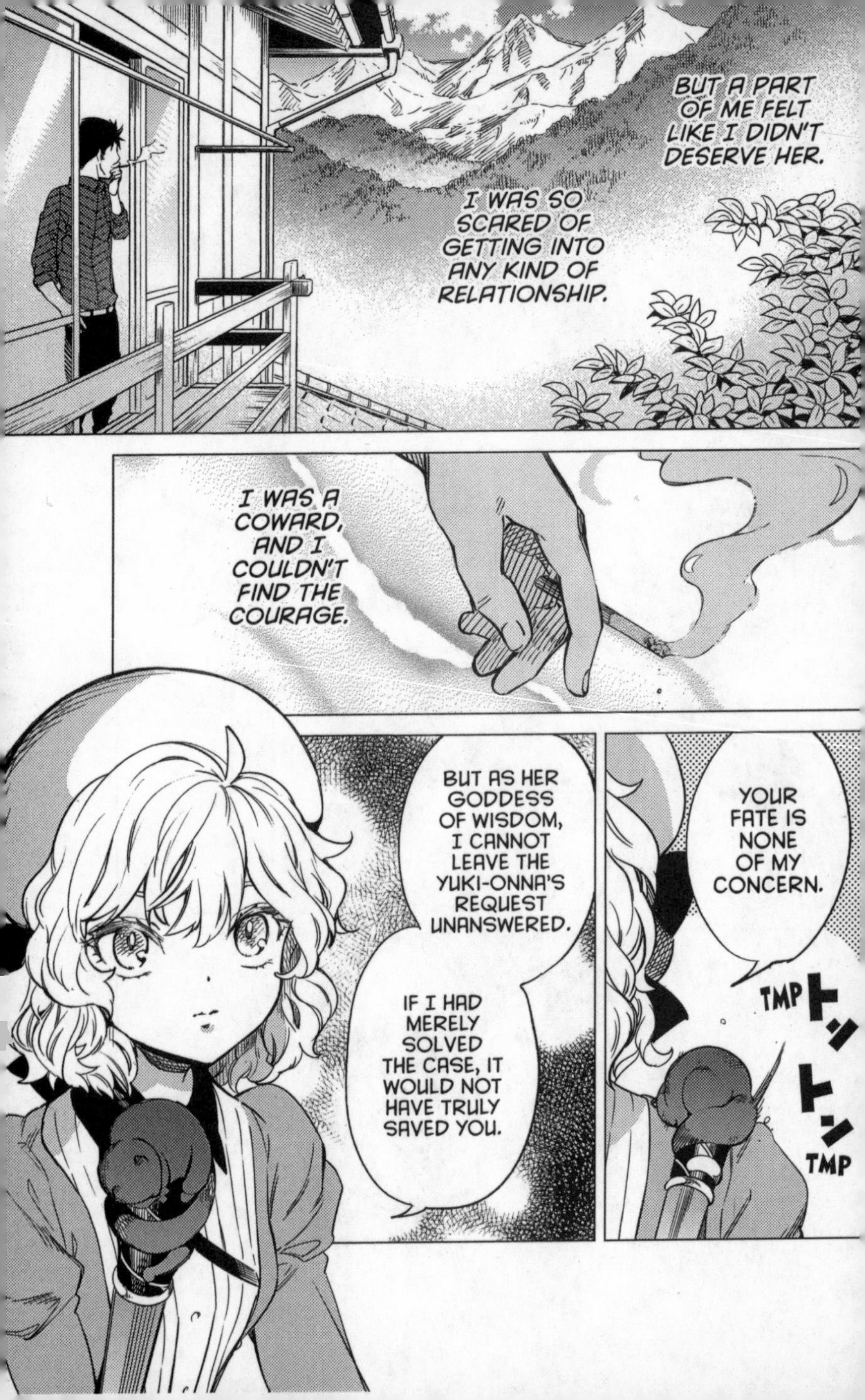
BUT A PART OF ME FELT LIKE I DIDN'T DESERVE HER.
I WAS SO SCARED OF GETTING INTO ANY KIND OF RELATIONSHIP.
I WAS A COWARD, AND I COULDN'T FIND THE COURAGE.
YOUR FATE IS NONE OF MY CONCERN.
TMP トッ
トン TMP
BUT AS HER GODDESS OF WISDOM, I CANNOT LEAVE THE YUKI-ONNA'S REQUEST UNANSWERED.
IF I HAD MERELY SOLVED THE CASE, IT WOULD NOT HAVE TRULY SAVED YOU.

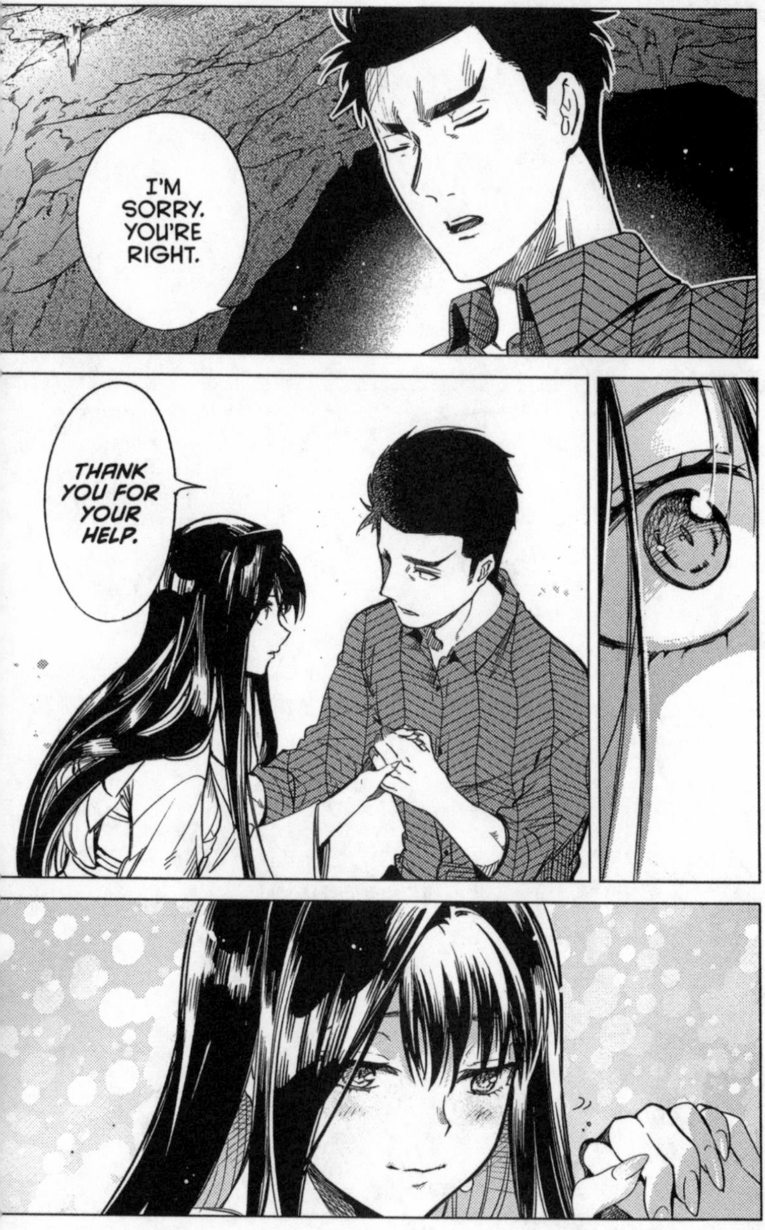
I'M SORRY. YOU'RE RIGHT.
THANK YOU FOR YOUR HELP.

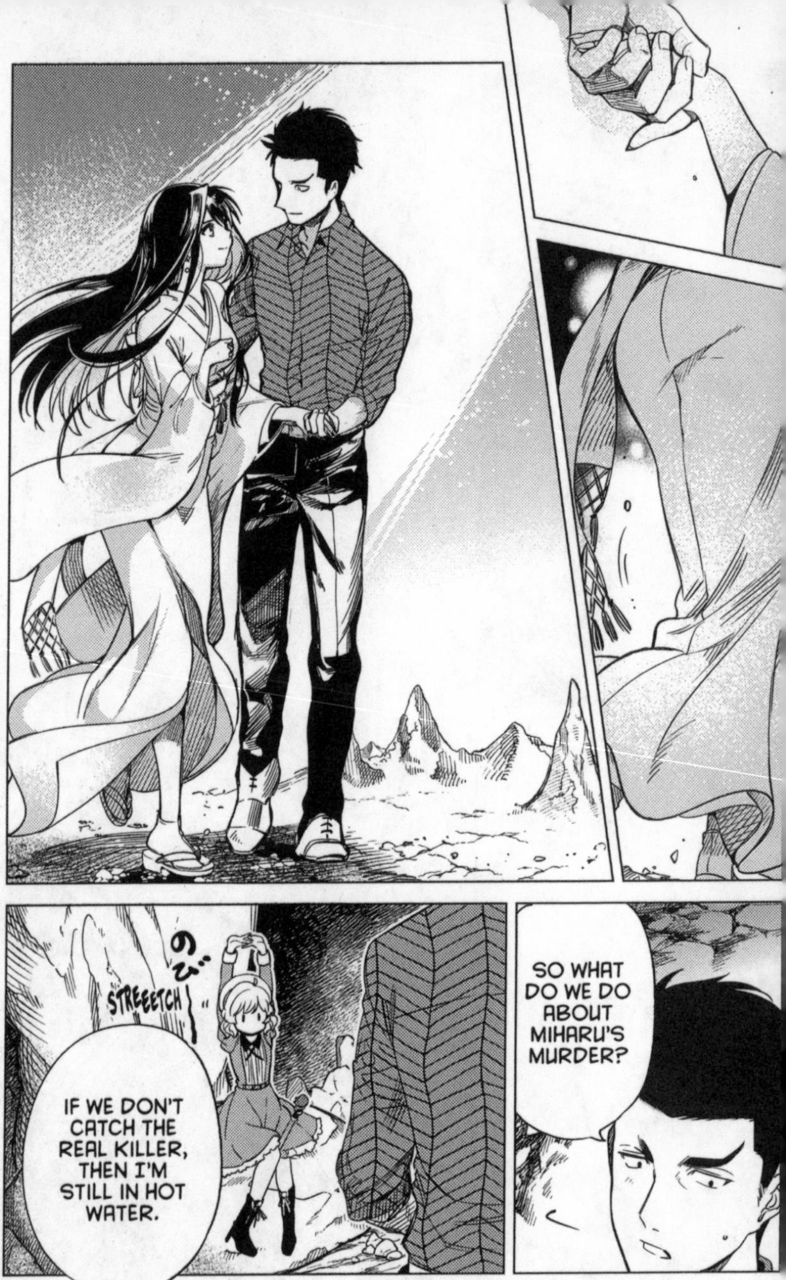
SO WHAT DO WE DO ABOUT MIHARU'S MURDER?
のび
STREEETCH
IF WE DON'T CATCH THE REAL KILLER, THEN I'M STILL IN HOT WATER.

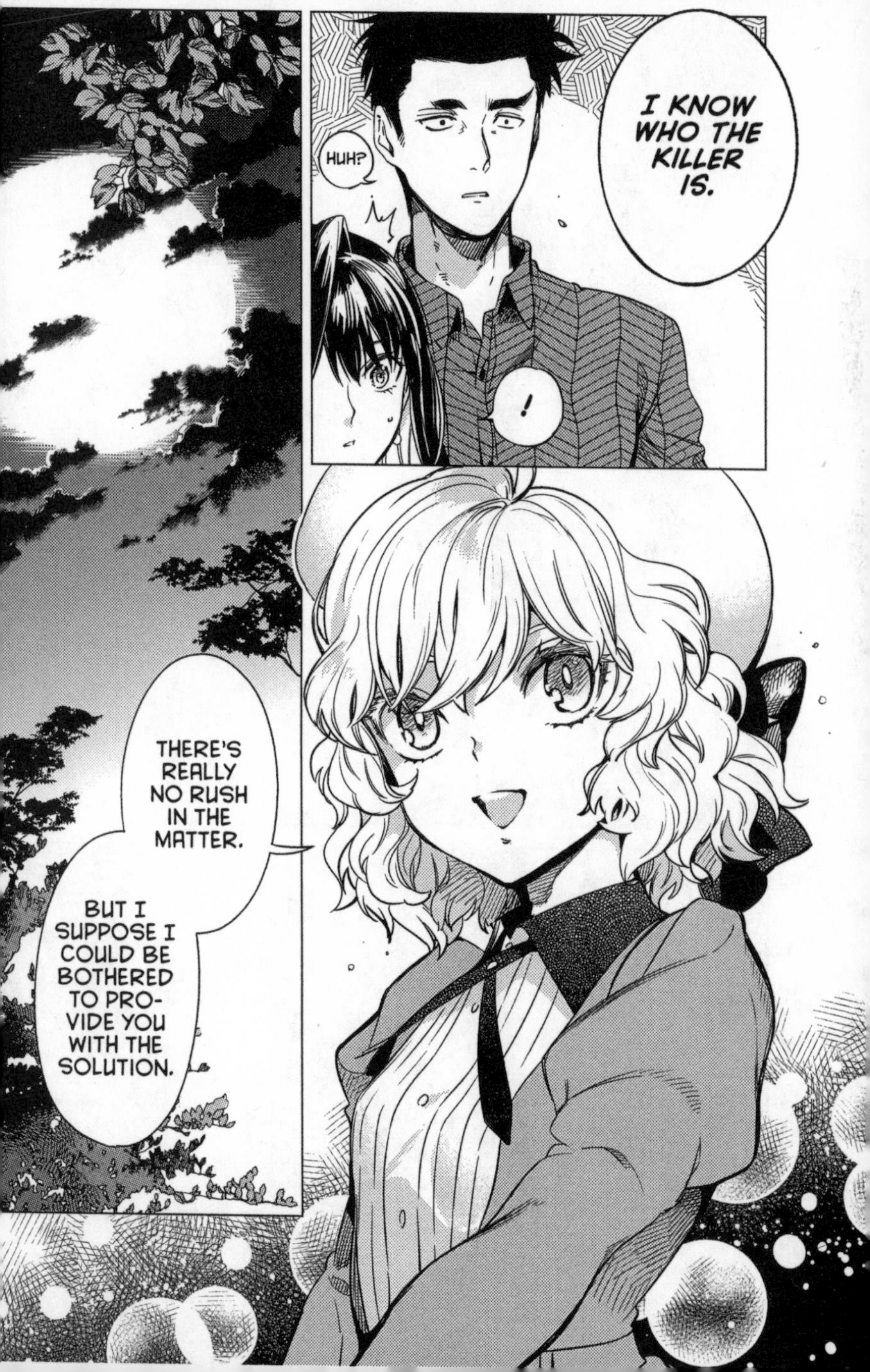
I KNOW WHO THE KILLER IS.
HUH?
!
THERE'S REALLY NO RUSH IN THE MATTER.
BUT I SUPPOSE I COULD BE BOTHERED TO PRO-VIDE YOU WITH THE SOLUTION.

CHAPTER 33: "THE YUKI-ONNA'S DILEMMA PART 4"

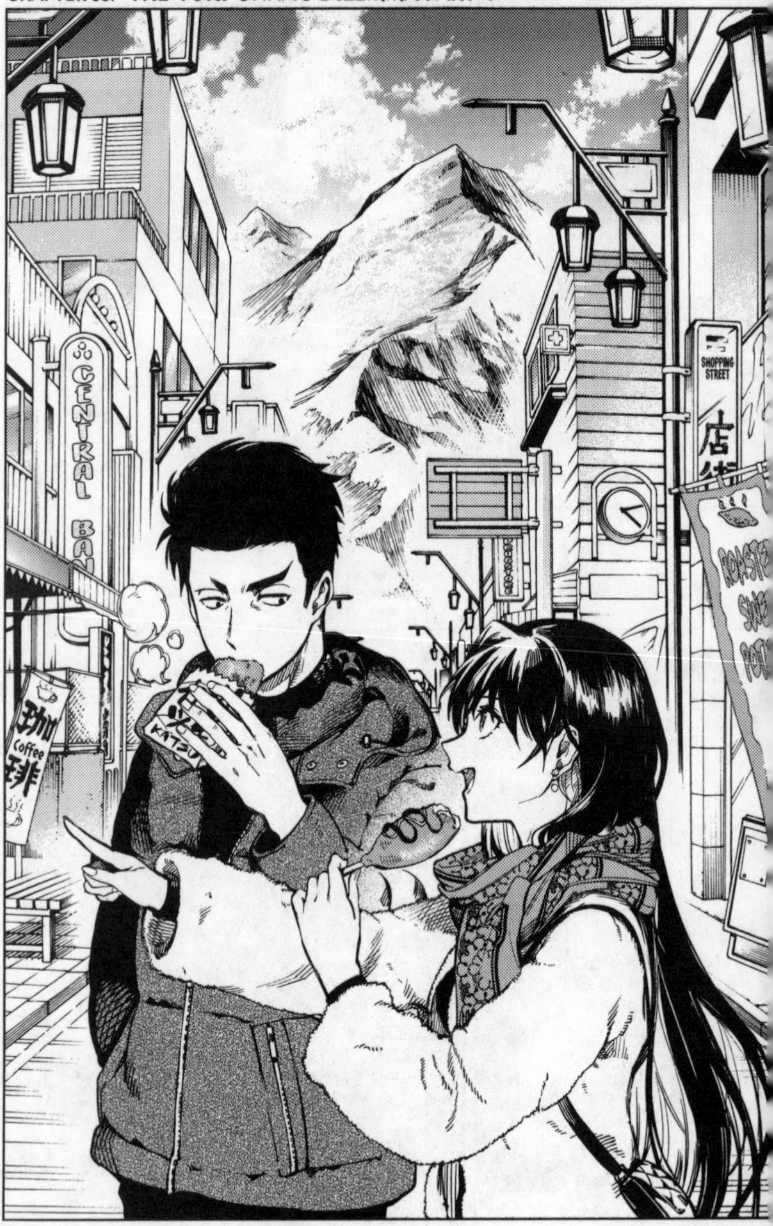

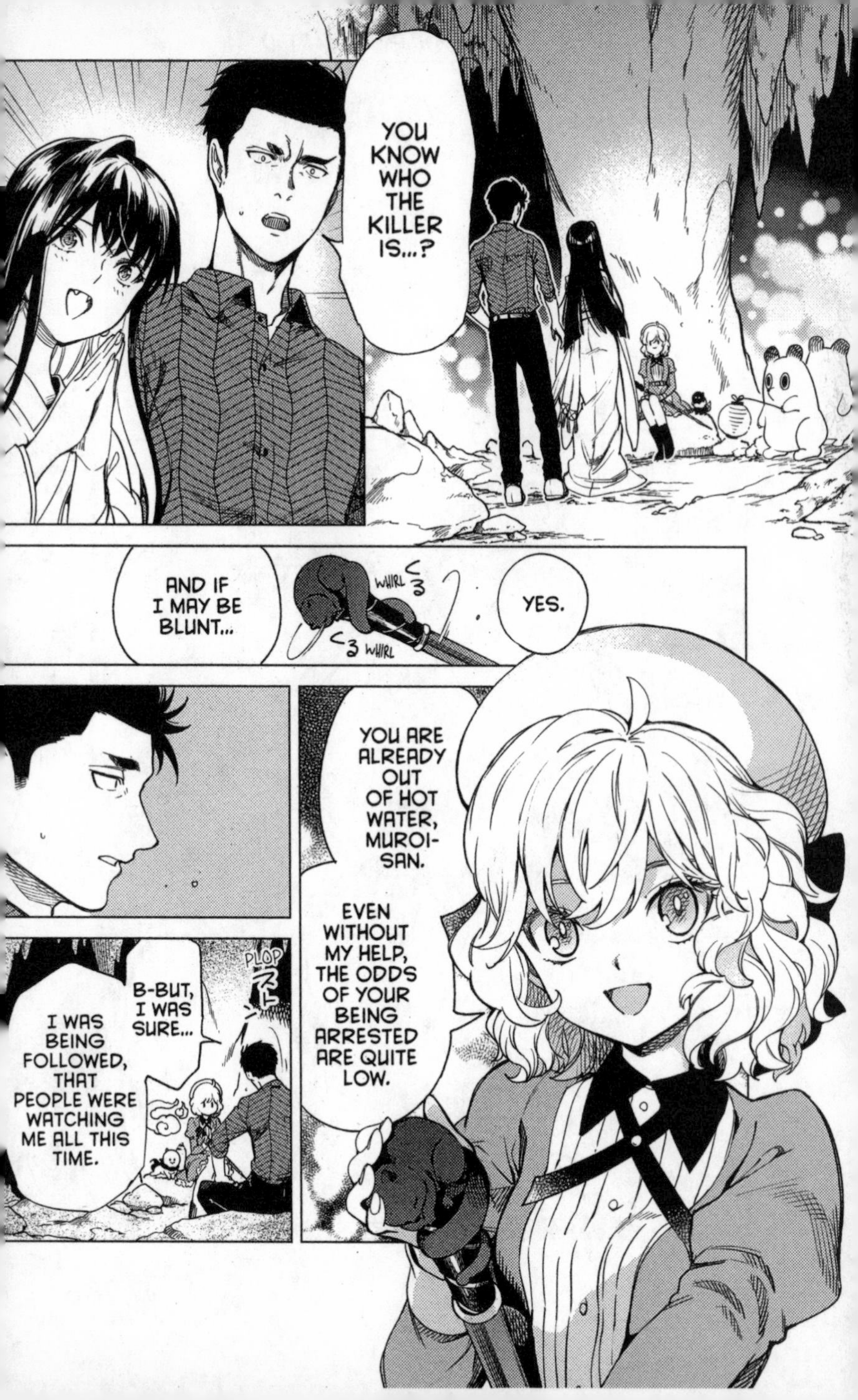
YOU KNOW WHO THE KILLER IS...?
YES.
WHIRL
WHIRL
AND IF I MAY BE BLUNT...
YOU ARE ALREADY OUT OF HOT WATER, MUROI-SAN.
EVEN WITHOUT MY HELP, THE ODDS OF YOUR BEING ARRESTED ARE QUITE LOW.
PLOP
B-BUT, I WAS SURE...
I WAS BEING FOLLOWED, THAT PEOPLE WERE WATCHING ME ALL THIS TIME.

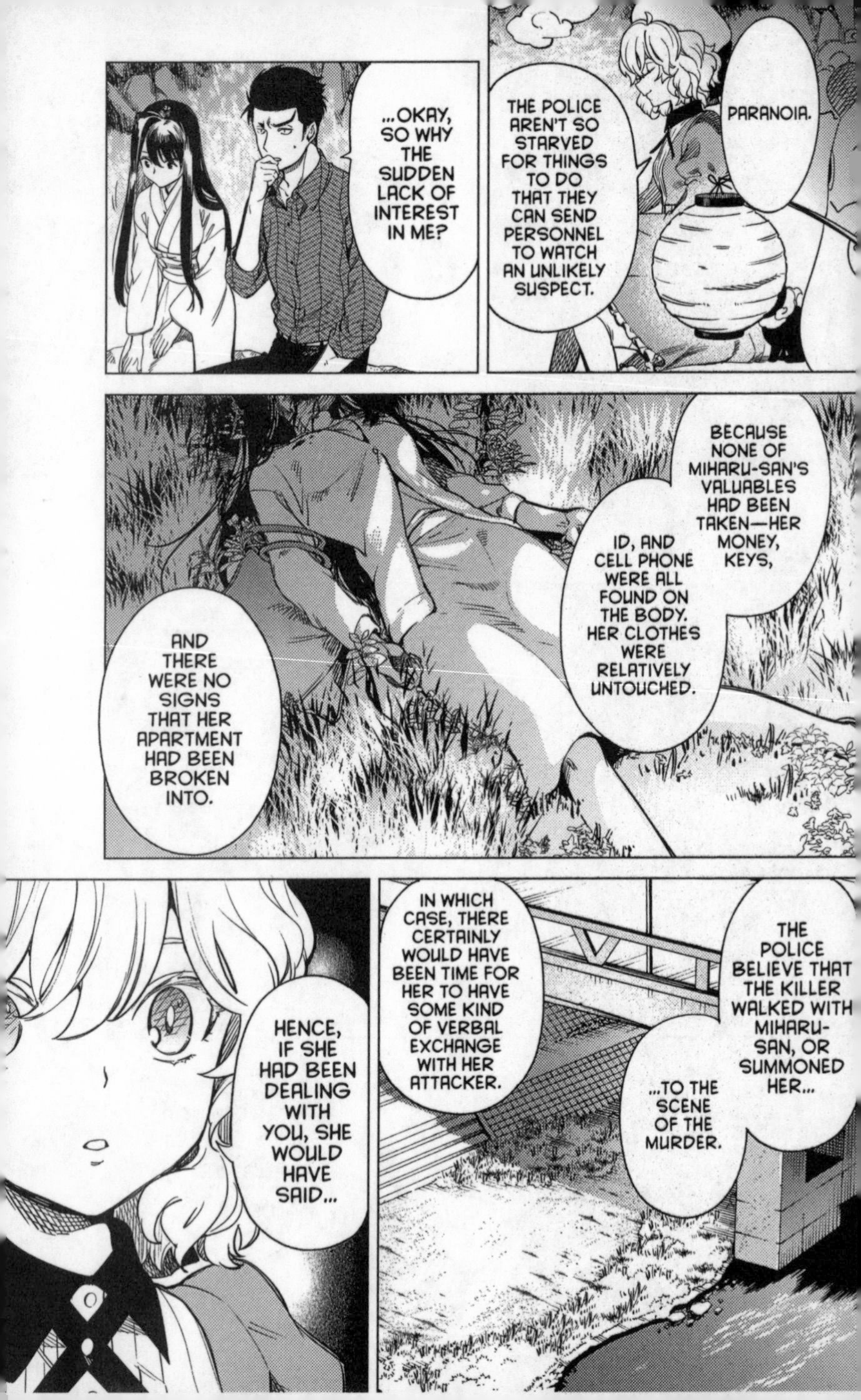
PARANOIA.
THE POLICE AREN'T SO STARVED FOR THINGS TO DO THAT THEY CAN SEND PERSONNEL TO WATCH AN UNLIKELY SUSPECT.
...OKAY, SO WHY THE SUDDEN LACK OF INTEREST IN ME?
BECAUSE NONE OF MIHARU-SAN'S VALUABLES HAD BEEN TAKEN—HER MONEY, KEYS,
ID, AND CELL PHONE WERE ALL FOUND ON THE BODY. HER CLOTHES WERE RELATIVELY UNTOUCHED.
AND THERE WERE NO SIGNS THAT HER APARTMENT HAD BEEN BROKEN INTO.
THE POLICE BELIEVE THAT THE KILLER WALKED WITH MIHARU-SAN, OR SUMMONED HER...
...TO THE SCENE OF THE MURDER.
IN WHICH CASE, THERE CERTAINLY WOULD HAVE BEEN TIME FOR HER TO HAVE SOME KIND OF VERBAL EXCHANGE WITH HER ATTACKER.
HENCE, IF SHE HAD BEEN DEALING WITH YOU, SHE WOULD HAVE SAID...

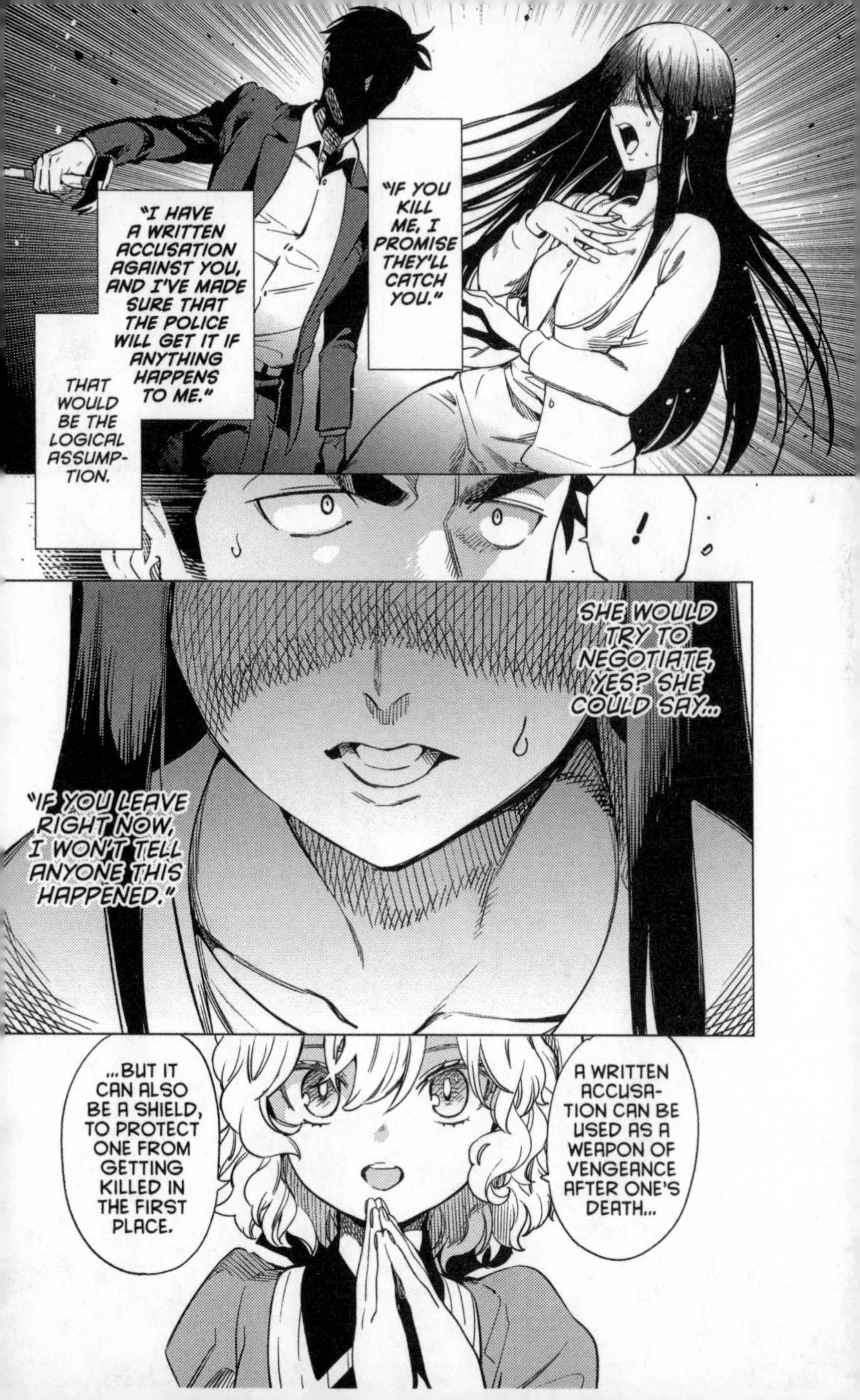
"IF YOU KILL ME, I PROMISE THEY'LL CATCH YOU."
"I HAVE A WRITTEN ACCUSATION AGAINST YOU, AND I'VE MADE SURE THAT THE POLICE WILL GET IT IF ANYTHING HAPPENS TO ME."
THAT WOULD BE THE LOGICAL ASSUMPTION.
!
SHE WOULD TRY TO NEGOTIATE, YES? SHE COULD SAY...
"IF YOU LEAVE RIGHT NOW, I WON'T TELL ANYONE THIS HAPPENED."
A WRITTEN ACCUSATION CAN BE USED AS A WEAPON OF VENGEANCE AFTER ONE'S DEATH...
...BUT IT CAN ALSO BE A SHIELD, TO PROTECT ONE FROM GETTING KILLED IN THE FIRST PLACE.

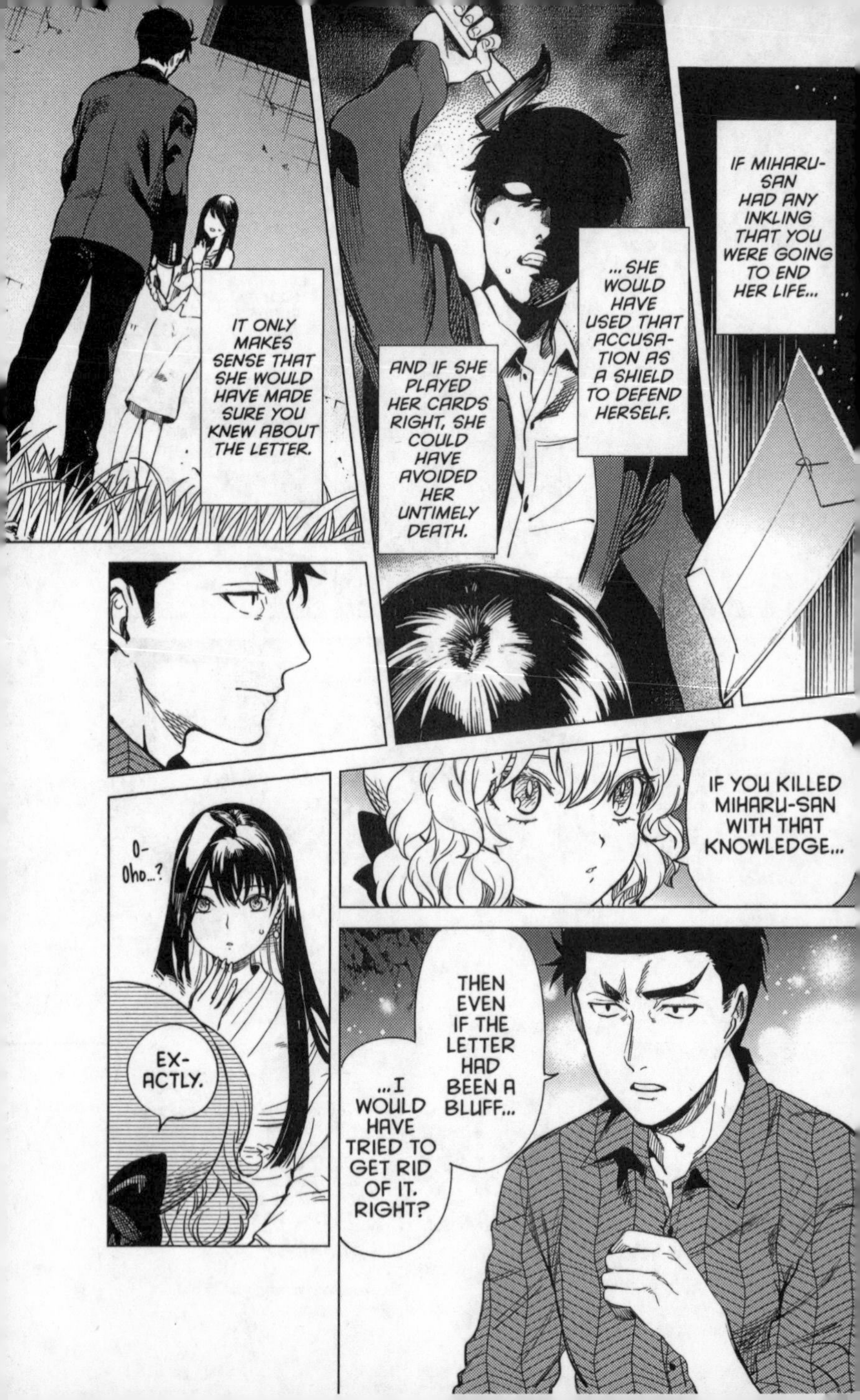

IF MIHARU-SAN HAD ANY INKLING THAT YOU WERE GOING TO END HER LIFE...
...SHE WOULD HAVE USED THAT ACCUSATION AS A SHIELD TO DEFEND HERSELF.
AND IF SHE PLAYED HER CARDS RIGHT, SHE COULD HAVE AVOIDED HER UNTIMELY DEATH.
IT ONLY MAKES SENSE THAT SHE WOULD HAVE MADE SURE YOU KNEW ABOUT THE LETTER.
IF YOU KILLED MIHARU-SAN WITH THAT KNOWLEDGE...
THEN EVEN IF THE LETTER HAD BEEN A BLUFF...
...I WOULD HAVE TRIED TO GET RID OF IT. RIGHT?
O-Oho...?
EX-ACTLY.

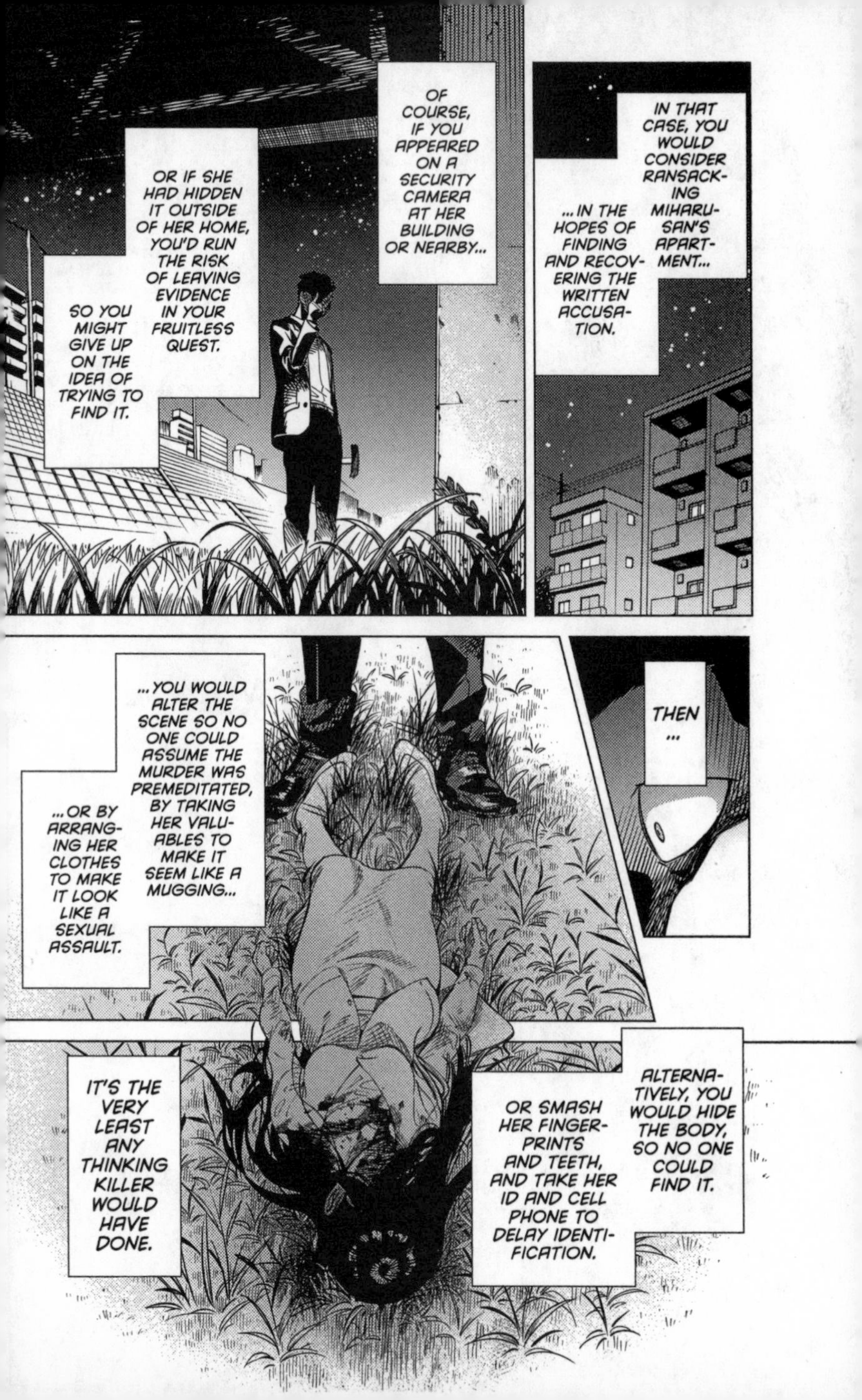
IN THAT CASE, YOU WOULD CONSIDER RANSACKING MIHARU-SAN'S APARTMENT...
...IN THE HOPES OF FINDING AND RECOVERING THE WRITTEN ACCUSATION.
OF COURSE, IF YOU APPEARED ON A SECURITY CAMERA AT HER BUILDING OR NEARBY...
OR IF SHE HAD HIDDEN IT OUTSIDE OF HER HOME, YOU'D RUN THE RISK OF LEAVING EVIDENCE IN YOUR FRUITLESS QUEST.
SO YOU MIGHT GIVE UP ON THE IDEA OF TRYING TO FIND IT.
THEN...
...YOU WOULD ALTER THE SCENE SO NO ONE COULD ASSUME THE MURDER WAS PREMEDITATED, BY TAKING HER VALUABLES TO MAKE IT SEEM LIKE A MUGGING...
...OR BY ARRANGING HER CLOTHES TO MAKE IT LOOK LIKE A SEXUAL ASSAULT.
ALTERNATIVELY, YOU WOULD HIDE THE BODY, SO NO ONE COULD FIND IT.
OR SMASH HER FINGERPRINTS AND TEETH, AND TAKE HER ID AND CELL PHONE TO DELAY IDENTIFICATION.
IT'S THE VERY LEAST ANY THINKING KILLER WOULD HAVE DONE.

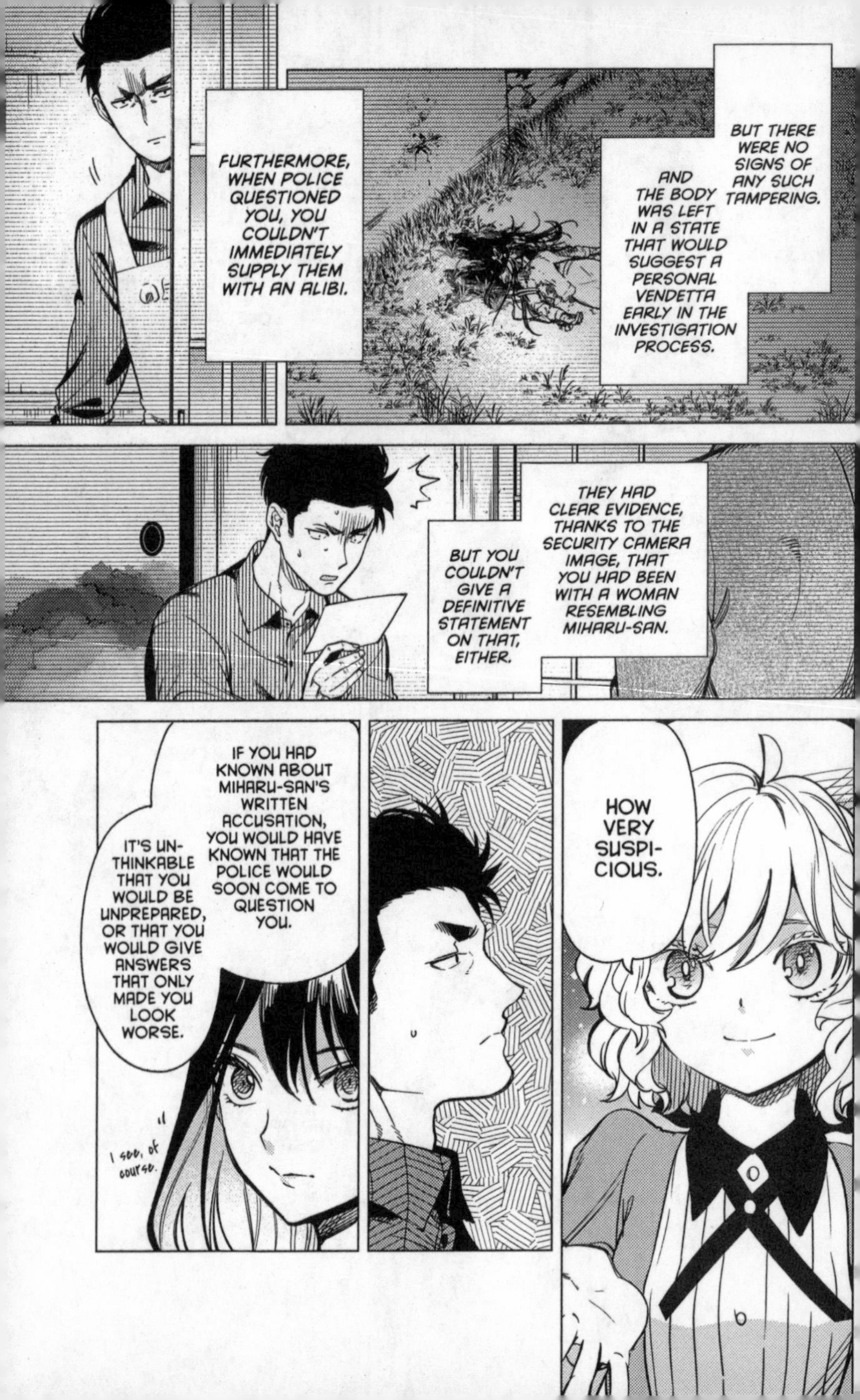
BUT THERE WERE NO SIGNS OF ANY SUCH TAMPERING.
AND THE BODY WAS LEFT IN A STATE THAT WOULD SUGGEST A PERSONAL VENDETTA EARLY IN THE INVESTIGATION PROCESS.
FURTHERMORE, WHEN POLICE QUESTIONED YOU, YOU COULDN'T IMMEDIATELY SUPPLY THEM WITH AN ALIBI.
THEY HAD CLEAR EVIDENCE, THANKS TO THE SECURITY CAMERA IMAGE, THAT YOU HAD BEEN WITH A WOMAN RESEMBLING MIHARU-SAN.
BUT YOU COULDN'T GIVE A DEFINITIVE STATEMENT ON THAT, EITHER.
HOW VERY SUSPICIOUS.
IF YOU HAD KNOWN ABOUT MIHARU-SAN'S WRITTEN ACCUSATION, YOU WOULD HAVE KNOWN THAT THE POLICE WOULD SOON COME TO QUESTION YOU.
IT'S UNTHINKABLE THAT YOU WOULD BE UNPREPARED, OR THAT YOU WOULD GIVE ANSWERS THAT ONLY MADE YOU LOOK WORSE.
I see, of course.

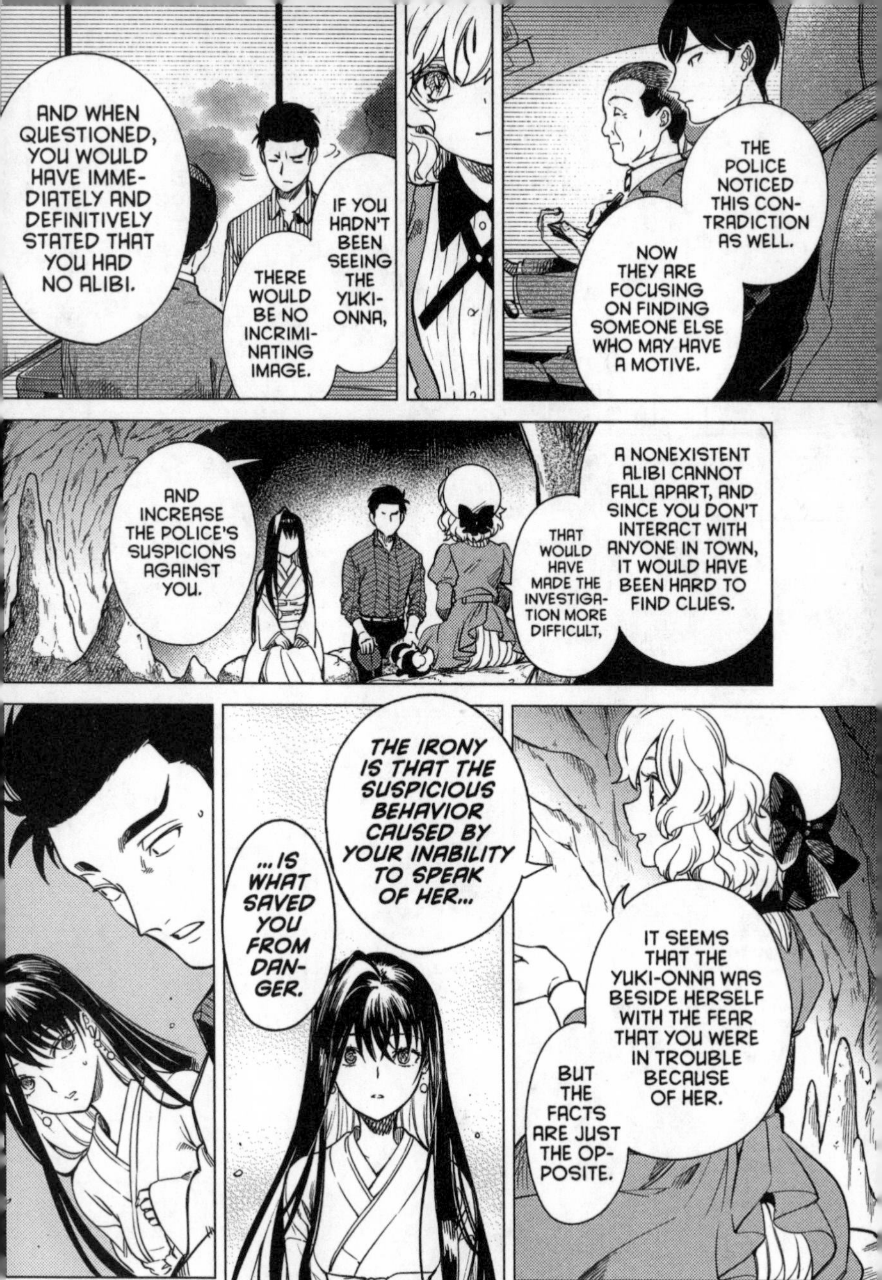
THE POLICE NOTICED THIS CONTRADICTION AS WELL.
NOW THEY ARE FOCUSING ON FINDING SOMEONE ELSE WHO MAY HAVE A MOTIVE.
IF YOU HADN'T BEEN SEEING THE YUKI-ONNA,
THERE WOULD BE NO INCRIMINATING IMAGE.
AND WHEN QUESTIONED, YOU WOULD HAVE IMMEDIATELY AND DEFINITIVELY STATED THAT YOU HAD NO ALIBI.
A NONEXISTENT ALIBI CANNOT FALL APART, AND SINCE YOU DON'T INTERACT WITH ANYONE IN TOWN, IT WOULD HAVE BEEN HARD TO FIND CLUES.
THAT WOULD HAVE MADE THE INVESTIGATION MORE DIFFICULT,
AND INCREASE THE POLICE'S SUSPICIONS AGAINST YOU.
IT SEEMS THAT THE YUKI-ONNA WAS BESIDE HERSELF WITH THE FEAR THAT YOU WERE IN TROUBLE BECAUSE OF HER.
BUT THE FACTS ARE JUST THE OPPOSITE.
THE IRONY IS THAT THE SUSPICIOUS BEHAVIOR CAUSED BY YOUR INABILITY TO SPEAK OF HER...
...IS WHAT SAVED YOU FROM DANGER.

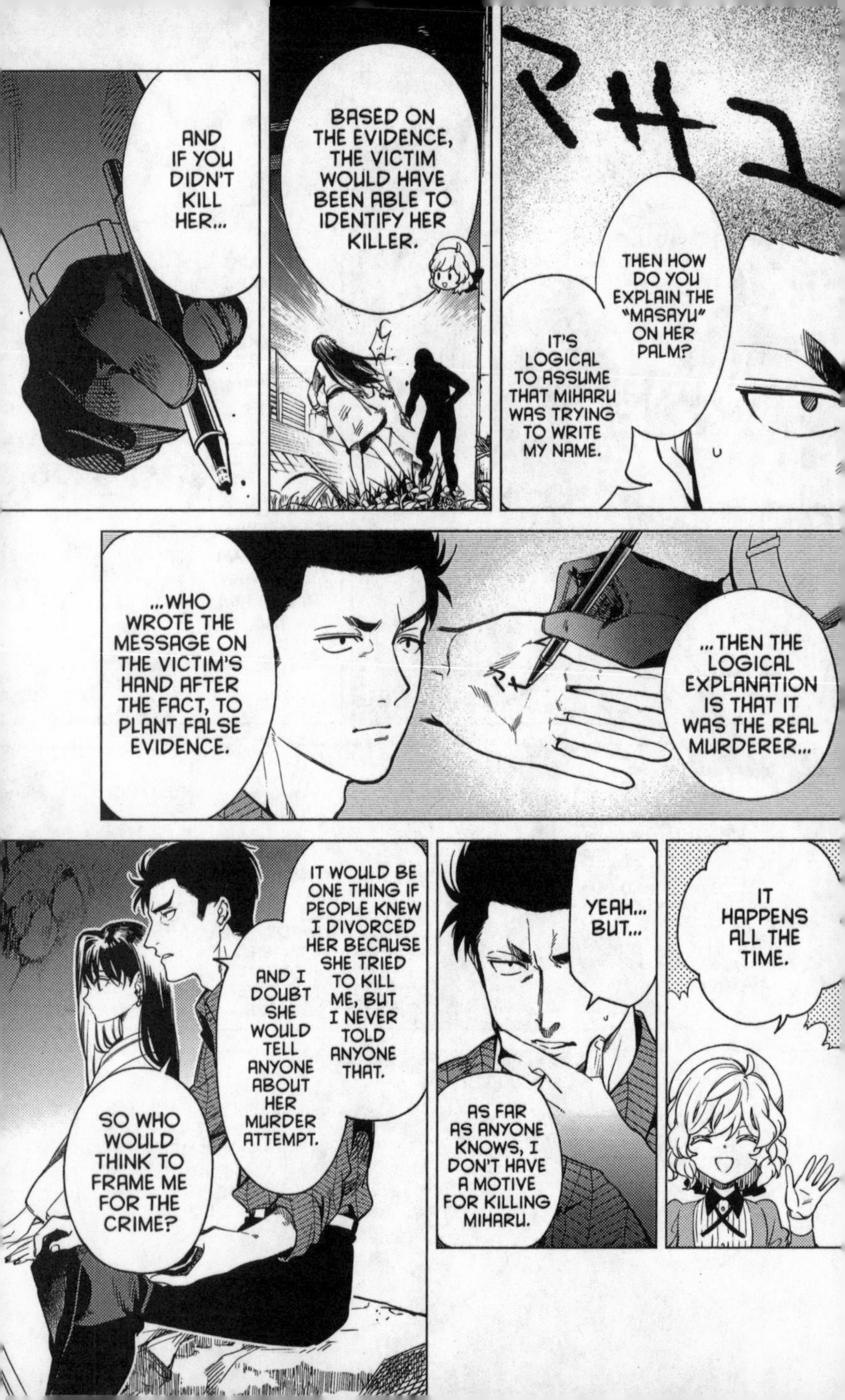
マサユ
THEN HOW DO YOU EXPLAIN THE "MASAYU" ON HER PALM?
IT'S LOGICAL TO ASSUME THAT MIHARU WAS TRYING TO WRITE MY NAME.
BASED ON THE EVIDENCE, THE VICTIM WOULD HAVE BEEN ABLE TO IDENTIFY HER KILLER.
AND IF YOU DIDN'T KILL HER...
...THEN THE LOGICAL EXPLANATION IS THAT IT WAS THE REAL MURDERER...
...WHO WROTE THE MESSAGE ON THE VICTIM'S HAND AFTER THE FACT, TO PLANT FALSE EVIDENCE.
IT HAPPENS ALL THE TIME.
YEAH... BUT...
AS FAR AS ANYONE KNOWS, I DON'T HAVE A MOTIVE FOR KILLING MIHARU.
IT WOULD BE ONE THING IF PEOPLE KNEW I DIVORCED HER BECAUSE SHE TRIED TO KILL ME, BUT I NEVER TOLD ANYONE THAT.
AND I DOUBT SHE WOULD TELL ANYONE ABOUT HER MURDER ATTEMPT.
SO WHO WOULD THINK TO FRAME ME FOR THE CRIME?

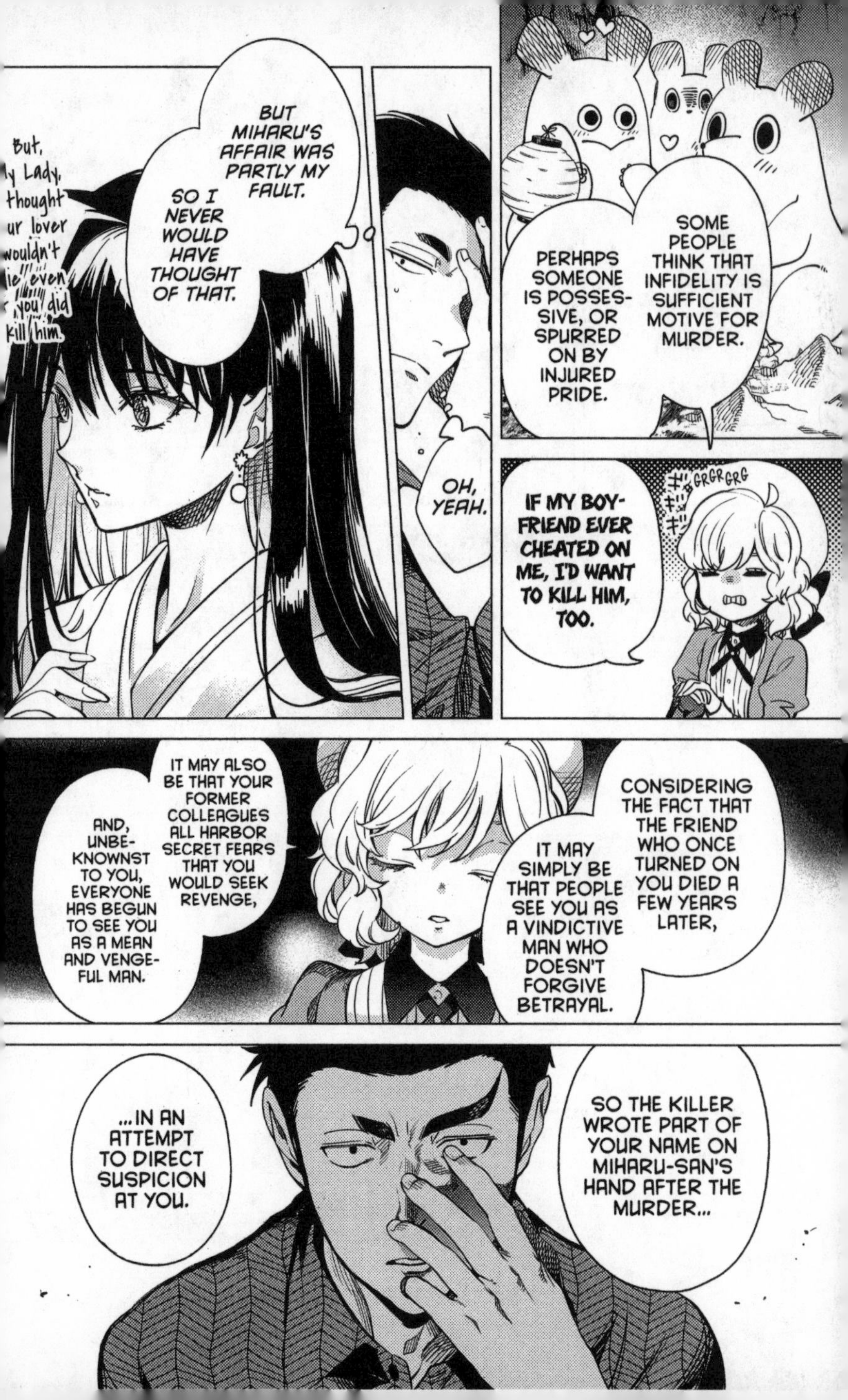

SOME PEOPLE THINK THAT INFIDELITY IS SUFFICIENT MOTIVE FOR MURDER.
PERHAPS SOMEONE IS POSSES-SIVE, OR SPURRED ON BY INJURED PRIDE.
ギギギ GRGRGRG
IF MY BOY-FRIEND EVER CHEATED ON ME, I'D WANT TO KILL HIM, TOO.
OH, YEAH.
BUT MIHARU'S AFFAIR WAS PARTLY MY FAULT.
SO I NEVER WOULD HAVE THOUGHT OF THAT.
But, ly Lady, thought ur lover wouldn't lie even you did kill him.
CONSIDERING THE FACT THAT THE FRIEND WHO ONCE TURNED ON YOU DIED A FEW YEARS LATER,
IT MAY SIMPLY BE THAT PEOPLE SEE YOU AS A VINDICTIVE MAN WHO DOESN'T FORGIVE BETRAYAL.
IT MAY ALSO BE THAT YOUR FORMER COLLEAGUES ALL HARBOR SECRET FEARS THAT YOU WOULD SEEK REVENGE,
AND, UNBE-KNOWNST TO YOU, EVERYONE HAS BEGUN TO SEE YOU AS A MEAN AND VENGE-FUL MAN.
SO THE KILLER WROTE PART OF YOUR NAME ON MIHARU-SAN'S HAND AFTER THE MURDER...
...IN AN ATTEMPT TO DIRECT SUSPICION AT YOU.

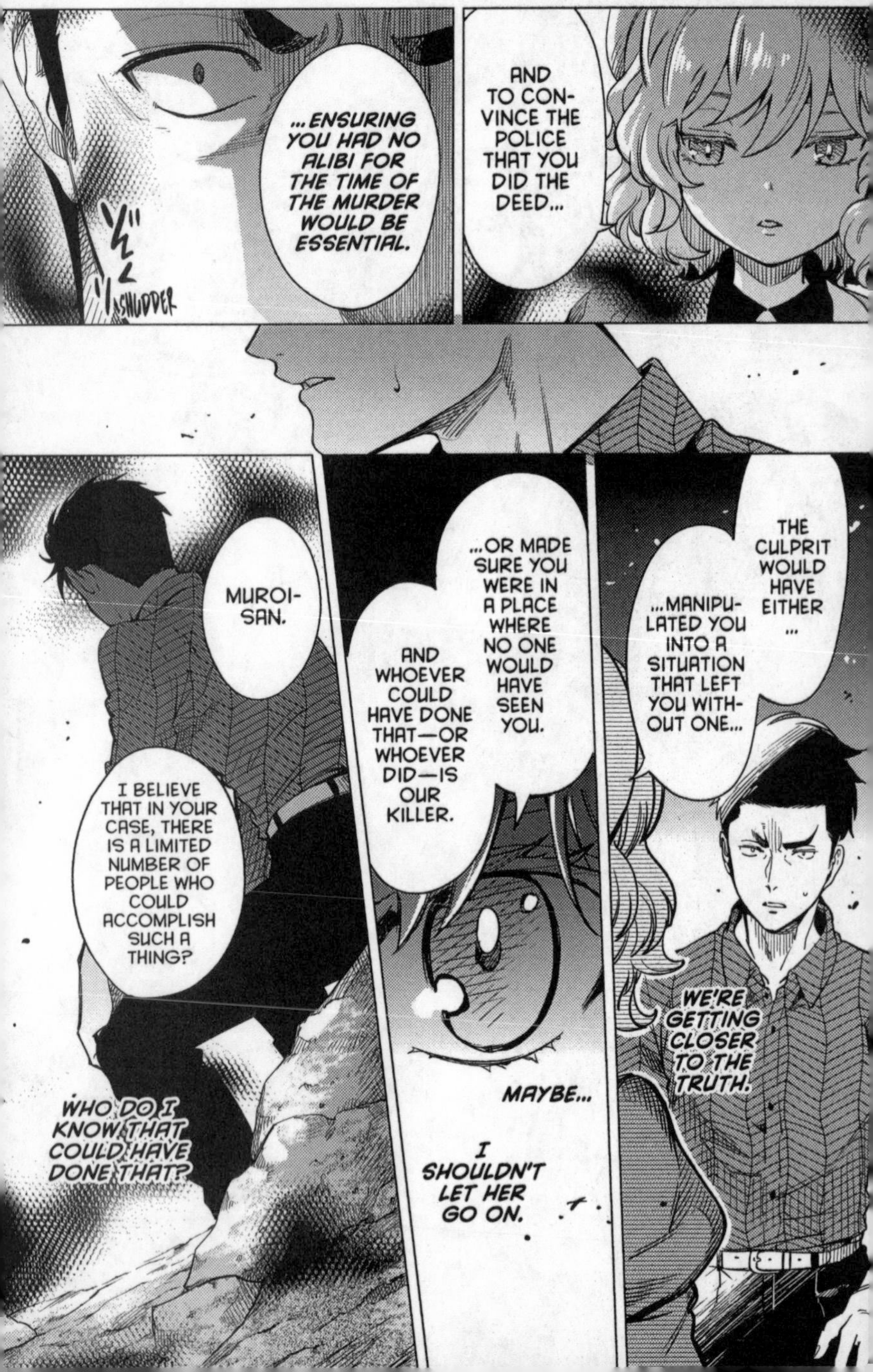
AND TO CONVINCE THE POLICE THAT YOU DID THE DEED...
...ENSURING YOU HAD NO ALIBI FOR THE TIME OF THE MURDER WOULD BE ESSENTIAL.
SHUDDER
THE CULPRIT WOULD HAVE EITHER...
...MANIPULATED YOU INTO A SITUATION THAT LEFT YOU WITHOUT ONE...
WE'RE GETTING CLOSER TO THE TRUTH.
...OR MADE SURE YOU WERE IN A PLACE WHERE NO ONE WOULD HAVE SEEN YOU.
AND WHOEVER COULD HAVE DONE THAT—OR WHOEVER DID—IS OUR KILLER.
MAYBE...
I SHOULDN'T LET HER GO ON.
MUROI-SAN.
I BELIEVE THAT IN YOUR CASE, THERE IS A LIMITED NUMBER OF PEOPLE WHO COULD ACCOMPLISH SUCH A THING?
WHO DO I KNOW THAT COULD HAVE DONE THAT?

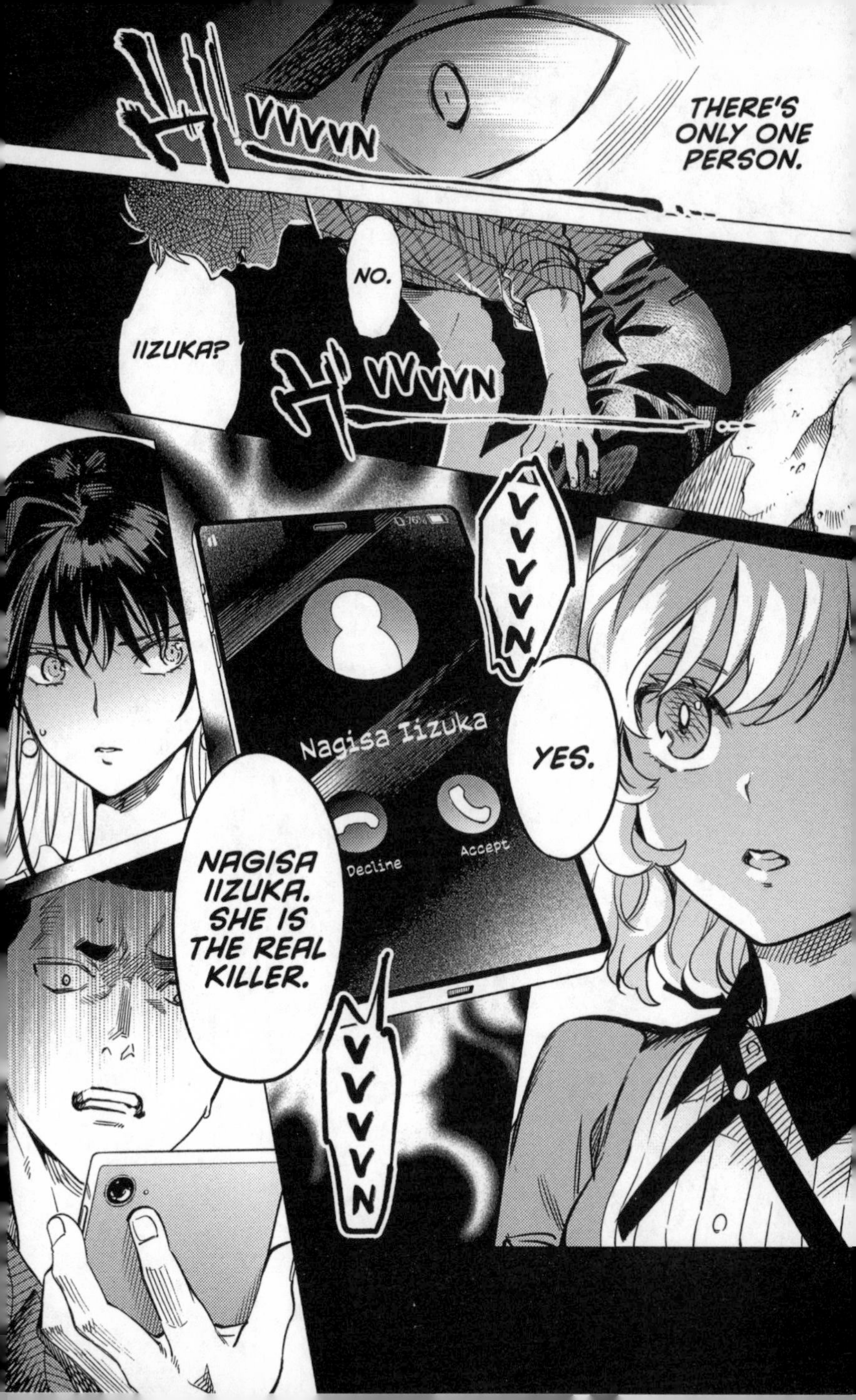
THERE'S ONLY ONE PERSON.
VVVVN
NO.
IIZUKA?
VVVVN
YES.
VVVVN
Nagisa Iizuka
Accept
Decline
NAGISA IIZUKA. SHE IS THE REAL KILLER.
VVVVN

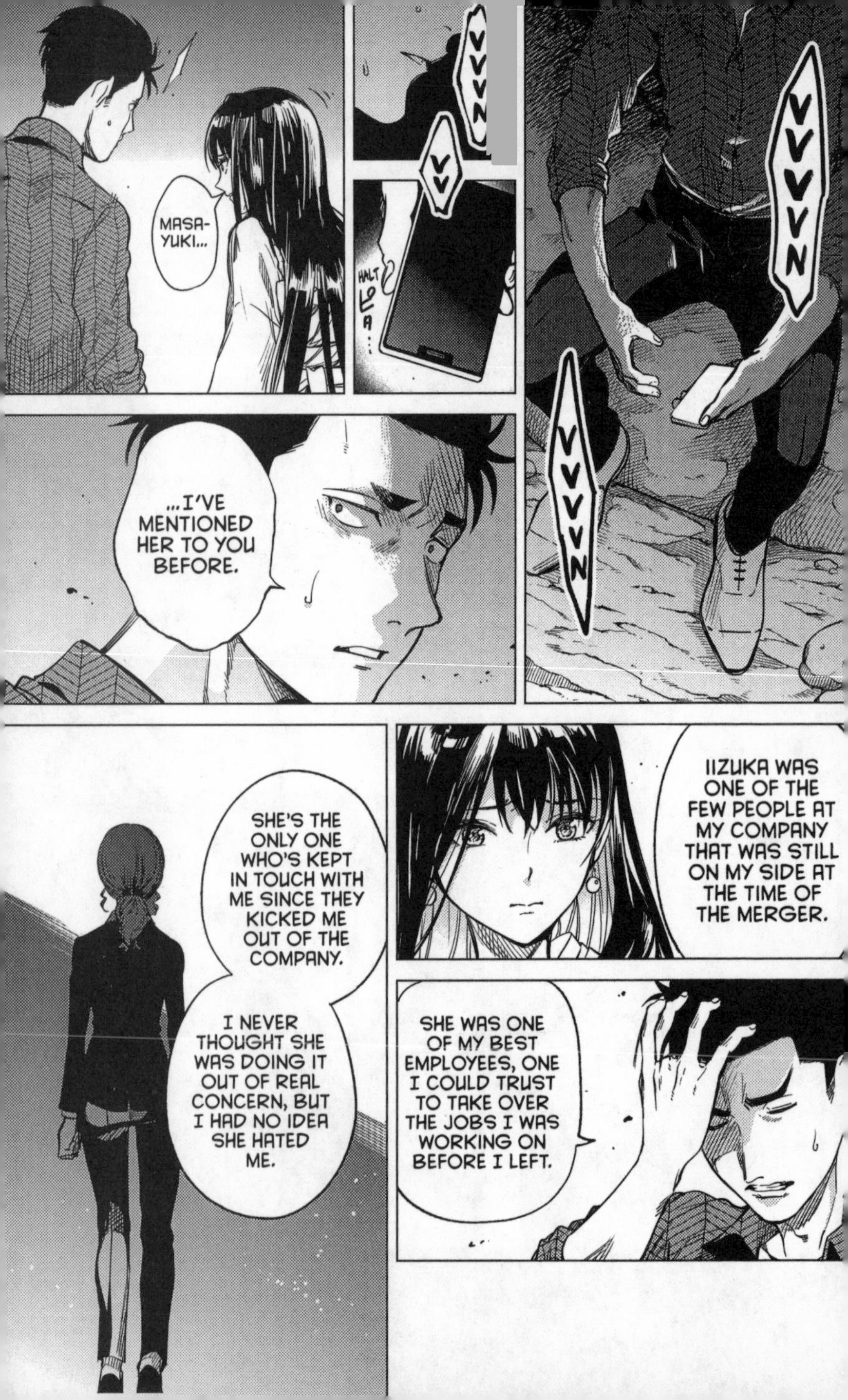
VVVVN
VVVVN
VVVVN
VVV
HALT
MASA-YUKI...
...I'VE MENTIONED HER TO YOU BEFORE.
IIZUKA WAS ONE OF THE FEW PEOPLE AT MY COMPANY THAT WAS STILL ON MY SIDE AT THE TIME OF THE MERGER.
SHE WAS ONE OF MY BEST EMPLOYEES, ONE I COULD TRUST TO TAKE OVER THE JOBS I WAS WORKING ON BEFORE I LEFT.
SHE'S THE ONLY ONE WHO'S KEPT IN TOUCH WITH ME SINCE THEY KICKED ME OUT OF THE COMPANY.
I NEVER THOUGHT SHE WAS DOING IT OUT OF REAL CONCERN, BUT I HAD NO IDEA SHE HATED ME.

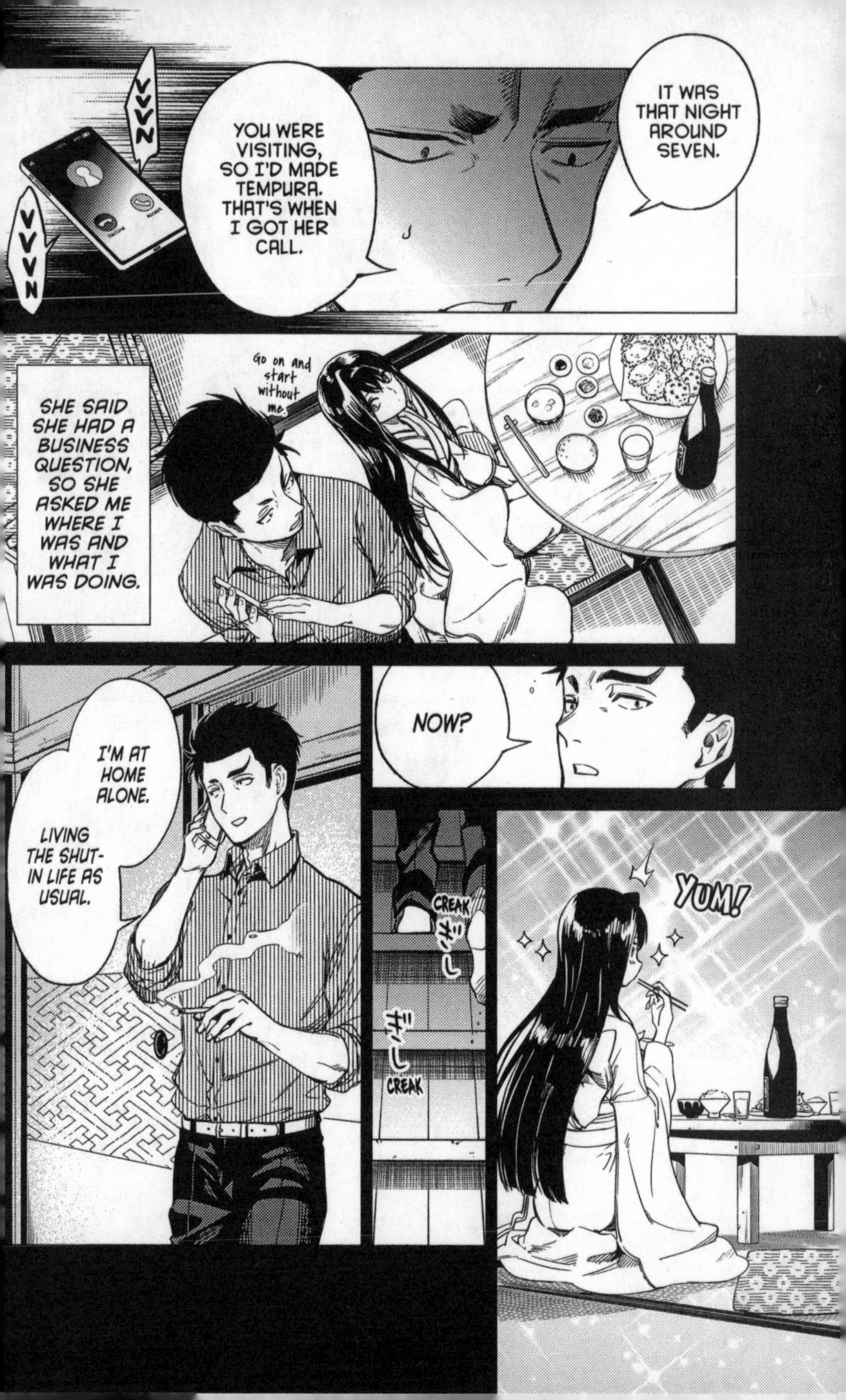
IT WAS THAT NIGHT AROUND SEVEN.
YOU WERE VISITING, SO I'D MADE TEMPURA. THAT'S WHEN I GOT HER CALL.
VVVN
VVVN
Go on and start without me.
SHE SAID SHE HAD A BUSINESS QUESTION, SO SHE ASKED ME WHERE I WAS AND WHAT I WAS DOING.
NOW?
YUM!
CREAK ぎし
ぎし CREAK
I'M AT HOME ALONE.
LIVING THE SHUT-IN LIFE AS USUAL.

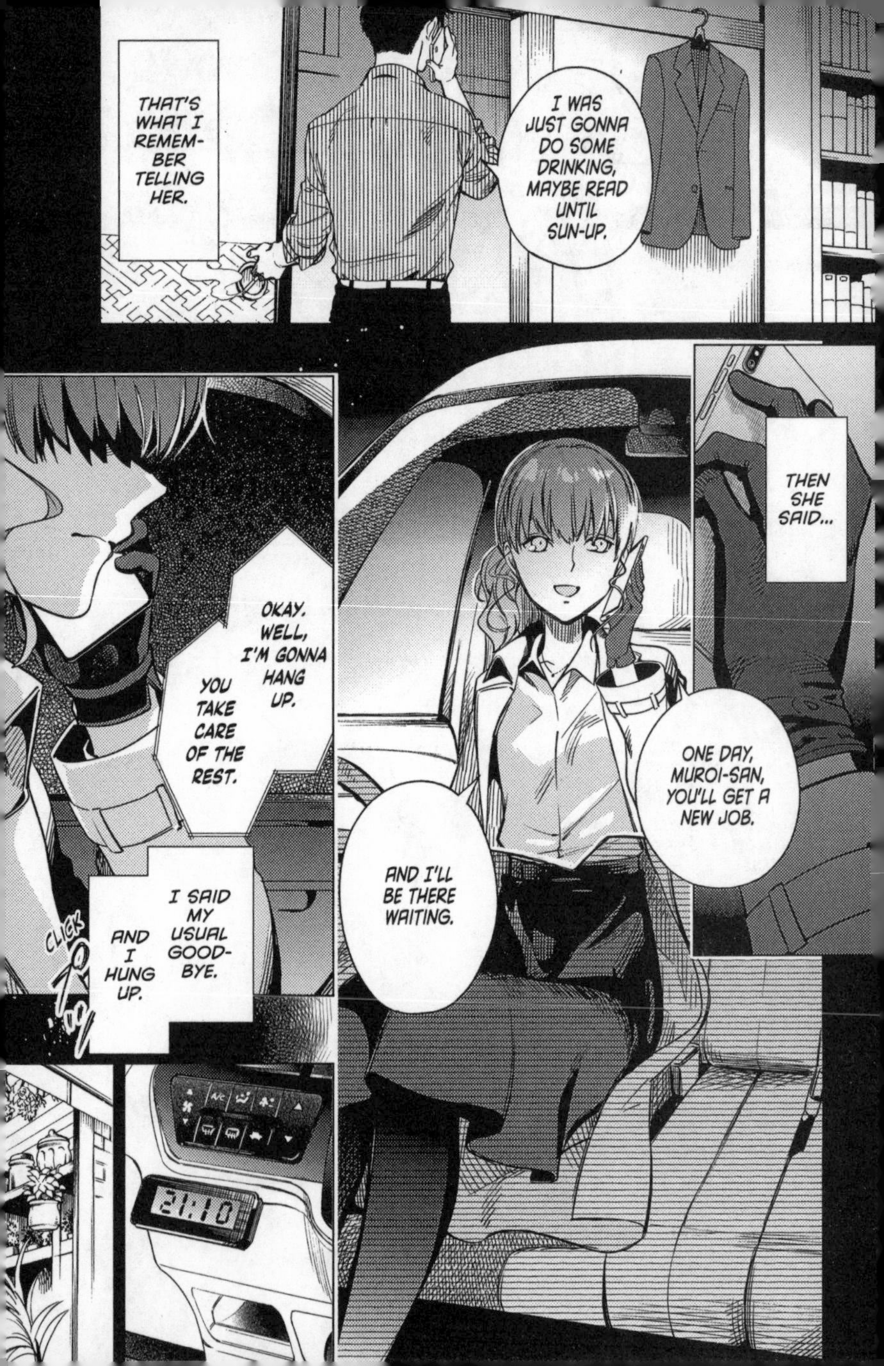
I WAS JUST GONNA DO SOME DRINKING, MAYBE READ UNTIL SUN-UP.
THAT'S WHAT I REMEMBER TELLING HER.
THEN SHE SAID...
ONE DAY, MUROI-SAN, YOU'LL GET A NEW JOB.
AND I'LL BE THERE WAITING.
OKAY. WELL, I'M GONNA HANG UP.
YOU TAKE CARE OF THE REST.
I SAID MY USUAL GOOD-BYE.
AND I HUNG UP.
CLICK
A/C
21:10

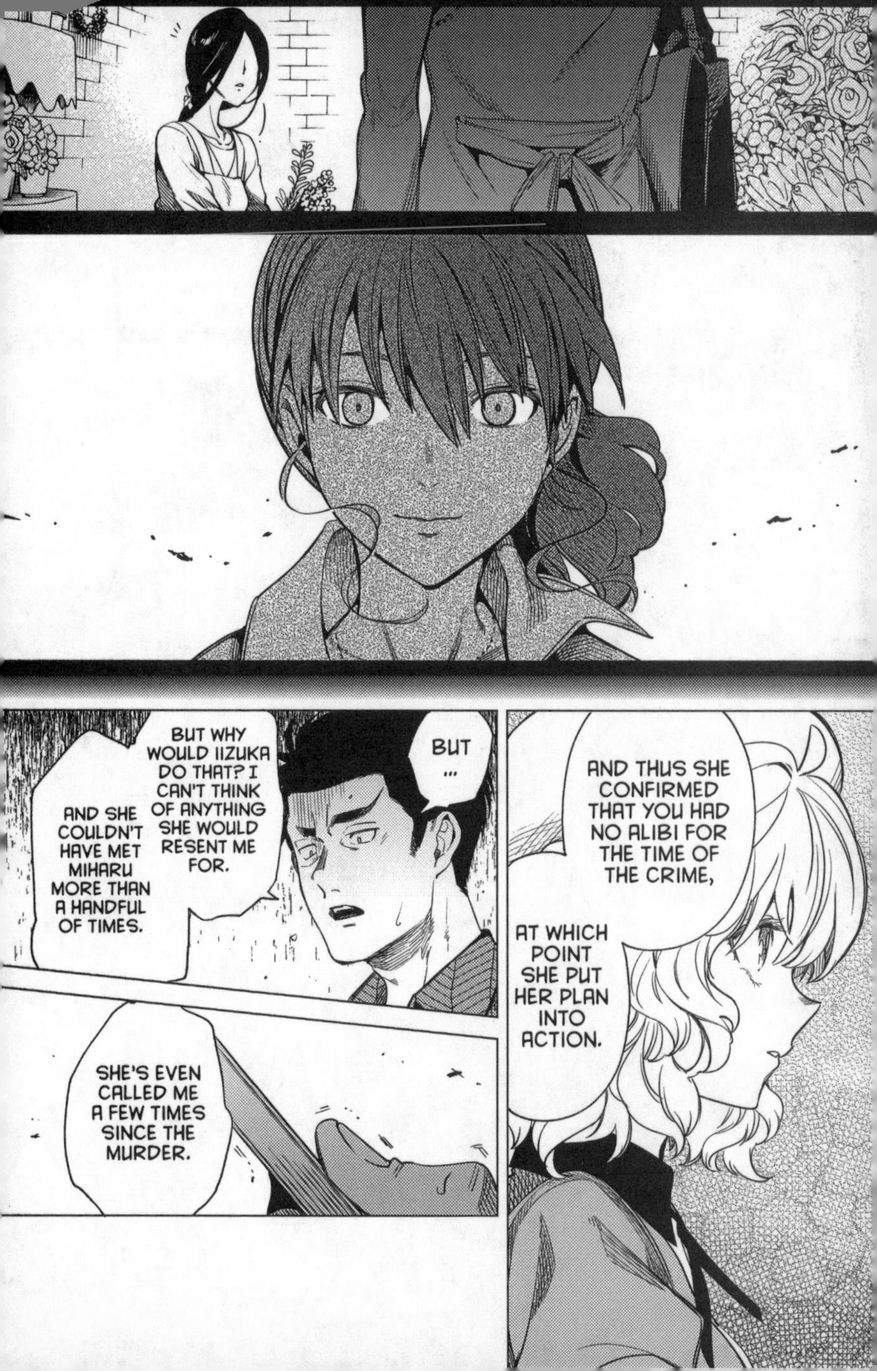
AND THUS SHE CONFIRMED THAT YOU HAD NO ALIBI FOR THE TIME OF THE CRIME,
AT WHICH POINT SHE PUT HER PLAN INTO ACTION.
BUT ...
BUT WHY WOULD IIZUKA DO THAT? I CAN'T THINK OF ANYTHING SHE WOULD RESENT ME FOR.
AND SHE COULDN'T HAVE MET MIHARU MORE THAN A HANDFUL OF TIMES.
SHE'S EVEN CALLED ME A FEW TIMES SINCE THE MURDER.

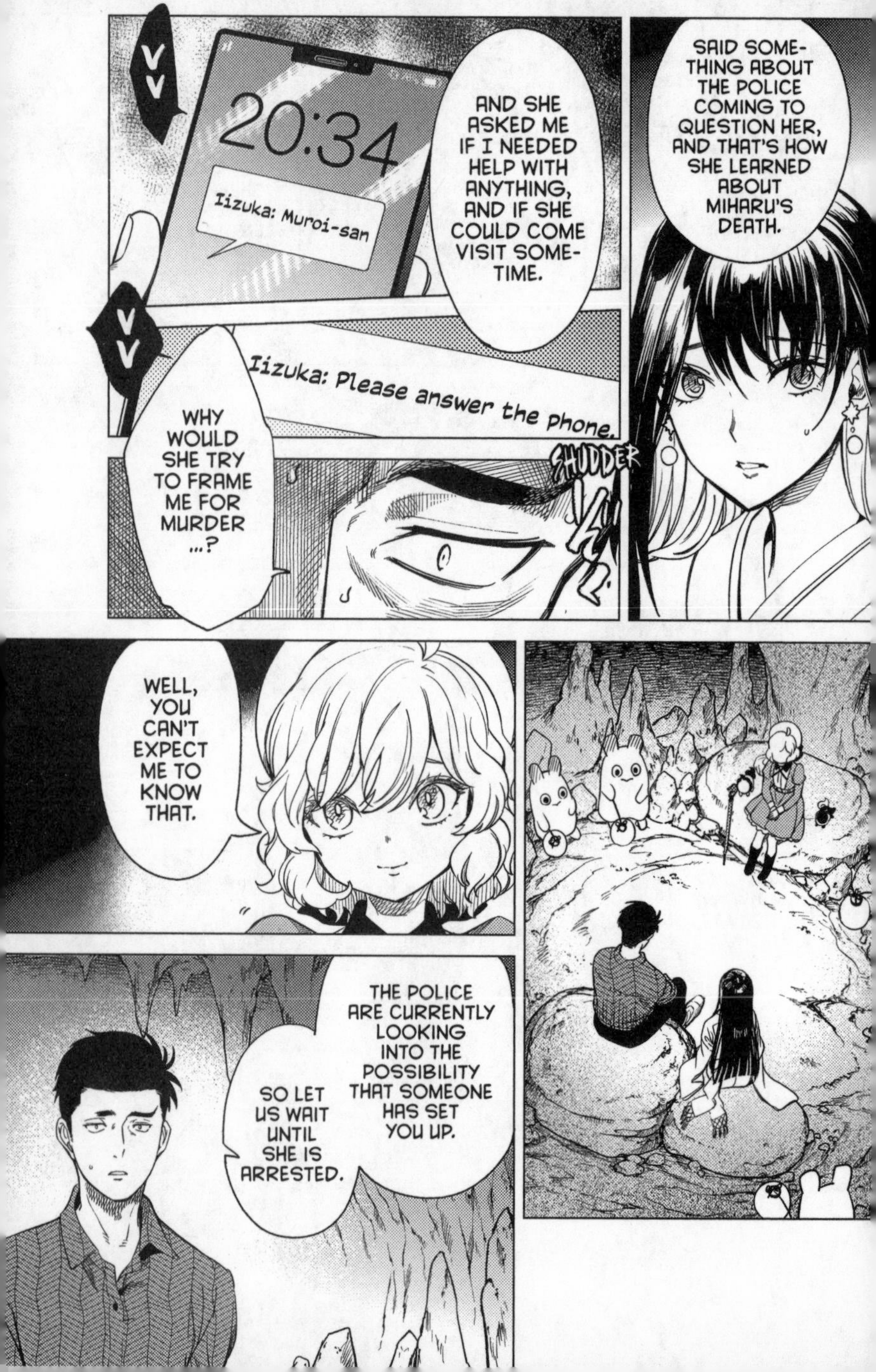
SAID SOMETHING ABOUT THE POLICE COMING TO QUESTION HER, AND THAT'S HOW SHE LEARNED ABOUT MIHARU'S DEATH.
20:34
Iizuka: Muroi-san
AND SHE ASKED ME IF I NEEDED HELP WITH ANYTHING, AND IF SHE COULD COME VISIT SOMETIME.
Iizuka: Please answer the phone.
SHUDDER
WHY WOULD SHE TRY TO FRAME ME FOR MURDER ...?
WELL, YOU CAN'T EXPECT ME TO KNOW THAT.
THE POLICE ARE CURRENTLY LOOKING INTO THE POSSIBILITY THAT SOMEONE HAS SET YOU UP.
SO LET US WAIT UNTIL SHE IS ARRESTED.

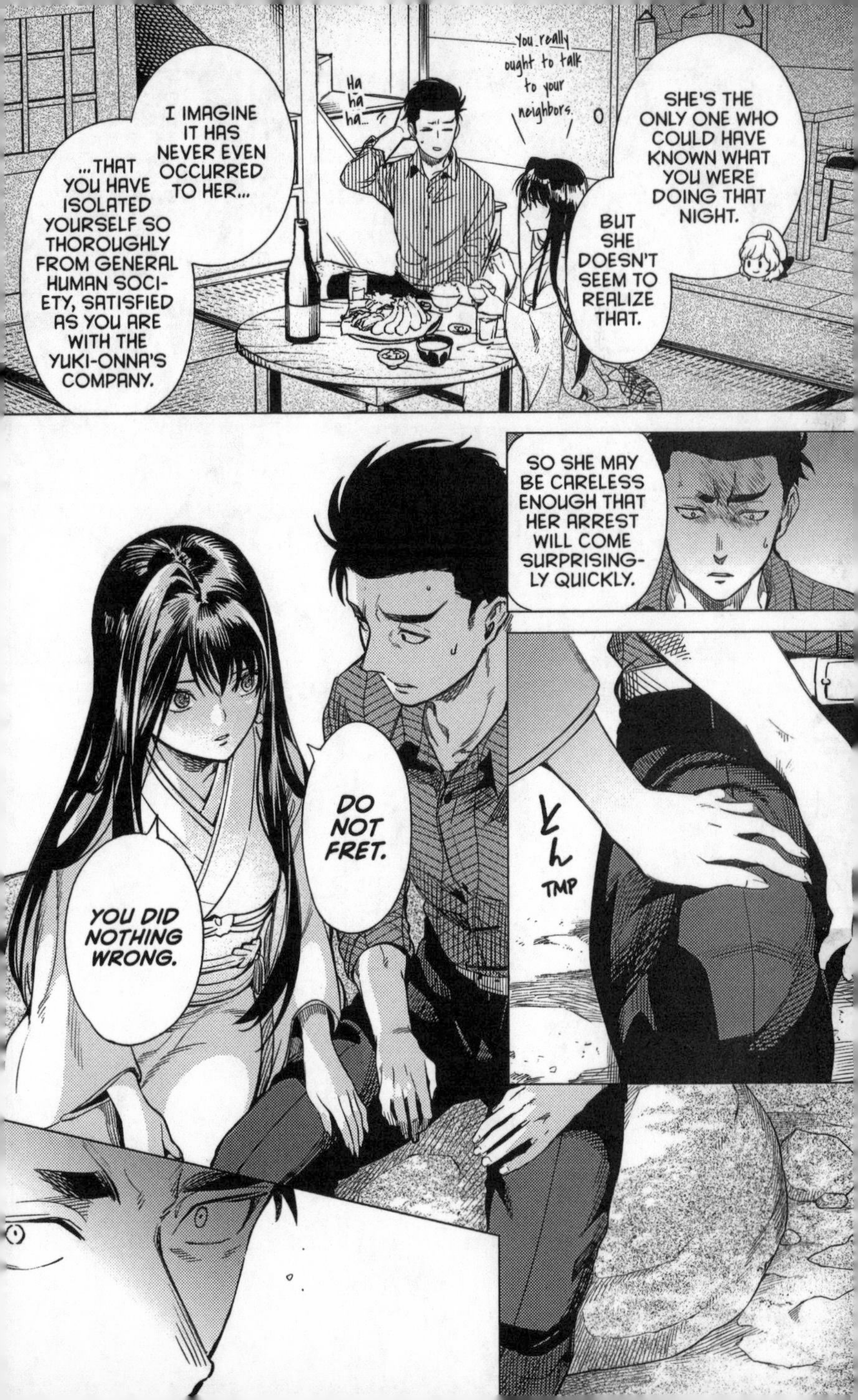
SHE'S THE ONLY ONE WHO COULD HAVE KNOWN WHAT YOU WERE DOING THAT NIGHT.
BUT SHE DOESN'T SEEM TO REALIZE THAT.
You really ought to talk to your neighbors.
Ha ha ha...
I IMAGINE IT HAS NEVER EVEN OCCURRED TO HER...
...THAT YOU HAVE ISOLATED YOURSELF SO THOROUGHLY FROM GENERAL HUMAN SOCI-ETY, SATISFIED AS YOU ARE WITH THE YUKI-ONNA'S COMPANY.
SO SHE MAY BE CARELESS ENOUGH THAT HER ARREST WILL COME SURPRISING-LY QUICKLY.
とん
TMP
DO NOT FRET.
YOU DID NOTHING WRONG.

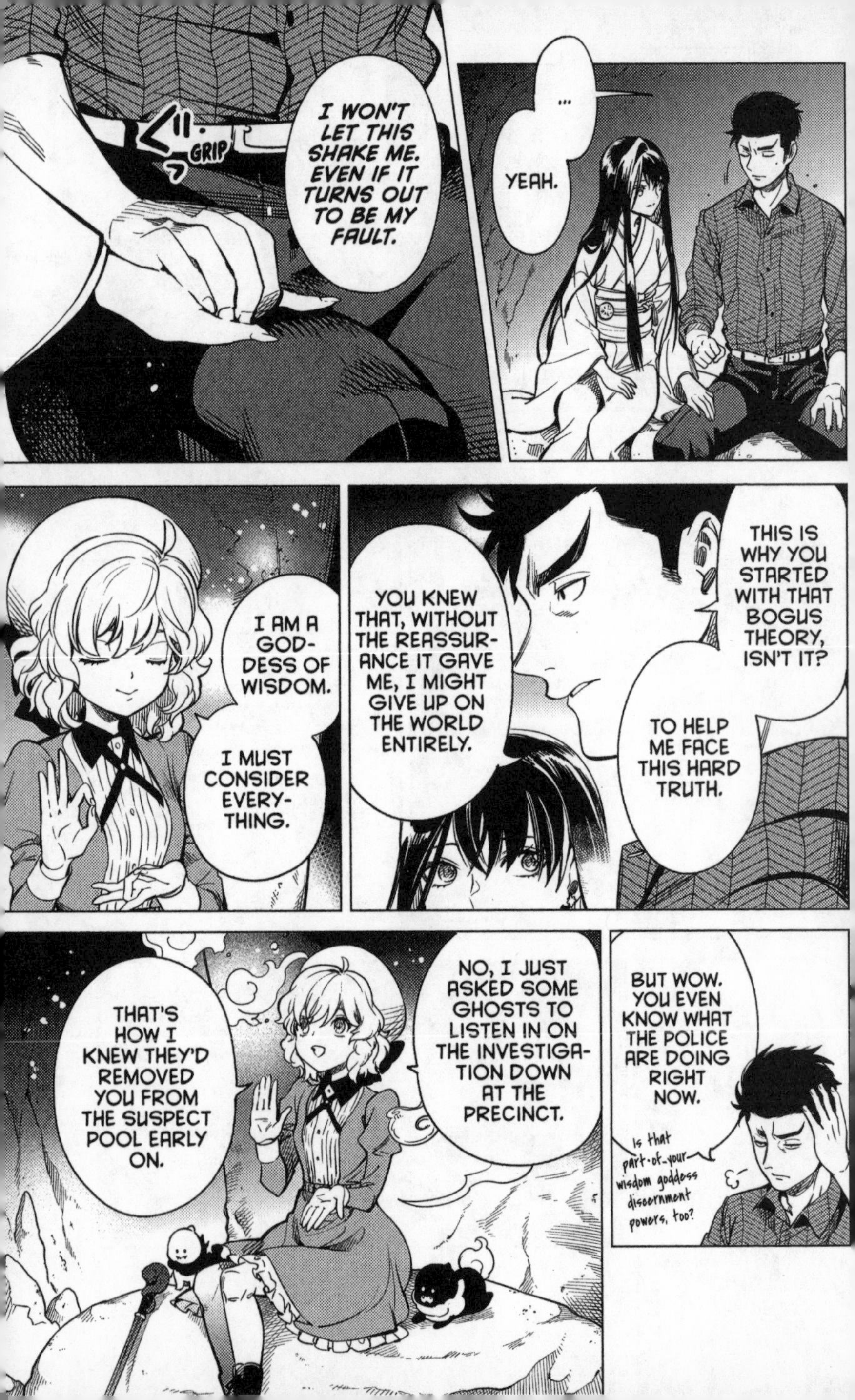
...
YEAH.
GRIP
I WON'T LET THIS SHAKE ME. EVEN IF IT TURNS OUT TO BE MY FAULT.
THIS IS WHY YOU STARTED WITH THAT BOGUS THEORY, ISN'T IT?
TO HELP ME FACE THIS HARD TRUTH.
YOU KNEW THAT, WITHOUT THE REASSUR-ANCE IT GAVE ME, I MIGHT GIVE UP ON THE WORLD ENTIRELY.
I AM A GOD-DESS OF WISDOM.
I MUST CONSIDER EVERY-THING.
BUT WOW. YOU EVEN KNOW WHAT THE POLICE ARE DOING RIGHT NOW.
Is that part of your wisdom goddess discernment powers, too?
NO, I JUST ASKED SOME GHOSTS TO LISTEN IN ON THE INVESTIGA-TION DOWN AT THE PRECINCT.
THAT'S HOW I KNEW THEY'D REMOVED YOU FROM THE SUSPECT POOL EARLY ON.

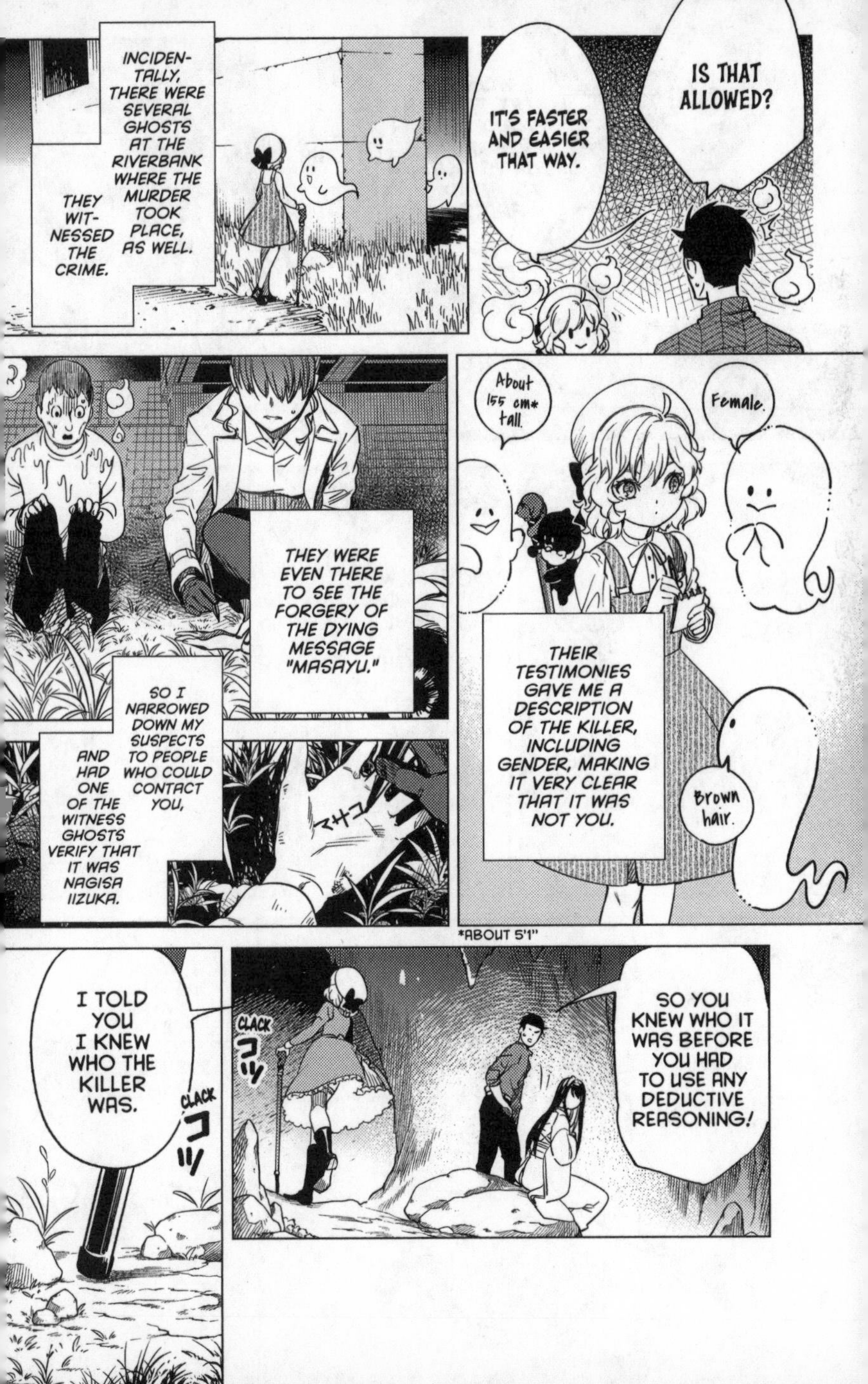
IS THAT ALLOWED?
IT'S FASTER AND EASIER THAT WAY.
INCIDENTALLY, THERE WERE SEVERAL GHOSTS AT THE RIVERBANK WHERE THE MURDER TOOK PLACE, AS WELL.
THEY WITNESSED THE CRIME.
Female.
About 155 cm* tall.
THEIR TESTIMONIES GAVE ME A DESCRIPTION OF THE KILLER, INCLUDING GENDER, MAKING IT VERY CLEAR THAT IT WAS NOT YOU.
Brown hair.
THEY WERE EVEN THERE TO SEE THE FORGERY OF THE DYING MESSAGE "MASAYU."
SO I NARROWED DOWN MY SUSPECTS TO PEOPLE WHO COULD CONTACT YOU,
AND HAD ONE OF THE WITNESS GHOSTS VERIFY THAT IT WAS NAGISA IIZUKA.
マサユ
SO YOU KNEW WHO IT WAS BEFORE YOU HAD TO USE ANY DEDUCTIVE REASONING!
CLACK コツ
I TOLD YOU I KNEW WHO THE KILLER WAS.
CLACK コツ

*ABOUT 5'1"

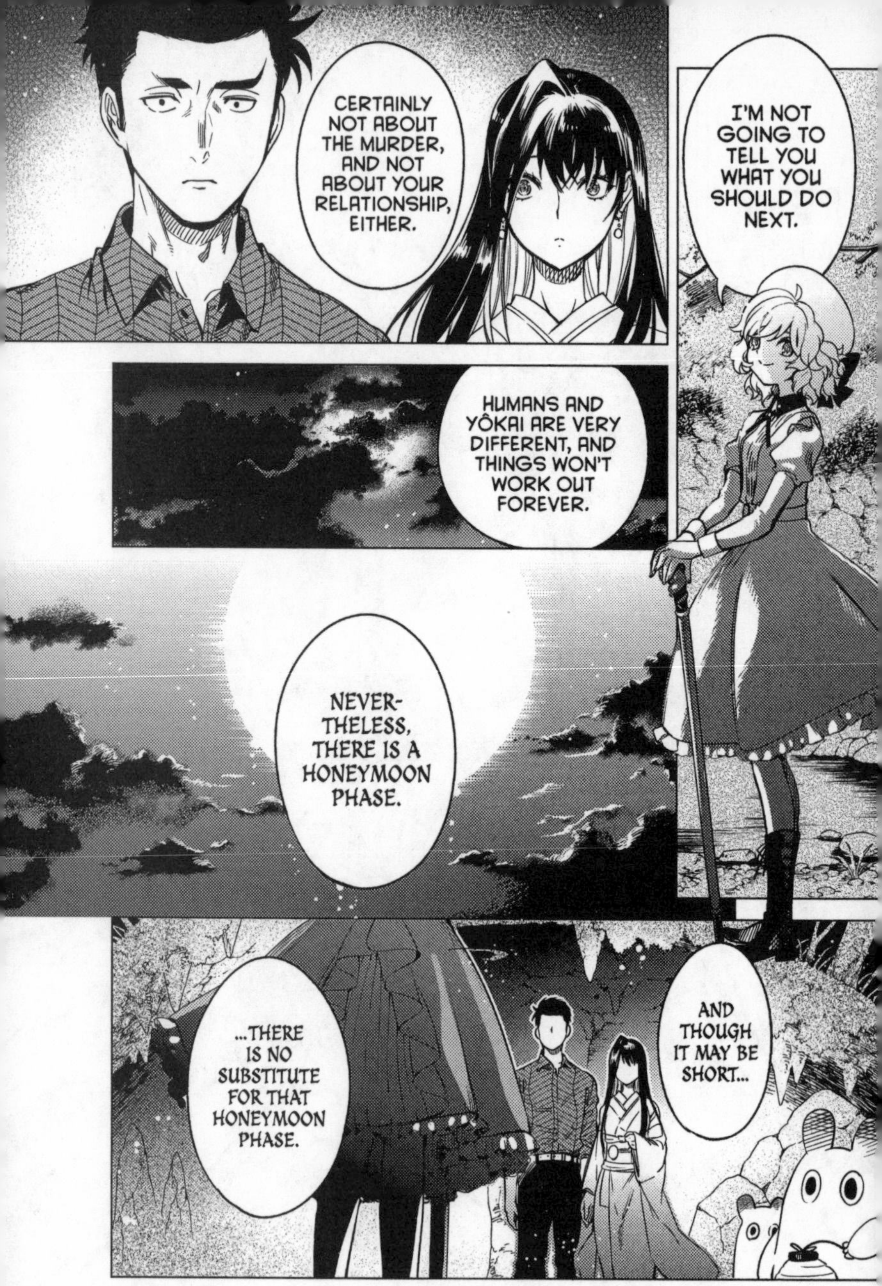
I'M NOT GOING TO TELL YOU WHAT YOU SHOULD DO NEXT.
CERTAINLY NOT ABOUT THE MURDER, AND NOT ABOUT YOUR RELATIONSHIP, EITHER.
HUMANS AND YÔKAI ARE VERY DIFFERENT, AND THINGS WON'T WORK OUT FOREVER.
NEVER-THELESS, THERE IS A HONEYMOON PHASE.
AND THOUGH IT MAY BE SHORT...
...THERE IS NO SUBSTITUTE FOR THAT HONEYMOON PHASE.

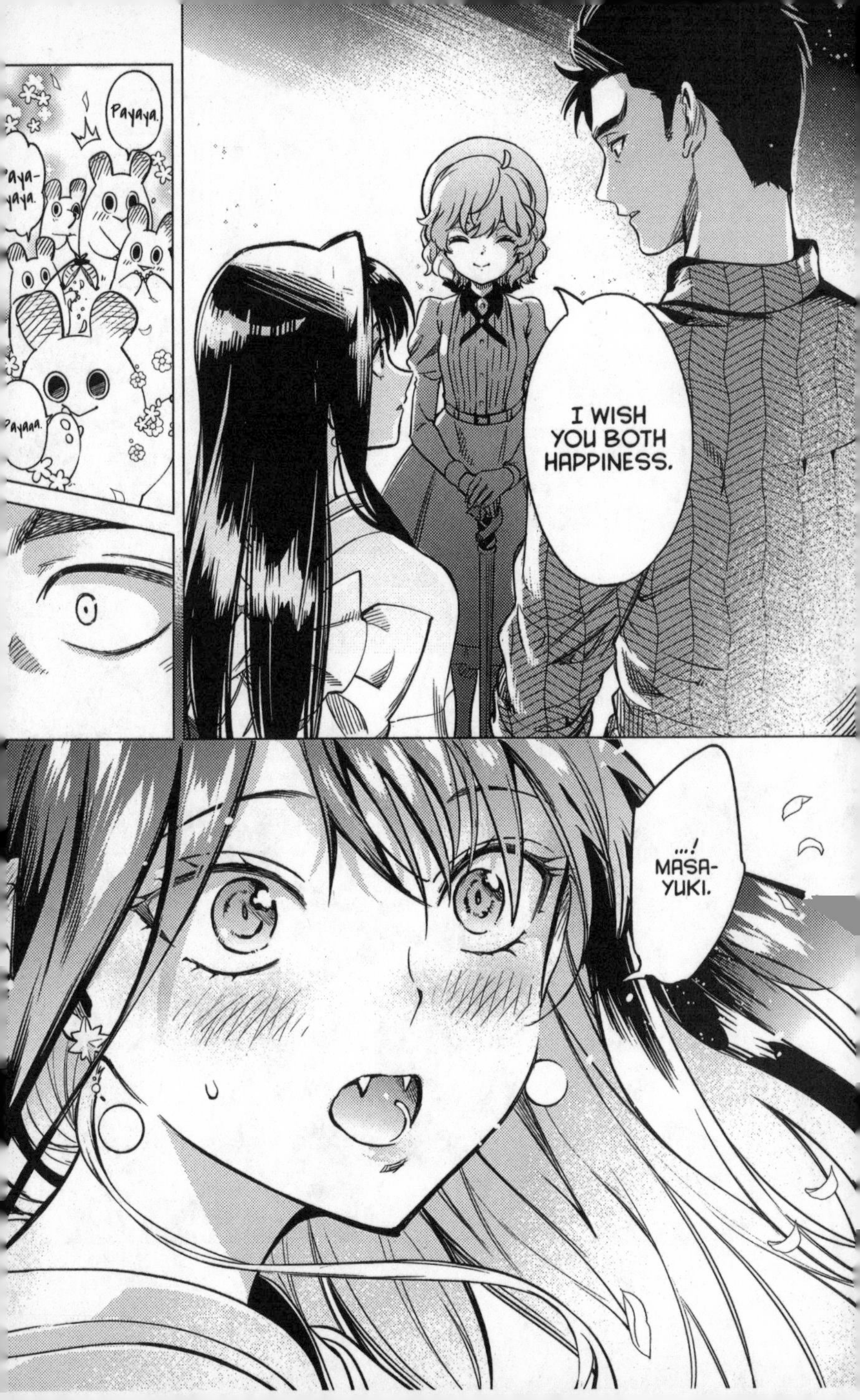

I WISH YOU BOTH HAPPINESS.
Payaya.
Paya-yaya.
Payaaa.
...! MASA-YUKI.

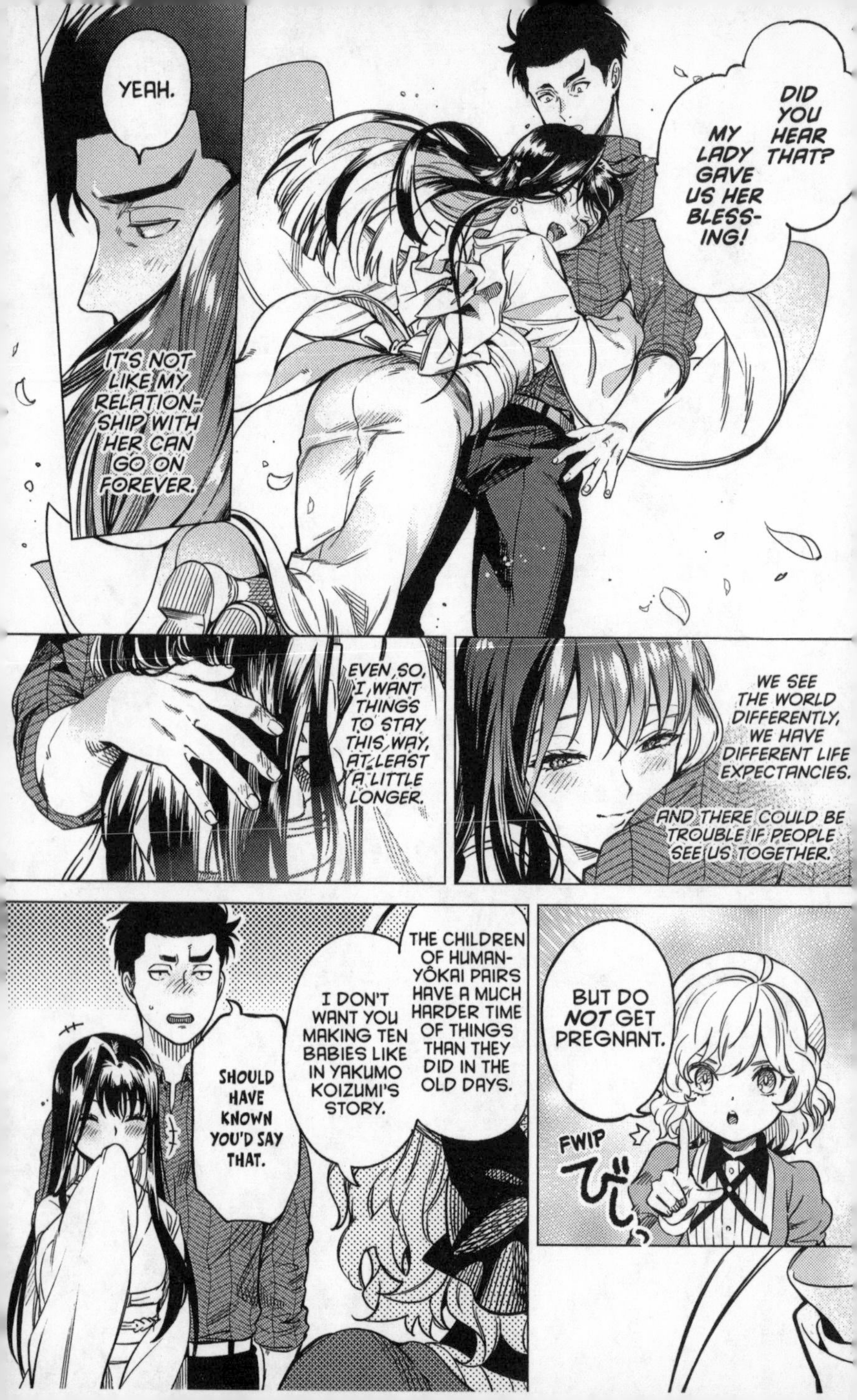
DID YOU HEAR THAT?
MY LADY GAVE US HER BLESSING!
YEAH.
IT'S NOT LIKE MY RELATIONSHIP WITH HER CAN GO ON FOREVER.
WE SEE THE WORLD DIFFERENTLY, WE HAVE DIFFERENT LIFE EXPECTANCIES.
AND THERE COULD BE TROUBLE IF PEOPLE SEE US TOGETHER.
EVEN SO, I WANT THINGS TO STAY THIS WAY, AT LEAST A LITTLE LONGER.
BUT DO NOT GET PREGNANT.
FWIP
びしっ
THE CHILDREN OF HUMAN-YÔKAI PAIRS HAVE A MUCH HARDER TIME OF THINGS THAN THEY DID IN THE OLD DAYS.
I DON'T WANT YOU MAKING TEN BABIES LIKE IN YAKUMO KOIZUMI'S STORY.
SHOULD HAVE KNOWN YOU'D SAY THAT.

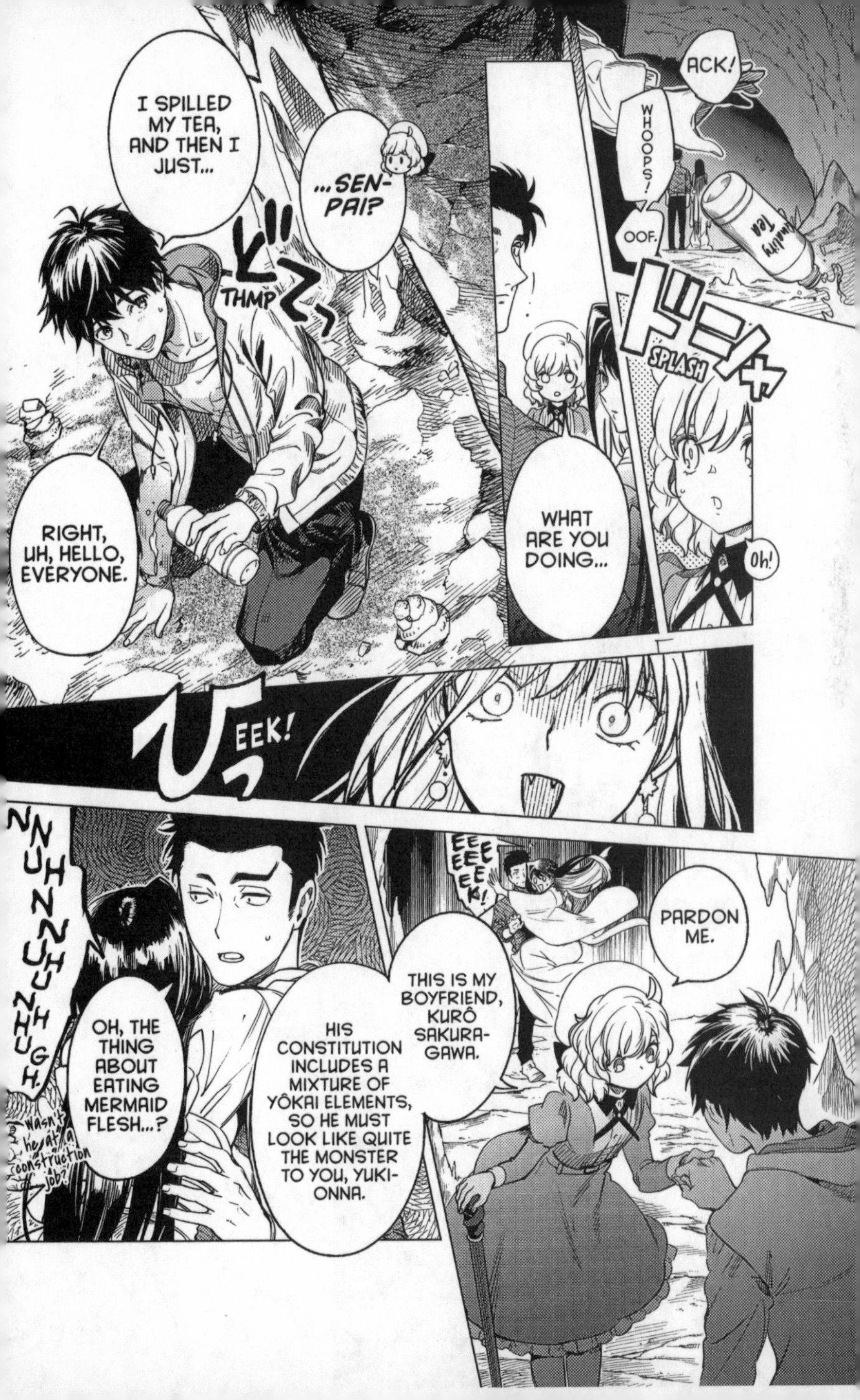
ACK!
WHOOPS!
OOF.
Quality Tea
SPLASH
Oh!
WHAT ARE YOU DOING...
...SEN-PAI?
I SPILLED MY TEA, AND THEN I JUST...
THMP
RIGHT, UH, HELLO, EVERYONE.
EEK!
PARDON ME.
EEEEEEEK!
THIS IS MY BOYFRIEND, KURÔ SAKURA-GAWA.
HIS CONSTITUTION INCLUDES A MIXTURE OF YÔKAI ELEMENTS, SO HE MUST LOOK LIKE QUITE THE MONSTER TO YOU, YUKI-ONNA.
OH, THE THING ABOUT EATING MERMAID FLESH...?
NNUHNNNUHUHNHUGH.
Wasn't he at a construction job?

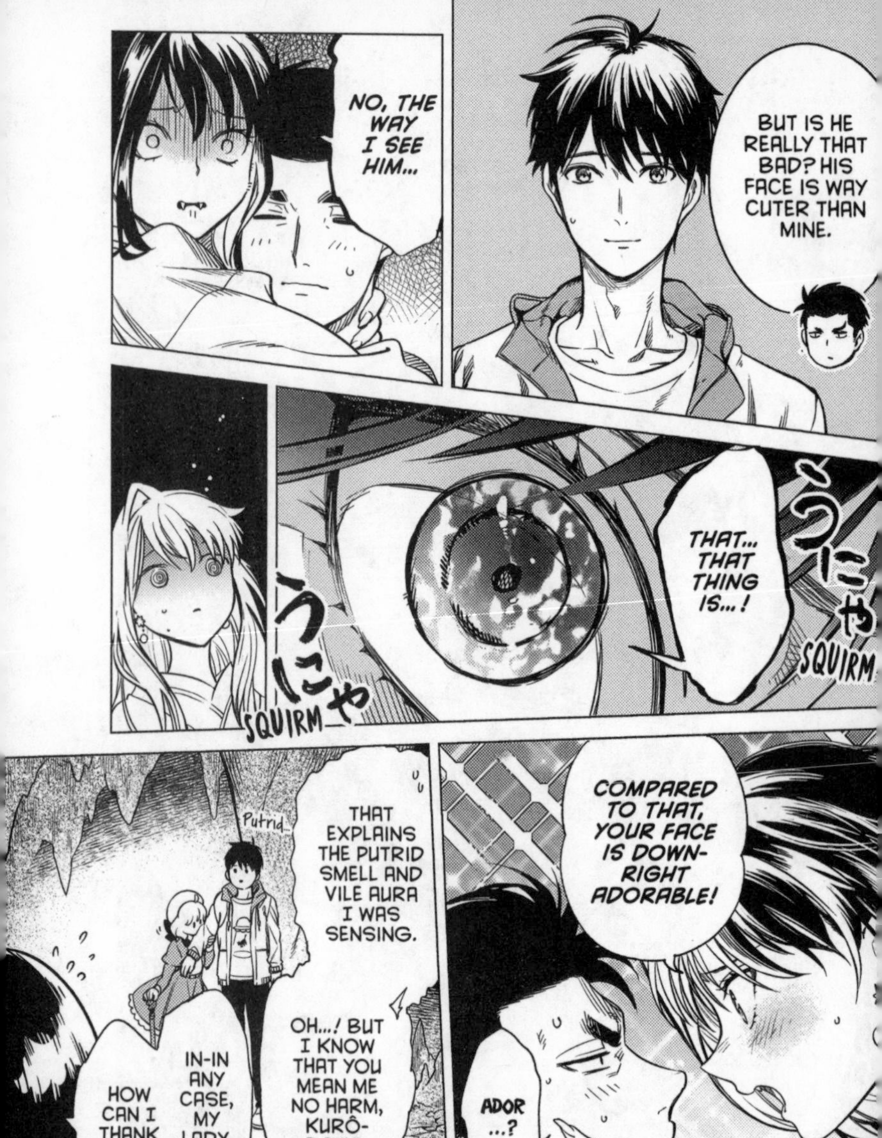
BUT IS HE REALLY THAT BAD? HIS FACE IS WAY CUTER THAN MINE.
NO, THE WAY I SEE HIM...
うにゃ
SQUIRM
THAT... THAT THING IS...!
うにゃ
SQUIRM
COMPARED TO THAT, YOUR FACE IS DOWN-RIGHT ADORABLE!
ADOR ...?
YANK
ぐい
Putrid...
THAT EXPLAINS THE PUTRID SMELL AND VILE AURA I WAS SENSING.
OH...! BUT I KNOW THAT YOU MEAN ME NO HARM, KURÔ-DONO.
IN-IN ANY CASE, MY LADY.
HOW CAN I THANK YOU FOR YOUR AID?

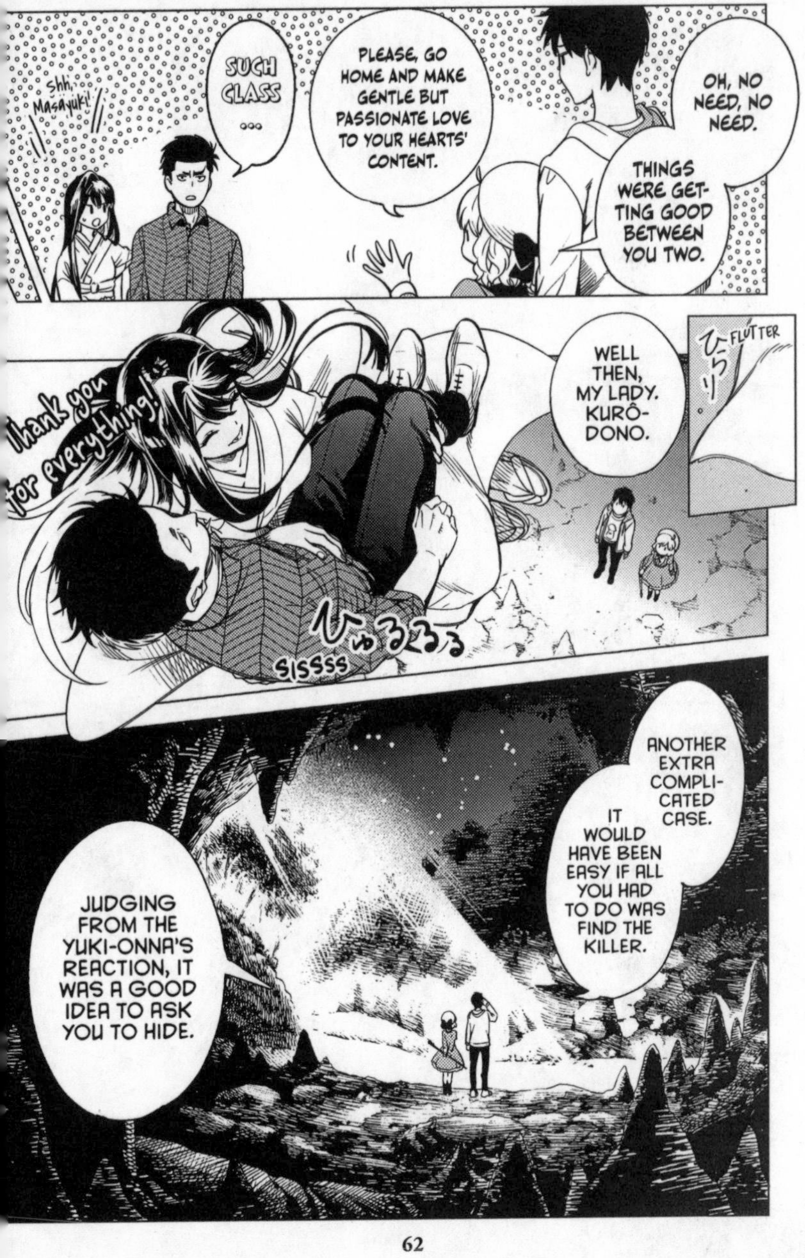

OH, NO NEED, NO NEED.
THINGS WERE GETTING GOOD BETWEEN YOU TWO.
PLEASE, GO HOME AND MAKE GENTLE BUT PASSIONATE LOVE TO YOUR HEARTS' CONTENT.
SUCH CLASS...
Shh, Masayuki!
ひらり FLUTTER
WELL THEN, MY LADY. KURÔ-DONO.
Thank you for everything!
ひゅるるる SISSSS
ANOTHER EXTRA COMPLICATED CASE.
IT WOULD HAVE BEEN EASY IF ALL YOU HAD TO DO WAS FIND THE KILLER.
JUDGING FROM THE YUKI-ONNA'S REACTION, IT WAS A GOOD IDEA TO ASK YOU TO HIDE.

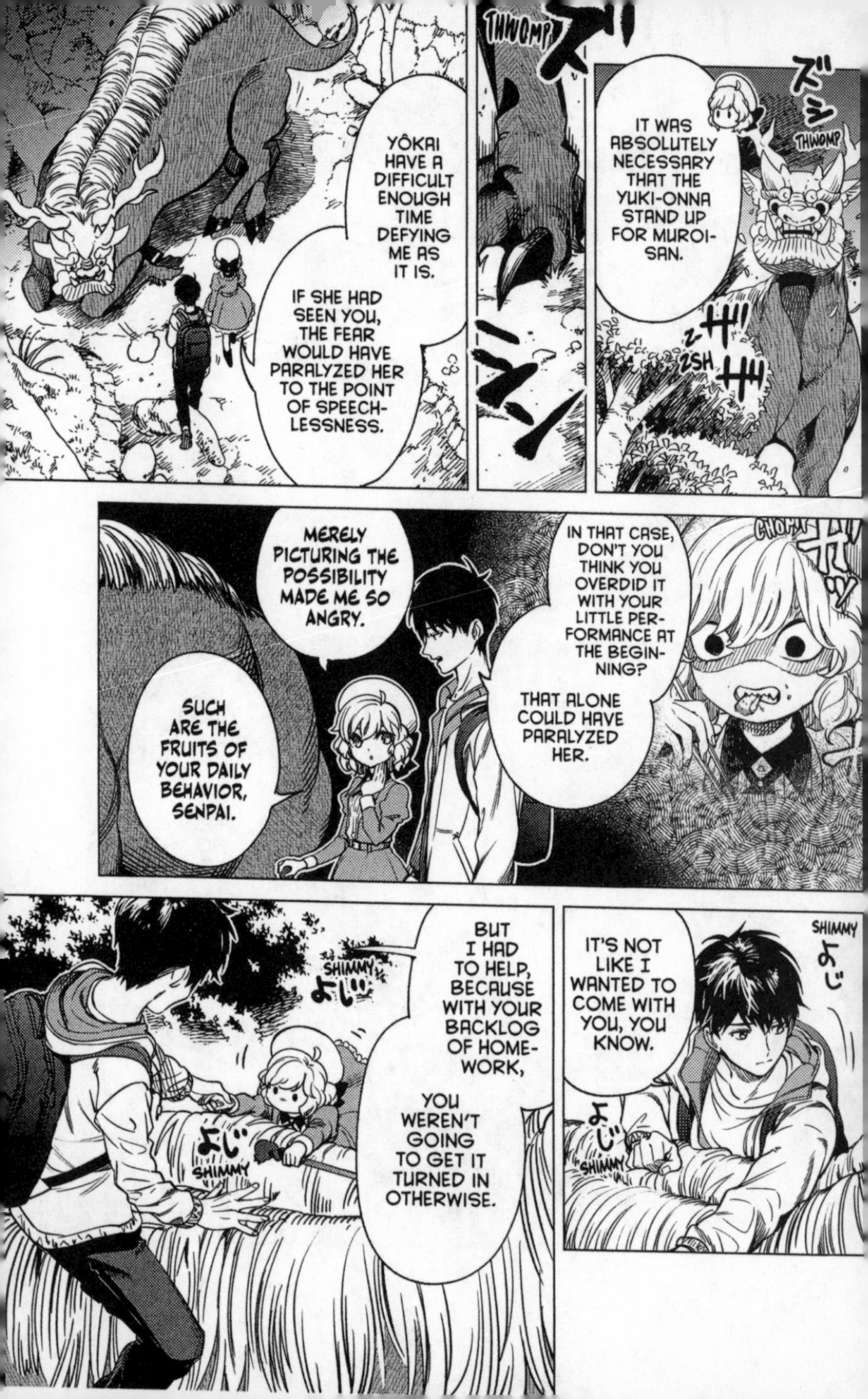
THWOMP
IT WAS ABSOLUTELY NECESSARY THAT THE YUKI-ONNA STAND UP FOR MUROI-SAN.
ZSH
THWOMP
YÔKAI HAVE A DIFFICULT ENOUGH TIME DEFYING ME AS IT IS.
IF SHE HAD SEEN YOU, THE FEAR WOULD HAVE PARALYZED HER TO THE POINT OF SPEECH-LESSNESS.
CHOMP
IN THAT CASE, DON'T YOU THINK YOU OVERDID IT WITH YOUR LITTLE PER-FORMANCE AT THE BEGIN-NING?
THAT ALONE COULD HAVE PARALYZED HER.
MERELY PICTURING THE POSSIBILITY MADE ME SO ANGRY.
SUCH ARE THE FRUITS OF YOUR DAILY BEHAVIOR, SENPAI.
SHIMMY
IT'S NOT LIKE I WANTED TO COME WITH YOU, YOU KNOW.
SHIMMY
BUT I HAD TO HELP, BECAUSE WITH YOUR BACKLOG OF HOME-WORK,
YOU WEREN'T GOING TO GET IT TURNED IN OTHERWISE.
SHIMMY
SHIMMY

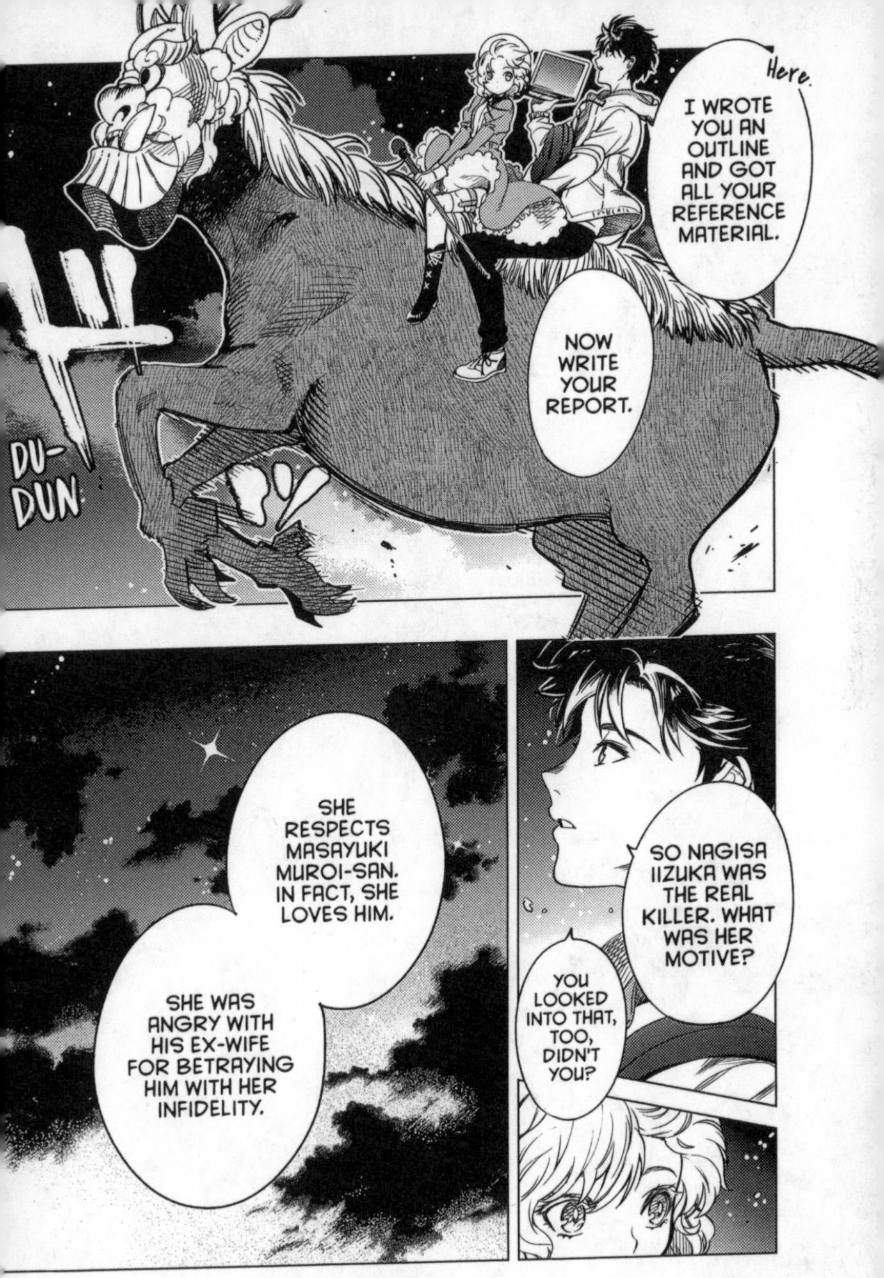
Here.
I WROTE YOU AN OUTLINE AND GOT ALL YOUR REFERENCE MATERIAL.
NOW WRITE YOUR REPORT.
DU-DUN
SO NAGISA IIZUKA WAS THE REAL KILLER. WHAT WAS HER MOTIVE?
YOU LOOKED INTO THAT, TOO, DIDN'T YOU?
SHE RESPECTS MASAYUKI MUROI-SAN. IN FACT, SHE LOVES HIM.
SHE WAS ANGRY WITH HIS EX-WIFE FOR BETRAYING HIM WITH HER INFIDELITY.

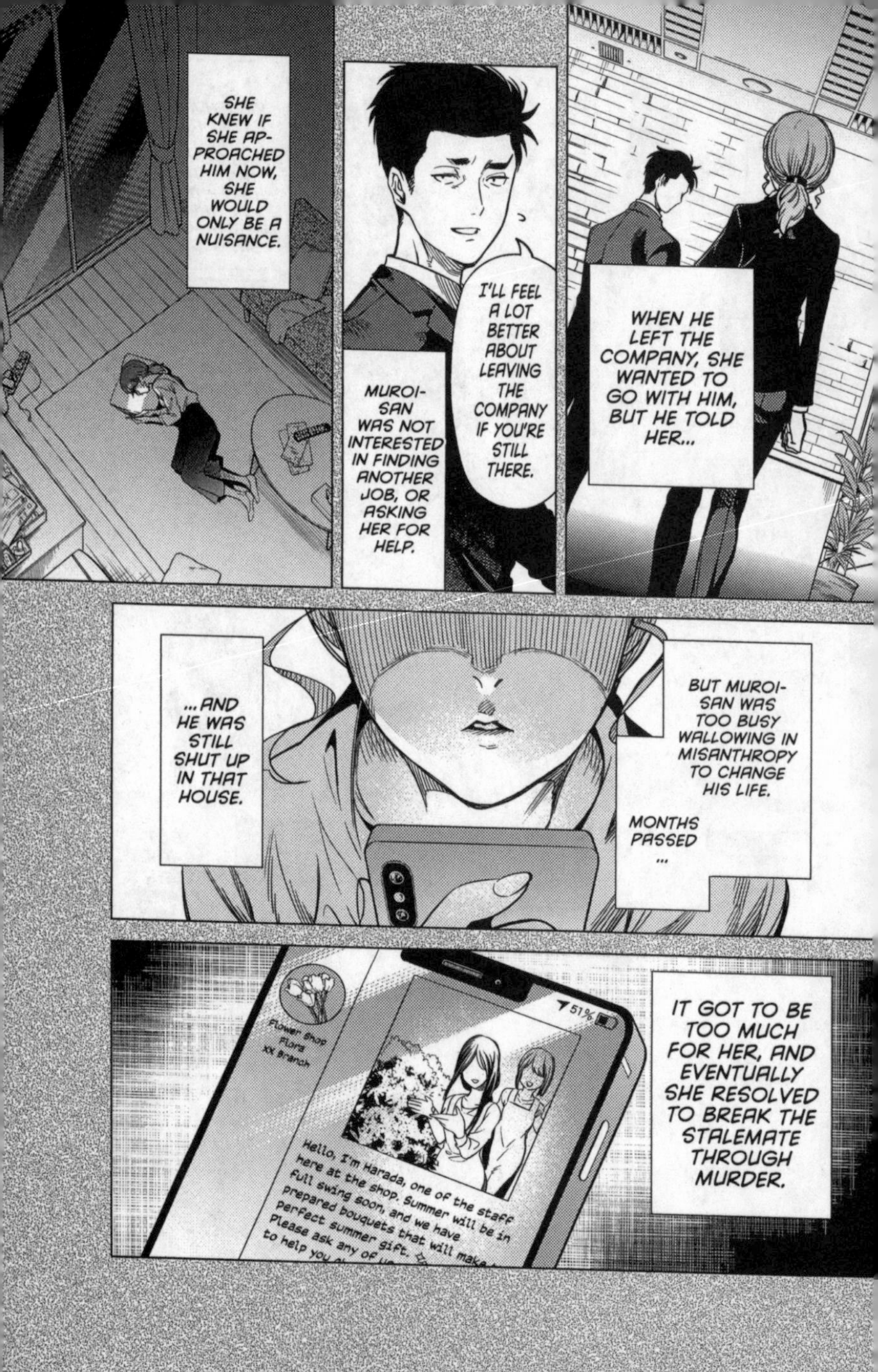
WHEN HE LEFT THE COMPANY, SHE WANTED TO GO WITH HIM, BUT HE TOLD HER...
I'LL FEEL A LOT BETTER ABOUT LEAVING THE COMPANY IF YOU'RE STILL THERE.
MUROI-SAN WAS NOT INTERESTED IN FINDING ANOTHER JOB, OR ASKING HER FOR HELP.
SHE KNEW IF SHE AP-PROACHED HIM NOW, SHE WOULD ONLY BE A NUISANCE.
BUT MUROI-SAN WAS TOO BUSY WALLOWING IN MISANTHROPY TO CHANGE HIS LIFE.
MONTHS PASSED ...
...AND HE WAS STILL SHUT UP IN THAT HOUSE.
IT GOT TO BE TOO MUCH FOR HER, AND EVENTUALLY SHE RESOLVED TO BREAK THE STALEMATE THROUGH MURDER.
51%
Flower Shop Flora XX Branch
Hello, I'm Harada, one of the staff here at the shop. Summer will be in full swing soon, and we have prepared bouquets that will make
perfect summer gift.
Please ask any of us
to help you

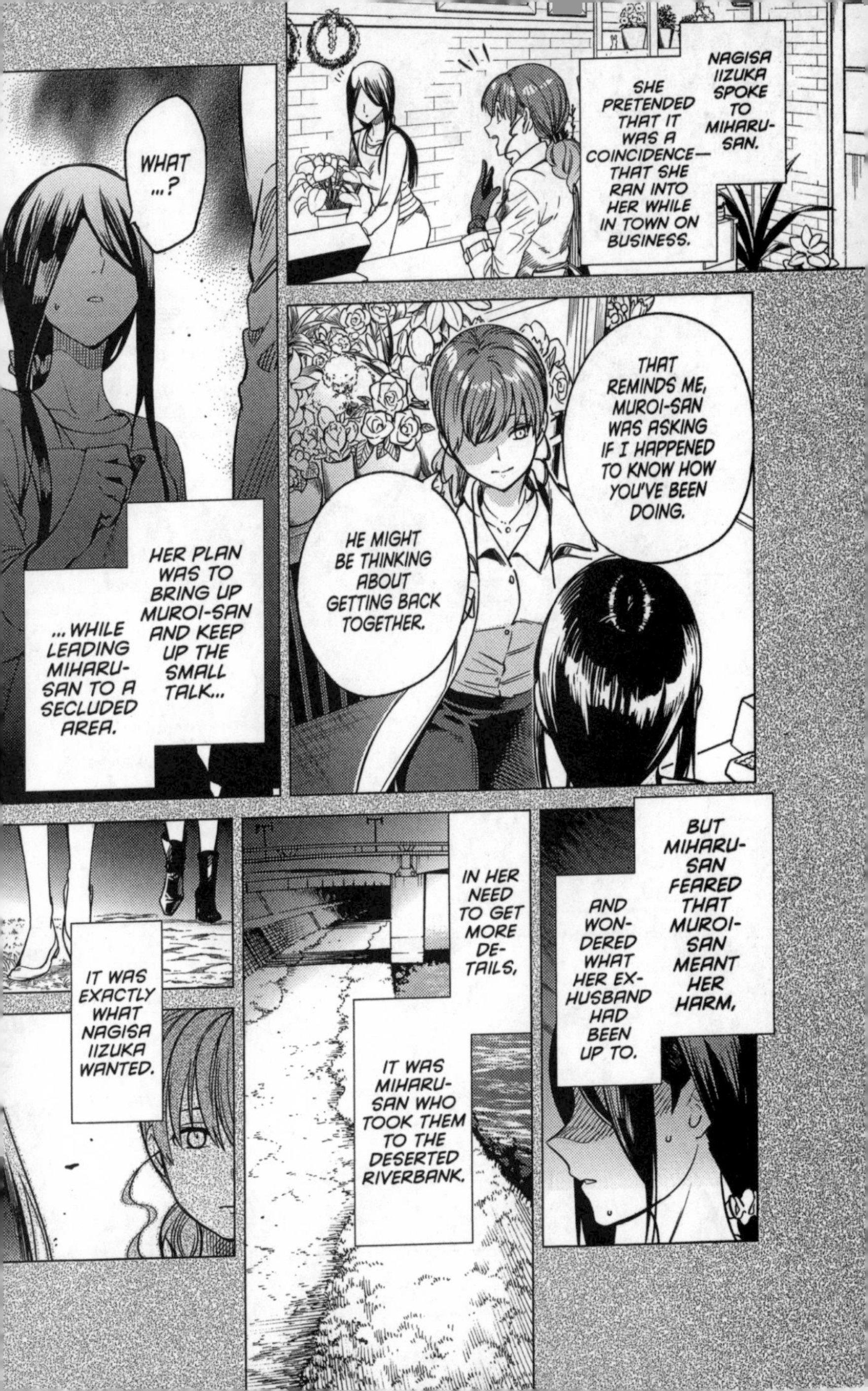
NAGISA IIZUKA SPOKE TO MIHARU-SAN.
SHE PRETENDED THAT IT WAS A COINCIDENCE— THAT SHE RAN INTO HER WHILE IN TOWN ON BUSINESS.
THAT REMINDS ME, MUROI-SAN WAS ASKING IF I HAPPENED TO KNOW HOW YOU'VE BEEN DOING.
HE MIGHT BE THINKING ABOUT GETTING BACK TOGETHER.
WHAT ...?
HER PLAN WAS TO BRING UP MUROI-SAN AND KEEP UP THE SMALL TALK...
...WHILE LEADING MIHARU-SAN TO A SECLUDED AREA.
BUT MIHARU-SAN FEARED THAT MUROI-SAN MEANT HER HARM,
AND WONDERED WHAT HER EX-HUSBAND HAD BEEN UP TO.
IN HER NEED TO GET MORE DETAILS,
IT WAS MIHARU-SAN WHO TOOK THEM TO THE DESERTED RIVERBANK.
IT WAS EXACTLY WHAT NAGISA IIZUKA WANTED.

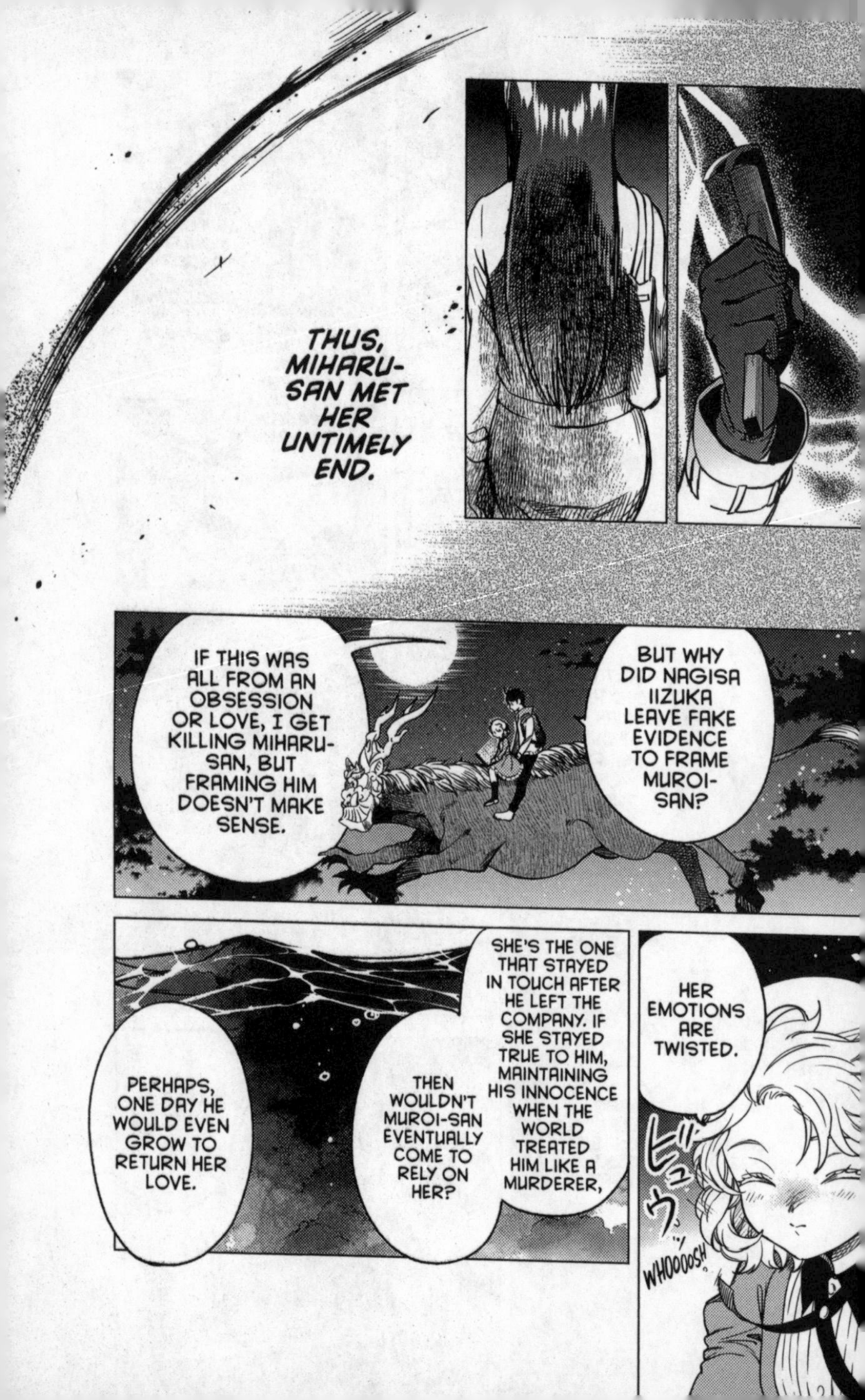
THUS, MIHARU-SAN MET HER UNTIMELY END.
BUT WHY DID NAGISA IIZUKA LEAVE FAKE EVIDENCE TO FRAME MUROI-SAN?
IF THIS WAS ALL FROM AN OBSESSION OR LOVE, I GET KILLING MIHARU-SAN, BUT FRAMING HIM DOESN'T MAKE SENSE.
HER EMOTIONS ARE TWISTED.
ヒュウ
WHOOOOSH
SHE'S THE ONE THAT STAYED IN TOUCH AFTER HE LEFT THE COMPANY. IF SHE STAYED TRUE TO HIM, MAINTAINING HIS INNOCENCE WHEN THE WORLD TREATED HIM LIKE A MURDERER,
THEN WOULDN'T MUROI-SAN EVENTUALLY COME TO RELY ON HER?
PERHAPS, ONE DAY HE WOULD EVEN GROW TO RETURN HER LOVE.

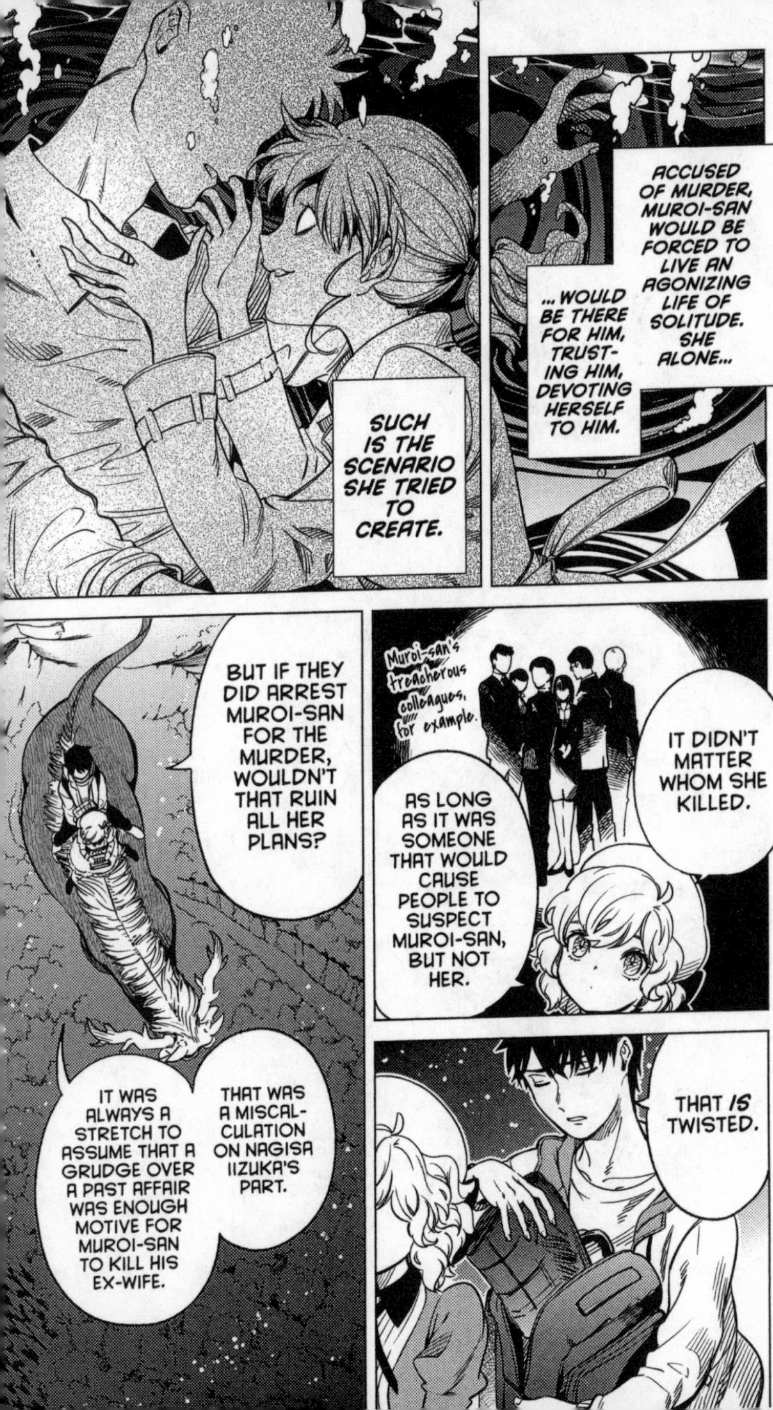
ACCUSED OF MURDER, MUROI-SAN WOULD BE FORCED TO LIVE AN AGONIZING LIFE OF SOLITUDE. SHE ALONE...
...WOULD BE THERE FOR HIM, TRUSTING HIM, DEVOTING HERSELF TO HIM.
SUCH IS THE SCENARIO SHE TRIED TO CREATE.
IT DIDN'T MATTER WHOM SHE KILLED.
AS LONG AS IT WAS SOMEONE THAT WOULD CAUSE PEOPLE TO SUSPECT MUROI-SAN, BUT NOT HER.
Muroi-san's treacherous colleagues, for example.
THAT *IS* TWISTED.
BUT IF THEY DID ARREST MUROI-SAN FOR THE MURDER, WOULDN'T THAT RUIN ALL HER PLANS?
THAT WAS A MISCALCULATION ON NAGISA IIZUKA'S PART.
IT WAS ALWAYS A STRETCH TO ASSUME THAT A GRUDGE OVER A PAST AFFAIR WAS ENOUGH MOTIVE FOR MUROI-SAN TO KILL HIS EX-WIFE.

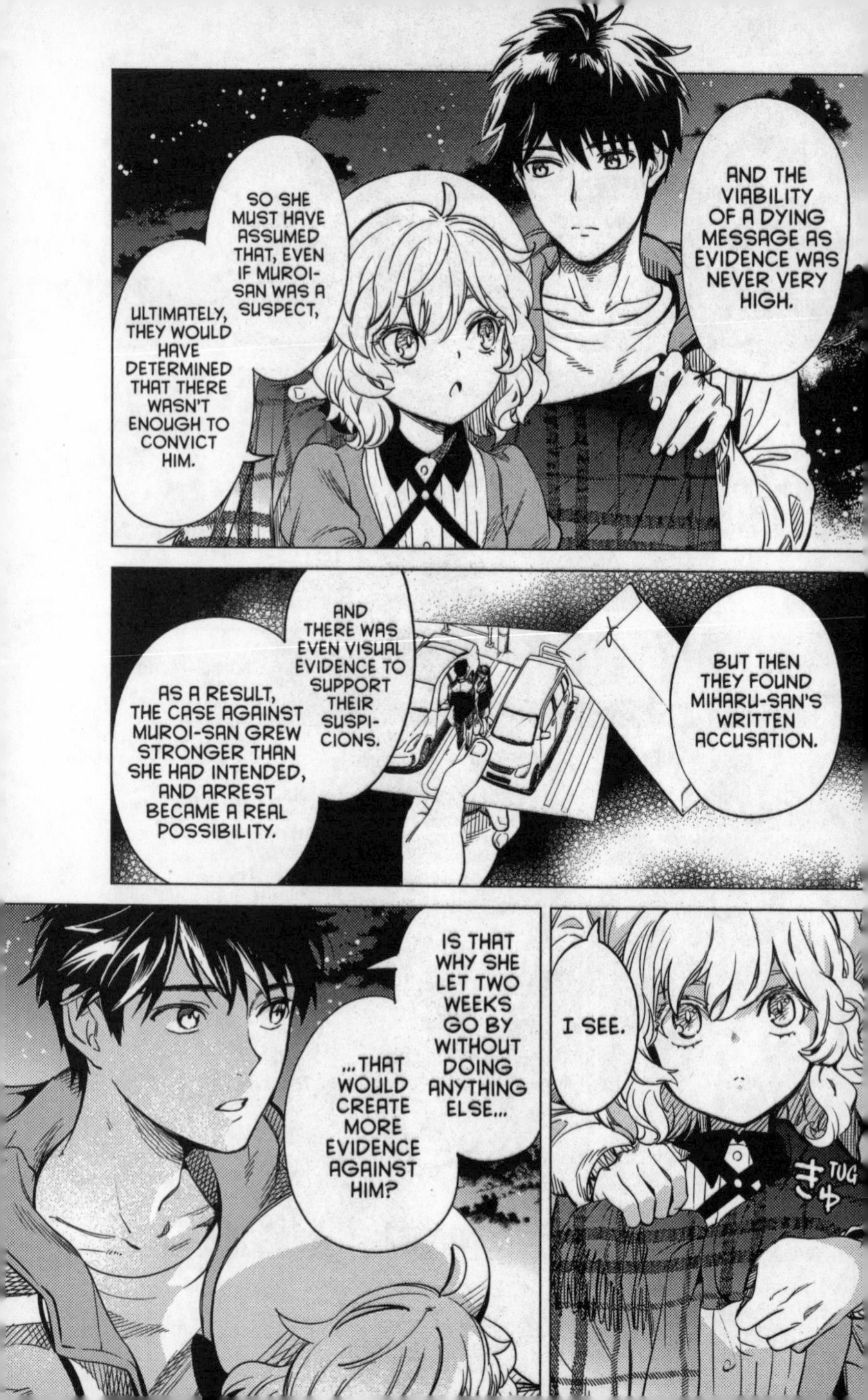
AND THE VIABILITY OF A DYING MESSAGE AS EVIDENCE WAS NEVER VERY HIGH.
SO SHE MUST HAVE ASSUMED THAT, EVEN IF MUROI-SAN WAS A SUSPECT,
ULTIMATELY, THEY WOULD HAVE DETERMINED THAT THERE WASN'T ENOUGH TO CONVICT HIM.
BUT THEN THEY FOUND MIHARU-SAN'S WRITTEN ACCUSATION.
AND THERE WAS EVEN VISUAL EVIDENCE TO SUPPORT THEIR SUSPICIONS.
AS A RESULT, THE CASE AGAINST MUROI-SAN GREW STRONGER THAN SHE HAD INTENDED, AND ARREST BECAME A REAL POSSIBILITY.
I SEE.
きゅ TUG
IS THAT WHY SHE LET TWO WEEKS GO BY WITHOUT DOING ANYTHING ELSE...
...THAT WOULD CREATE MORE EVIDENCE AGAINST HIM?

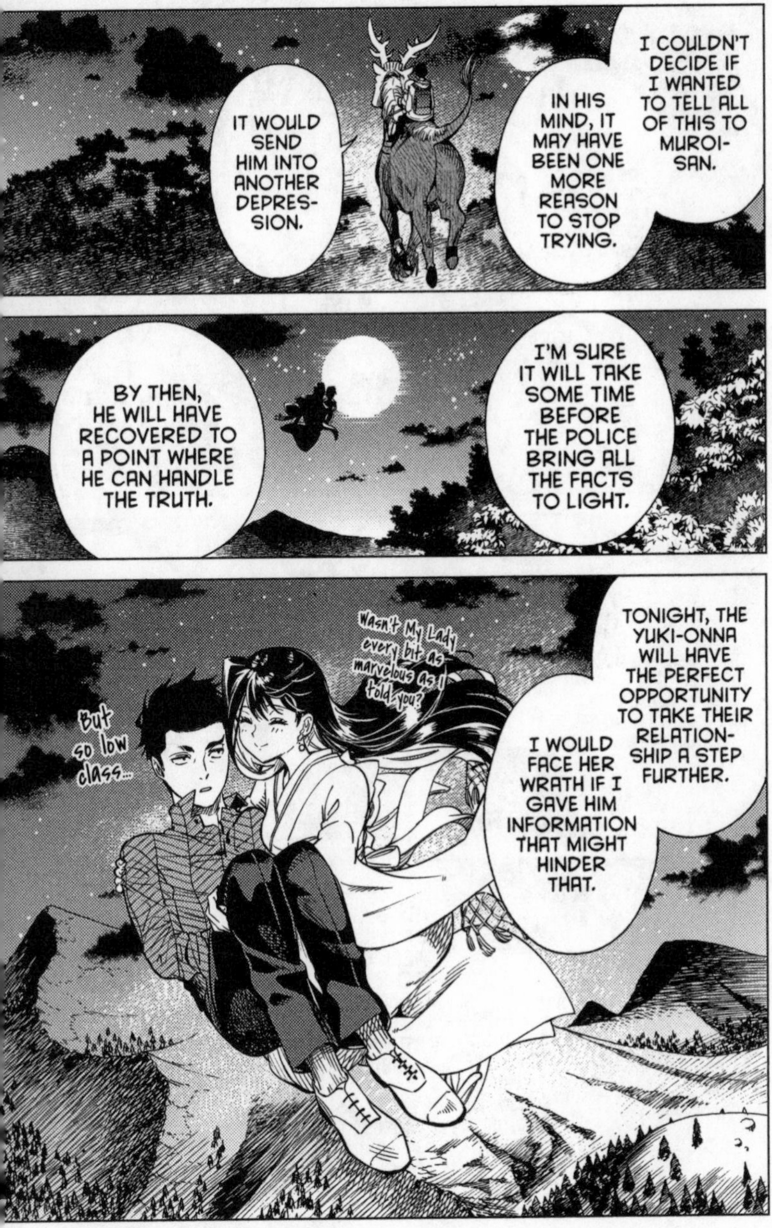
I COULDN'T DECIDE IF I WANTED TO TELL ALL OF THIS TO MUROI-SAN.
IN HIS MIND, IT MAY HAVE BEEN ONE MORE REASON TO STOP TRYING.
IT WOULD SEND HIM INTO ANOTHER DEPRES-SION.
I'M SURE IT WILL TAKE SOME TIME BEFORE THE POLICE BRING ALL THE FACTS TO LIGHT.
BY THEN, HE WILL HAVE RECOVERED TO A POINT WHERE HE CAN HANDLE THE TRUTH.
TONIGHT, THE YUKI-ONNA WILL HAVE THE PERFECT OPPORTUNITY TO TAKE THEIR RELATION-SHIP A STEP FURTHER.
I WOULD FACE HER WRATH IF I GAVE HIM INFORMATION THAT MIGHT HINDER THAT.
Wasn't My Lady every bit as marvelous as I told you?
But so low class...

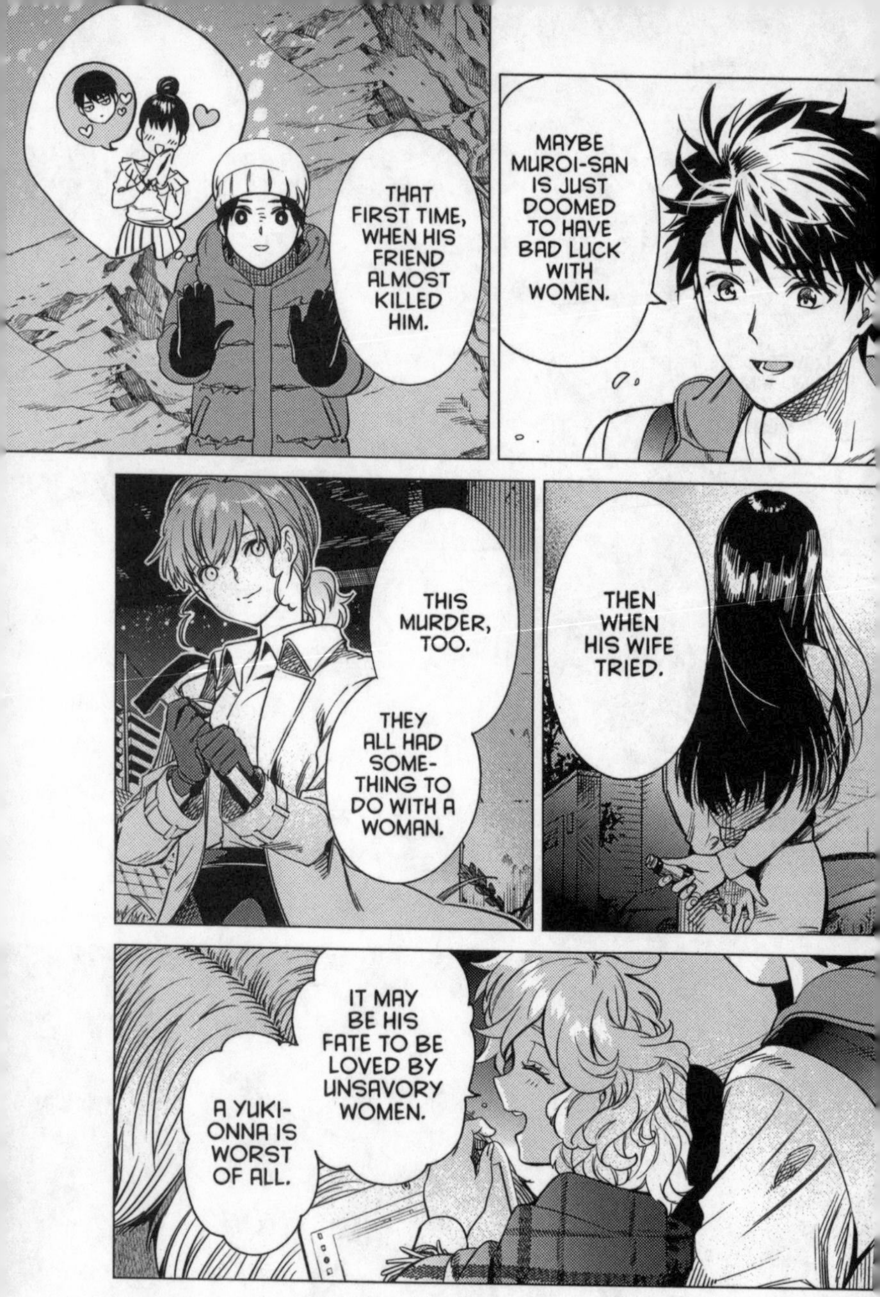
MAYBE MUROI-SAN IS JUST DOOMED TO HAVE BAD LUCK WITH WOMEN.
THAT FIRST TIME, WHEN HIS FRIEND ALMOST KILLED HIM.
THEN WHEN HIS WIFE TRIED.
THIS MURDER, TOO.
THEY ALL HAD SOME-THING TO DO WITH A WOMAN.
IT MAY BE HIS FATE TO BE LOVED BY UNSAVORY WOMEN.
A YUKI-ONNA IS WORST OF ALL.

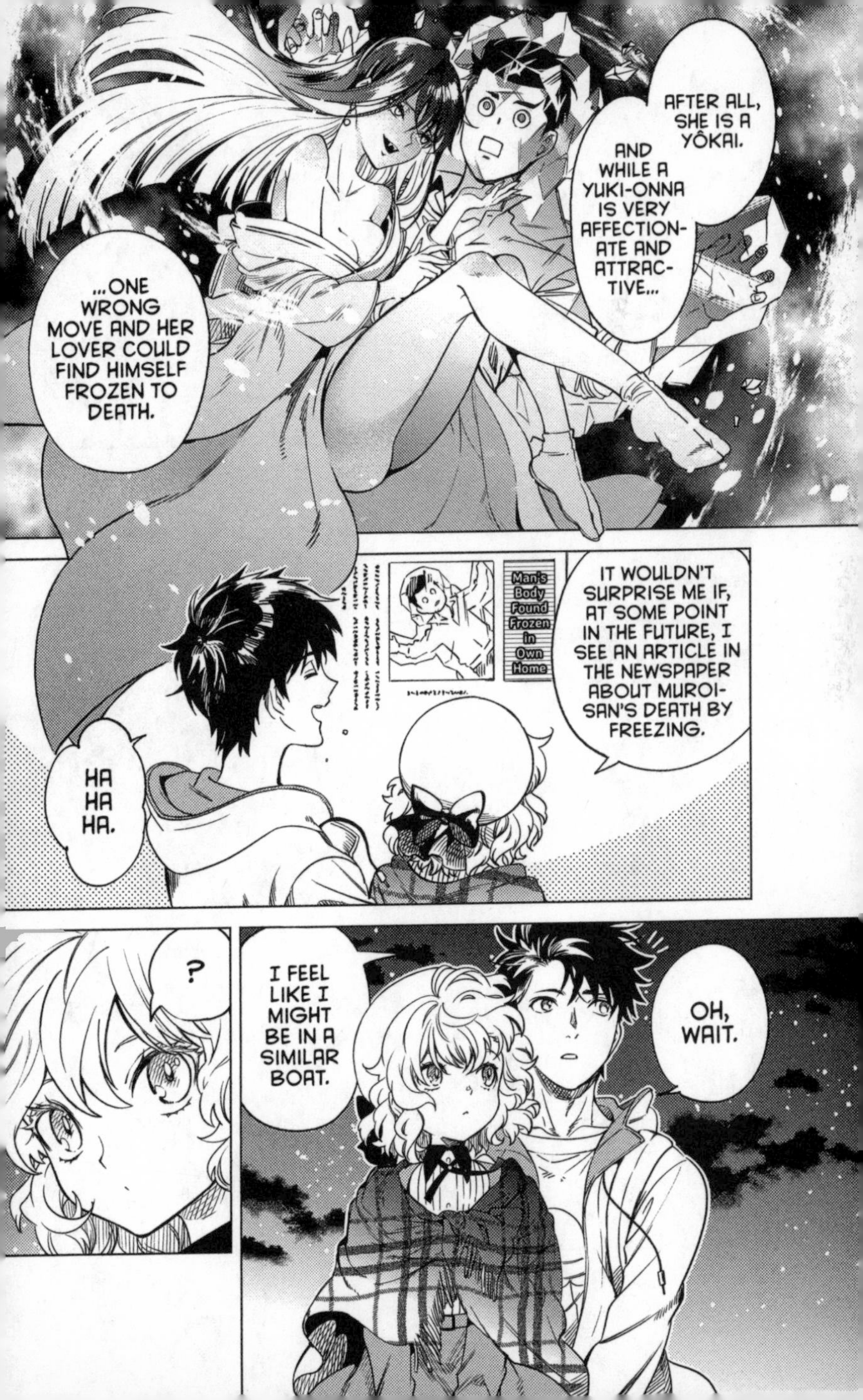
AFTER ALL, SHE IS A YÔKAI.
AND WHILE A YUKI-ONNA IS VERY AFFECTION-ATE AND ATTRAC-TIVE...
...ONE WRONG MOVE AND HER LOVER COULD FIND HIMSELF FROZEN TO DEATH.
IT WOULDN'T SURPRISE ME IF, AT SOME POINT IN THE FUTURE, I SEE AN ARTICLE IN THE NEWSPAPER ABOUT MUROI-SAN'S DEATH BY FREEZING.
Man's Body Found Frozen in Own Home
HA HA HA.
OH, WAIT.
I FEEL LIKE I MIGHT BE IN A SIMILAR BOAT.
?

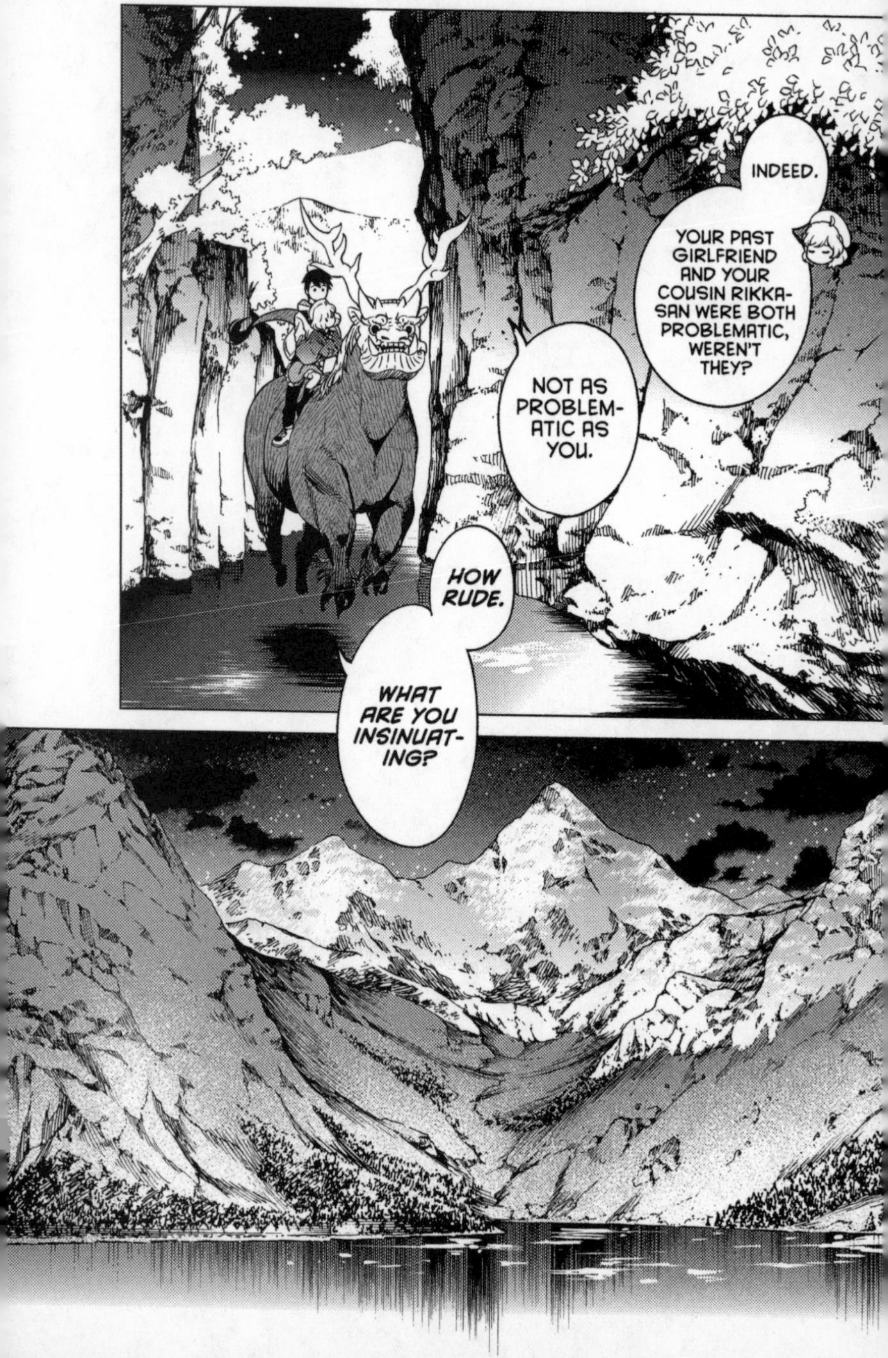
INDEED.
YOUR PAST GIRLFRIEND AND YOUR COUSIN RIKKA-SAN WERE BOTH PROBLEMATIC, WEREN'T THEY?
NOT AS PROBLEM-ATIC AS YOU.
HOW RUDE.
WHAT ARE YOU INSINUAT-ING?

Happy ending?

CHAPTER 34: "A STORY THAT'S NOT NOT-SCARY IF YOU REALLY THINK ABOUT IT"

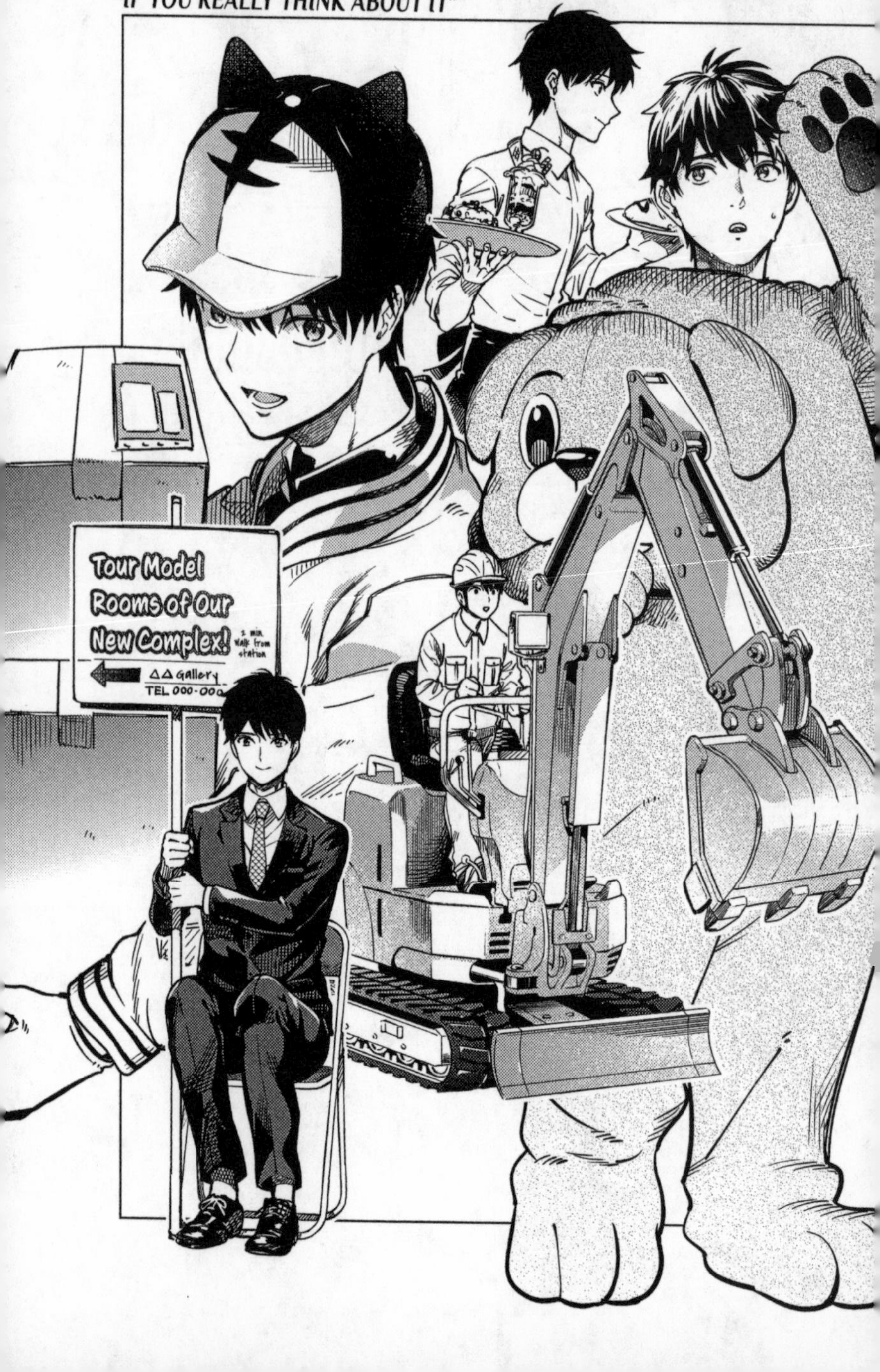
Tour Model Rooms of Our New Complex!
1 min. walk from station
ΔΔ Gallery
TEL 000-000

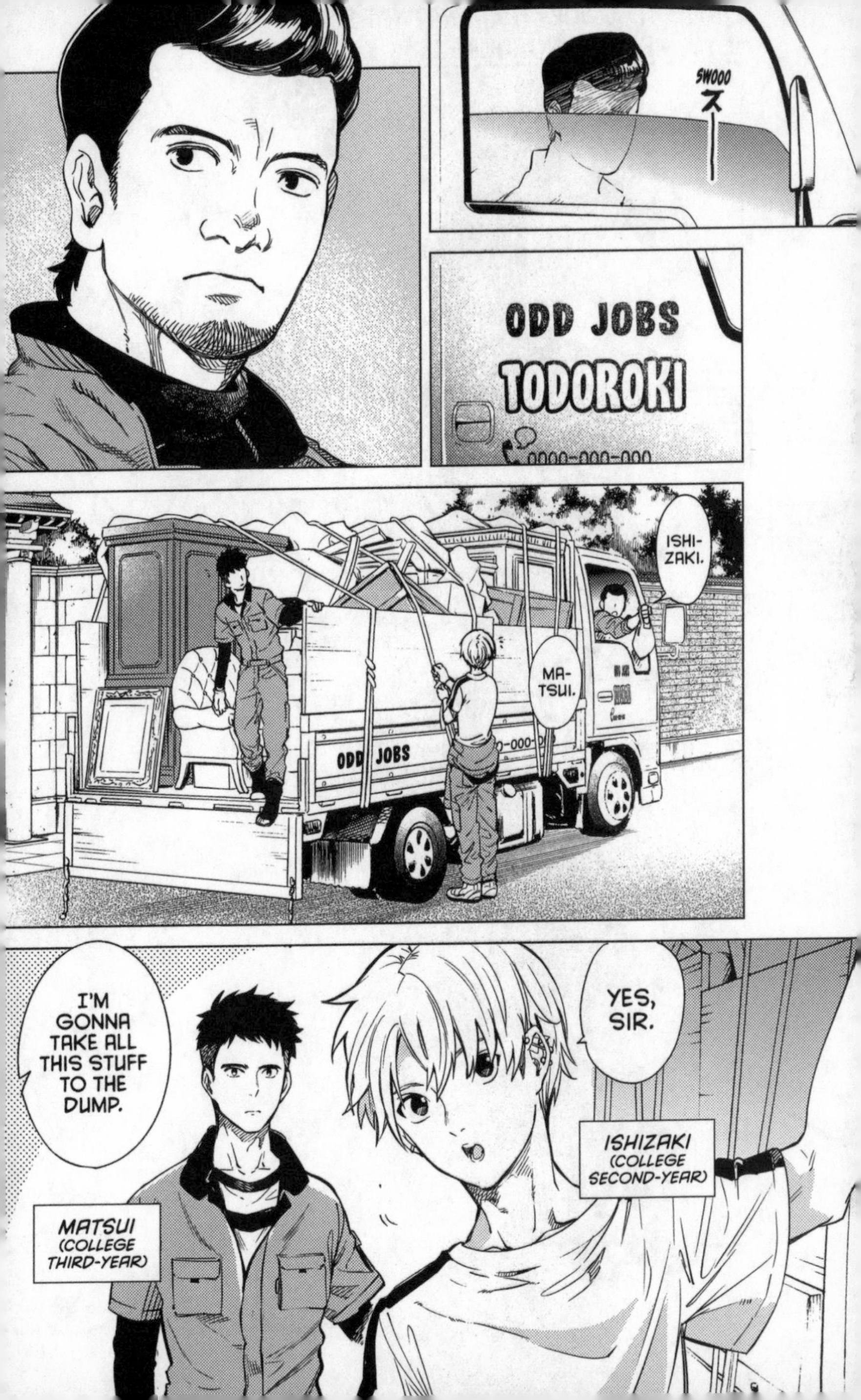
SWOOO
スー
ODD JOBS
TODOROKI
0000-000-000
ISHI-ZAKI.
MA-TSUI.
ODD JOBS
YES, SIR.
ISHIZAKI (COLLEGE SECOND-YEAR)
I'M GONNA TAKE ALL THIS STUFF TO THE DUMP.
MATSUI (COLLEGE THIRD-YEAR)

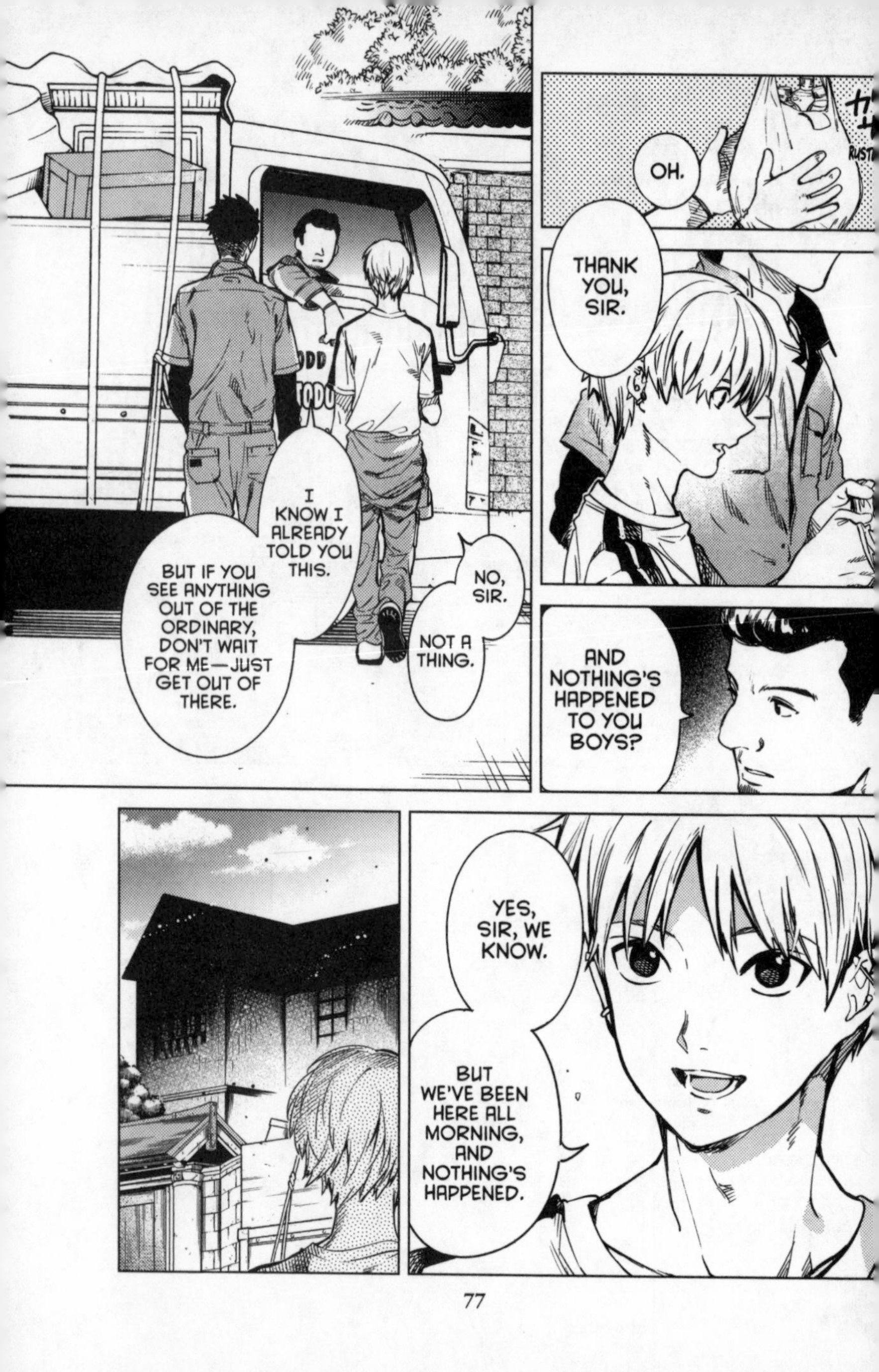

RUST
OH.
THANK YOU, SIR.
AND NOTHING'S HAPPENED TO YOU BOYS?
NO, SIR.
NOT A THING.
I KNOW I ALREADY TOLD YOU THIS.
BUT IF YOU SEE ANYTHING OUT OF THE ORDINARY, DON'T WAIT FOR ME—JUST GET OUT OF THERE.
YES, SIR, WE KNOW.
BUT WE'VE BEEN HERE ALL MORNING, AND NOTHING'S HAPPENED.

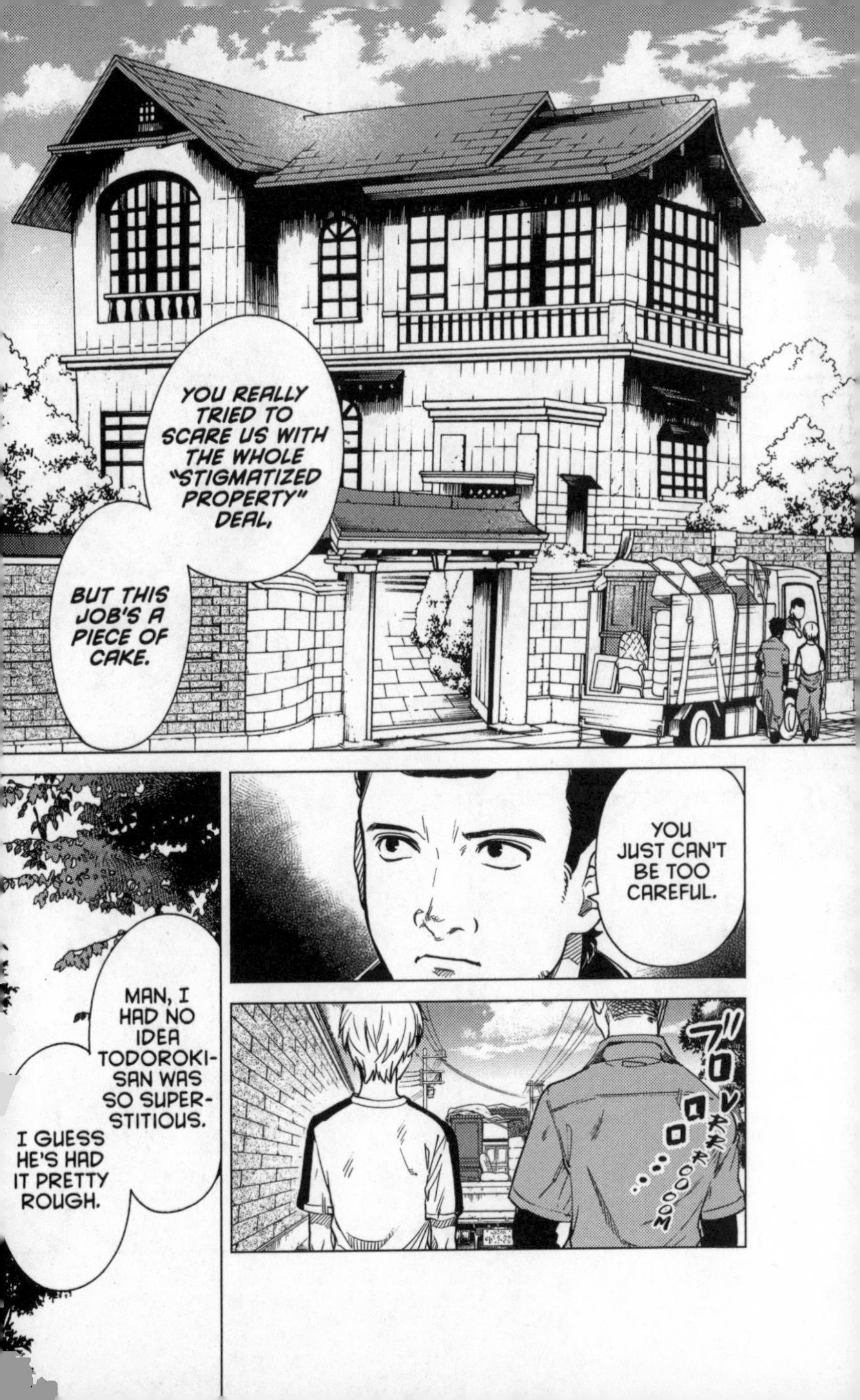
YOU REALLY TRIED TO SCARE US WITH THE WHOLE "STIGMATIZED PROPERTY" DEAL,
BUT THIS JOB'S A PIECE OF CAKE.
YOU JUST CAN'T BE TOO CAREFUL.
ブロロロ…
VRRROOOOOM
MAN, I HAD NO IDEA TODOROKI-SAN WAS SO SUPER-STITIOUS.
I GUESS HE'S HAD IT PRETTY ROUGH.

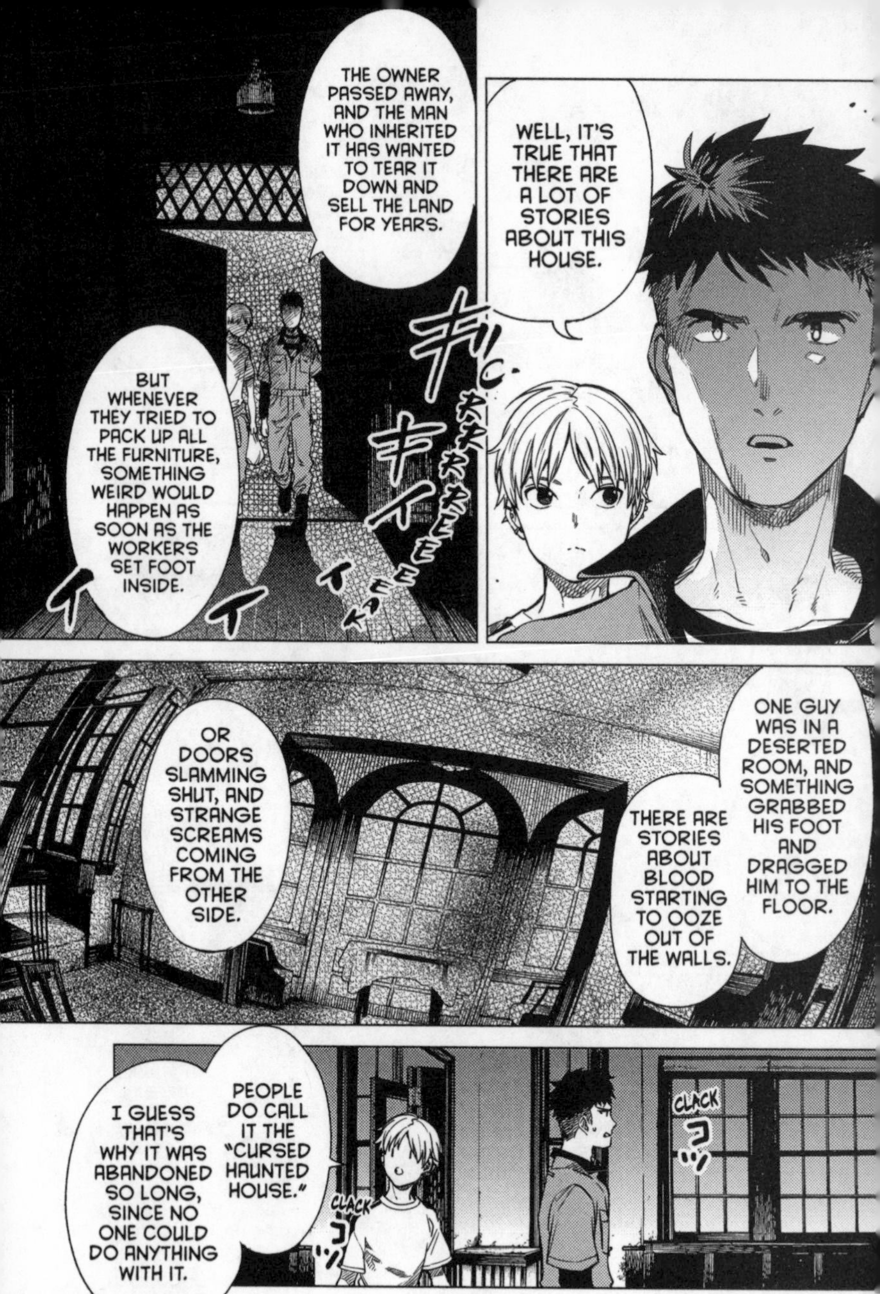
WELL, IT'S TRUE THAT THERE ARE A LOT OF STORIES ABOUT THIS HOUSE.
THE OWNER PASSED AWAY, AND THE MAN WHO INHERITED IT HAS WANTED TO TEAR IT DOWN AND SELL THE LAND FOR YEARS.
CRRREEEEAK
BUT WHENEVER THEY TRIED TO PACK UP ALL THE FURNITURE, SOMETHING WEIRD WOULD HAPPEN AS SOON AS THE WORKERS SET FOOT INSIDE.
ONE GUY WAS IN A DESERTED ROOM, AND SOMETHING GRABBED HIS FOOT AND DRAGGED HIM TO THE FLOOR.
THERE ARE STORIES ABOUT BLOOD STARTING TO OOZE OUT OF THE WALLS.
OR DOORS SLAMMING SHUT, AND STRANGE SCREAMS COMING FROM THE OTHER SIDE.
CLACK
PEOPLE DO CALL IT THE "CURSED HAUNTED HOUSE."
I GUESS THAT'S WHY IT WAS ABANDONED SO LONG, SINCE NO ONE COULD DO ANYTHING WITH IT.
CLACK

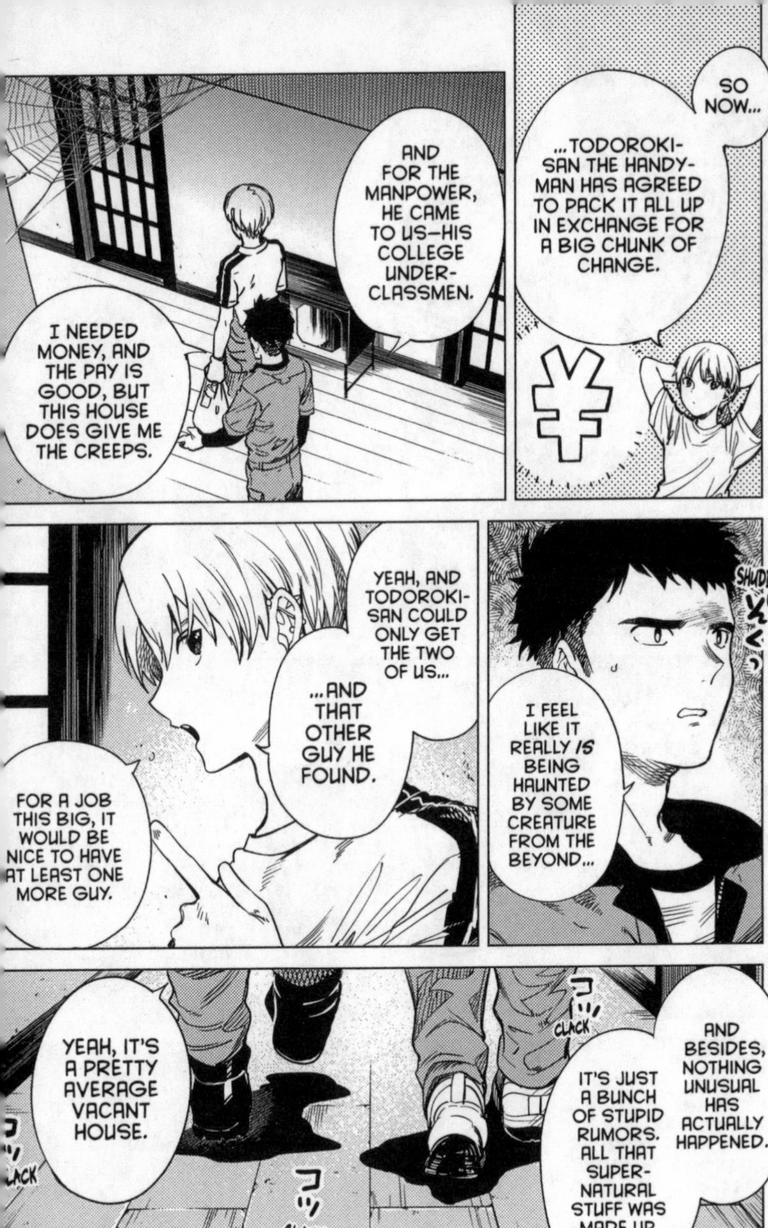
SO NOW...
...TODOROKI-SAN THE HANDYMAN HAS AGREED TO PACK IT ALL UP IN EXCHANGE FOR A BIG CHUNK OF CHANGE.
AND FOR THE MANPOWER, HE CAME TO US—HIS COLLEGE UNDERCLASSMEN.
I NEEDED MONEY, AND THE PAY IS GOOD, BUT THIS HOUSE DOES GIVE ME THE CREEPS.
SHUDDER
I FEEL LIKE IT REALLY *IS* BEING HAUNTED BY SOME CREATURE FROM THE BEYOND...
YEAH, AND TODOROKI-SAN COULD ONLY GET THE TWO OF US...
...AND THAT OTHER GUY HE FOUND.
FOR A JOB THIS BIG, IT WOULD BE NICE TO HAVE AT LEAST ONE MORE GUY.
AND BESIDES, NOTHING UNUSUAL HAS ACTUALLY HAPPENED.
IT'S JUST A BUNCH OF STUPID RUMORS. ALL THAT SUPERNATURAL STUFF WAS MADE UP.
CLACK
CLACK
YEAH, IT'S A PRETTY AVERAGE VACANT HOUSE.
CLACK

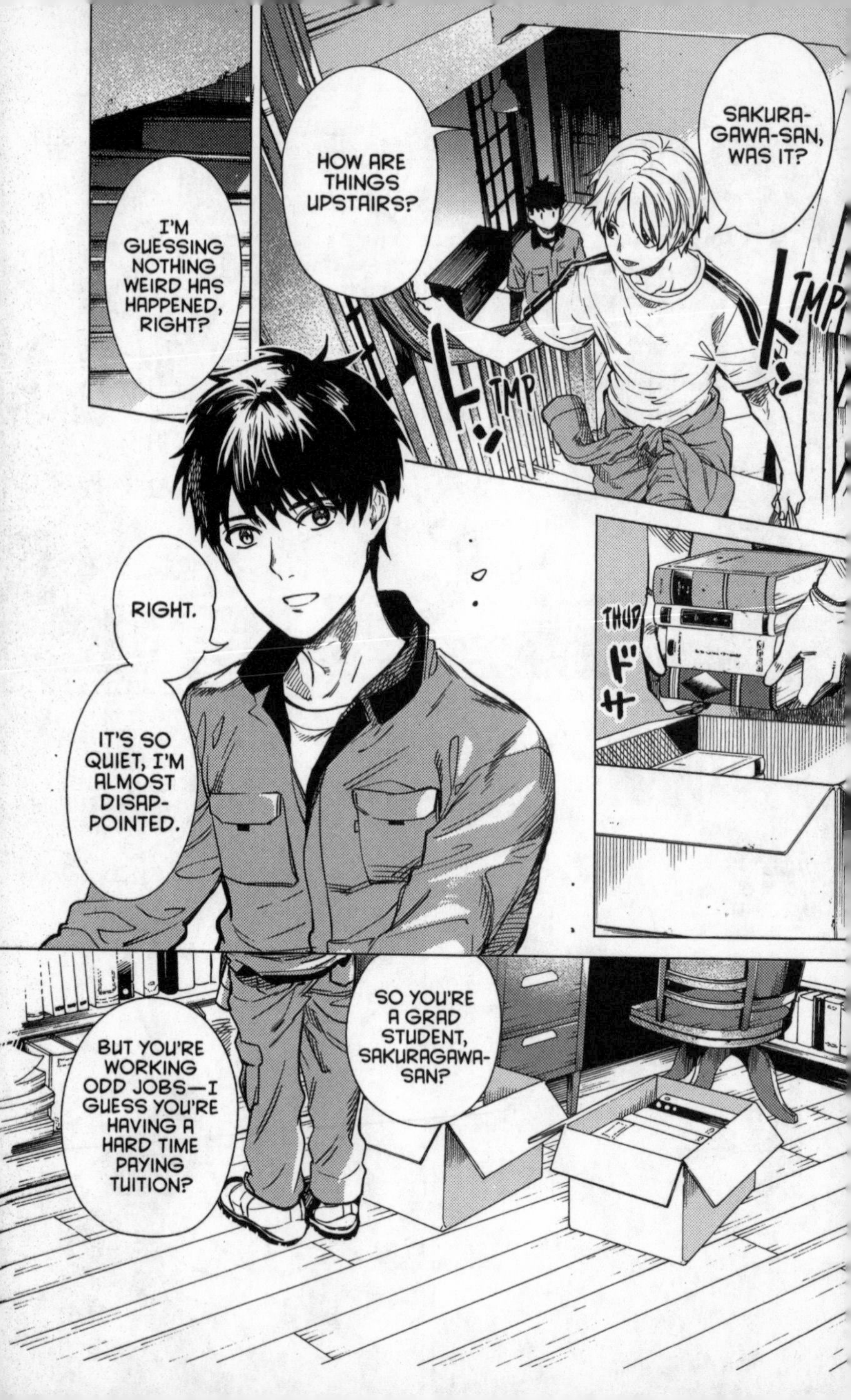
SAKURA-GAWA-SAN, WAS IT?
TMP
HOW ARE THINGS UPSTAIRS?
TMP
I'M GUESSING NOTHING WEIRD HAS HAPPENED, RIGHT?
THUD
ドサ
RIGHT.
IT'S SO QUIET, I'M ALMOST DISAP-POINTED.
SO YOU'RE A GRAD STUDENT, SAKURAGAWA-SAN?
BUT YOU'RE WORKING ODD JOBS—I GUESS YOU'RE HAVING A HARD TIME PAYING TUITION?

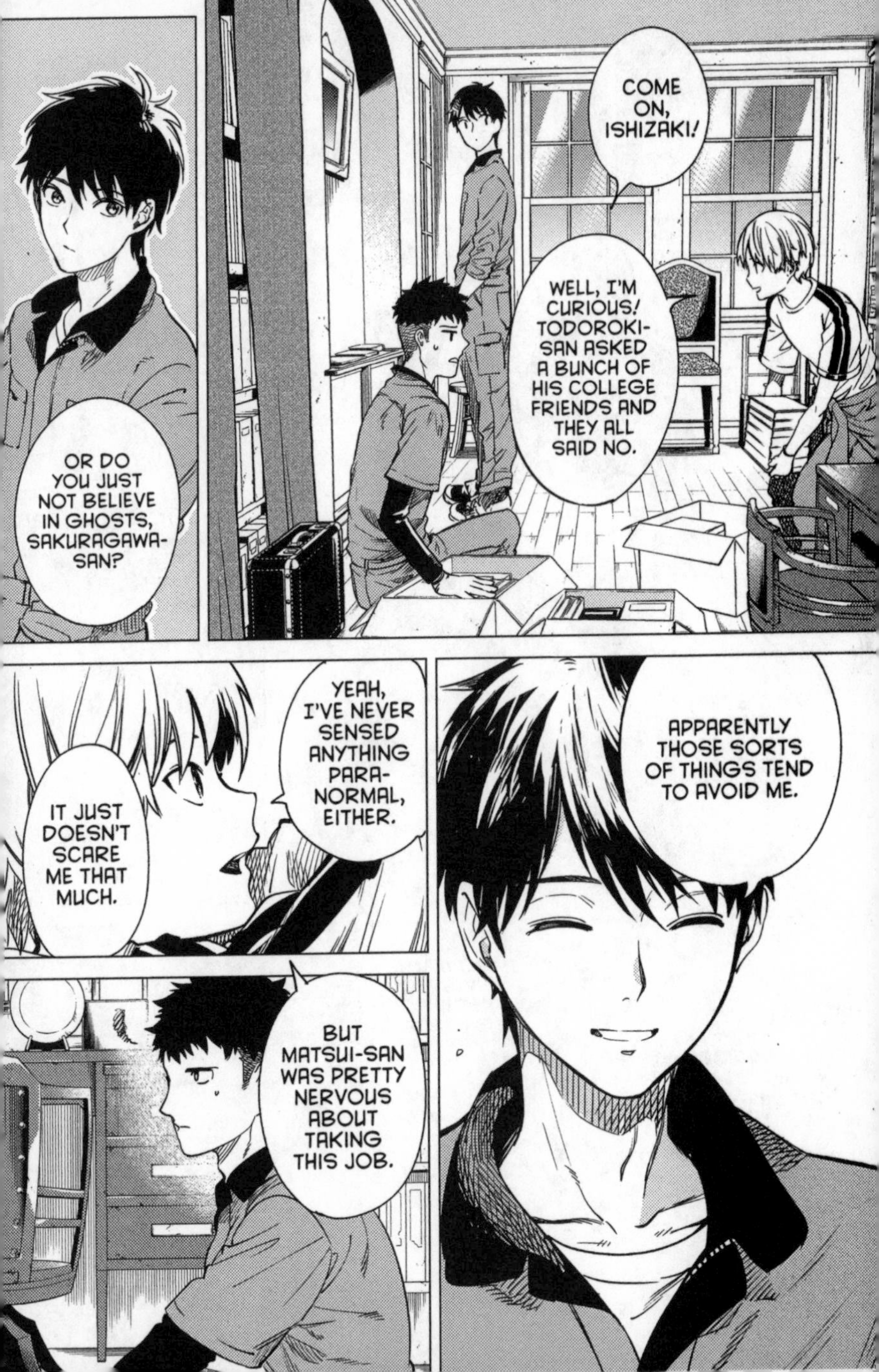
COME ON, ISHIZAKI!
WELL, I'M CURIOUS! TODOROKI-SAN ASKED A BUNCH OF HIS COLLEGE FRIENDS AND THEY ALL SAID NO.
OR DO YOU JUST NOT BELIEVE IN GHOSTS, SAKURAGAWA-SAN?
APPARENTLY THOSE SORTS OF THINGS TEND TO AVOID ME.
YEAH, I'VE NEVER SENSED ANYTHING PARA-NORMAL, EITHER.
IT JUST DOESN'T SCARE ME THAT MUCH.
BUT MATSUI-SAN WAS PRETTY NERVOUS ABOUT TAKING THIS JOB.

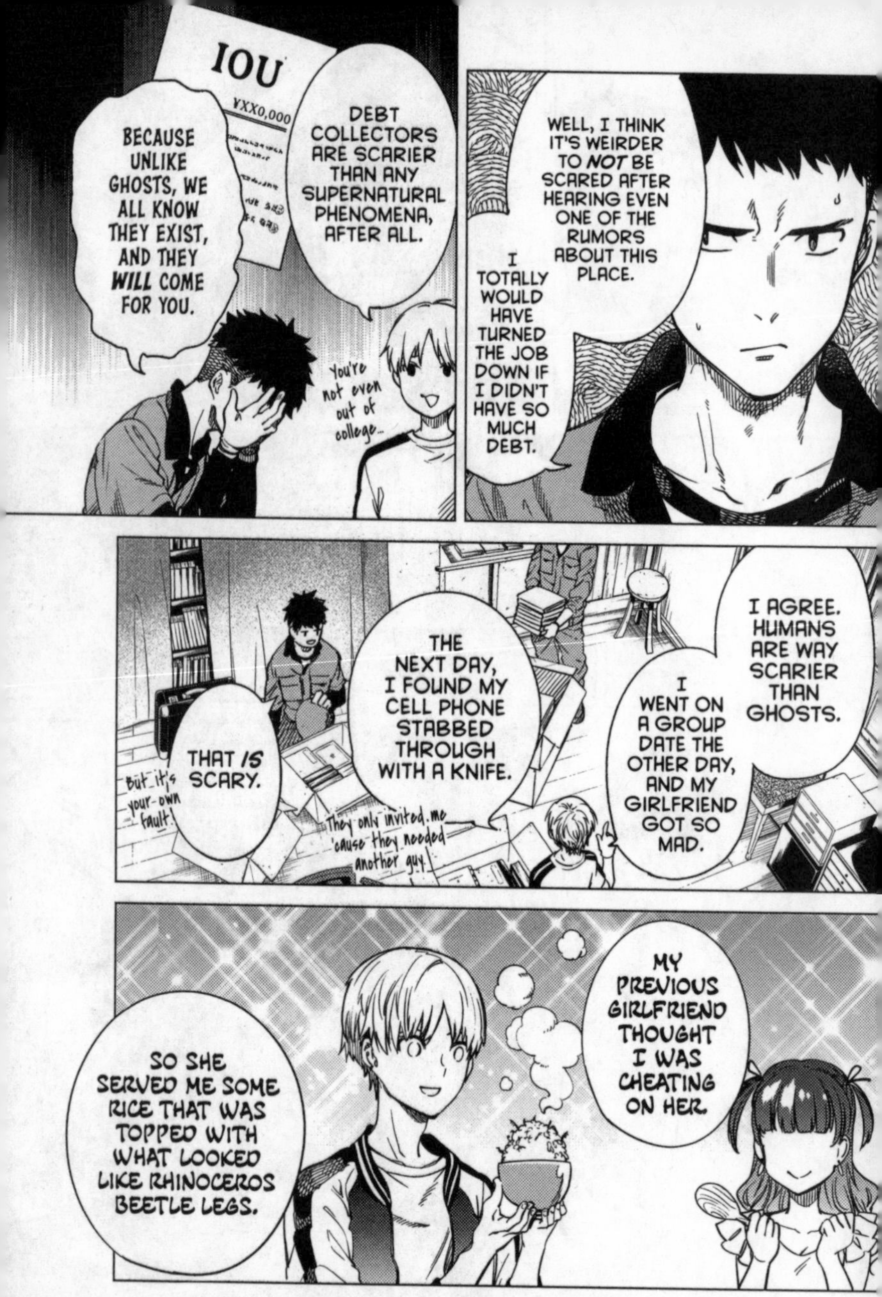
WELL, I THINK IT'S WEIRDER TO *NOT* BE SCARED AFTER HEARING EVEN ONE OF THE RUMORS ABOUT THIS PLACE.
I TOTALLY WOULD HAVE TURNED THE JOB DOWN IF I DIDN'T HAVE SO MUCH DEBT.
IOU
¥XX0,000
DEBT COLLECTORS ARE SCARIER THAN ANY SUPERNATURAL PHENOMENA, AFTER ALL.
BECAUSE UNLIKE GHOSTS, WE ALL KNOW THEY EXIST, AND THEY *WILL* COME FOR YOU.
You're not even out of college...
I AGREE. HUMANS ARE WAY SCARIER THAN GHOSTS.
I WENT ON A GROUP DATE THE OTHER DAY, AND MY GIRLFRIEND GOT SO MAD.
THE NEXT DAY, I FOUND MY CELL PHONE STABBED THROUGH WITH A KNIFE.
They only invited me 'cause they needed another guy.
THAT *IS* SCARY.
But it's your own fault.
MY PREVIOUS GIRLFRIEND THOUGHT I WAS CHEATING ON HER.
SO SHE SERVED ME SOME RICE THAT WAS TOPPED WITH WHAT LOOKED LIKE RHINOCEROS BEETLE LEGS.

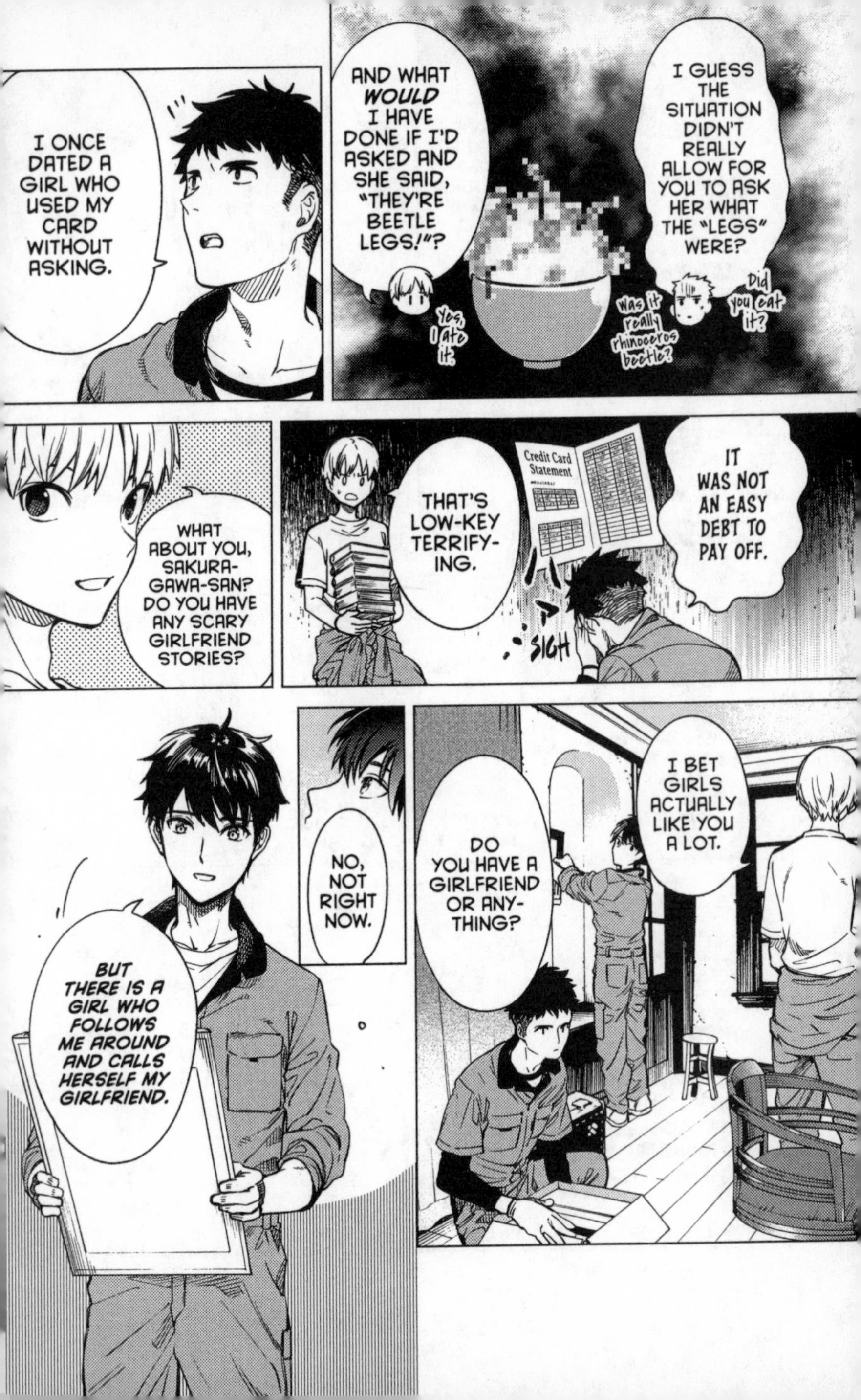
I GUESS THE SITUATION DIDN'T REALLY ALLOW FOR YOU TO ASK HER WHAT THE "LEGS" WERE?
AND WHAT *WOULD* I HAVE DONE IF I'D ASKED AND SHE SAID, "THEY'RE BEETLE LEGS!"?
Did you eat it?
Was it really rhinoceros beetle?
Yes, I ate it.
I ONCE DATED A GIRL WHO USED MY CARD WITHOUT ASKING.
IT WAS NOT AN EASY DEBT TO PAY OFF.
Credit Card Statement
SIGH
THAT'S LOW-KEY TERRIFY-ING.
WHAT ABOUT YOU, SAKURA-GAWA-SAN? DO YOU HAVE ANY SCARY GIRLFRIEND STORIES?
I BET GIRLS ACTUALLY LIKE YOU A LOT.
DO YOU HAVE A GIRLFRIEND OR ANY-THING?
NO, NOT RIGHT NOW.
BUT THERE IS A GIRL WHO FOLLOWS ME AROUND AND CALLS HERSELF MY GIRLFRIEND.

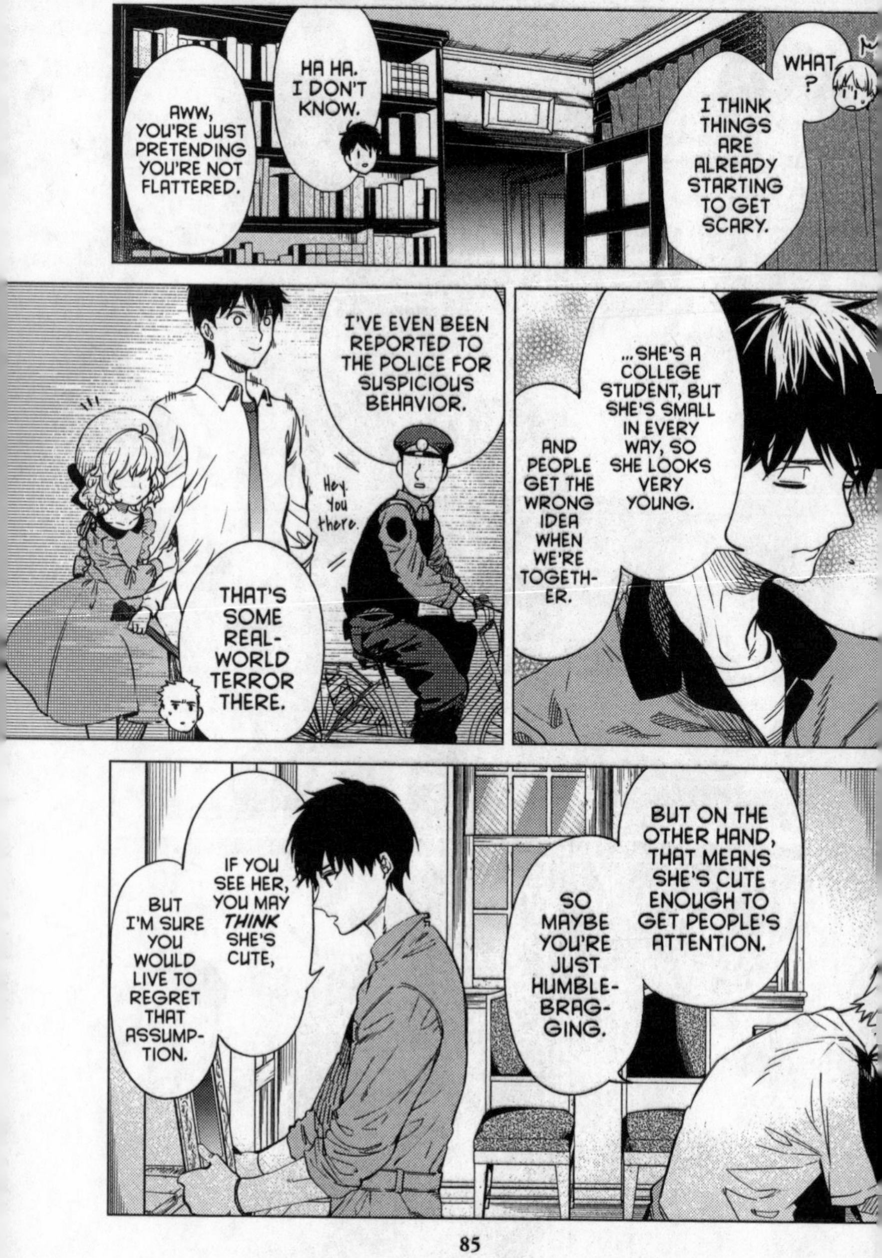
WHAT ?
I THINK THINGS ARE ALREADY STARTING TO GET SCARY.
HA HA. I DON'T KNOW.
AWW, YOU'RE JUST PRETENDING YOU'RE NOT FLATTERED.
...SHE'S A COLLEGE STUDENT, BUT SHE'S SMALL IN EVERY WAY, SO SHE LOOKS VERY YOUNG.
AND PEOPLE GET THE WRONG IDEA WHEN WE'RE TOGETH-ER.
I'VE EVEN BEEN REPORTED TO THE POLICE FOR SUSPICIOUS BEHAVIOR.
Hey. You there.
THAT'S SOME REAL-WORLD TERROR THERE.
BUT ON THE OTHER HAND, THAT MEANS SHE'S CUTE ENOUGH TO GET PEOPLE'S ATTENTION.
SO MAYBE YOU'RE JUST HUMBLE-BRAG-GING.
IF YOU SEE HER, YOU MAY *THINK* SHE'S CUTE,
BUT I'M SURE YOU WOULD LIVE TO REGRET THAT ASSUMP-TION.

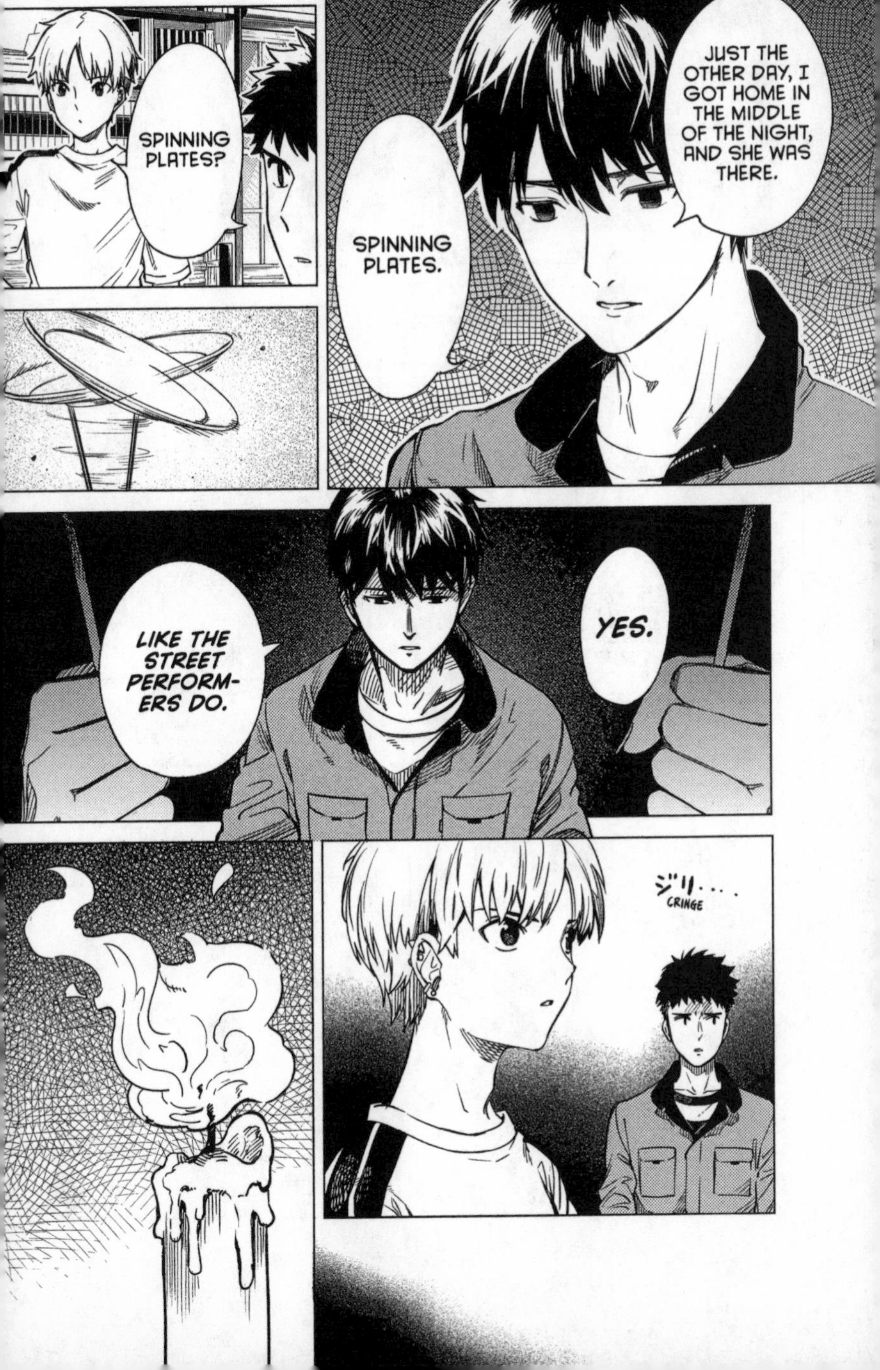
JUST THE OTHER DAY, I GOT HOME IN THE MIDDLE OF THE NIGHT, AND SHE WAS THERE.
SPINNING PLATES.
SPINNING PLATES?
YES.
LIKE THE STREET PERFORMERS DO.
ジリ……
CRINGE

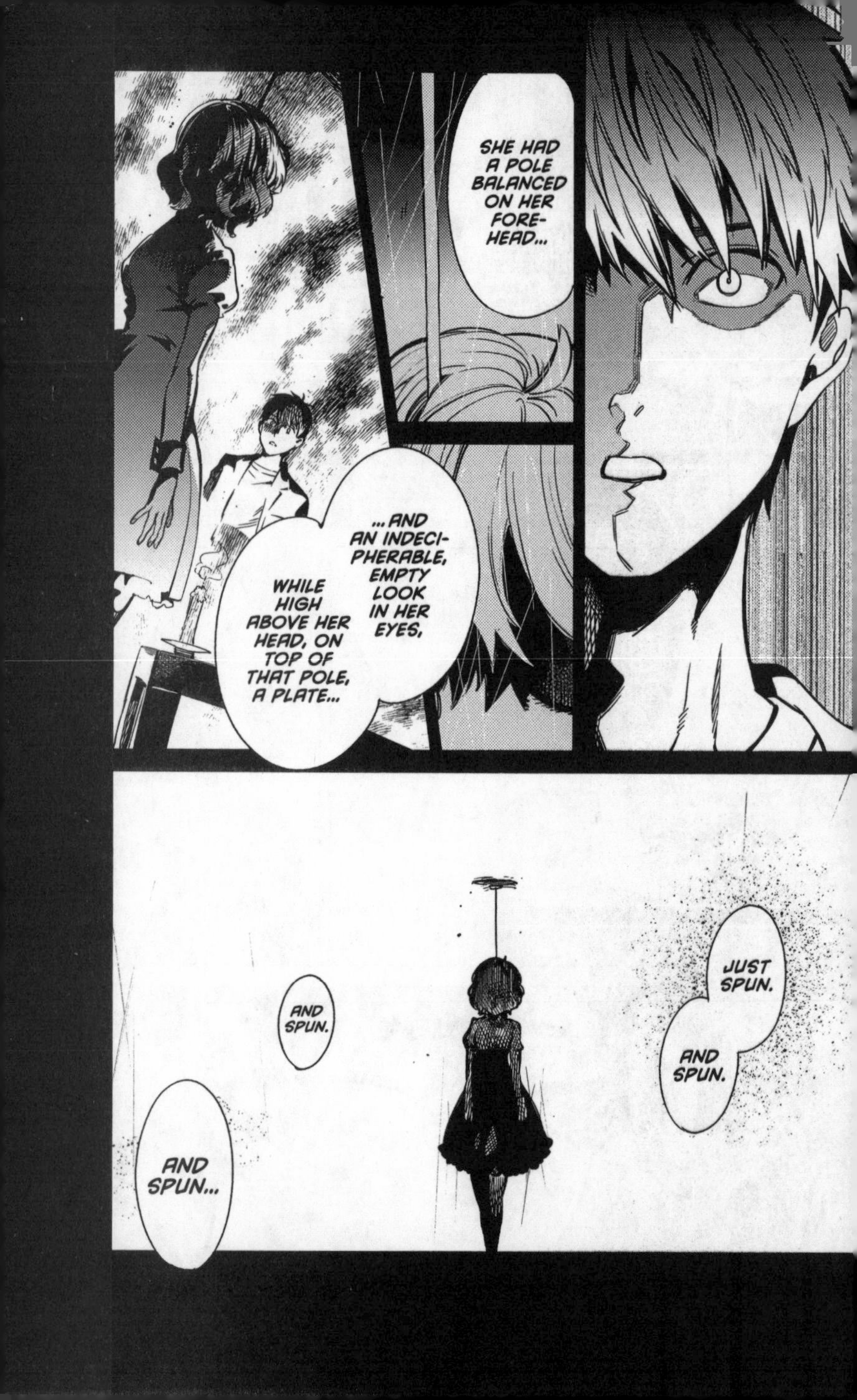
SHE HAD A POLE BALANCED ON HER FOREHEAD...
...AND AN INDECIPHERABLE, EMPTY LOOK IN HER EYES,
WHILE HIGH ABOVE HER HEAD, ON TOP OF THAT POLE, A PLATE...
JUST SPUN.
AND SPUN.
AND SPUN.
AND SPUN...

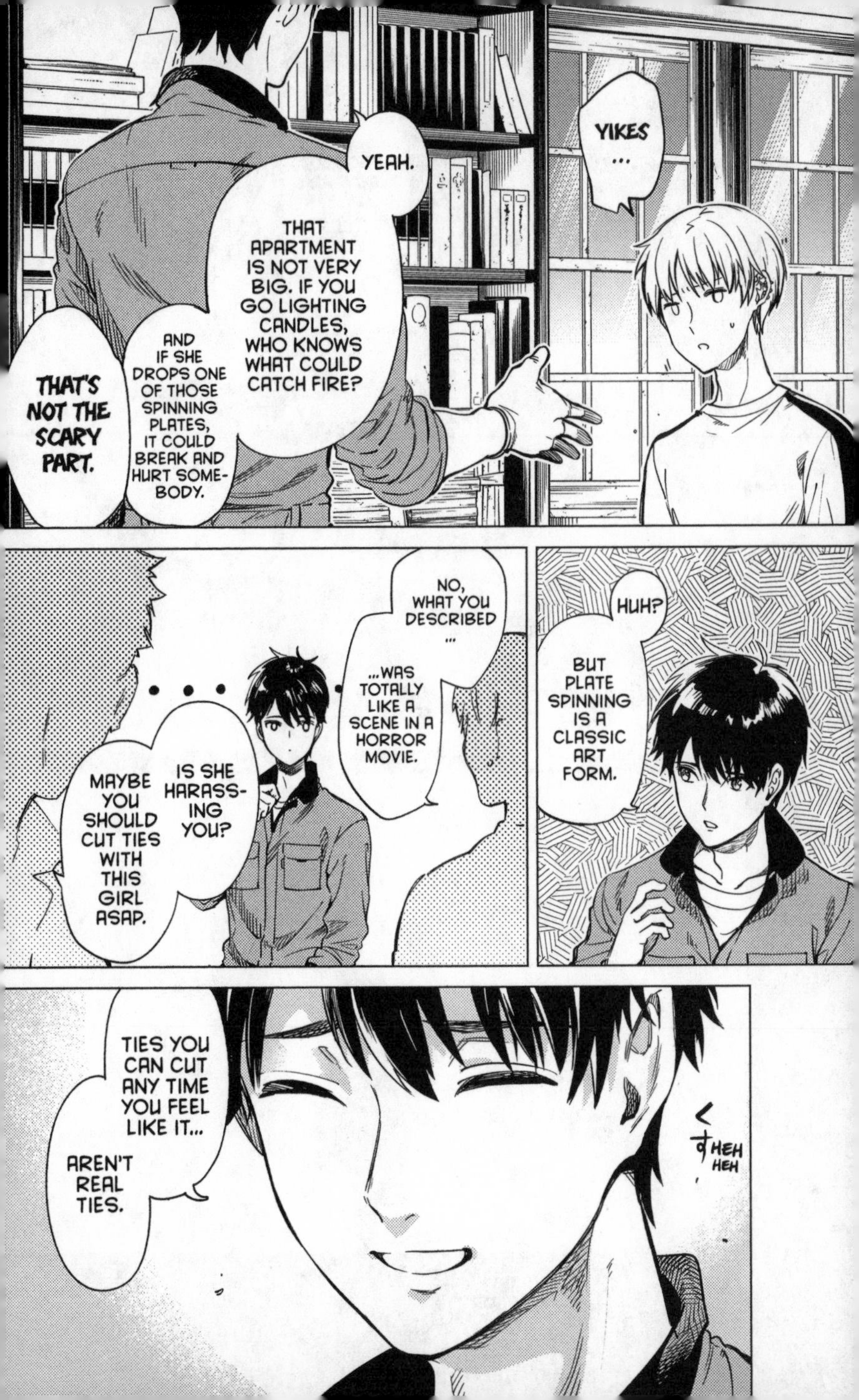
YIKES...
YEAH.
THAT APARTMENT IS NOT VERY BIG. IF YOU GO LIGHTING CANDLES, WHO KNOWS WHAT COULD CATCH FIRE?
AND IF SHE DROPS ONE OF THOSE SPINNING PLATES, IT COULD BREAK AND HURT SOMEBODY.
THAT'S NOT THE SCARY PART.
HUH?
BUT PLATE SPINNING IS A CLASSIC ART FORM.
NO, WHAT YOU DESCRIBED ...
...WAS TOTALLY LIKE A SCENE IN A HORROR MOVIE.
• • •
IS SHE HARASSING YOU?
MAYBE YOU SHOULD CUT TIES WITH THIS GIRL ASAP.
くす HEH HEH
TIES YOU CAN CUT ANY TIME YOU FEEL LIKE IT...
AREN'T REAL TIES.

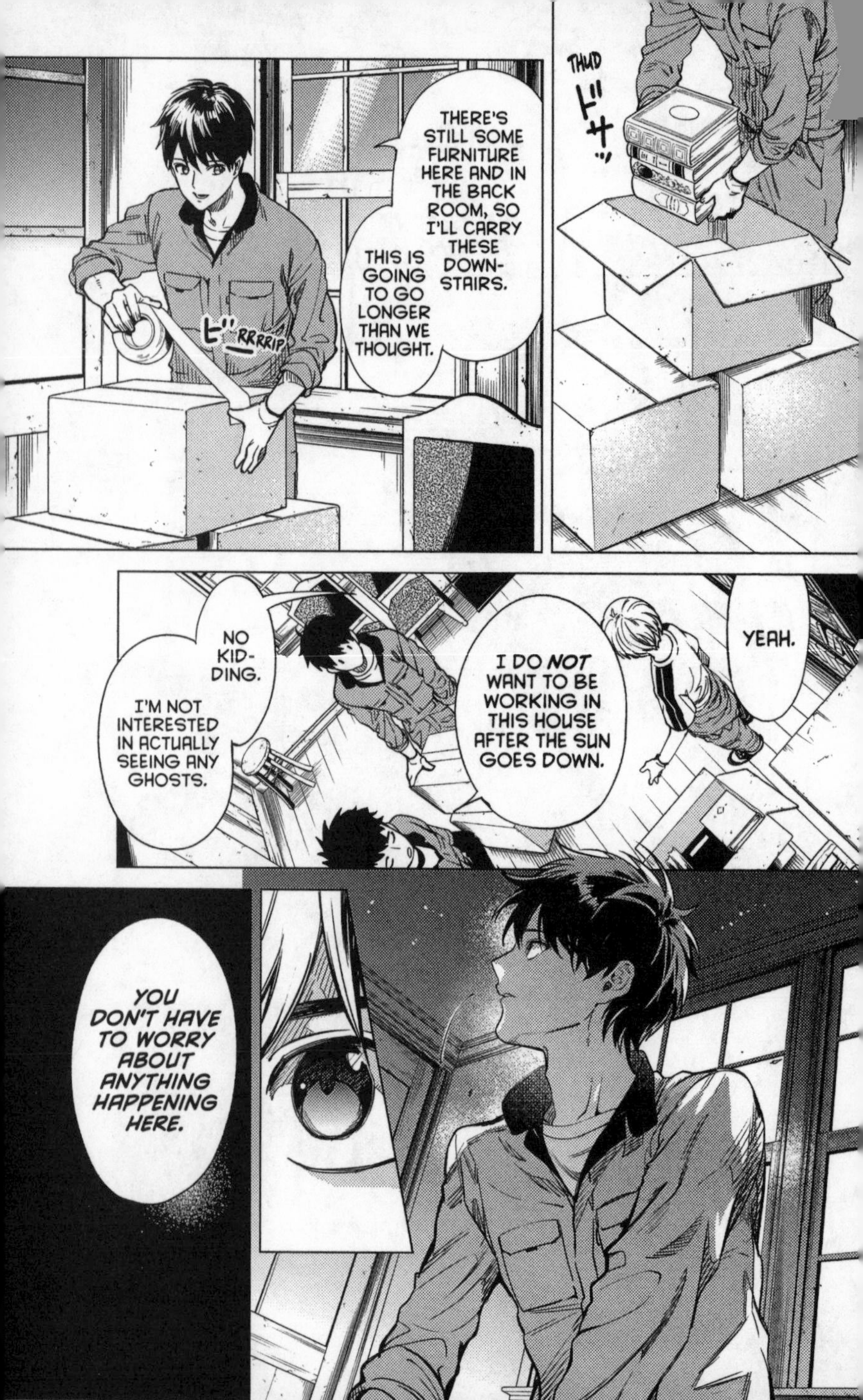

THUD
ドサッ
THERE'S STILL SOME FURNITURE HERE AND IN THE BACK ROOM, SO I'LL CARRY THESE DOWN-STAIRS.
THIS IS GOING TO GO LONGER THAN WE THOUGHT.
ビー RRRRIP
YEAH.
I DO *NOT* WANT TO BE WORKING IN THIS HOUSE AFTER THE SUN GOES DOWN.
NO KID-DING.
I'M NOT INTERESTED IN ACTUALLY SEEING ANY GHOSTS.
YOU DON'T HAVE TO WORRY ABOUT ANYTHING HAPPENING HERE.

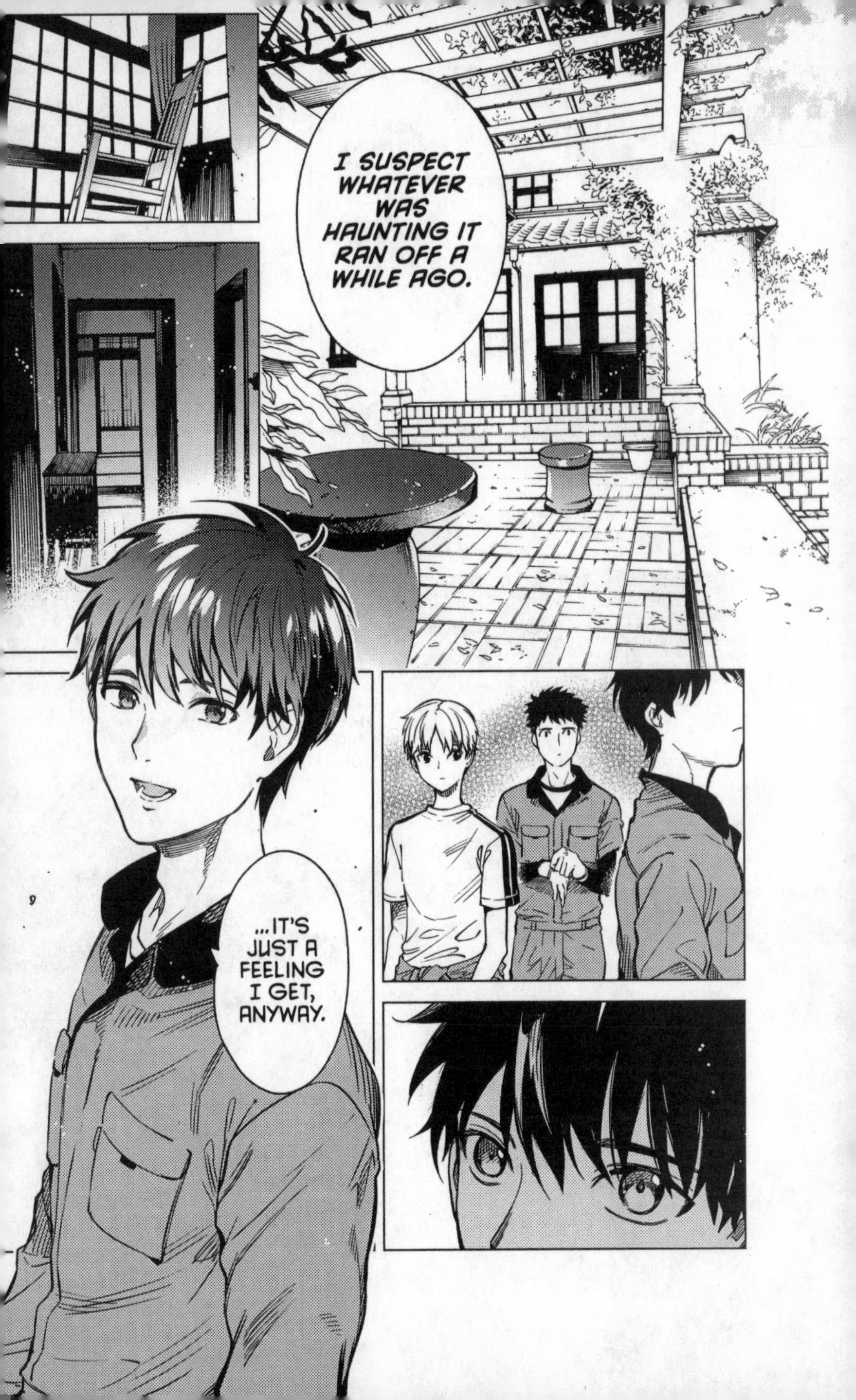
I SUSPECT WHATEVER WAS HAUNTING IT RAN OFF A WHILE AGO.
...IT'S JUST A FEELING I GET, ANYWAY.

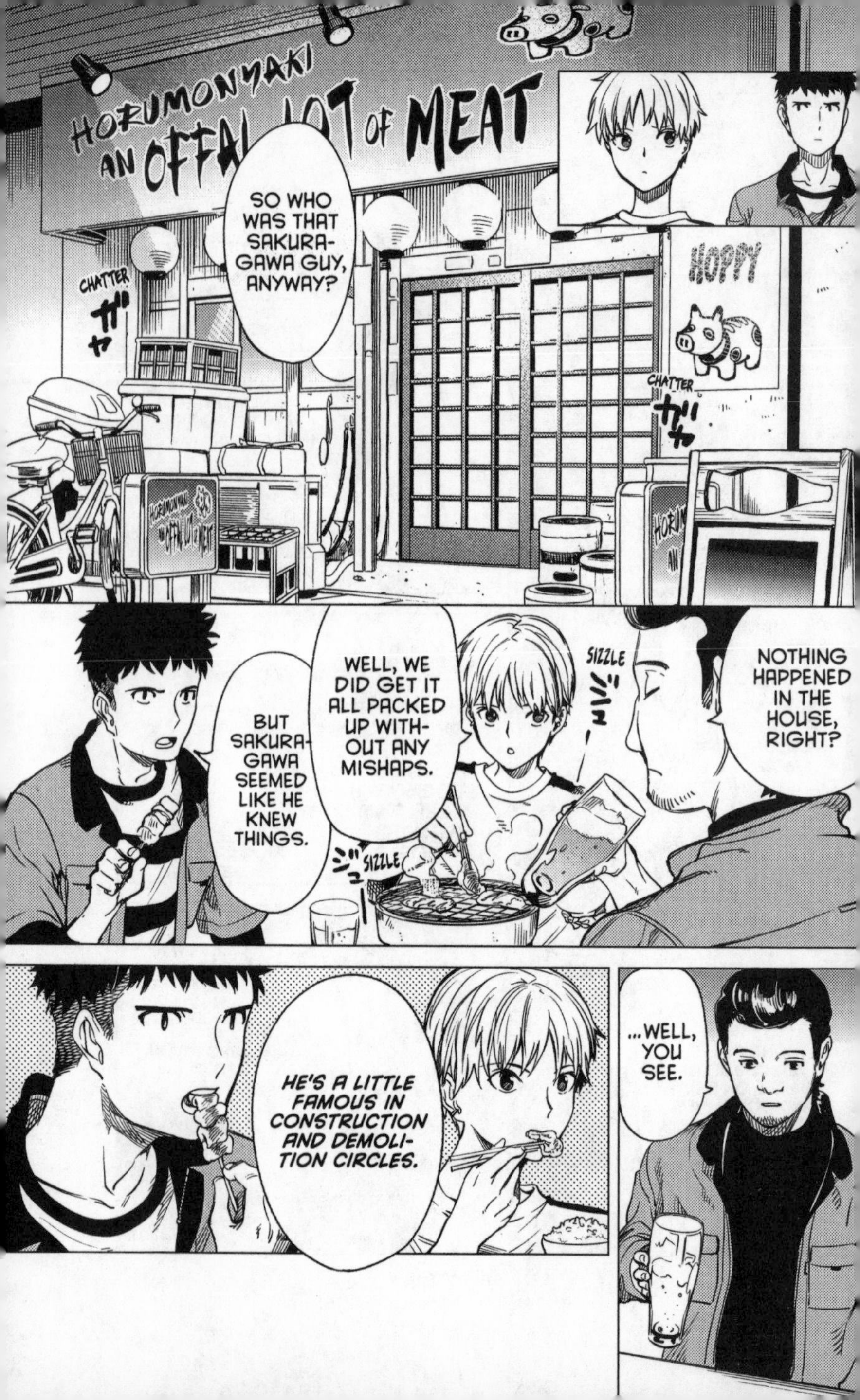
HORUMONYAKI AN OFFAL LOT OF MEAT
SO WHO WAS THAT SAKURA-GAWA GUY, ANYWAY?
HOPPY
CHATTER
CHATTER
NOTHING HAPPENED IN THE HOUSE, RIGHT?
SIZZLE
WELL, WE DID GET IT ALL PACKED UP WITH-OUT ANY MISHAPS.
BUT SAKURA-GAWA SEEMED LIKE HE KNEW THINGS.
SIZZLE
...WELL, YOU SEE.
HE'S A LITTLE FAMOUS IN CONSTRUCTION AND DEMOLI-TION CIRCLES.

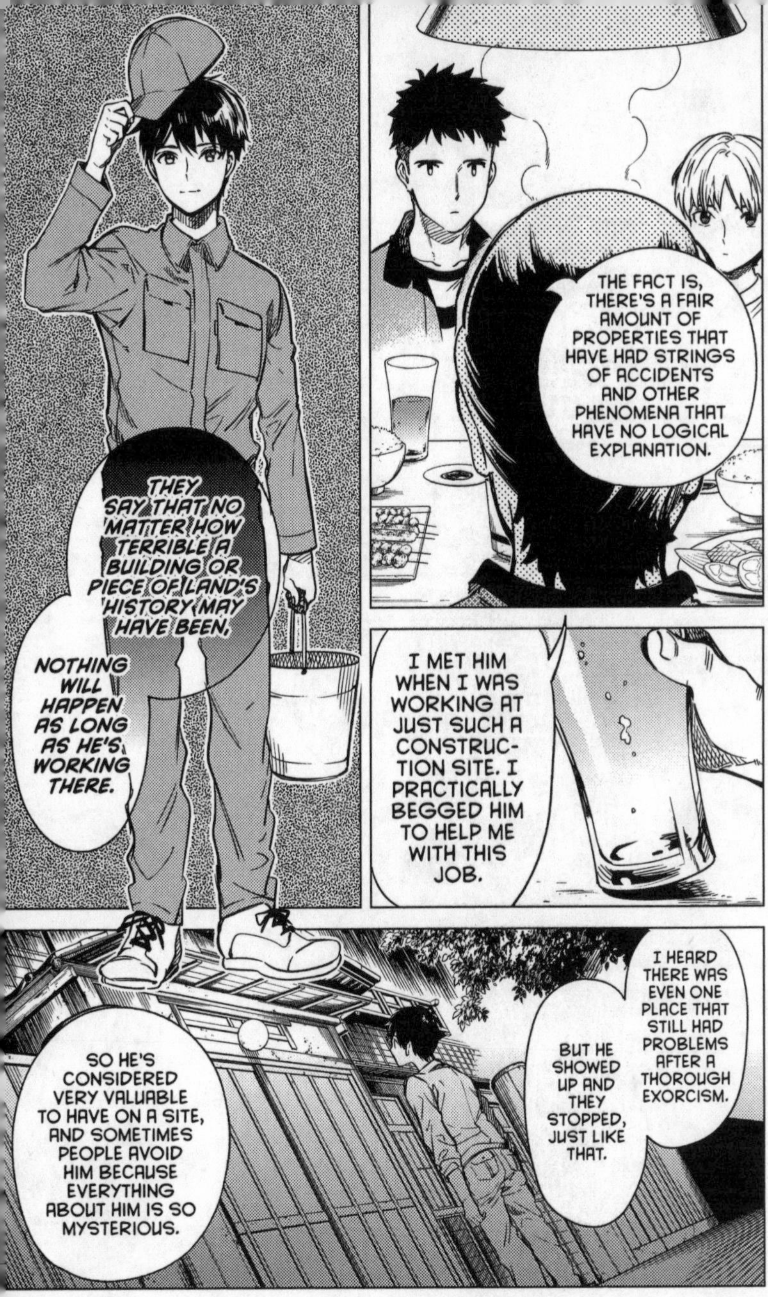
THE FACT IS, THERE'S A FAIR AMOUNT OF PROPERTIES THAT HAVE HAD STRINGS OF ACCIDENTS AND OTHER PHENOMENA THAT HAVE NO LOGICAL EXPLANATION.
I MET HIM WHEN I WAS WORKING AT JUST SUCH A CONSTRUC-TION SITE. I PRACTICALLY BEGGED HIM TO HELP ME WITH THIS JOB.
THEY SAY THAT NO MATTER HOW TERRIBLE A BUILDING OR PIECE OF LAND'S HISTORY MAY HAVE BEEN,
NOTHING WILL HAPPEN AS LONG AS HE'S WORKING THERE.
I HEARD THERE WAS EVEN ONE PLACE THAT STILL HAD PROBLEMS AFTER A THOROUGH EXORCISM.
BUT HE SHOWED UP AND THEY STOPPED, JUST LIKE THAT.
SO HE'S CONSIDERED VERY VALUABLE TO HAVE ON A SITE, AND SOMETIMES PEOPLE AVOID HIM BECAUSE EVERYTHING ABOUT HIM IS SO MYSTERIOUS.

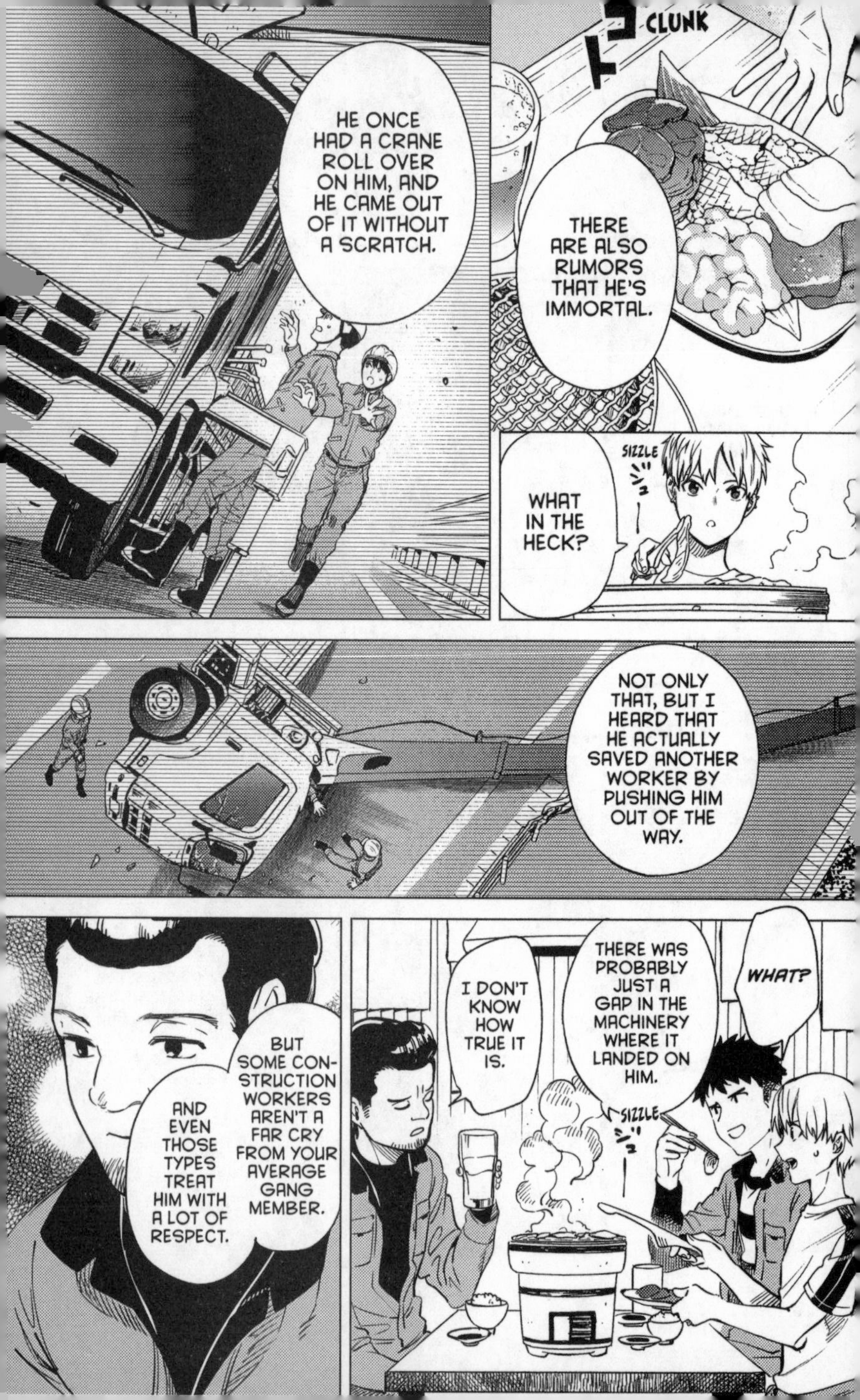
CLUNK
THERE ARE ALSO RUMORS THAT HE'S IMMORTAL.
SIZZLE
WHAT IN THE HECK?
HE ONCE HAD A CRANE ROLL OVER ON HIM, AND HE CAME OUT OF IT WITHOUT A SCRATCH.
NOT ONLY THAT, BUT I HEARD THAT HE ACTUALLY SAVED ANOTHER WORKER BY PUSHING HIM OUT OF THE WAY.
WHAT?
THERE WAS PROBABLY JUST A GAP IN THE MACHINERY WHERE IT LANDED ON HIM.
I DON'T KNOW HOW TRUE IT IS.
SIZZLE
BUT SOME CON-STRUCTION WORKERS AREN'T A FAR CRY FROM YOUR AVERAGE GANG MEMBER.
AND EVEN THOSE TYPES TREAT HIM WITH A LOT OF RESPECT.

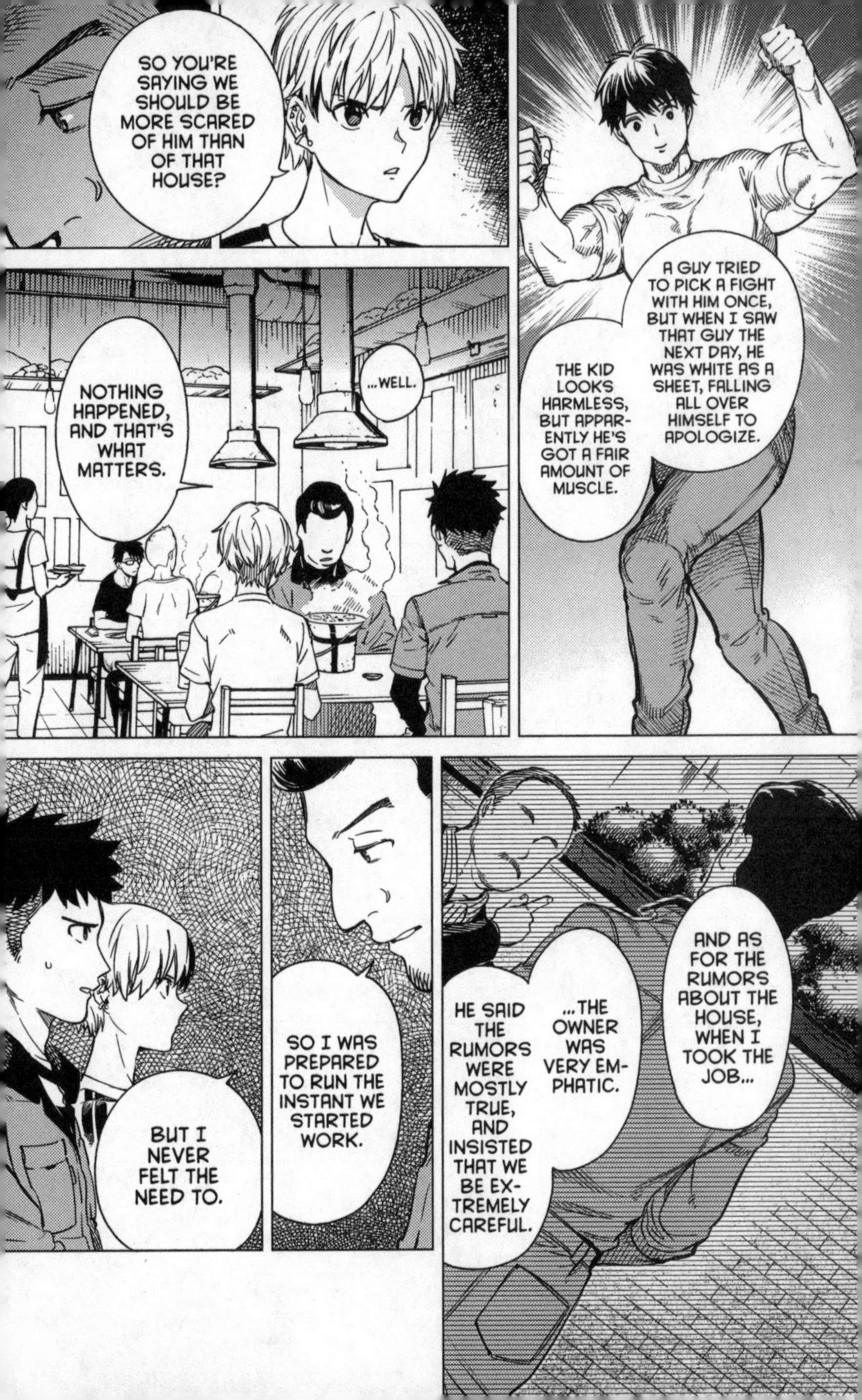
A GUY TRIED TO PICK A FIGHT WITH HIM ONCE, BUT WHEN I SAW THAT GUY THE NEXT DAY, HE WAS WHITE AS A SHEET, FALLING ALL OVER HIMSELF TO APOLOGIZE.
THE KID LOOKS HARMLESS, BUT APPARENTLY HE'S GOT A FAIR AMOUNT OF MUSCLE.
SO YOU'RE SAYING WE SHOULD BE MORE SCARED OF HIM THAN OF THAT HOUSE?
...WELL.
NOTHING HAPPENED, AND THAT'S WHAT MATTERS.
AND AS FOR THE RUMORS ABOUT THE HOUSE, WHEN I TOOK THE JOB...
...THE OWNER WAS VERY EMPHATIC.
HE SAID THE RUMORS WERE MOSTLY TRUE, AND INSISTED THAT WE BE EXTREMELY CAREFUL.
SO I WAS PREPARED TO RUN THE INSTANT WE STARTED WORK.
BUT I NEVER FELT THE NEED TO.

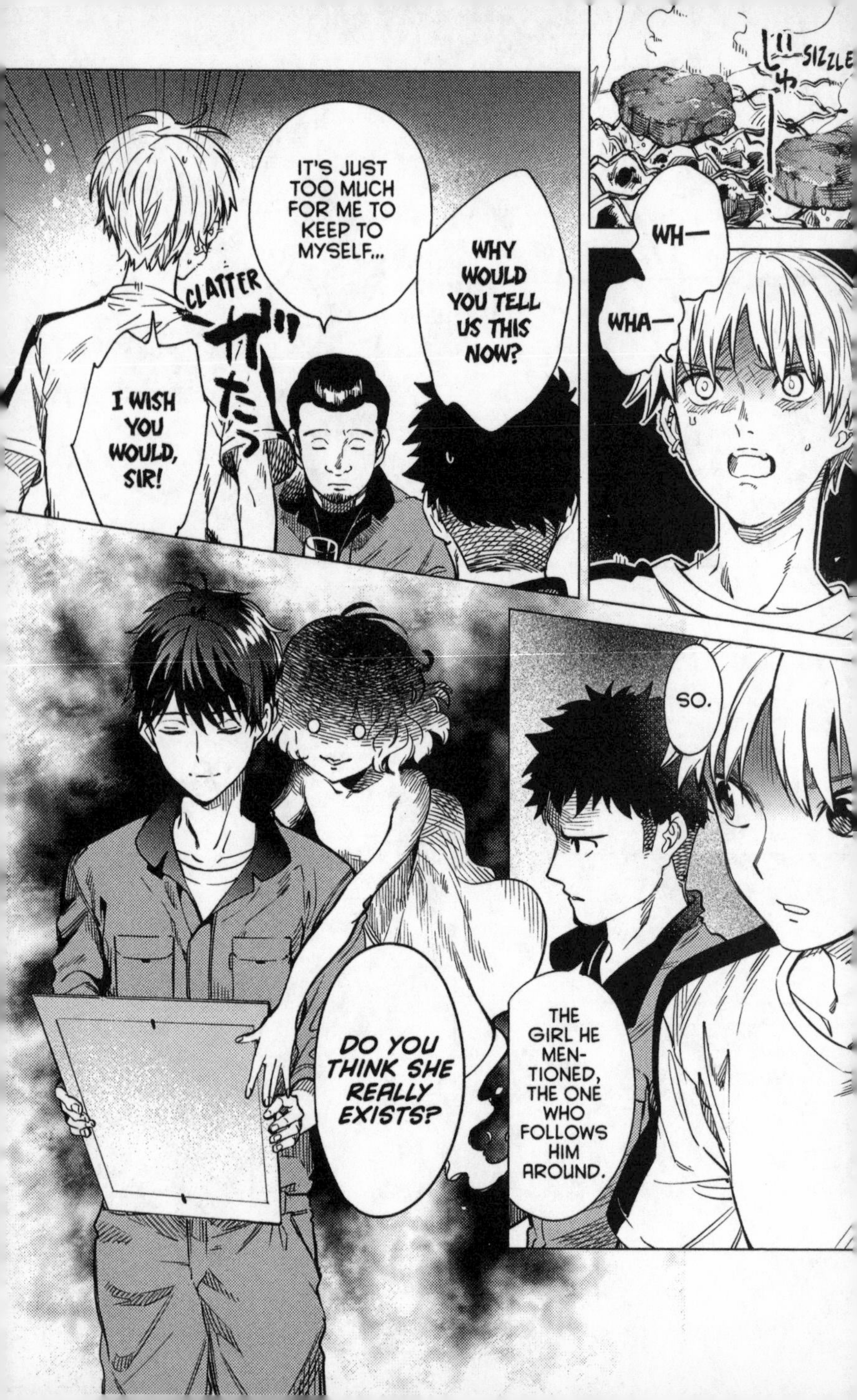
SIZZLE
WH—
WHA—
WHY WOULD YOU TELL US THIS NOW?
IT'S JUST TOO MUCH FOR ME TO KEEP TO MYSELF...
CLATTER
I WISH YOU WOULD, SIR!
SO.
THE GIRL HE MEN-TIONED, THE ONE WHO FOLLOWS HIM AROUND.
DO YOU THINK SHE REALLY EXISTS?

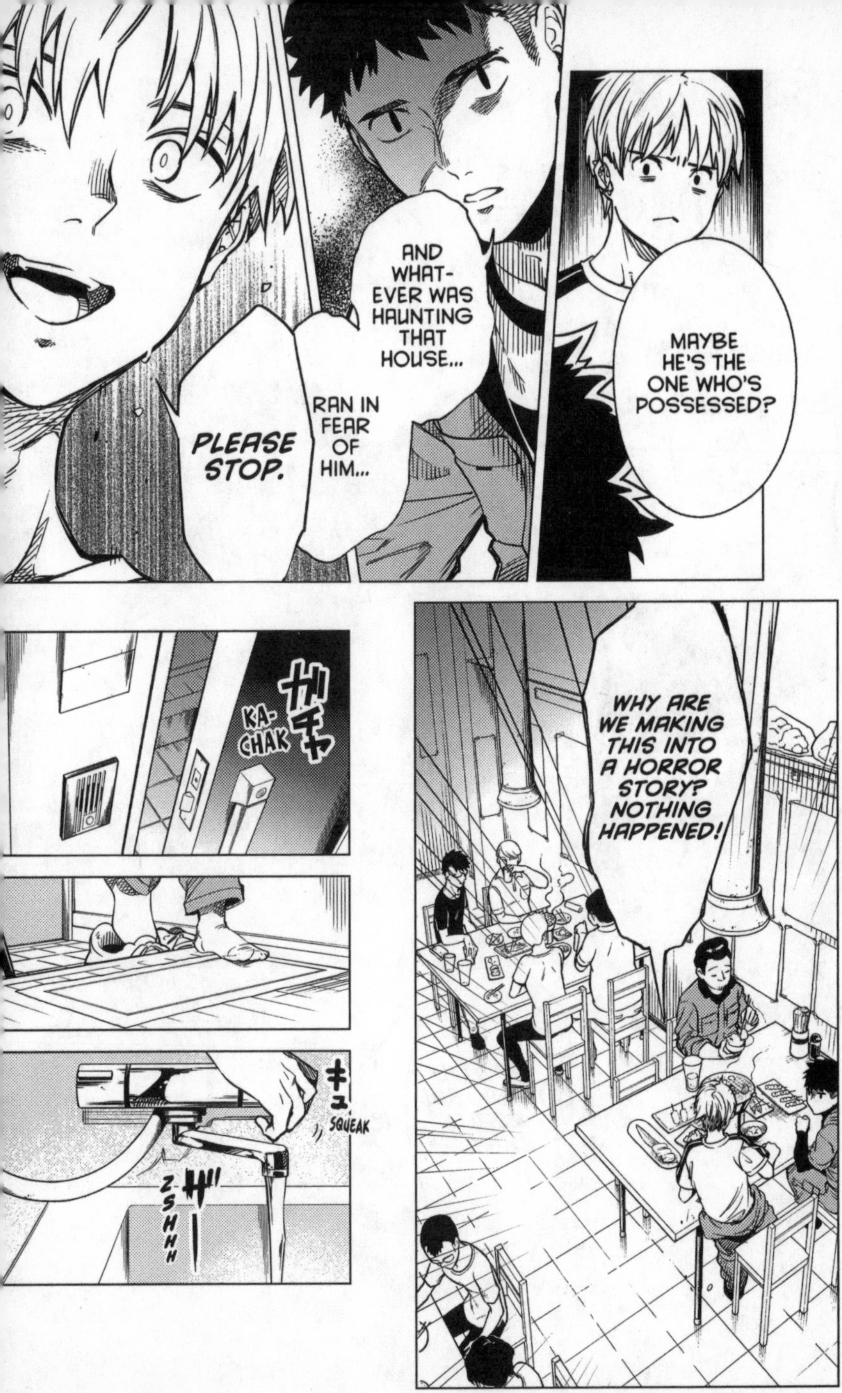
MAYBE HE'S THE ONE WHO'S POSSESSED?
AND WHAT-EVER WAS HAUNTING THAT HOUSE...
RAN IN FEAR OF HIM...
PLEASE STOP.
WHY ARE WE MAKING THIS INTO A HORROR STORY? NOTHING HAPPENED!
ガチャ
KA-CHAK
キュ
SQUEAK
ZSHHH

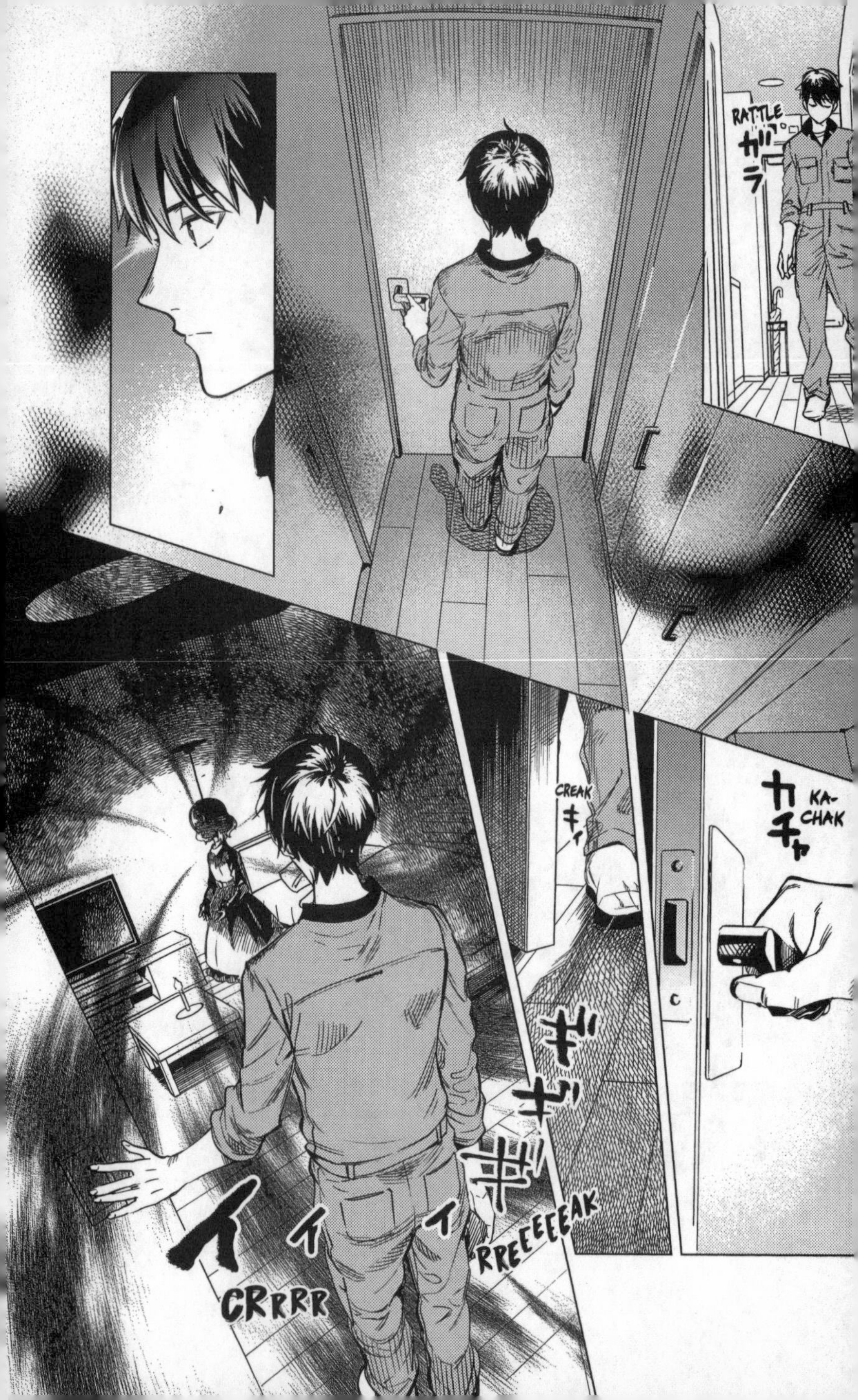
RATTLE
ガラ
KA-CHAK
カチャ
CREAK
キィ
ギギギ
RREEEEEAK
イイイ
CRRRR

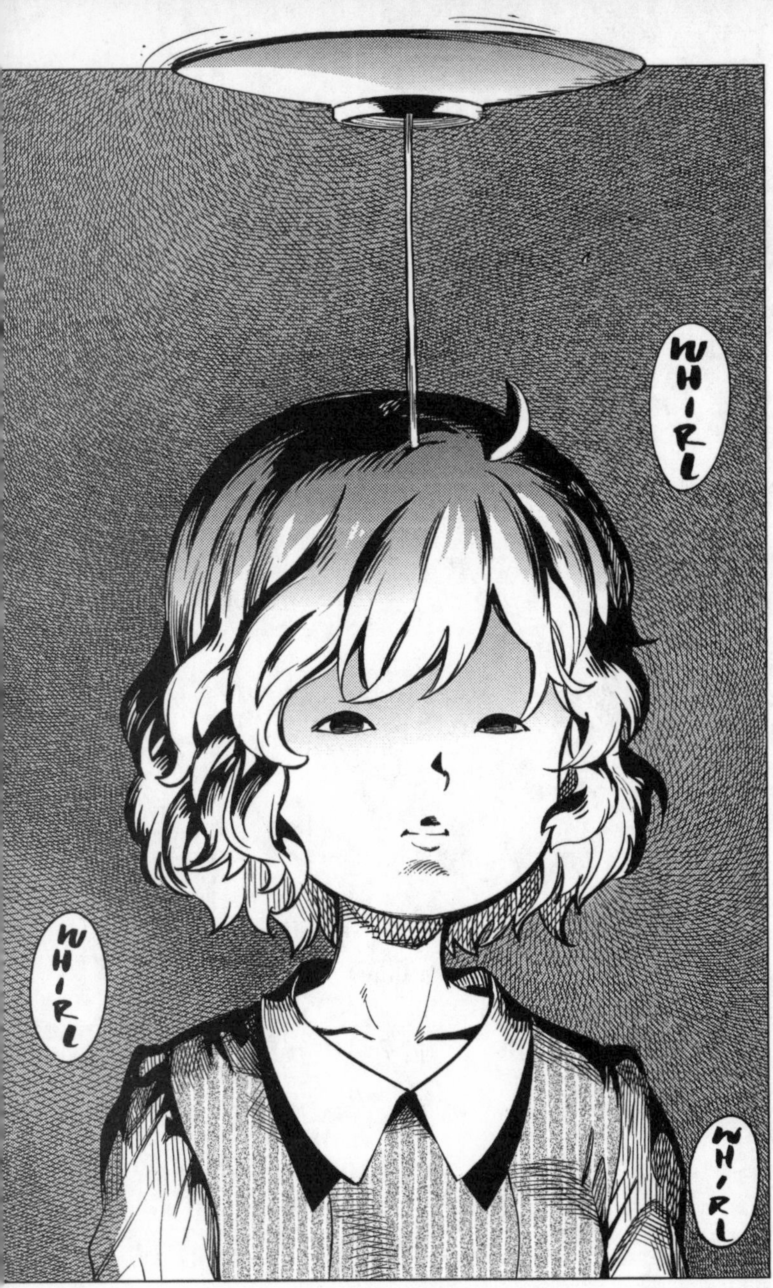
WHIRL
WHIRL
WHIRL

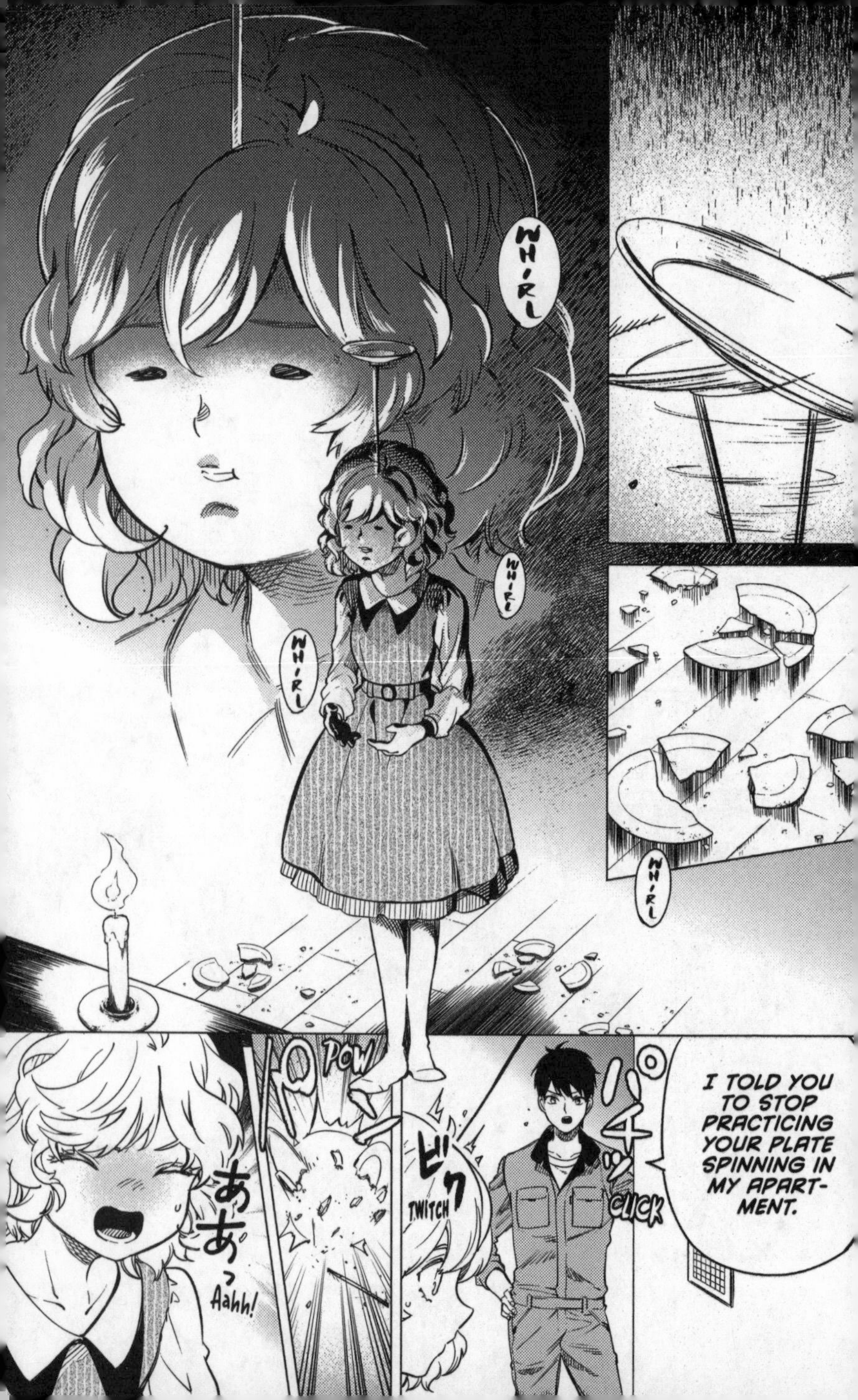
WHIRL
WHIRL
WHIRL
WHIRL
I TOLD YOU TO STOP PRACTICING YOUR PLATE SPINNING IN MY APART-MENT.
CLICK
ビク
TWITCH
POW
あぁっ
Aahh!

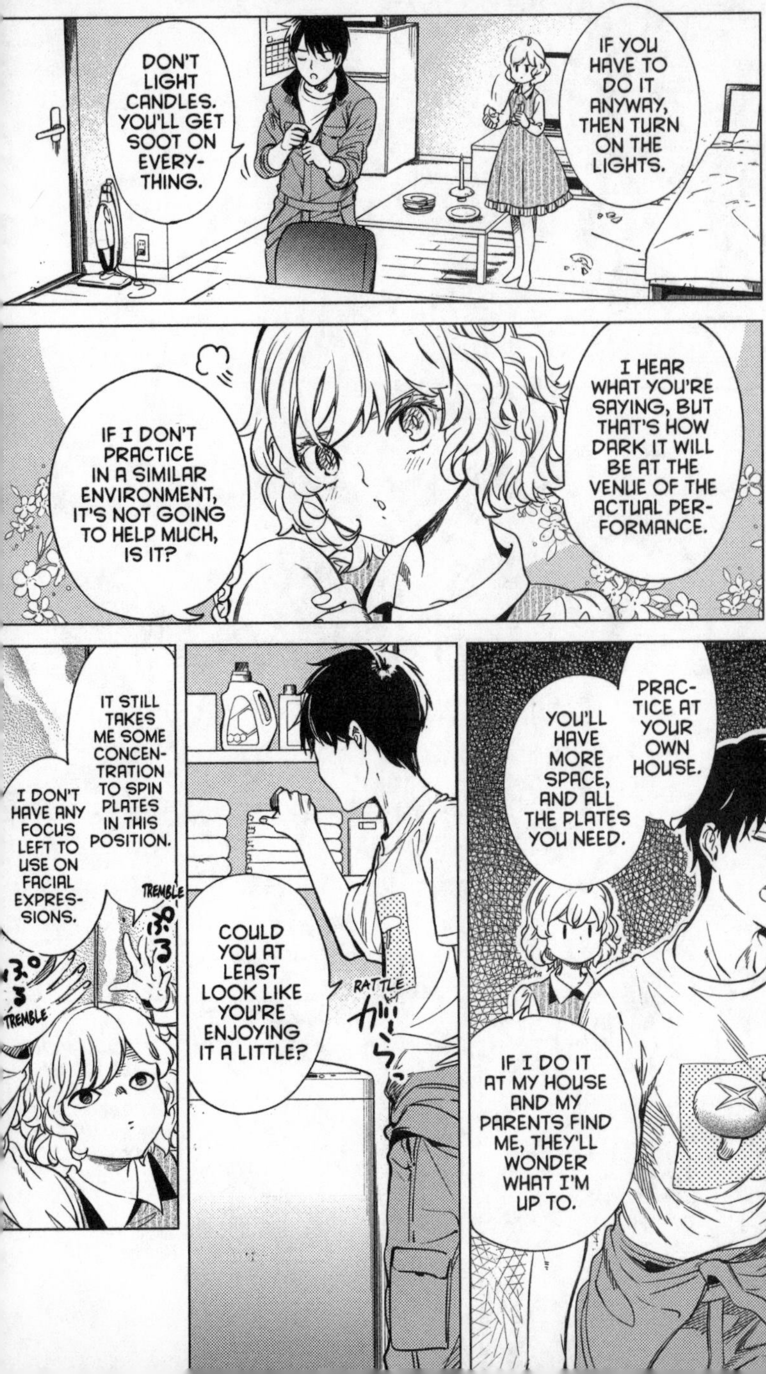
IF YOU HAVE TO DO IT ANYWAY, THEN TURN ON THE LIGHTS.
DON'T LIGHT CANDLES. YOU'LL GET SOOT ON EVERY-THING.
I HEAR WHAT YOU'RE SAYING, BUT THAT'S HOW DARK IT WILL BE AT THE VENUE OF THE ACTUAL PER-FORMANCE.
IF I DON'T PRACTICE IN A SIMILAR ENVIRONMENT, IT'S NOT GOING TO HELP MUCH, IS IT?
PRAC-TICE AT YOUR OWN HOUSE.
YOU'LL HAVE MORE SPACE, AND ALL THE PLATES YOU NEED.
IF I DO IT AT MY HOUSE AND MY PARENTS FIND ME, THEY'LL WONDER WHAT I'M UP TO.
RATTLE
COULD YOU AT LEAST LOOK LIKE YOU'RE ENJOYING IT A LITTLE?
IT STILL TAKES ME SOME CONCEN-TRATION TO SPIN PLATES IN THIS POSITION.
I DON'T HAVE ANY FOCUS LEFT TO USE ON FACIAL EXPRES-SIONS.
TREMBLE
TREMBLE

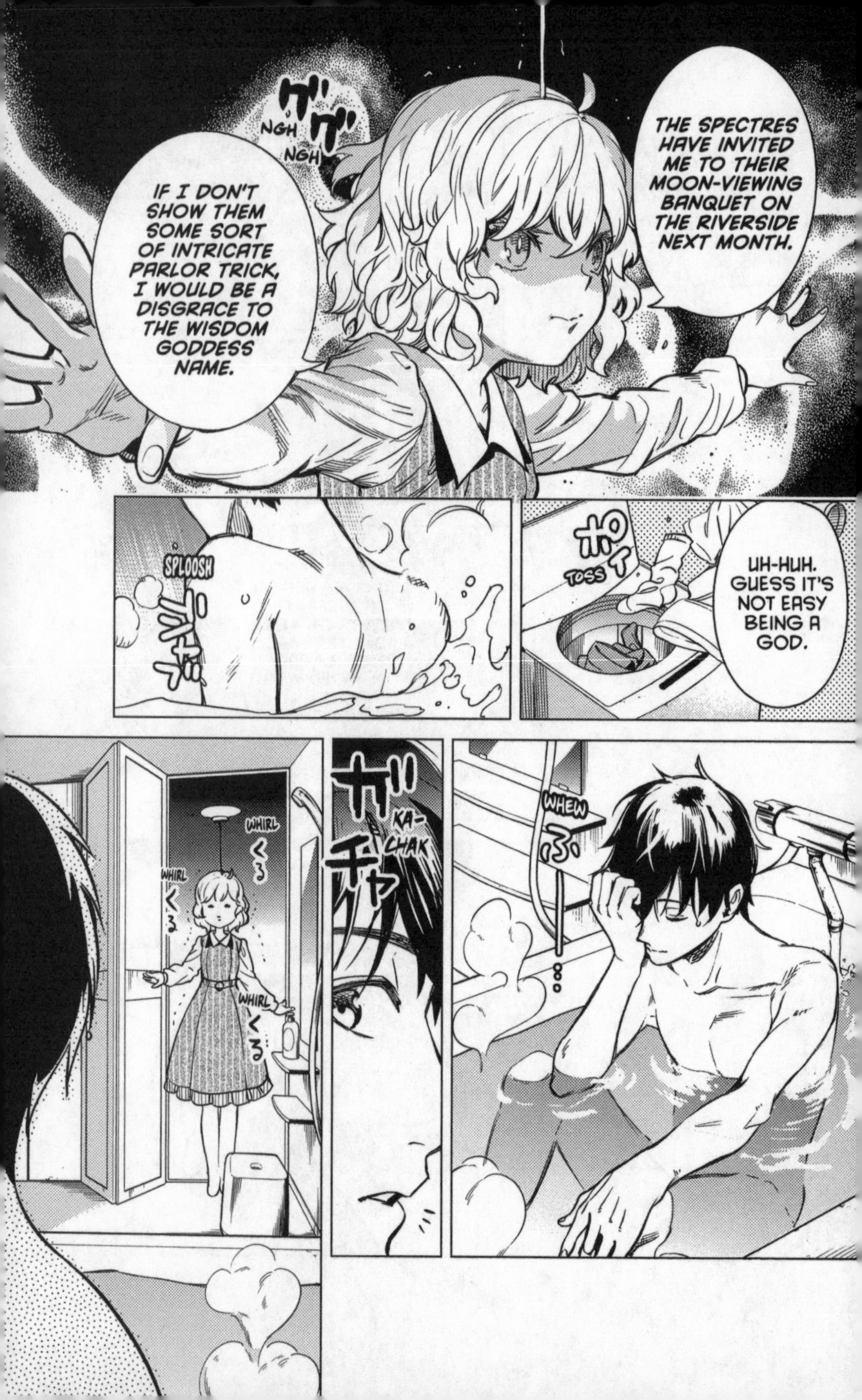
THE SPECTRES HAVE INVITED ME TO THEIR MOON-VIEWING BANQUET ON THE RIVERSIDE NEXT MONTH.
NGH
NGH
IF I DON'T SHOW THEM SOME SORT OF INTRICATE PARLOR TRICK, I WOULD BE A DISGRACE TO THE WISDOM GODDESS NAME.
TOSS
UH-HUH. GUESS IT'S NOT EASY BEING A GOD.
SPLOOSH
WHEW
...
KA-CHAK
WHIRL
WHIRL
WHIRL

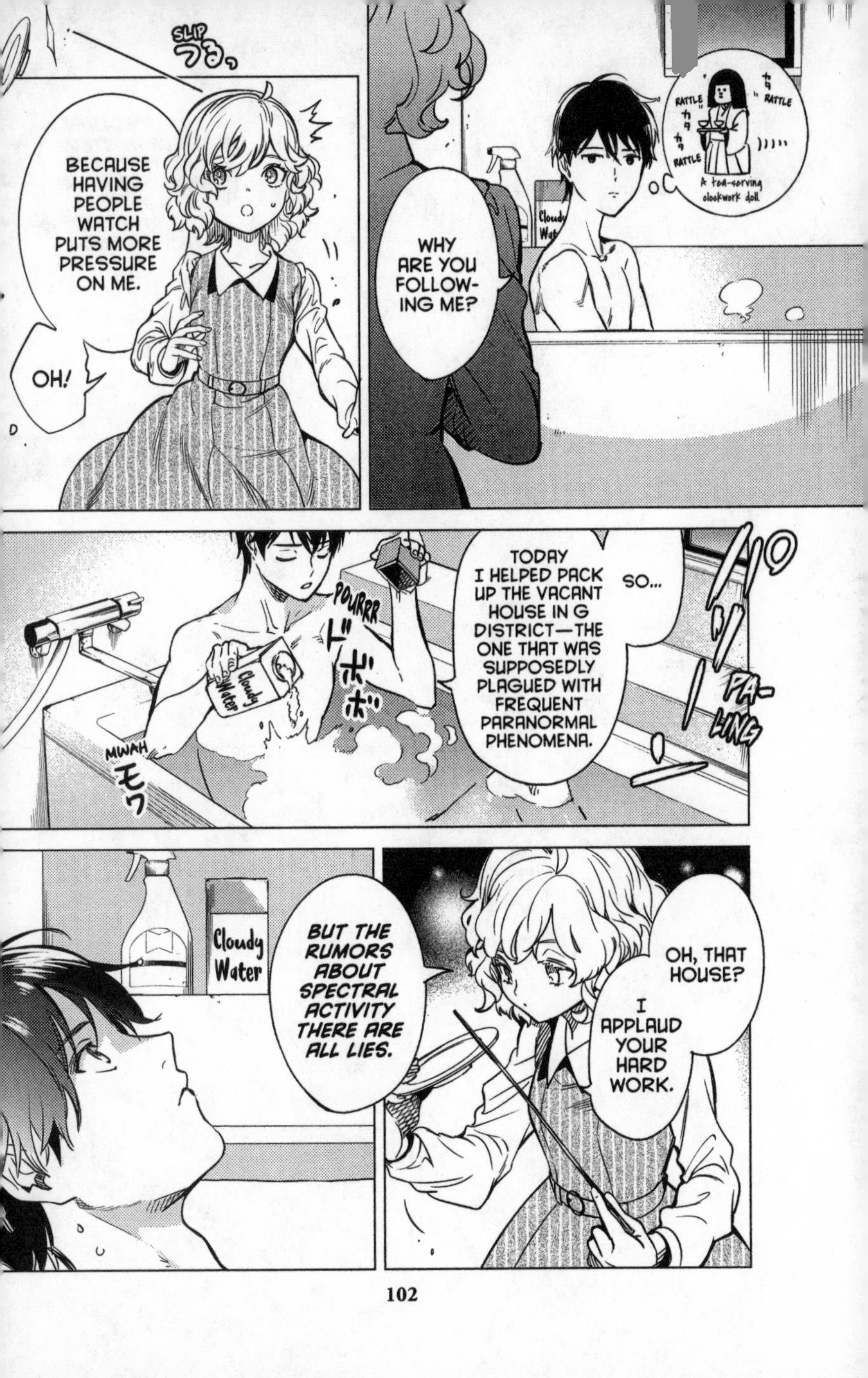

RATTLE カタ RATTLE カタ カタ RATTLE
A tea-serving clockwork doll.
Cloudy Water
WHY ARE YOU FOLLOWING ME?
SLIP つるっ
BECAUSE HAVING PEOPLE WATCH PUTS MORE PRESSURE ON ME.
OH!
PA-LING
SO...
TODAY I HELPED PACK UP THE VACANT HOUSE IN G DISTRICT—THE ONE THAT WAS SUPPOSEDLY PLAGUED WITH FREQUENT PARANORMAL PHENOMENA.
POURRR ドボボ
Cloudy Water
MWAH モワ
OH, THAT HOUSE?
I APPLAUD YOUR HARD WORK.
BUT THE RUMORS ABOUT SPECTRAL ACTIVITY THERE ARE ALL LIES.
Cloudy Water

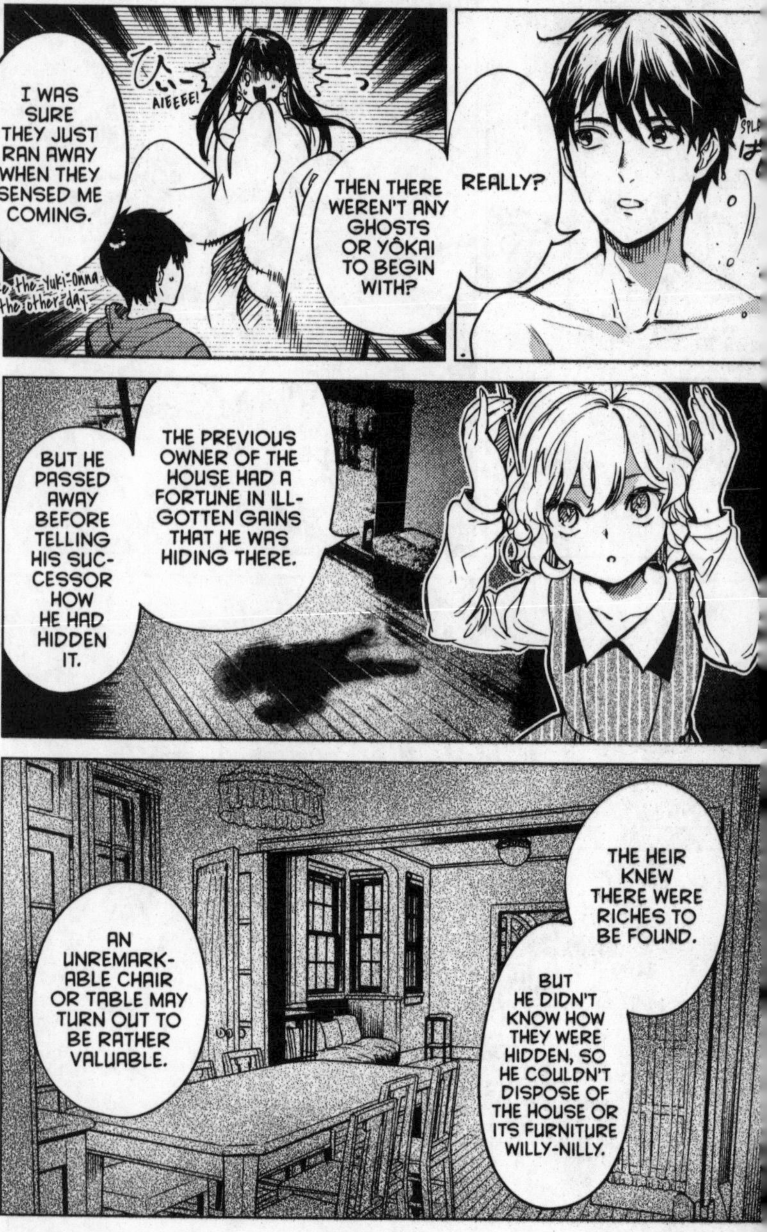
REALLY?
THEN THERE WEREN'T ANY GHOSTS OR YÔKAI TO BEGIN WITH?
AIEEEE!
I WAS SURE THEY JUST RAN AWAY WHEN THEY SENSED ME COMING.
Like the Yuki-Onna the other day.
THE PREVIOUS OWNER OF THE HOUSE HAD A FORTUNE IN ILL-GOTTEN GAINS THAT HE WAS HIDING THERE.
BUT HE PASSED AWAY BEFORE TELLING HIS SUCCESSOR HOW HE HAD HIDDEN IT.
THE HEIR KNEW THERE WERE RICHES TO BE FOUND.
BUT HE DIDN'T KNOW HOW THEY WERE HIDDEN, SO HE COULDN'T DISPOSE OF THE HOUSE OR ITS FURNITURE WILLY-NILLY.
AN UNREMARKABLE CHAIR OR TABLE MAY TURN OUT TO BE RATHER VALUABLE.

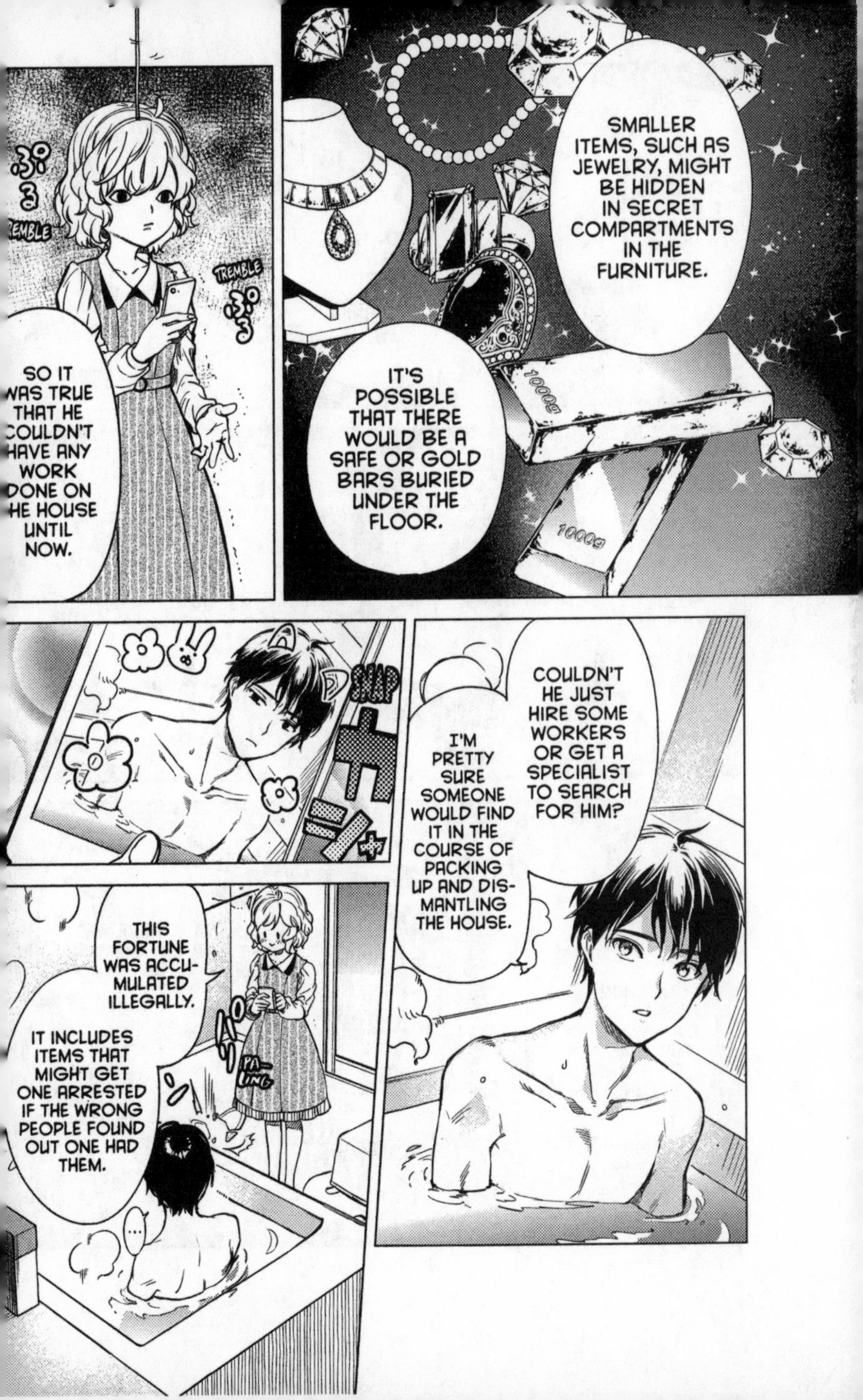
SMALLER ITEMS, SUCH AS JEWELRY, MIGHT BE HIDDEN IN SECRET COMPARTMENTS IN THE FURNITURE.
IT'S POSSIBLE THAT THERE WOULD BE A SAFE OR GOLD BARS BURIED UNDER THE FLOOR.
1000g
1000g
TREMBLE
TREMBLE
SO IT WAS TRUE THAT HE COULDN'T HAVE ANY WORK DONE ON HE HOUSE UNTIL NOW.
COULDN'T HE JUST HIRE SOME WORKERS OR GET A SPECIALIST TO SEARCH FOR HIM?
I'M PRETTY SURE SOMEONE WOULD FIND IT IN THE COURSE OF PACKING UP AND DIS-MANTLING THE HOUSE.
SNAP
THIS FORTUNE WAS ACCU-MULATED ILLEGALLY.
IT INCLUDES ITEMS THAT MIGHT GET ONE ARRESTED IF THE WRONG PEOPLE FOUND OUT ONE HAD THEM.
PA-LING
...

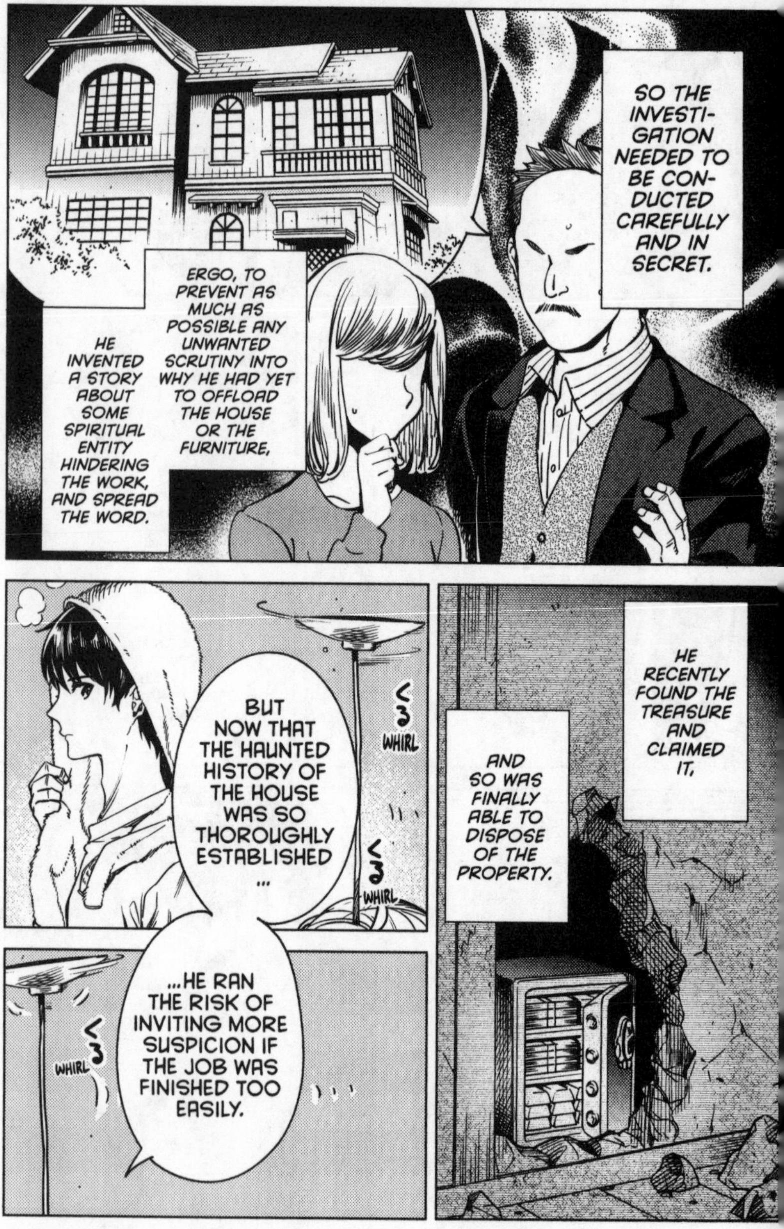
SO THE INVESTIGATION NEEDED TO BE CONDUCTED CAREFULLY AND IN SECRET.
ERGO, TO PREVENT AS MUCH AS POSSIBLE ANY UNWANTED SCRUTINY INTO WHY HE HAD YET TO OFFLOAD THE HOUSE OR THE FURNITURE,
HE INVENTED A STORY ABOUT SOME SPIRITUAL ENTITY HINDERING THE WORK, AND SPREAD THE WORD.
HE RECENTLY FOUND THE TREASURE AND CLAIMED IT,
AND SO WAS FINALLY ABLE TO DISPOSE OF THE PROPERTY.
WHIRL
BUT NOW THAT THE HAUNTED HISTORY OF THE HOUSE WAS SO THOROUGHLY ESTABLISHED...
WHIRL
...HE RAN THE RISK OF INVITING MORE SUSPICION IF THE JOB WAS FINISHED TOO EASILY.
WHIRL

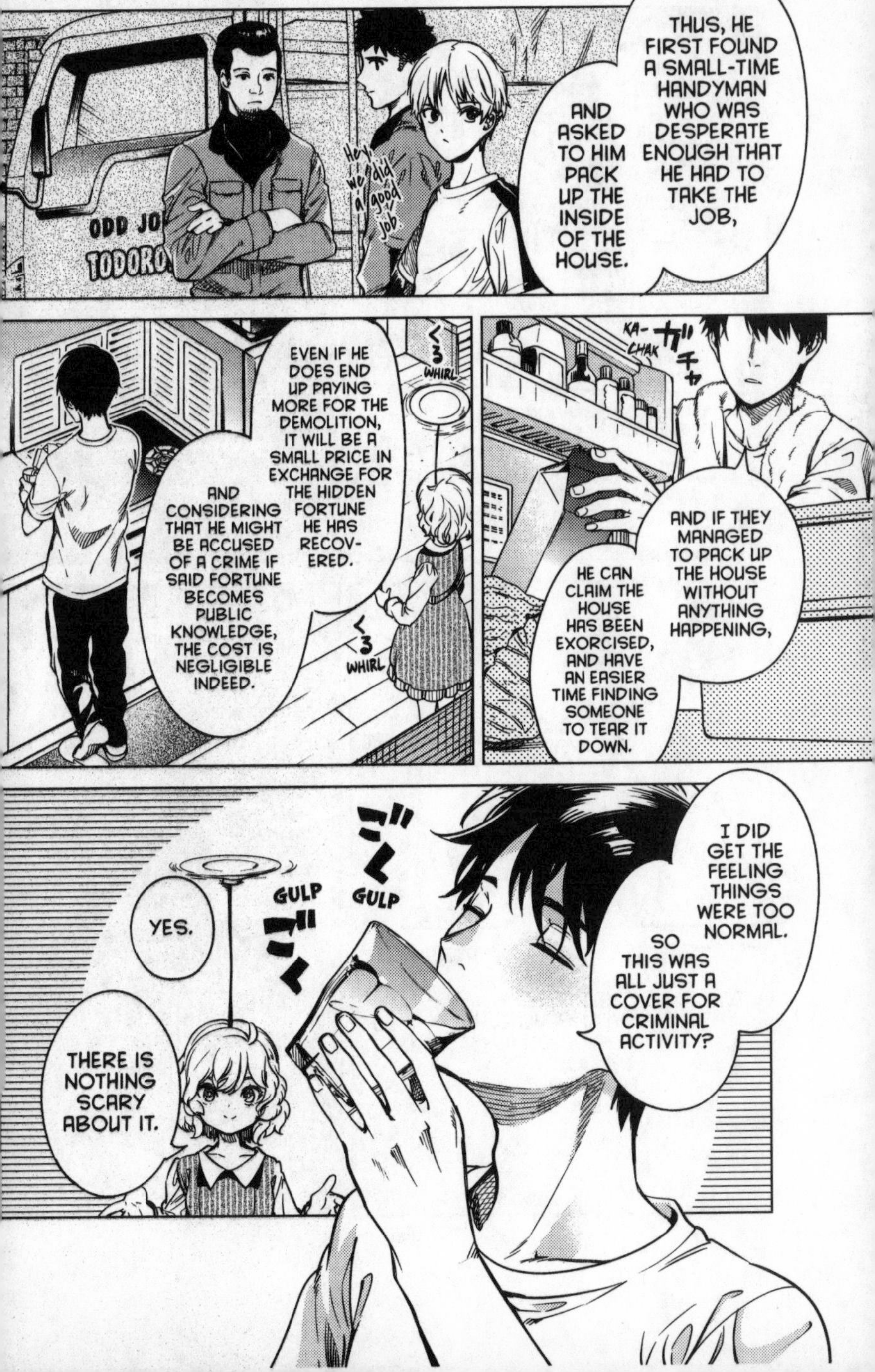
THUS, HE FIRST FOUND A SMALL-TIME HANDYMAN WHO WAS DESPERATE ENOUGH THAT HE HAD TO TAKE THE JOB,
AND ASKED TO HIM PACK UP THE INSIDE OF THE HOUSE.
Hey, we did a good job
ODD JO
TODORO
ガチャ KA-CHAK
AND IF THEY MANAGED TO PACK UP THE HOUSE WITHOUT ANYTHING HAPPENING,
HE CAN CLAIM THE HOUSE HAS BEEN EXORCISED, AND HAVE AN EASIER TIME FINDING SOMEONE TO TEAR IT DOWN.
くる WHIRL
EVEN IF HE DOES END UP PAYING MORE FOR THE DEMOLITION, IT WILL BE A SMALL PRICE IN EXCHANGE FOR THE HIDDEN FORTUNE HE HAS RECOVERED.
AND CONSIDERING THAT HE MIGHT BE ACCUSED OF A CRIME IF SAID FORTUNE BECOMES PUBLIC KNOWLEDGE, THE COST IS NEGLIGIBLE INDEED.
くる WHIRL
I DID GET THE FEELING THINGS WERE TOO NORMAL.
SO THIS WAS ALL JUST A COVER FOR CRIMINAL ACTIVITY?
ごく GULP
ごく GULP
YES.
THERE IS NOTHING SCARY ABOUT IT.

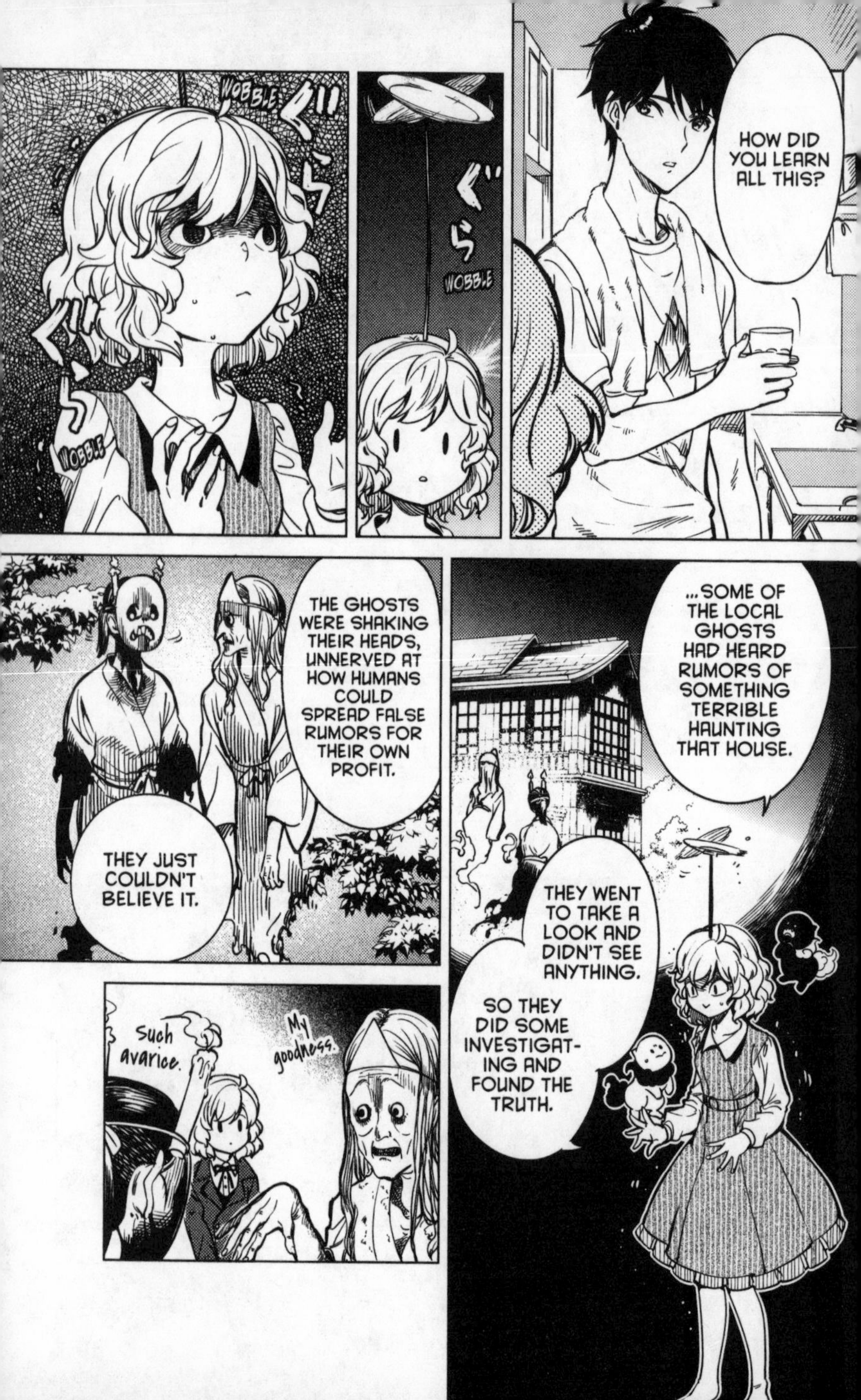
HOW DID YOU LEARN ALL THIS?
ぐら
WOBBLE
WOBBLE
ぐら
WOBBLE
...SOME OF THE LOCAL GHOSTS HAD HEARD RUMORS OF SOMETHING TERRIBLE HAUNTING THAT HOUSE.
THEY WENT TO TAKE A LOOK AND DIDN'T SEE ANYTHING.
SO THEY DID SOME INVESTIGAT-ING AND FOUND THE TRUTH.
THE GHOSTS WERE SHAKING THEIR HEADS, UNNERVED AT HOW HUMANS COULD SPREAD FALSE RUMORS FOR THEIR OWN PROFIT.
THEY JUST COULDN'T BELIEVE IT.
My goodness.
Such avarice.

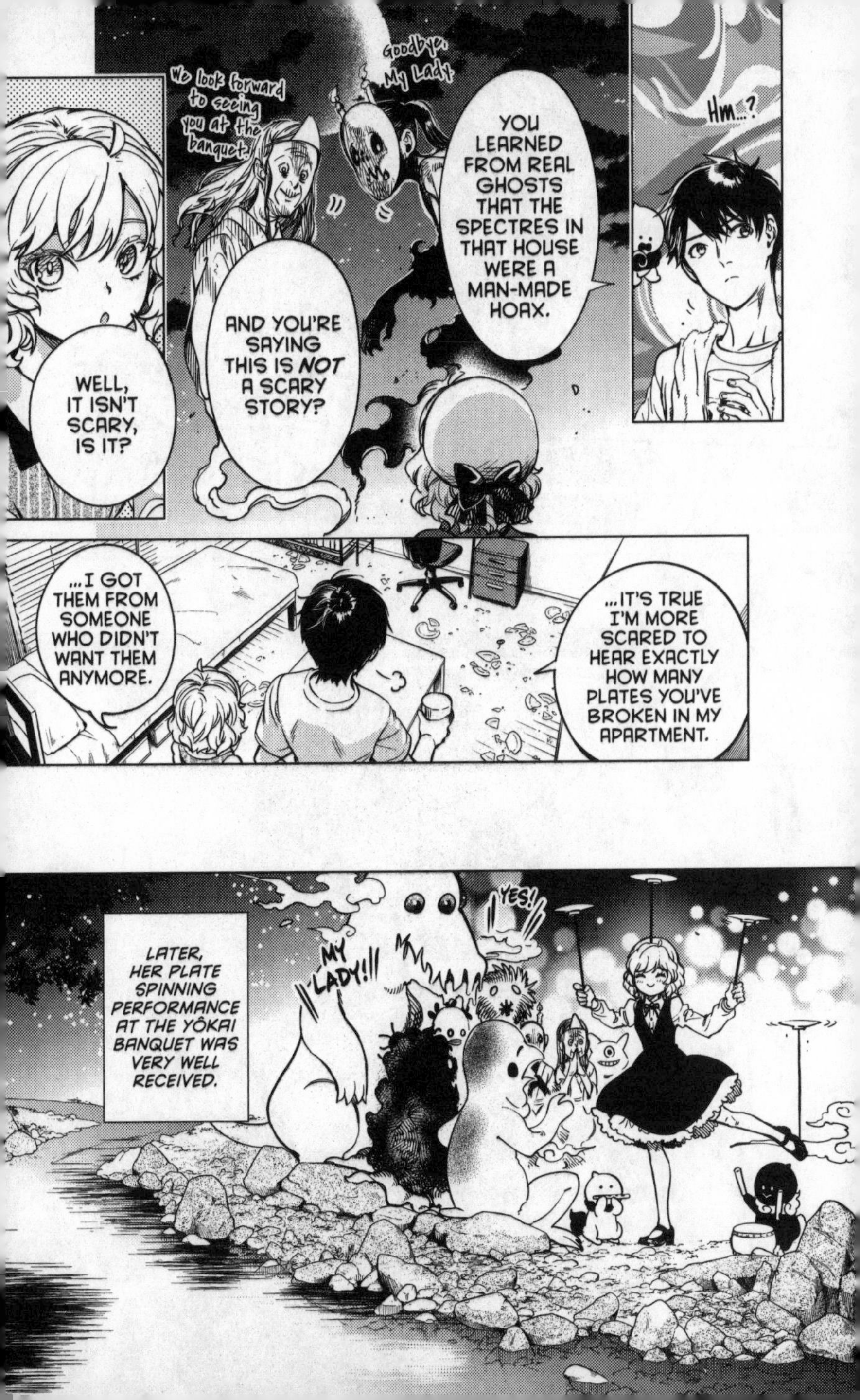
Hm...?
Goodbye, My Lady.
We look forward to seeing you at the banquet.
YOU LEARNED FROM REAL GHOSTS THAT THE SPECTRES IN THAT HOUSE WERE A MAN-MADE HOAX.
AND YOU'RE SAYING THIS IS *NOT* A SCARY STORY?
WELL, IT ISN'T SCARY, IS IT?
...IT'S TRUE I'M MORE SCARED TO HEAR EXACTLY HOW MANY PLATES YOU'VE BROKEN IN MY APARTMENT.
...I GOT THEM FROM SOMEONE WHO DIDN'T WANT THEM ANYMORE.
YES!
MY LADY!!
LATER, HER PLATE SPINNING PERFORMANCE AT THE YÔKAI BANQUET WAS VERY WELL RECEIVED.

(This
is a
copy)

According to Shirodaira-sensei, Iwanaga's
look and facial expression when spinning
plates were based on this Shunsō
Jōshu's Plate Spinning Hotei.

"Apologies for the Volume 12 Bonus Manga"

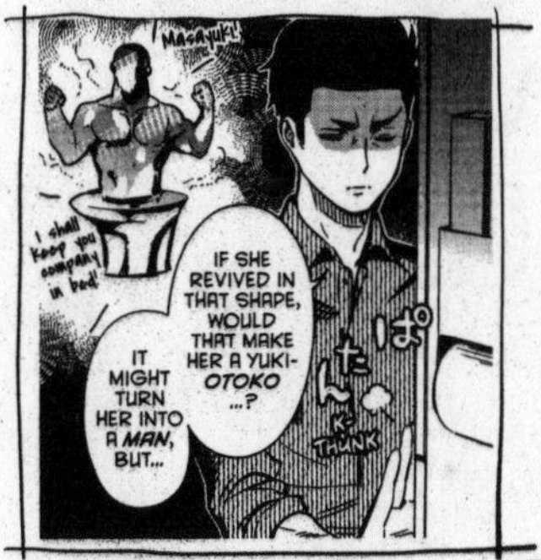
Masayuki!
I shall keep you company in bed!
IF SHE REVIVED IN THAT SHAPE, WOULD THAT MAKE HER A YUKI-*OTOKO* ...?
IT MIGHT TURN HER INTO A *MAN*, BUT...
K-THUNK

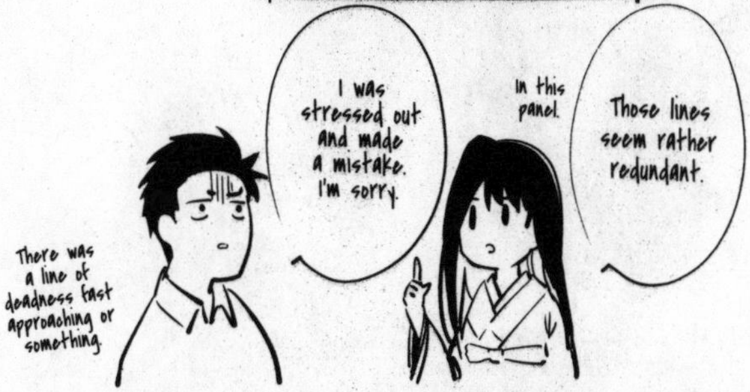
In this panel.
Those lines seem rather redundant.
I was stressed out and made a mistake. I'm sorry.
There was a line of deadness fast approaching or something.

*In the original Japanese, "yuki-otoko" was written twice in this panel, once in each balloon.

CHAPTER 35: "WHAT WAS SEEN PART 1"

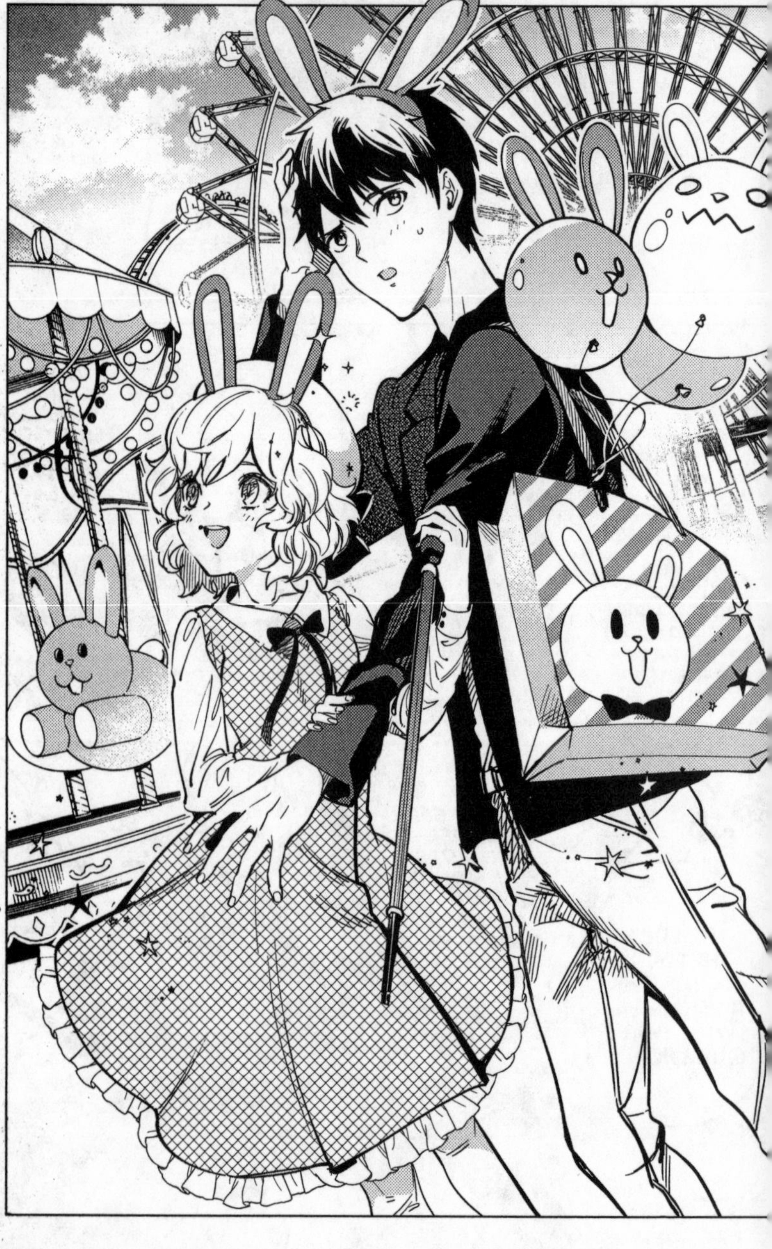

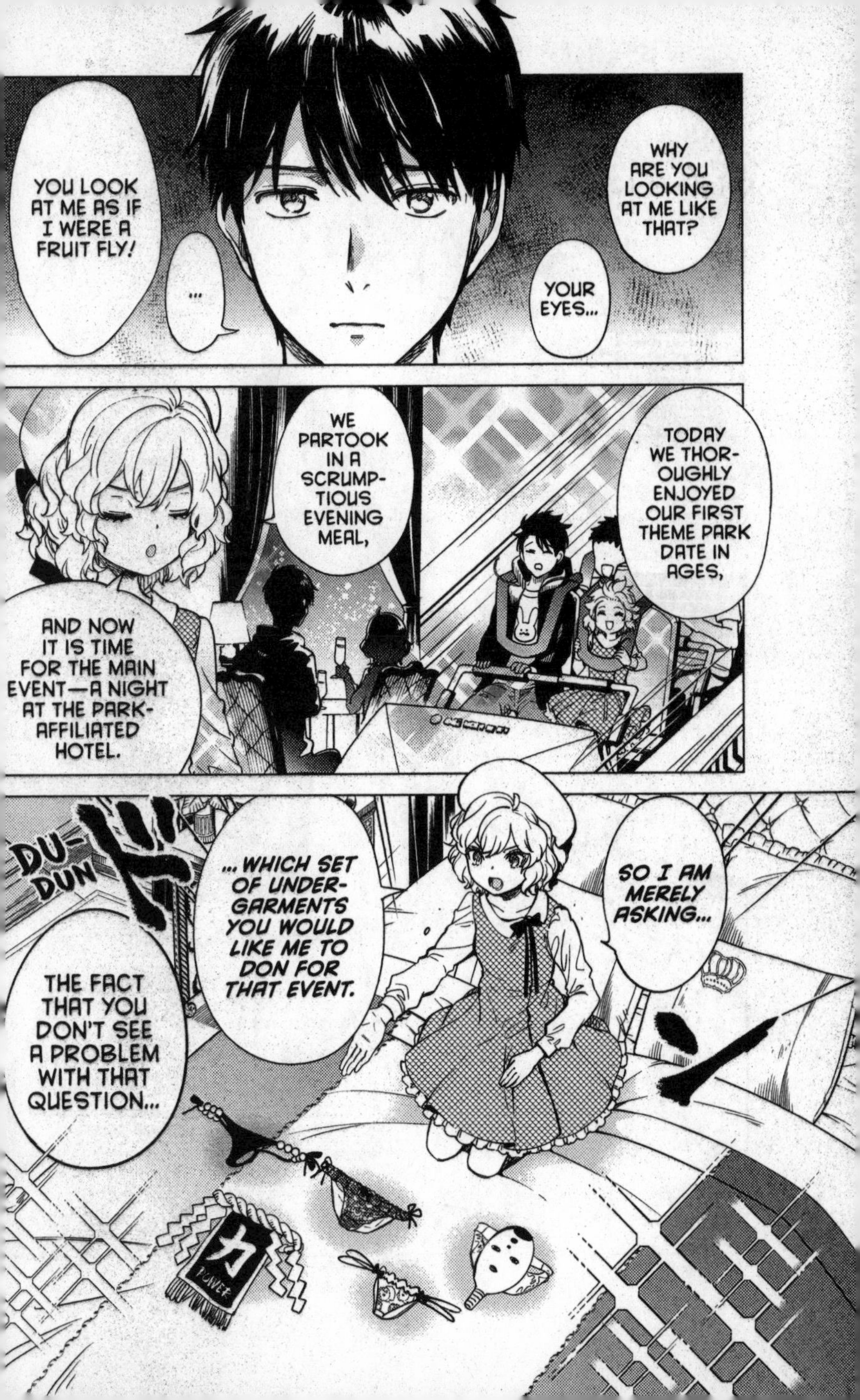
WHY ARE YOU LOOKING AT ME LIKE THAT?
YOUR EYES...
...
YOU LOOK AT ME AS IF I WERE A FRUIT FLY!
TODAY WE THOROUGHLY ENJOYED OUR FIRST THEME PARK DATE IN AGES,
WE PARTOOK IN A SCRUMPTIOUS EVENING MEAL,
AND NOW IT IS TIME FOR THE MAIN EVENT—A NIGHT AT THE PARK-AFFILIATED HOTEL.
SO I AM MERELY ASKING...
...WHICH SET OF UNDERGARMENTS YOU WOULD LIKE ME TO DON FOR THAT EVENT.
DU-DUN
THE FACT THAT YOU DON'T SEE A PROBLEM WITH THAT QUESTION...
力
POWER

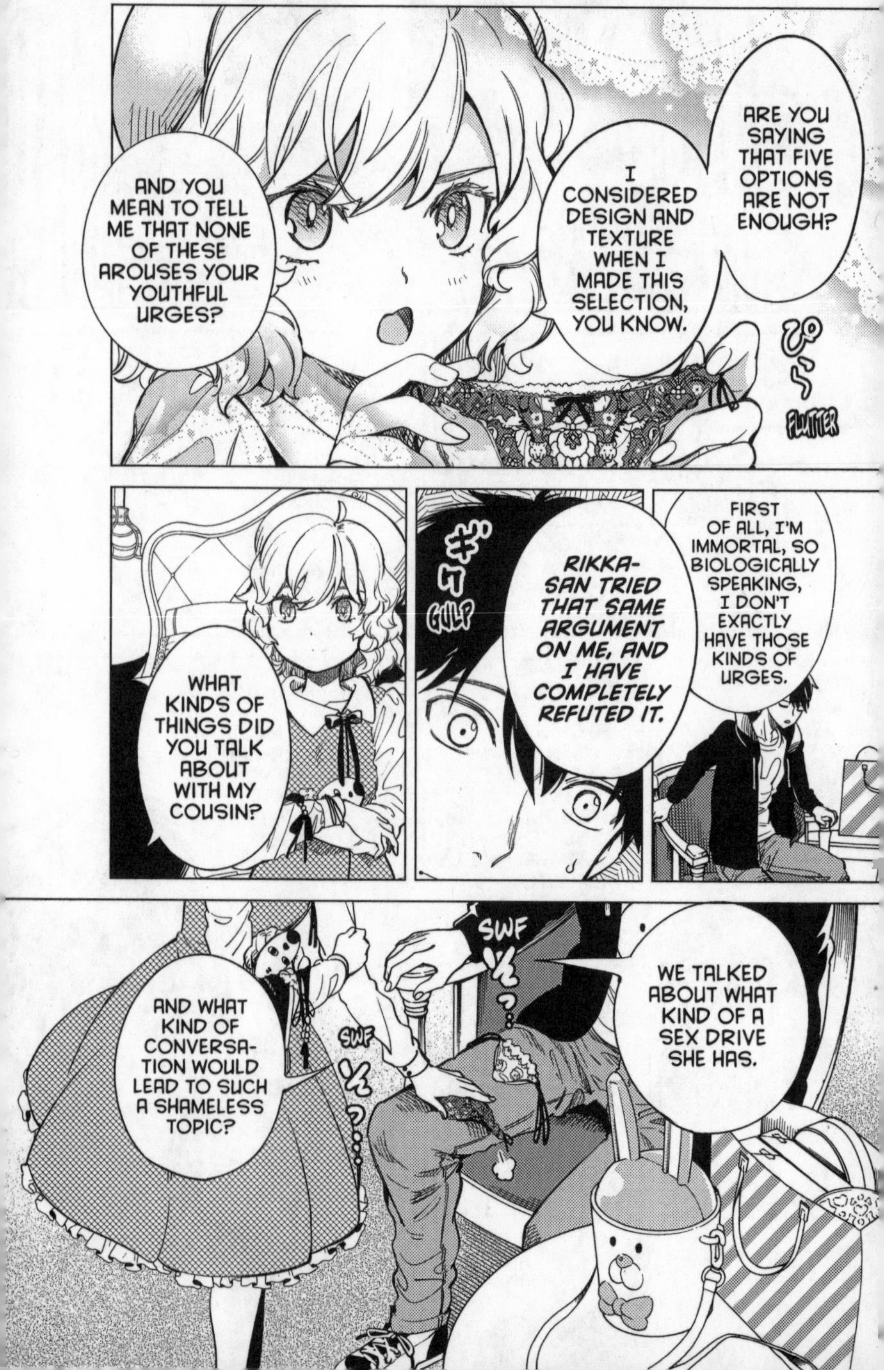
ARE YOU SAYING THAT FIVE OPTIONS ARE NOT ENOUGH?
I CONSIDERED DESIGN AND TEXTURE WHEN I MADE THIS SELECTION, YOU KNOW.
AND YOU MEAN TO TELL ME THAT NONE OF THESE AROUSES YOUR YOUTHFUL URGES?
FLUTTER
FIRST OF ALL, I'M IMMORTAL, SO BIOLOGICALLY SPEAKING, I DON'T EXACTLY HAVE THOSE KINDS OF URGES.
RIKKA-SAN TRIED THAT SAME ARGUMENT ON ME, AND I HAVE COMPLETELY REFUTED IT.
GULP
WHAT KINDS OF THINGS DID YOU TALK ABOUT WITH MY COUSIN?
WE TALKED ABOUT WHAT KIND OF A SEX DRIVE SHE HAS.
SWF
AND WHAT KIND OF CONVERSA-TION WOULD LEAD TO SUCH A SHAMELESS TOPIC?
SWF

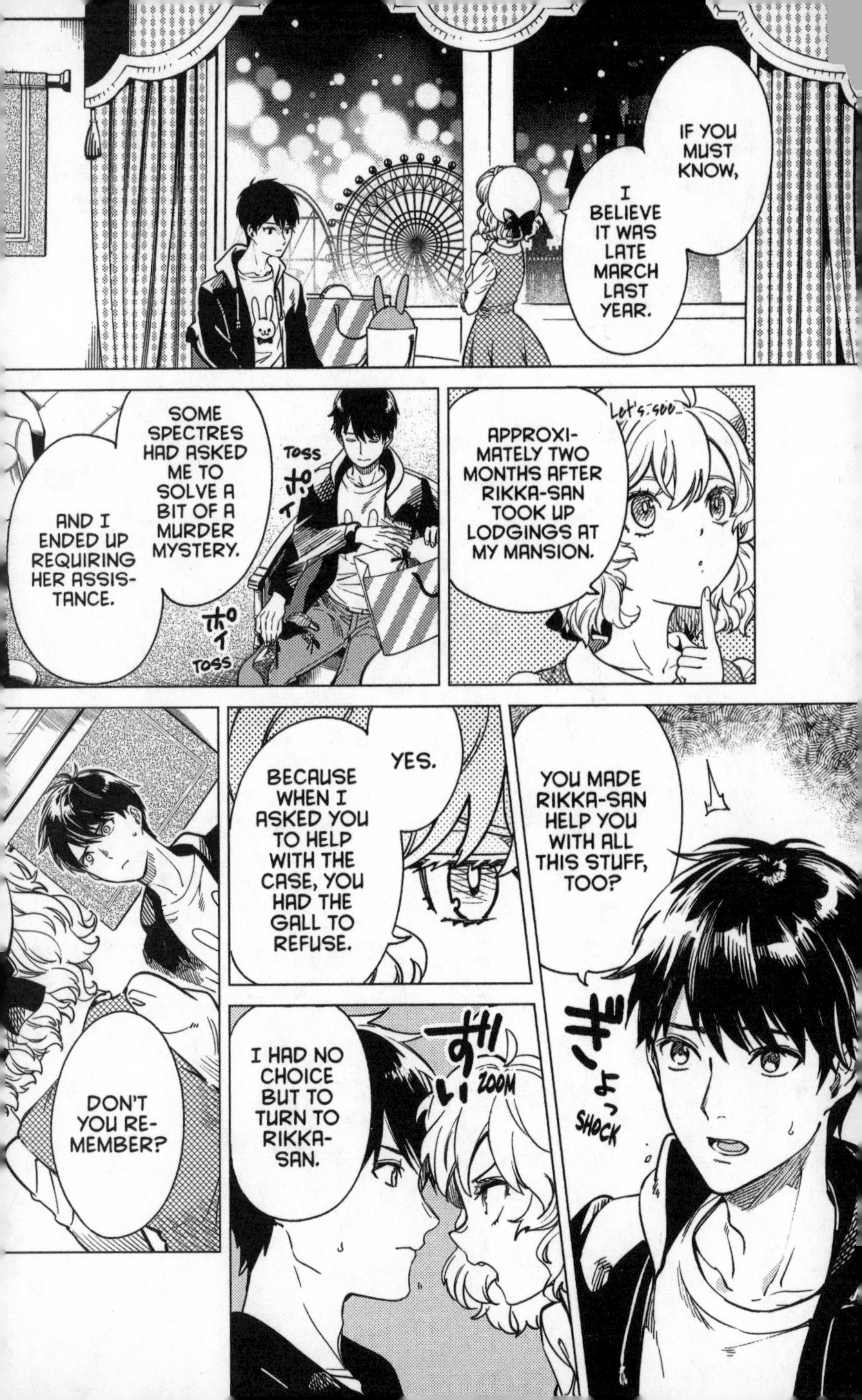
IF YOU MUST KNOW,
I BELIEVE IT WAS LATE MARCH LAST YEAR.
Let's see...
APPROXIMATELY TWO MONTHS AFTER RIKKA-SAN TOOK UP LODGINGS AT MY MANSION.
SOME SPECTRES HAD ASKED ME TO SOLVE A BIT OF A MURDER MYSTERY.
TOSS
AND I ENDED UP REQUIRING HER ASSISTANCE.
TOSS
YOU MADE RIKKA-SAN HELP YOU WITH ALL THIS STUFF, TOO?
SHOCK
YES.
BECAUSE WHEN I ASKED YOU TO HELP WITH THE CASE, YOU HAD THE GALL TO REFUSE.
ZOOM
I HAD NO CHOICE BUT TO TURN TO RIKKA-SAN.
DON'T YOU REMEMBER?

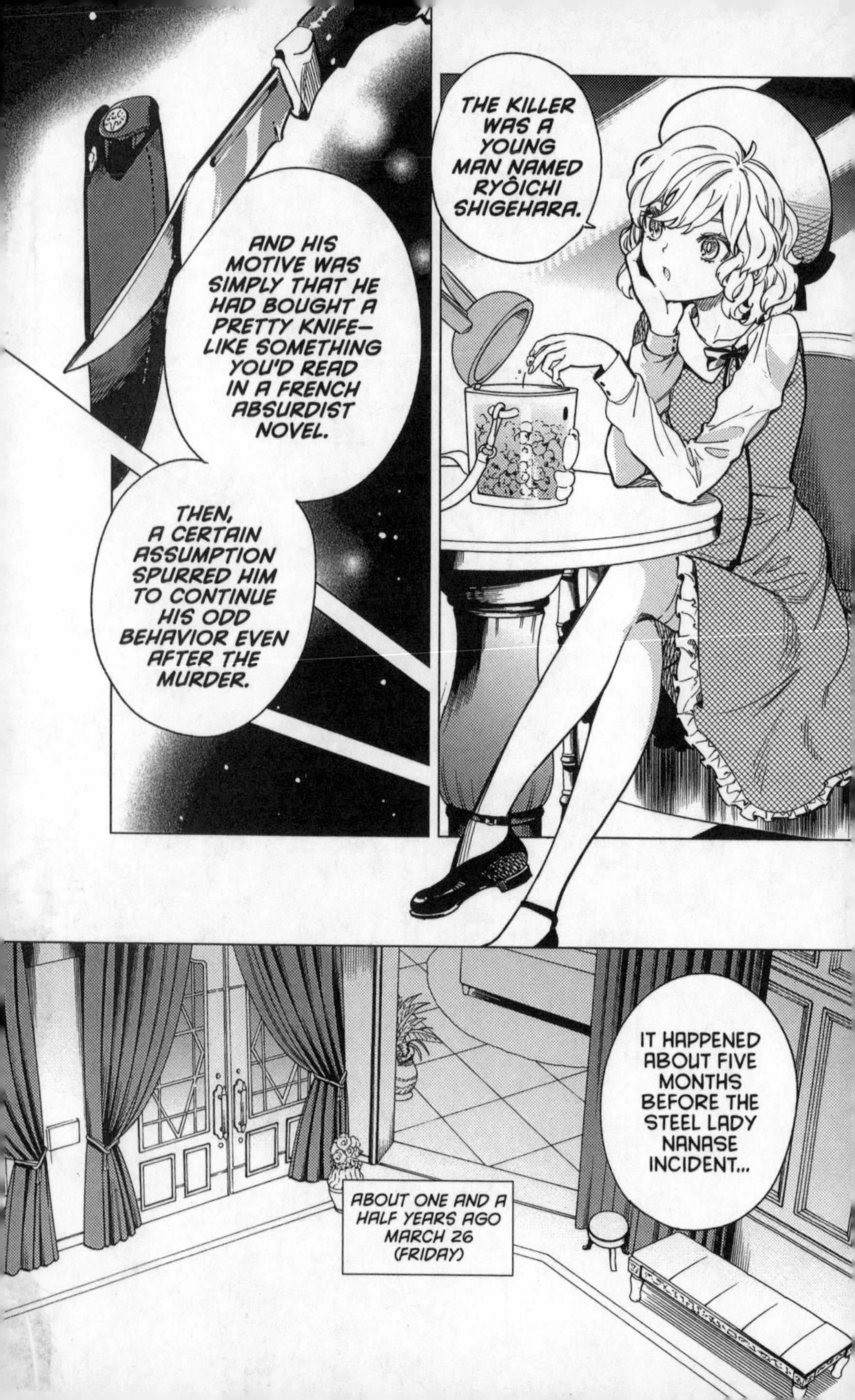
THE KILLER WAS A YOUNG MAN NAMED RYÔICHI SHIGEHARA.
AND HIS MOTIVE WAS SIMPLY THAT HE HAD BOUGHT A PRETTY KNIFE—LIKE SOMETHING YOU'D READ IN A FRENCH ABSURDIST NOVEL.
THEN, A CERTAIN ASSUMPTION SPURRED HIM TO CONTINUE HIS ODD BEHAVIOR EVEN AFTER THE MURDER.
IT HAPPENED ABOUT FIVE MONTHS BEFORE THE STEEL LADY NANASE INCIDENT...
ABOUT ONE AND A HALF YEARS AGO MARCH 26 (FRIDAY)

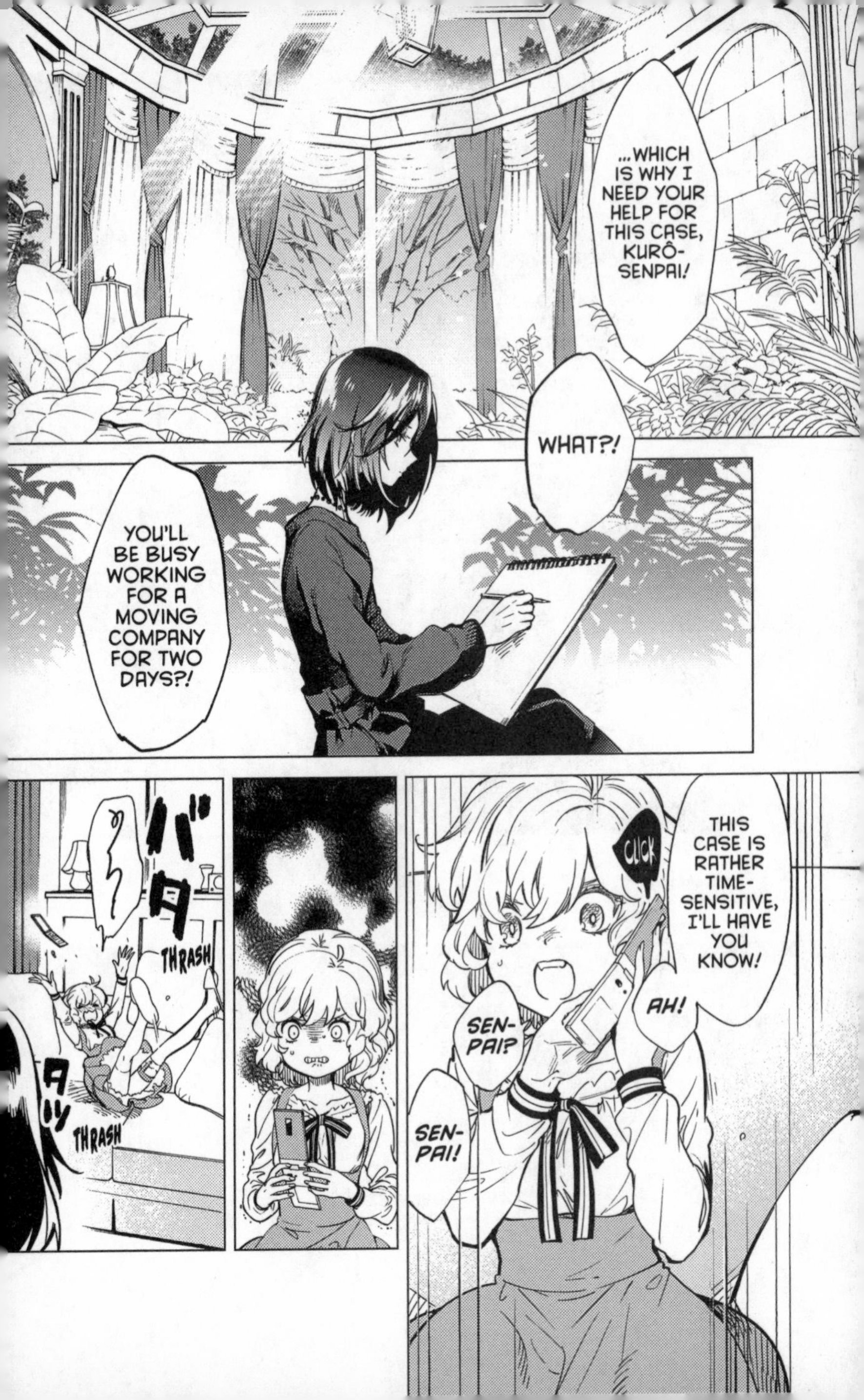

...WHICH IS WHY I NEED YOUR HELP FOR THIS CASE, KURÔ-SENPAI!
WHAT?!
YOU'LL BE BUSY WORKING FOR A MOVING COMPANY FOR TWO DAYS?!
THIS CASE IS RATHER TIME-SENSITIVE, I'LL HAVE YOU KNOW!
CLICK
AH!
SEN-PAI?
SEN-PAI!
THRASH
THRASH

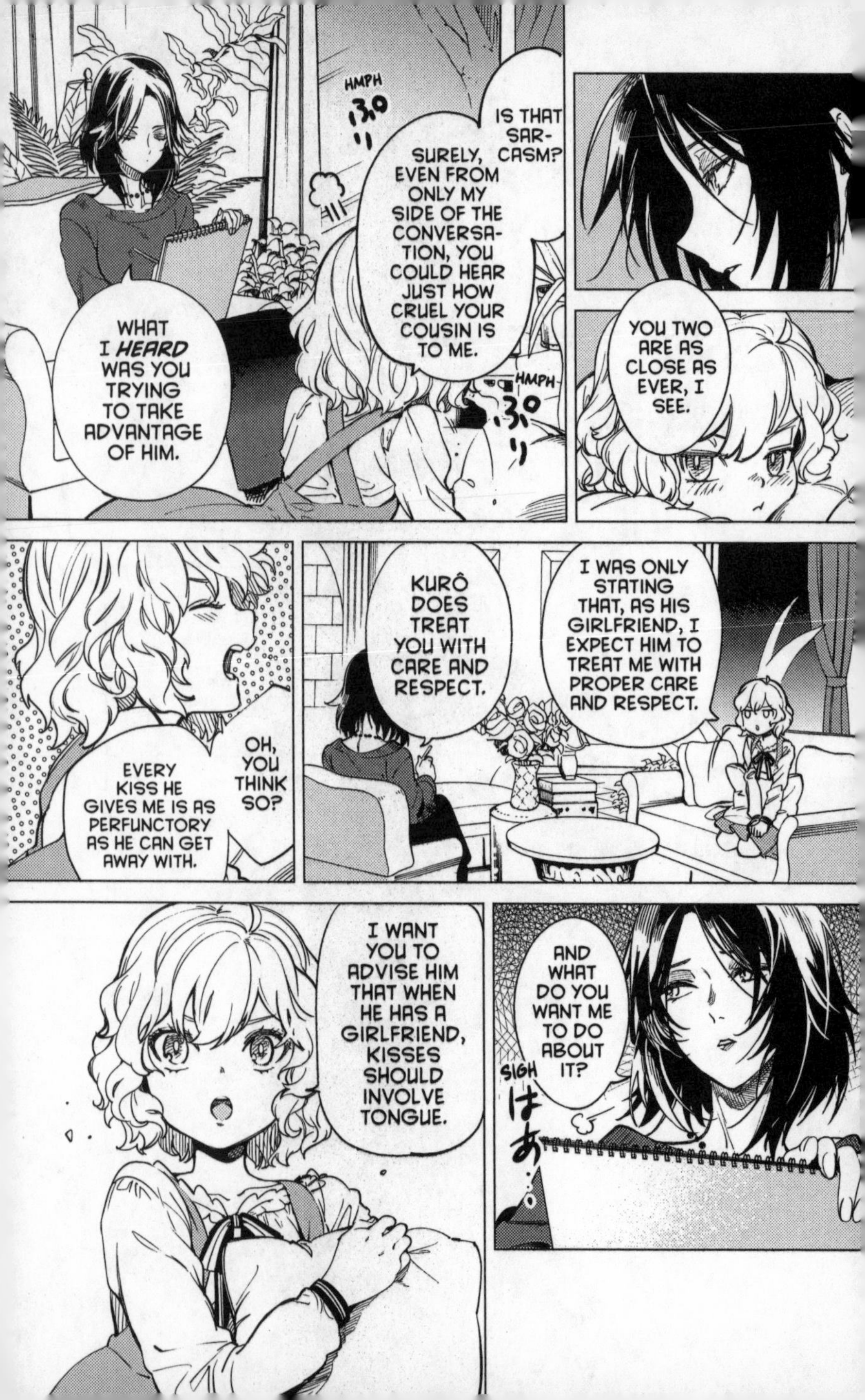
YOU TWO ARE AS CLOSE AS EVER, I SEE.
IS THAT SARCASM?
HMPH
SURELY, EVEN FROM ONLY MY SIDE OF THE CONVERSATION, YOU COULD HEAR JUST HOW CRUEL YOUR COUSIN IS TO ME.
HMPH
WHAT I *HEARD* WAS YOU TRYING TO TAKE ADVANTAGE OF HIM.
I WAS ONLY STATING THAT, AS HIS GIRLFRIEND, I EXPECT HIM TO TREAT ME WITH PROPER CARE AND RESPECT.
KURÔ DOES TREAT YOU WITH CARE AND RESPECT.
OH, YOU THINK SO?
EVERY KISS HE GIVES ME IS AS PERFUNCTORY AS HE CAN GET AWAY WITH.
AND WHAT DO YOU WANT ME TO DO ABOUT IT?
SIGH
I WANT YOU TO ADVISE HIM THAT WHEN HE HAS A GIRLFRIEND, KISSES SHOULD INVOLVE TONGUE.

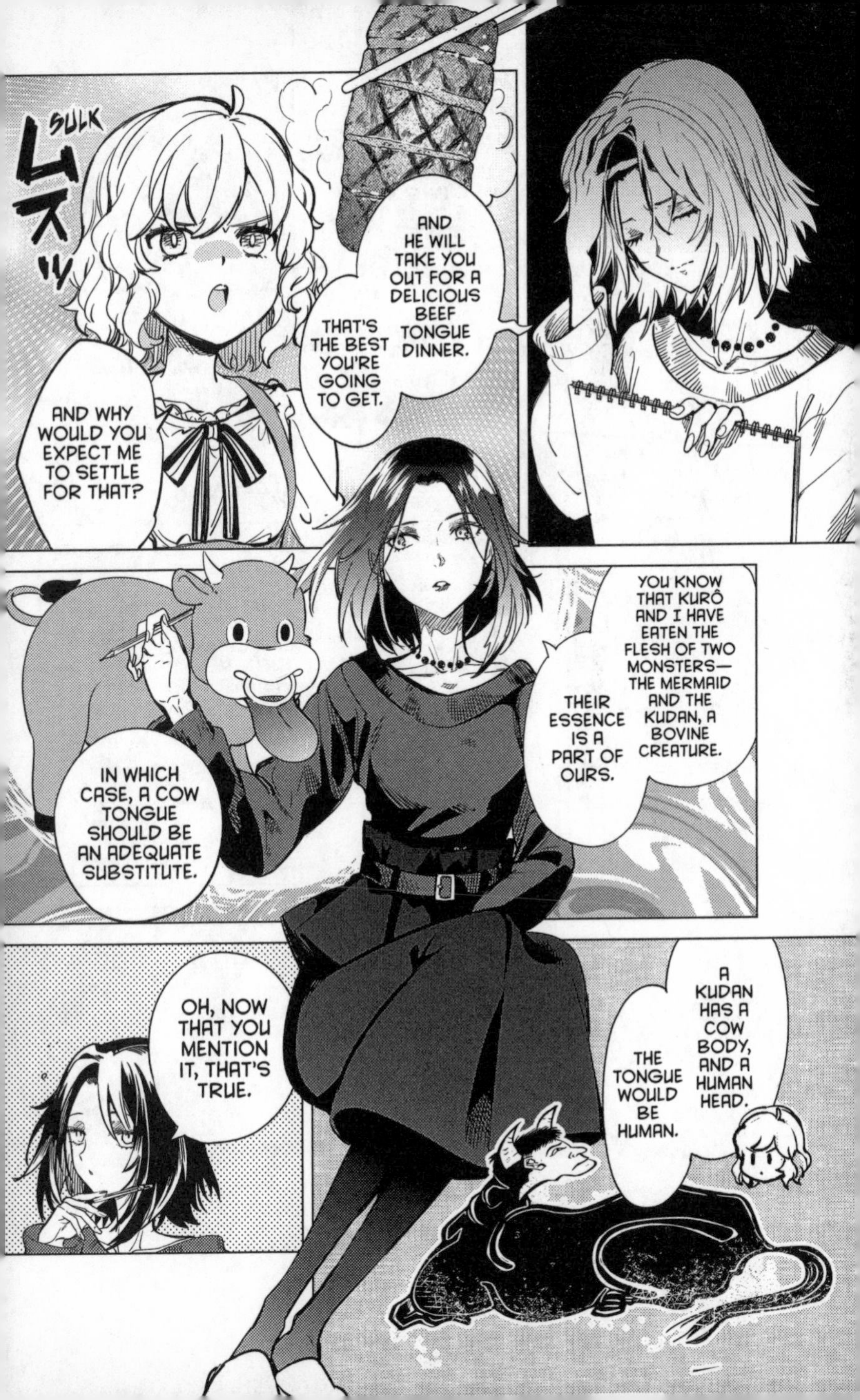

AND HE WILL TAKE YOU OUT FOR A DELICIOUS BEEF TONGUE DINNER.
THAT'S THE BEST YOU'RE GOING TO GET.
ムスッ SULK
AND WHY WOULD YOU EXPECT ME TO SETTLE FOR THAT?
YOU KNOW THAT KURÔ AND I HAVE EATEN THE FLESH OF TWO MONSTERS—THE MERMAID AND THE KUDAN, A BOVINE CREATURE.
THEIR ESSENCE IS A PART OF OURS.
IN WHICH CASE, A COW TONGUE SHOULD BE AN ADEQUATE SUBSTITUTE.
A KUDAN HAS A COW BODY, AND A HUMAN HEAD.
THE TONGUE WOULD BE HUMAN.
OH, NOW THAT YOU MENTION IT, THAT'S TRUE.

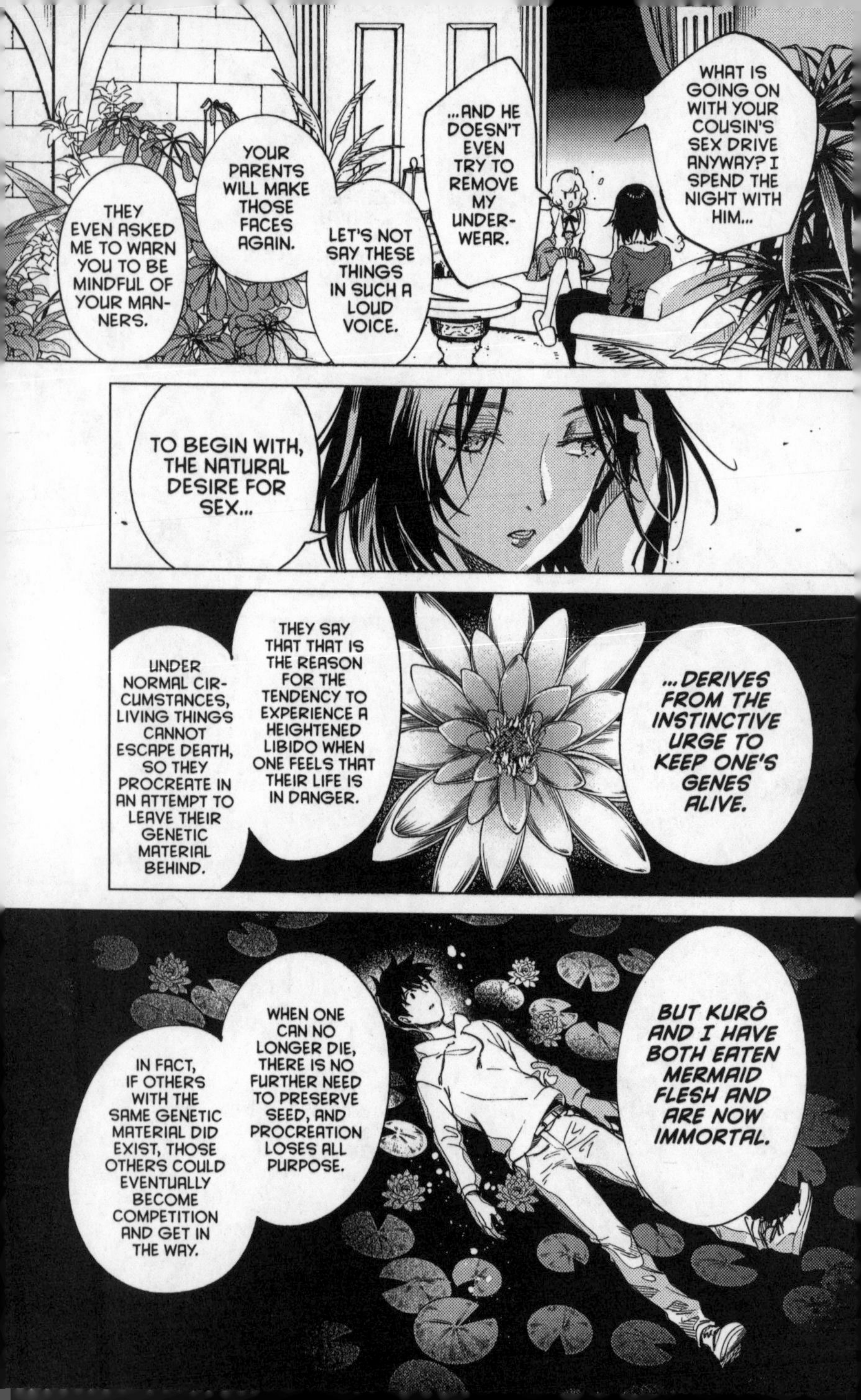
WHAT IS GOING ON WITH YOUR COUSIN'S SEX DRIVE ANYWAY? I SPEND THE NIGHT WITH HIM...
...AND HE DOESN'T EVEN TRY TO REMOVE MY UNDER-WEAR.
LET'S NOT SAY THESE THINGS IN SUCH A LOUD VOICE.
YOUR PARENTS WILL MAKE THOSE FACES AGAIN.
THEY EVEN ASKED ME TO WARN YOU TO BE MINDFUL OF YOUR MAN-NERS.
TO BEGIN WITH, THE NATURAL DESIRE FOR SEX...
...DERIVES FROM THE INSTINCTIVE URGE TO KEEP ONE'S GENES ALIVE.
THEY SAY THAT THAT IS THE REASON FOR THE TENDENCY TO EXPERIENCE A HEIGHTENED LIBIDO WHEN ONE FEELS THAT THEIR LIFE IS IN DANGER.
UNDER NORMAL CIR-CUMSTANCES, LIVING THINGS CANNOT ESCAPE DEATH, SO THEY PROCREATE IN AN ATTEMPT TO LEAVE THEIR GENETIC MATERIAL BEHIND.
BUT KURÔ AND I HAVE BOTH EATEN MERMAID FLESH AND ARE NOW IMMORTAL.
WHEN ONE CAN NO LONGER DIE, THERE IS NO FURTHER NEED TO PRESERVE SEED, AND PROCREATION LOSES ALL PURPOSE.
IN FACT, IF OTHERS WITH THE SAME GENETIC MATERIAL DID EXIST, THOSE OTHERS COULD EVENTUALLY BECOME COMPETITION AND GET IN THE WAY.

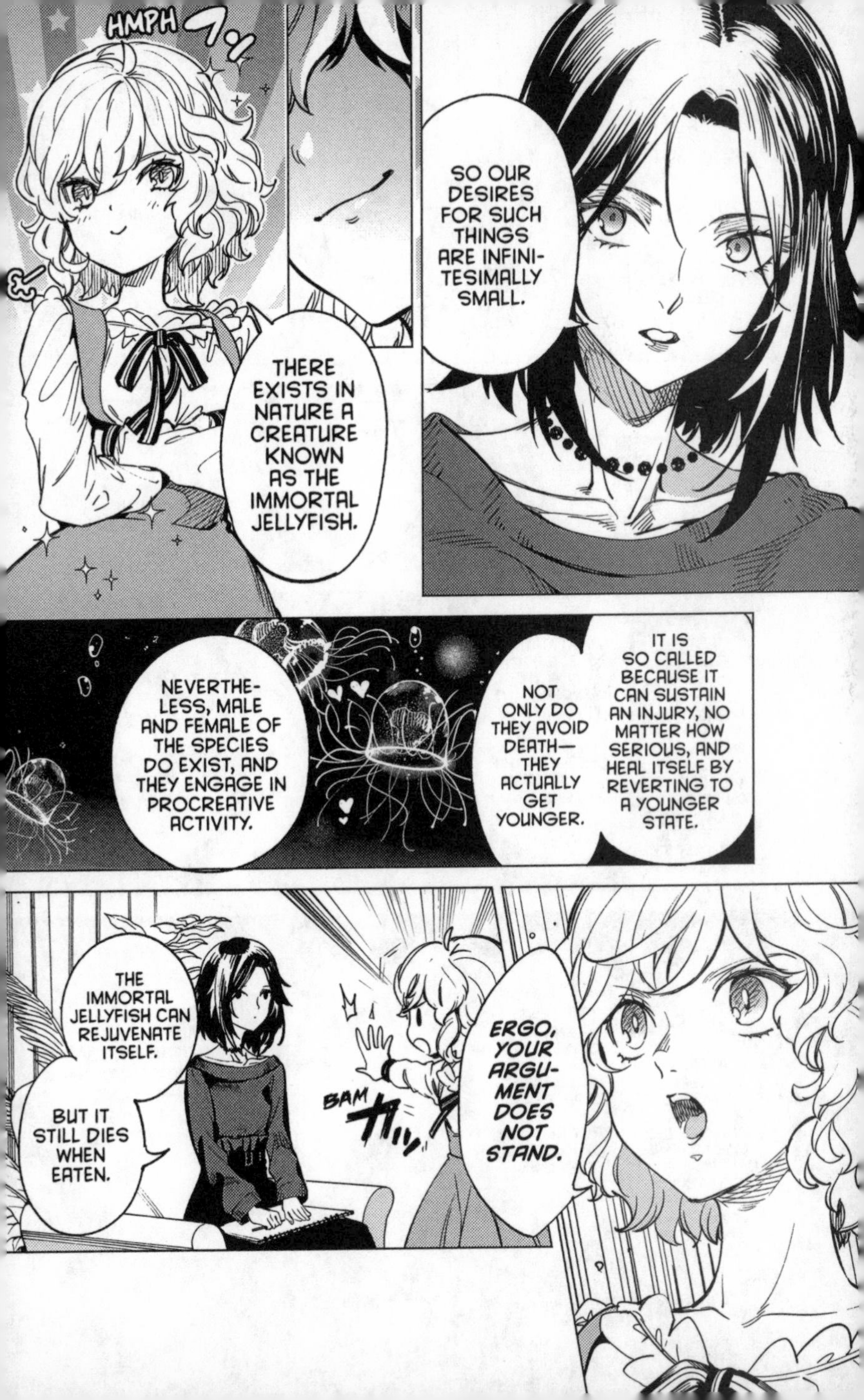
SO OUR DESIRES FOR SUCH THINGS ARE INFINITESIMALLY SMALL.
HMPH
THERE EXISTS IN NATURE A CREATURE KNOWN AS THE IMMORTAL JELLYFISH.
IT IS SO CALLED BECAUSE IT CAN SUSTAIN AN INJURY, NO MATTER HOW SERIOUS, AND HEAL ITSELF BY REVERTING TO A YOUNGER STATE.
NOT ONLY DO THEY AVOID DEATH—THEY ACTUALLY GET YOUNGER.
NEVERTHELESS, MALE AND FEMALE OF THE SPECIES DO EXIST, AND THEY ENGAGE IN PROCREATIVE ACTIVITY.
ERGO, YOUR ARGUMENT DOES NOT STAND.
BAM
THE IMMORTAL JELLYFISH CAN REJUVENATE ITSELF.
BUT IT STILL DIES WHEN EATEN.

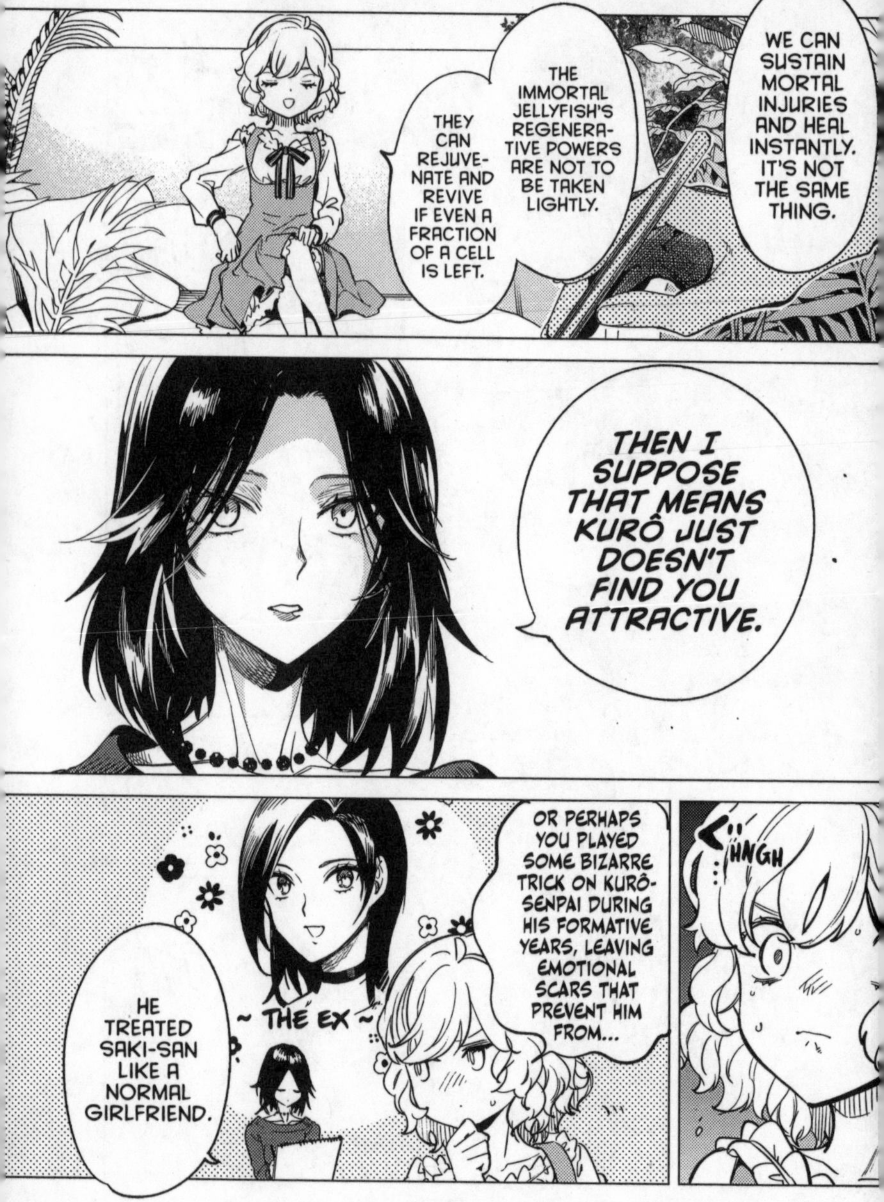
WE CAN SUSTAIN MORTAL INJURIES AND HEAL INSTANTLY. IT'S NOT THE SAME THING.
THE IMMORTAL JELLYFISH'S REGENERA-TIVE POWERS ARE NOT TO BE TAKEN LIGHTLY.
THEY CAN REJUVE-NATE AND REVIVE IF EVEN A FRACTION OF A CELL IS LEFT.
THEN I SUPPOSE THAT MEANS KURÔ JUST DOESN'T FIND YOU ATTRACTIVE.
HNGH
OR PERHAPS YOU PLAYED SOME BIZARRE TRICK ON KURÔ-SENPAI DURING HIS FORMATIVE YEARS, LEAVING EMOTIONAL SCARS THAT PREVENT HIM FROM...
~ THE EX ~
HE TREATED SAKI-SAN LIKE A NORMAL GIRLFRIEND.

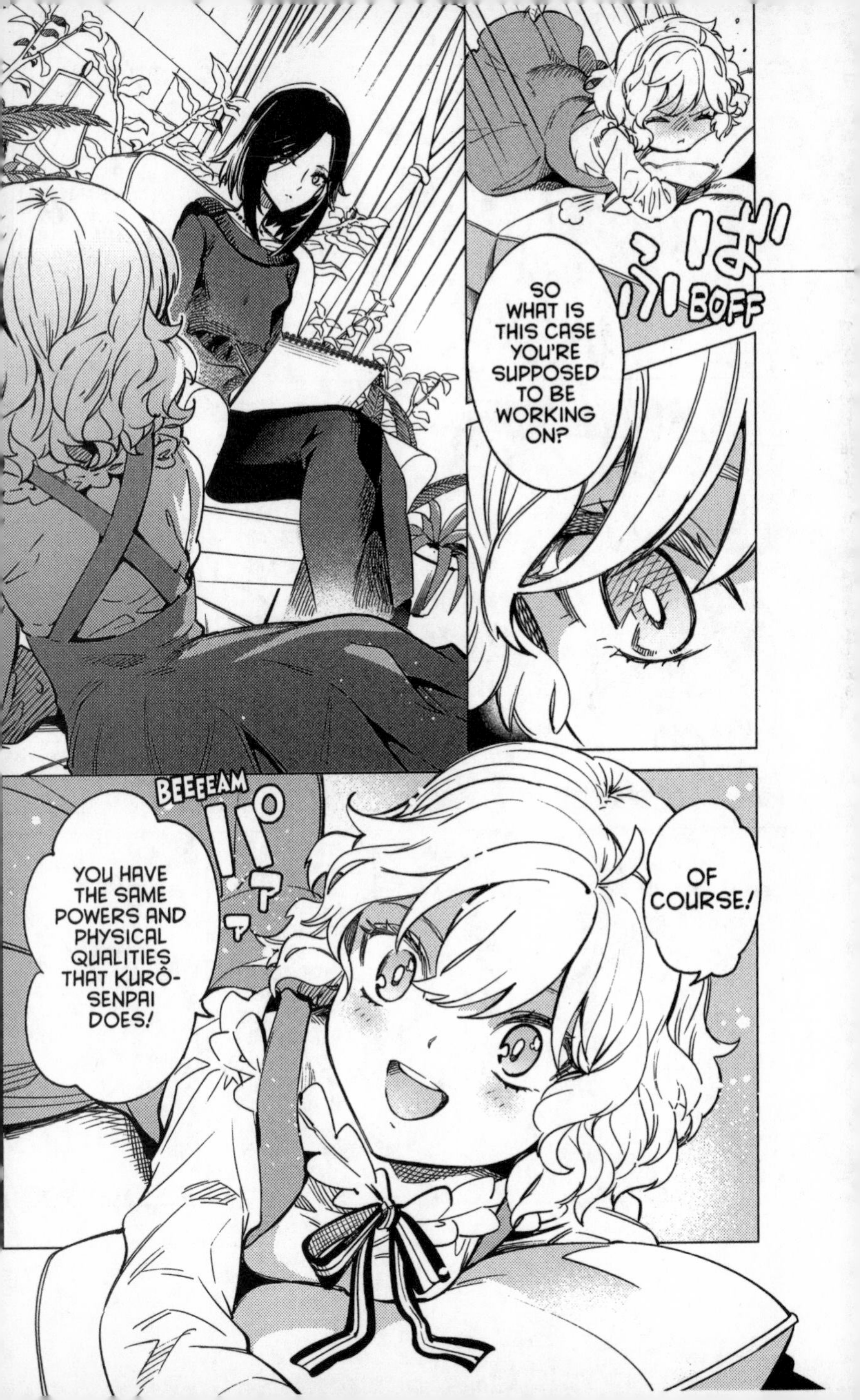ぼふ BOFF
SO WHAT IS THIS CASE YOU'RE SUPPOSED TO BE WORKING ON?
OF COURSE!
BEEEEAM パァァ
YOU HAVE THE SAME POWERS AND PHYSICAL QUALITIES THAT KURÔ-SENPAI DOES!

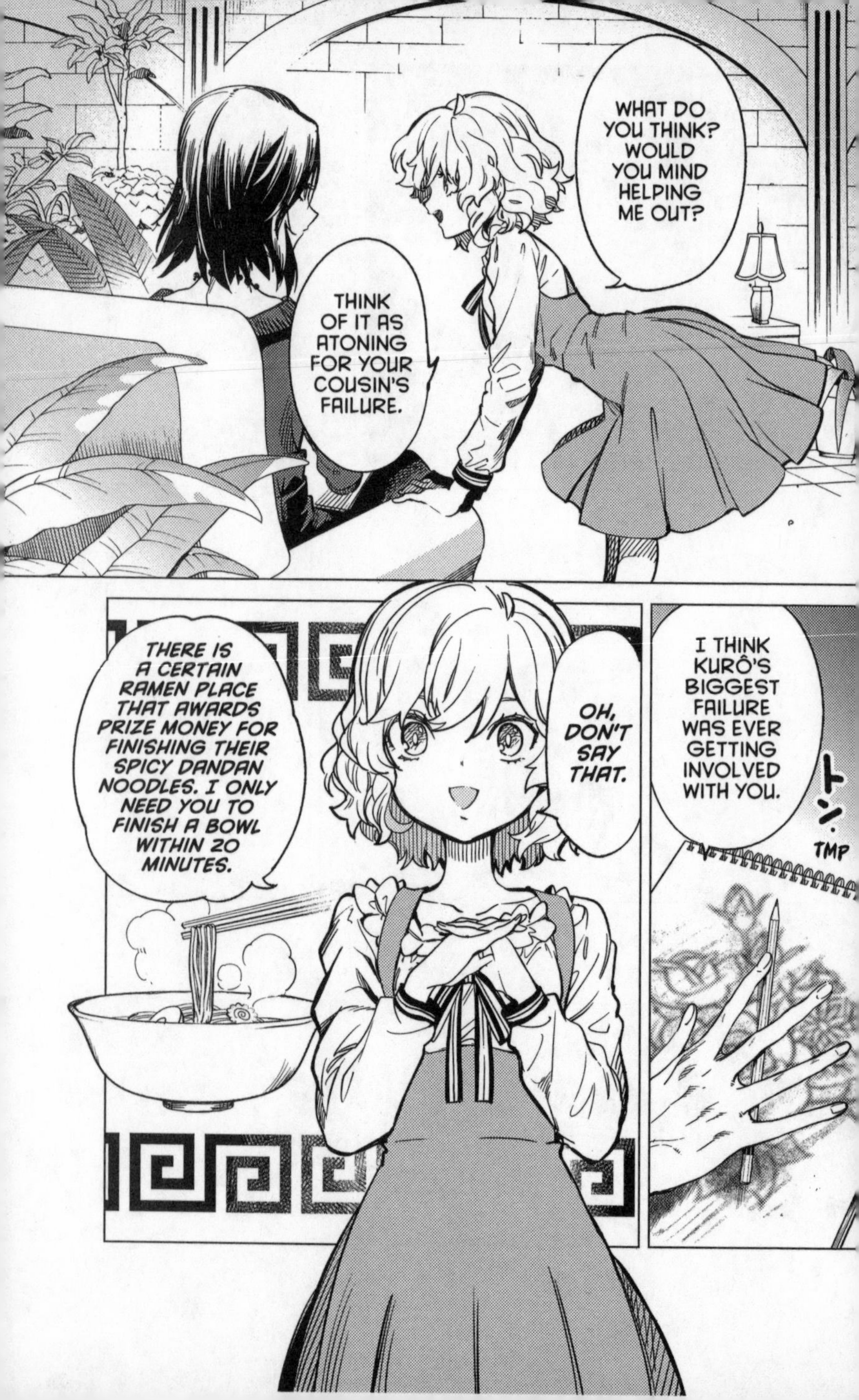

WHAT DO YOU THINK? WOULD YOU MIND HELPING ME OUT?
THINK OF IT AS ATONING FOR YOUR COUSIN'S FAILURE.
I THINK KURÔ'S BIGGEST FAILURE WAS EVER GETTING INVOLVED WITH YOU.
TMP
OH, DON'T SAY THAT.
THERE IS A CERTAIN RAMEN PLACE THAT AWARDS PRIZE MONEY FOR FINISHING THEIR SPICY DANDAN NOODLES. I ONLY NEED YOU TO FINISH A BOWL WITHIN 20 MINUTES.

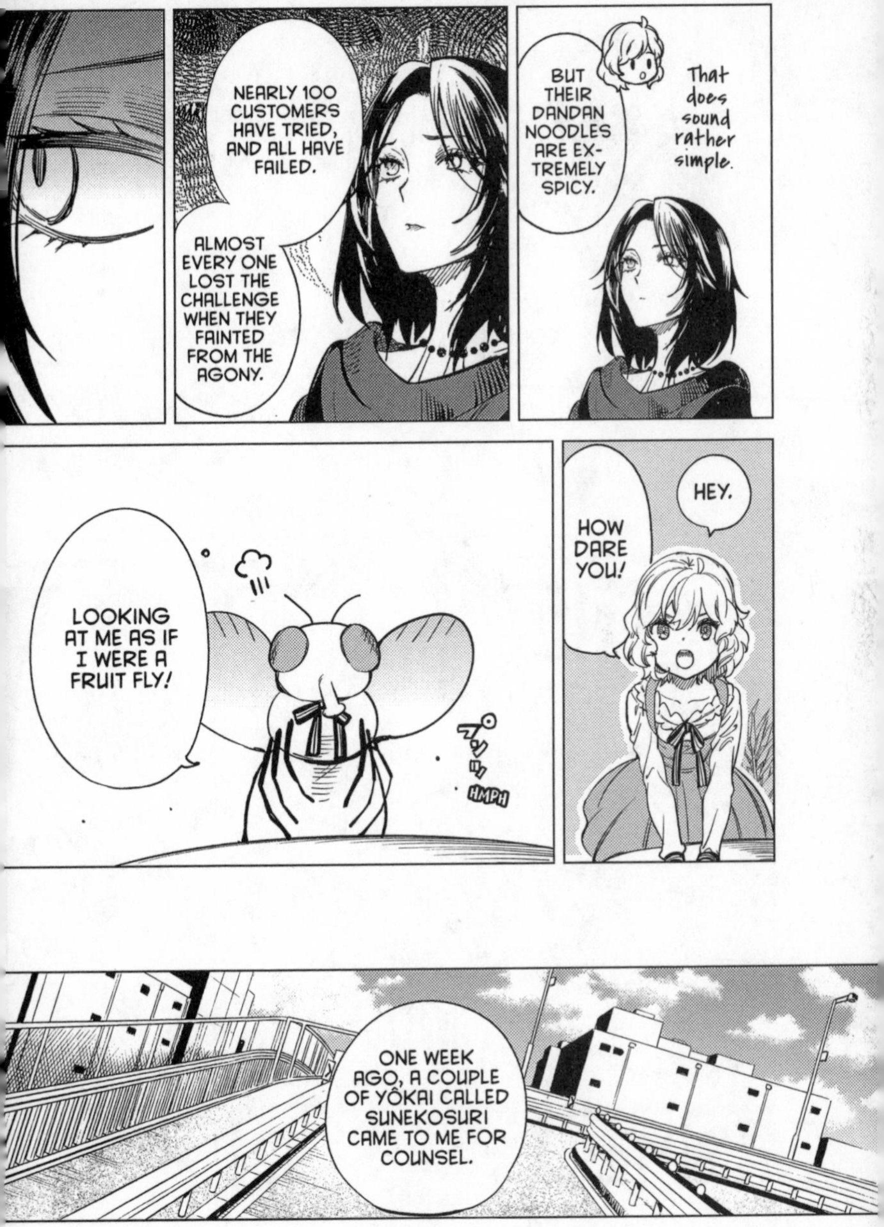
That does sound rather simple.
BUT THEIR DANDAN NOODLES ARE EXTREMELY SPICY.
NEARLY 100 CUSTOMERS HAVE TRIED, AND ALL HAVE FAILED.
ALMOST EVERY ONE LOST THE CHALLENGE WHEN THEY FAINTED FROM THE AGONY.
HEY.
HOW DARE YOU!
LOOKING AT ME AS IF I WERE A FRUIT FLY!
HMPH
ONE WEEK AGO, A COUPLE OF YÔKAI CALLED SUNEKOSURI CAME TO ME FOR COUNSEL.

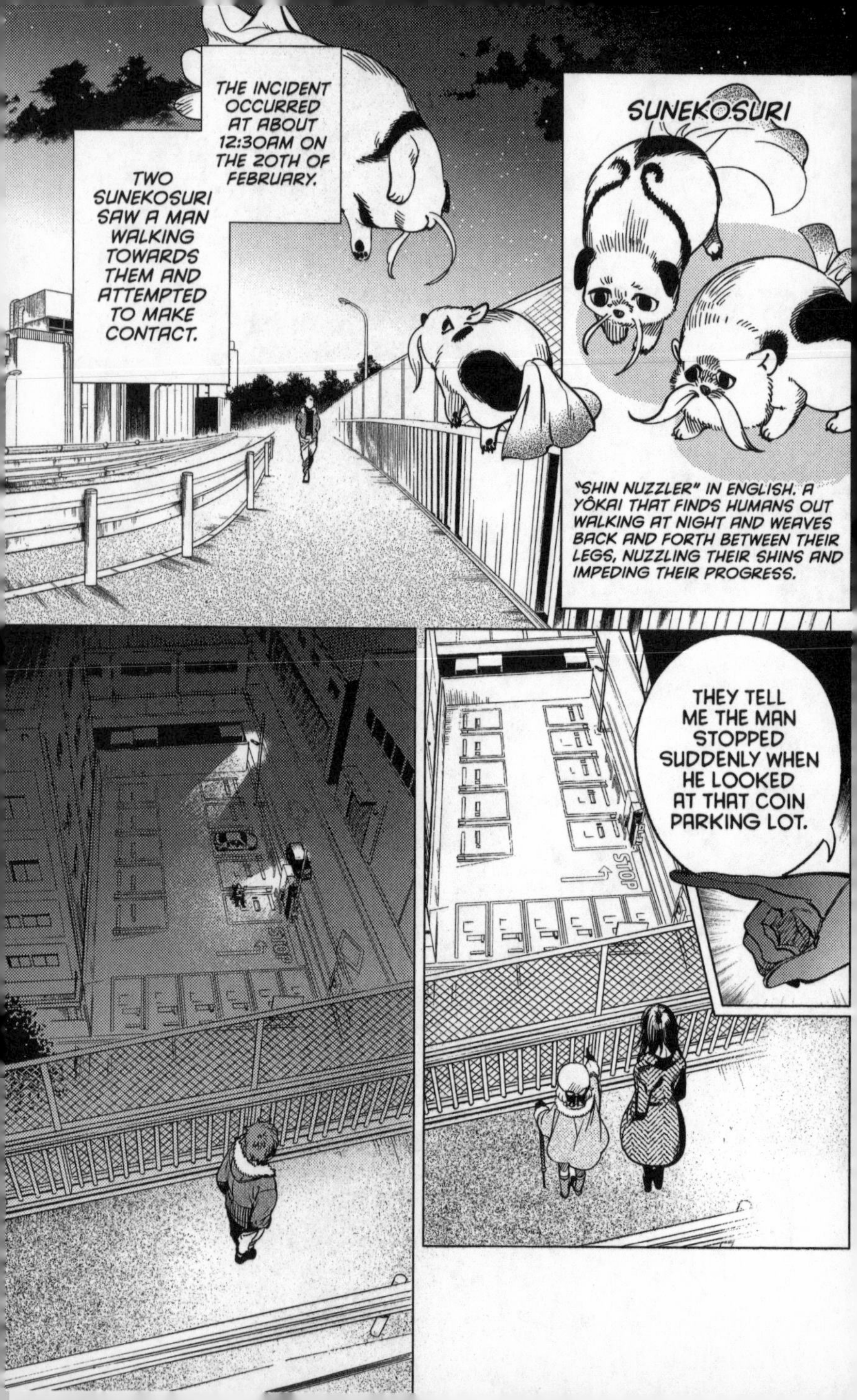
SUNEKOSURI
"SHIN NUZZLER" IN ENGLISH. A YÔKAI THAT FINDS HUMANS OUT WALKING AT NIGHT AND WEAVES BACK AND FORTH BETWEEN THEIR LEGS, NUZZLING THEIR SHINS AND IMPEDING THEIR PROGRESS.
THE INCIDENT OCCURRED AT ABOUT 12:30AM ON THE 20TH OF FEBRUARY.
TWO SUNEKOSURI SAW A MAN WALKING TOWARDS THEM AND ATTEMPTED TO MAKE CONTACT.
THEY TELL ME THE MAN STOPPED SUDDENLY WHEN HE LOOKED AT THAT COIN PARKING LOT.
STOP

WHEN THEY LOOKED TO SEE WHAT CAUGHT HIS ATTENTION...

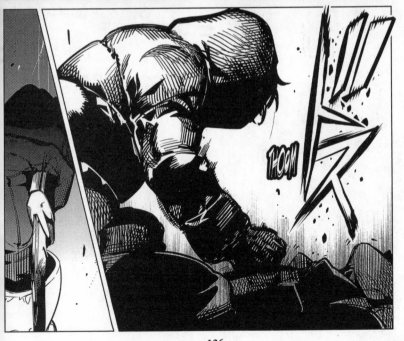

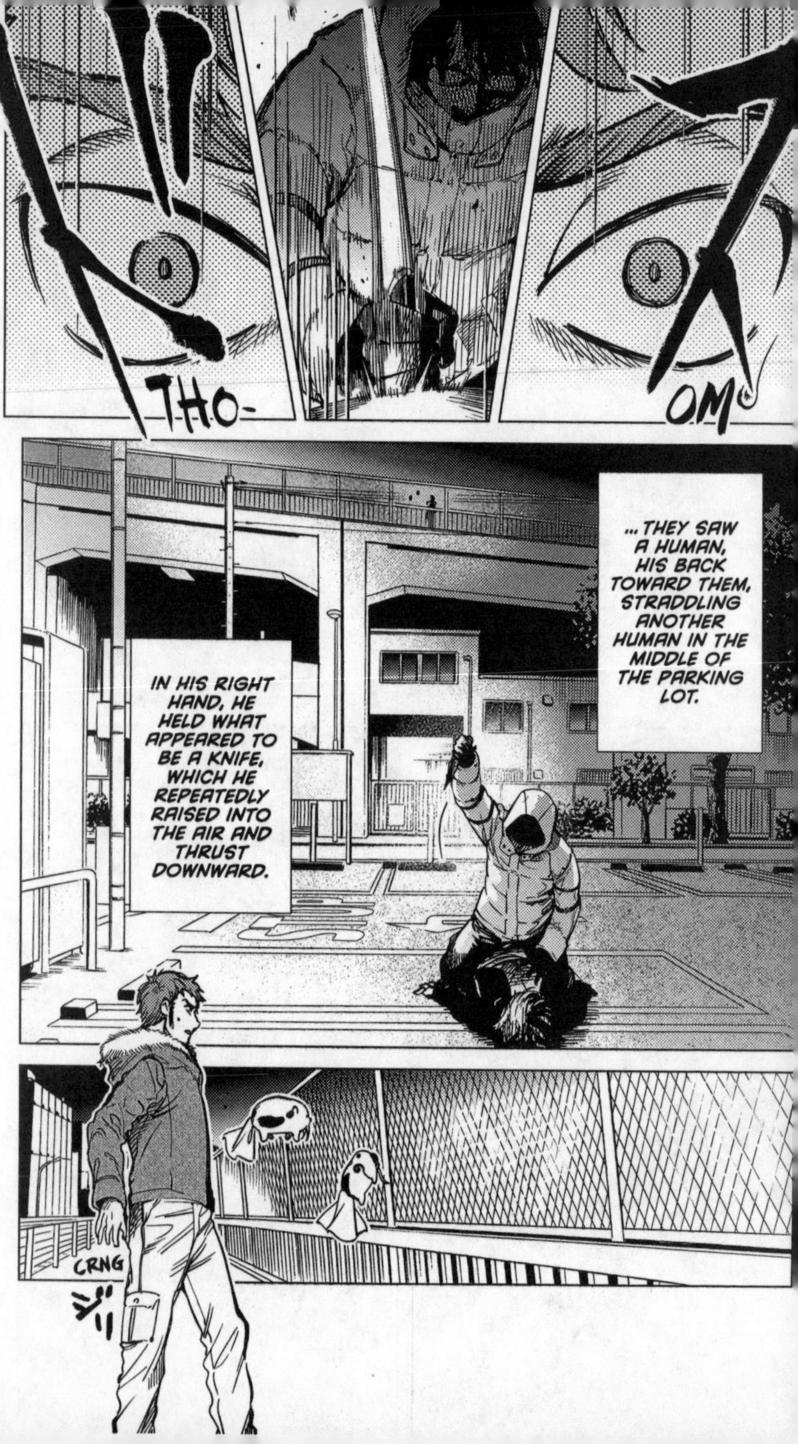
OM
THO-
...THEY SAW A HUMAN, HIS BACK TOWARD THEM, STRADDLING ANOTHER HUMAN IN THE MIDDLE OF THE PARKING LOT.
IN HIS RIGHT HAND, HE HELD WHAT APPEARED TO BE A KNIFE, WHICH HE REPEATEDLY RAISED INTO THE AIR AND THRUST DOWNWARD.
CRNG

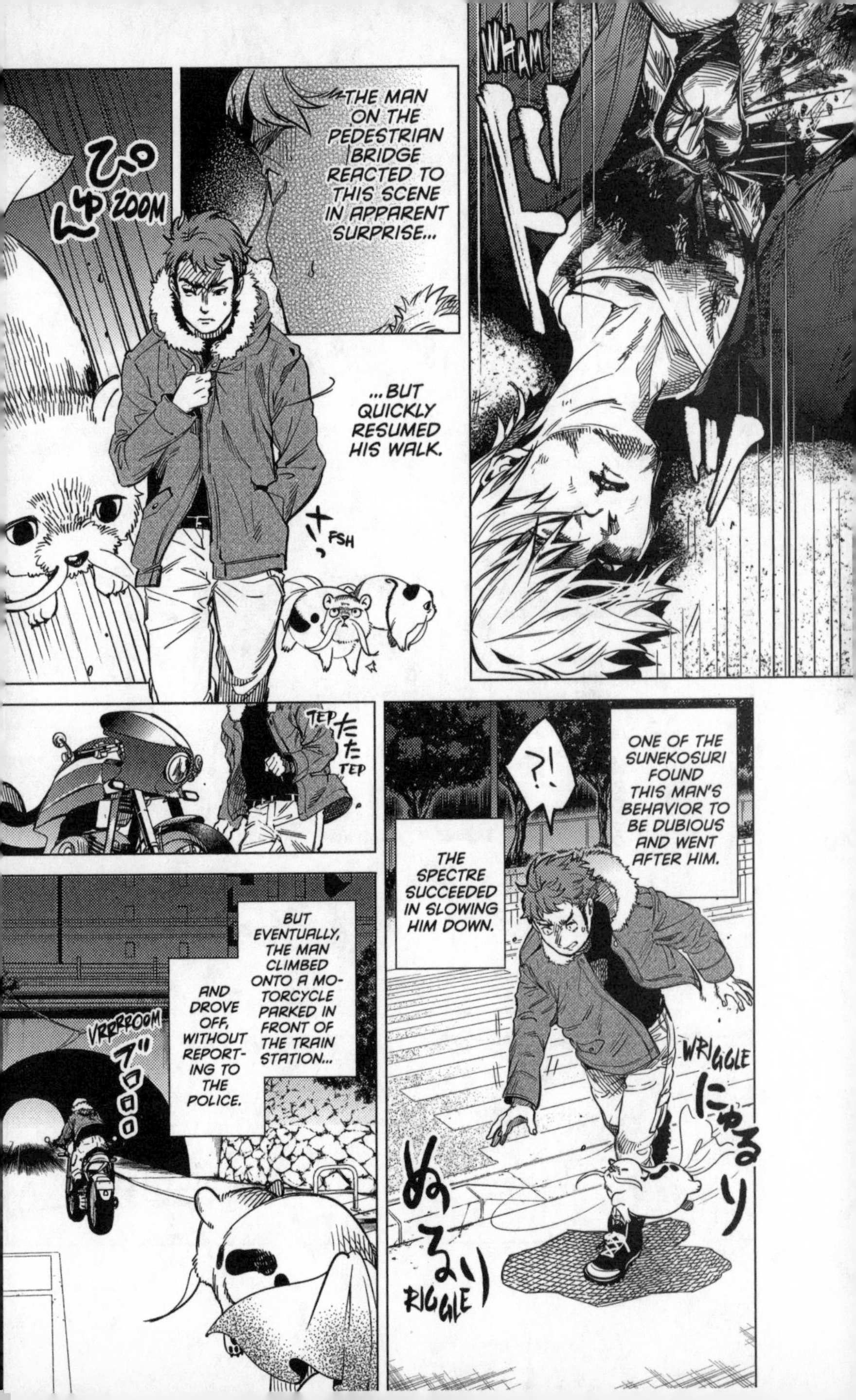
WHAM
THE MAN ON THE PEDESTRIAN BRIDGE REACTED TO THIS SCENE IN APPARENT SURPRISE...
ぴゅん ZOOM
...BUT QUICKLY RESUMED HIS WALK.
FSH
?!
ONE OF THE SUNEKOSURI FOUND THIS MAN'S BEHAVIOR TO BE DUBIOUS AND WENT AFTER HIM.
THE SPECTRE SUCCEEDED IN SLOWING HIM DOWN.
WRIGGLE にゅるり
ぬるり RIGGLE
TEP たた TEP
BUT EVENTUALLY, THE MAN CLIMBED ONTO A MOTORCYCLE PARKED IN FRONT OF THE TRAIN STATION...
AND DROVE OFF, WITHOUT REPORTING TO THE POLICE.
VRRRROOM ブロロロ

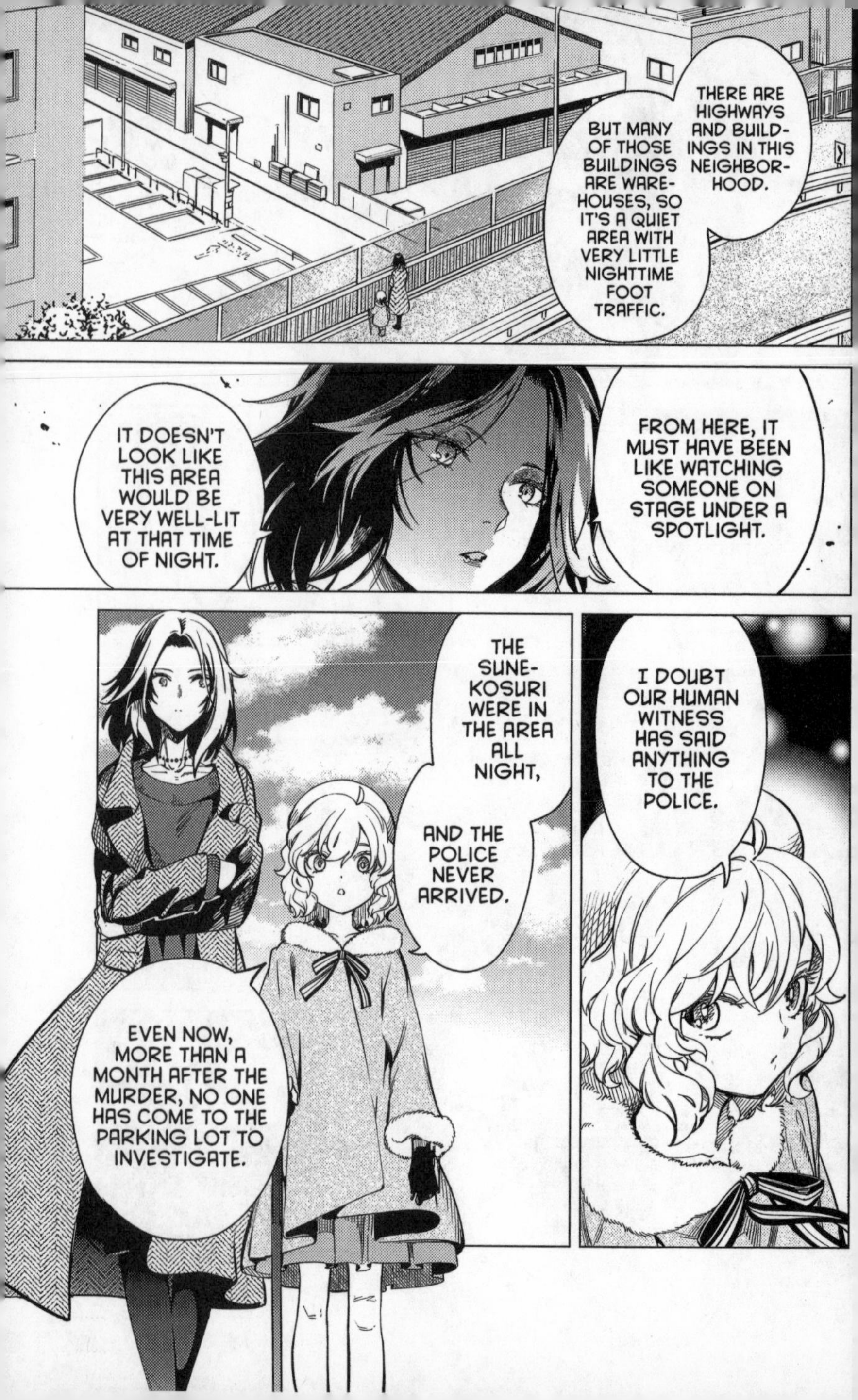
THERE ARE HIGHWAYS AND BUILDINGS IN THIS NEIGHBORHOOD.
BUT MANY OF THOSE BUILDINGS ARE WAREHOUSES, SO IT'S A QUIET AREA WITH VERY LITTLE NIGHTTIME FOOT TRAFFIC.
FROM HERE, IT MUST HAVE BEEN LIKE WATCHING SOMEONE ON STAGE UNDER A SPOTLIGHT.
IT DOESN'T LOOK LIKE THIS AREA WOULD BE VERY WELL-LIT AT THAT TIME OF NIGHT.
I DOUBT OUR HUMAN WITNESS HAS SAID ANYTHING TO THE POLICE.
THE SUNE-KOSURI WERE IN THE AREA ALL NIGHT,
AND THE POLICE NEVER ARRIVED.
EVEN NOW, MORE THAN A MONTH AFTER THE MURDER, NO ONE HAS COME TO THE PARKING LOT TO INVESTIGATE.

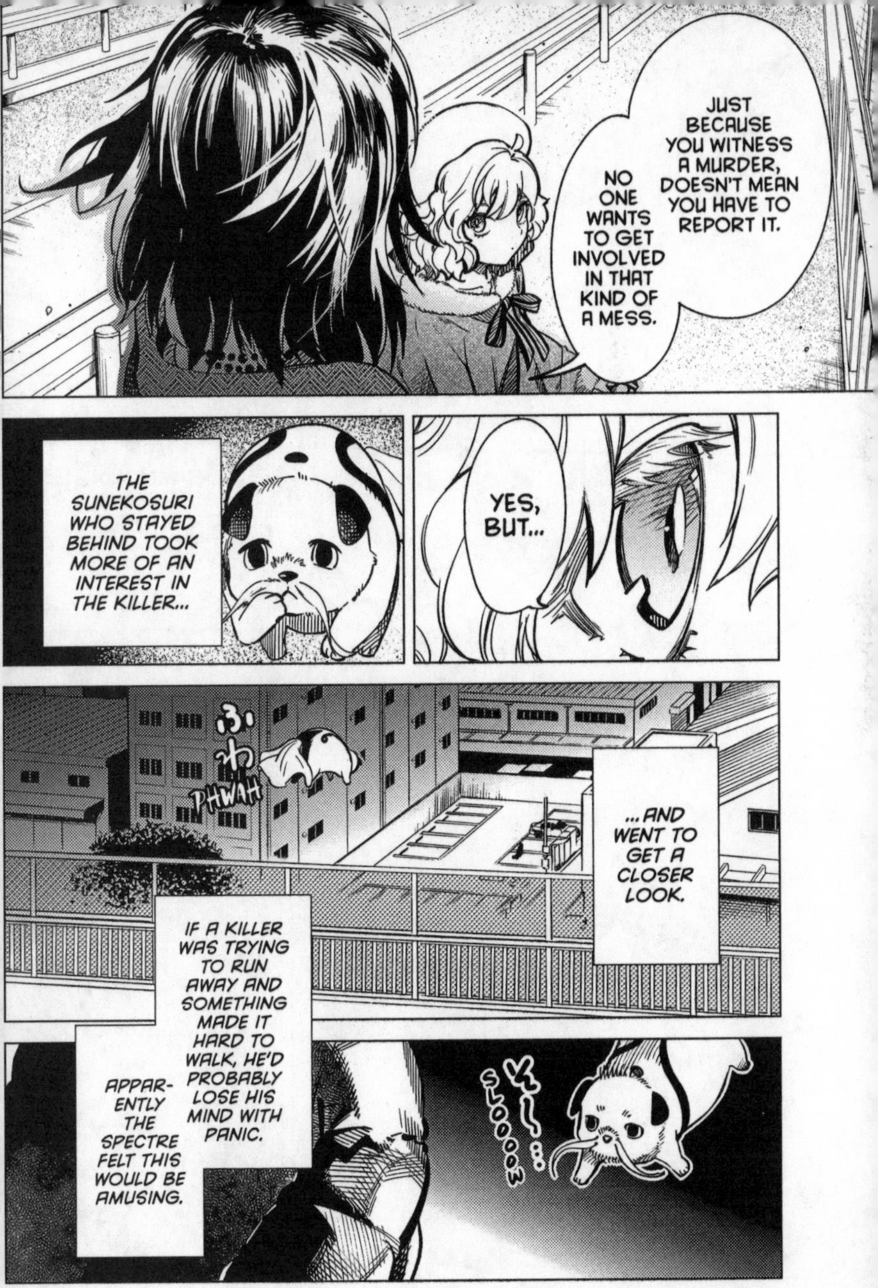
JUST BECAUSE YOU WITNESS A MURDER, DOESN'T MEAN YOU HAVE TO REPORT IT.
NO ONE WANTS TO GET INVOLVED IN THAT KIND OF A MESS.
YES, BUT...
THE SUNEKOSURI WHO STAYED BEHIND TOOK MORE OF AN INTEREST IN THE KILLER...
...AND WENT TO GET A CLOSER LOOK.
ふわ
PHWAH
IF A KILLER WAS TRYING TO RUN AWAY AND SOMETHING MADE IT HARD TO WALK, HE'D PROBABLY LOSE HIS MIND WITH PANIC.
SLOOOOOW
APPARENTLY THE SPECTRE FELT THIS WOULD BE AMUSING.

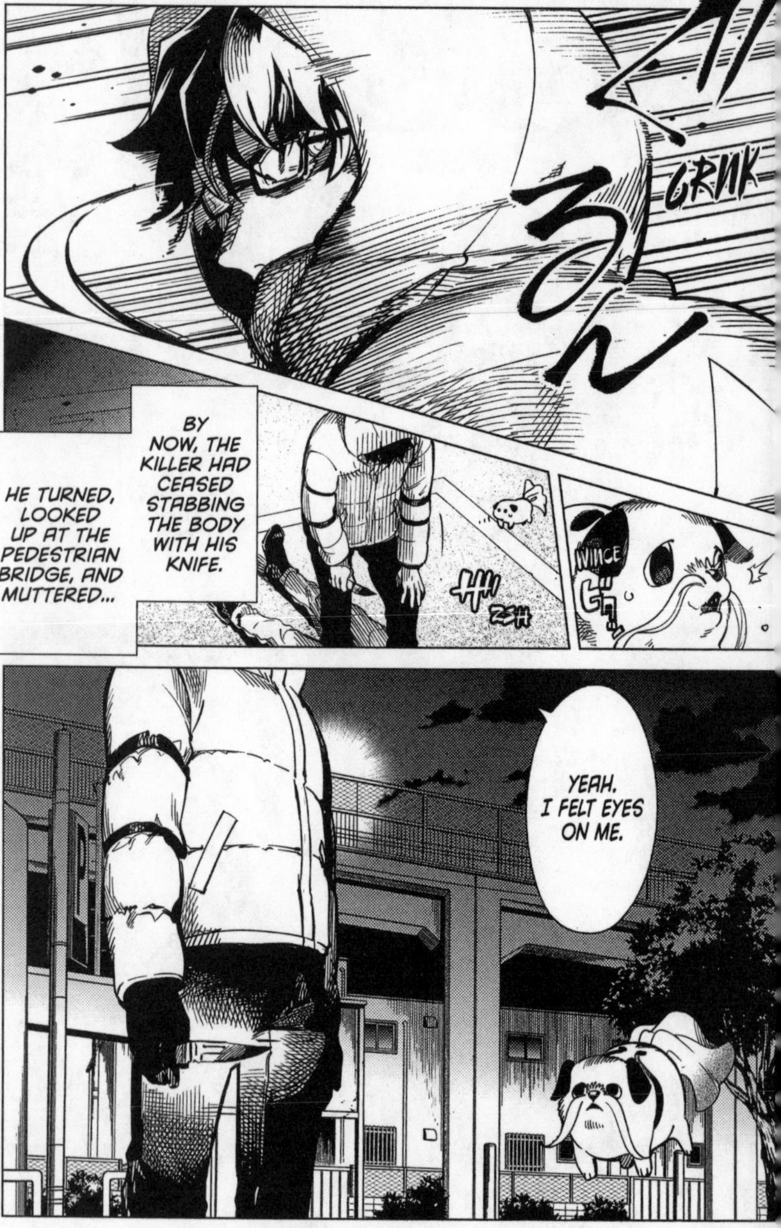
GRUNK
WINCE
BY NOW, THE KILLER HAD CEASED STABBING THE BODY WITH HIS KNIFE.
HE TURNED, LOOKED UP AT THE PEDESTRIAN BRIDGE, AND MUTTERED...
YEAH. I FELT EYES ON ME.

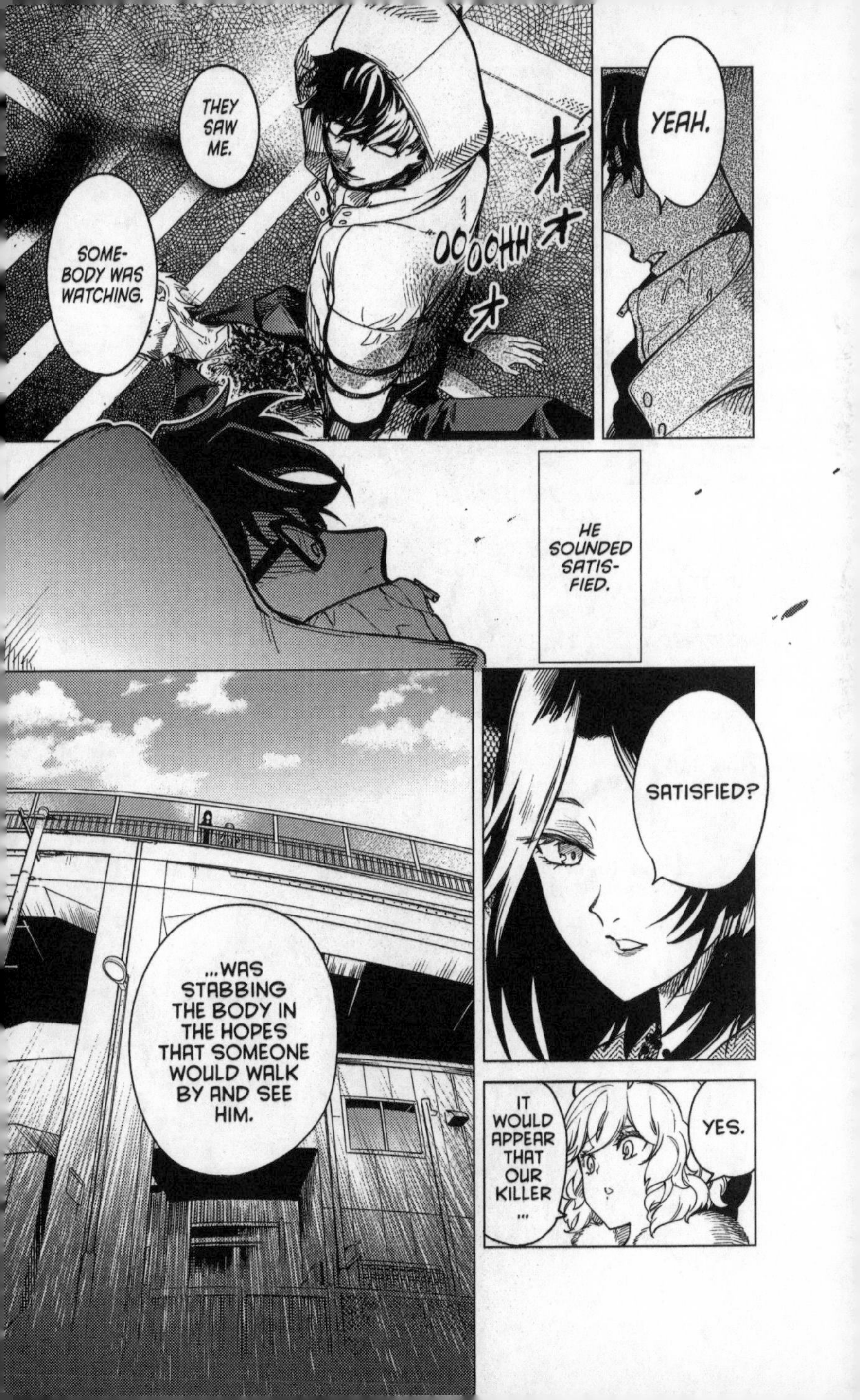
YEAH.
THEY SAW ME.
OOOOHH
オオオ
SOME-BODY WAS WATCHING.
HE SOUNDED SATIS-FIED.
SATISFIED?
YES.
IT WOULD APPEAR THAT OUR KILLER ...
...WAS STABBING THE BODY IN THE HOPES THAT SOMEONE WOULD WALK BY AND SEE HIM.

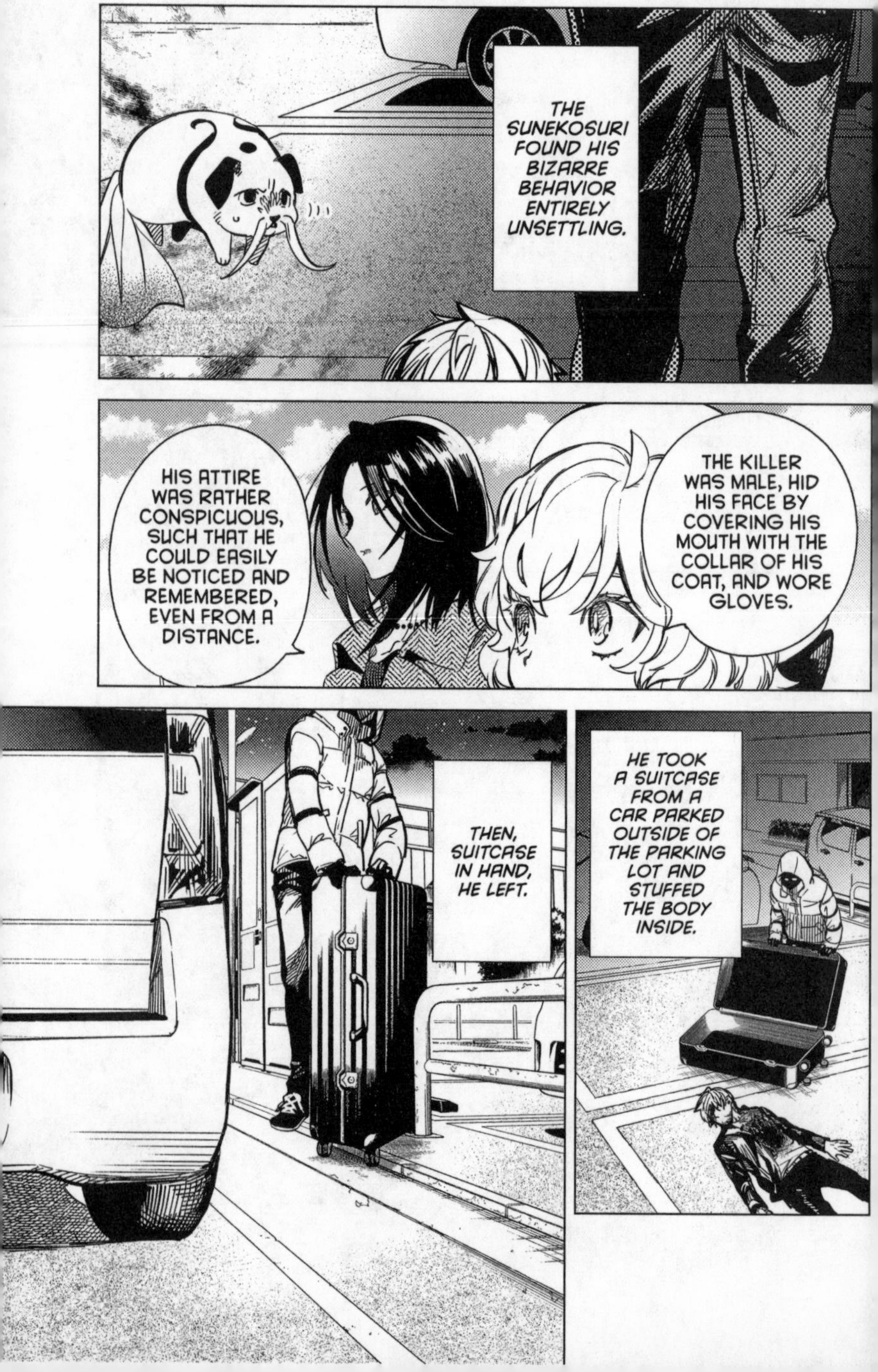
THE SUNEKOSURI FOUND HIS BIZARRE BEHAVIOR ENTIRELY UNSETTLING.
THE KILLER WAS MALE, HID HIS FACE BY COVERING HIS MOUTH WITH THE COLLAR OF HIS COAT, AND WORE GLOVES.
HIS ATTIRE WAS RATHER CONSPICUOUS, SUCH THAT HE COULD EASILY BE NOTICED AND REMEMBERED, EVEN FROM A DISTANCE.
HE TOOK A SUITCASE FROM A CAR PARKED OUTSIDE OF THE PARKING LOT AND STUFFED THE BODY INSIDE.
THEN, SUITCASE IN HAND, HE LEFT.

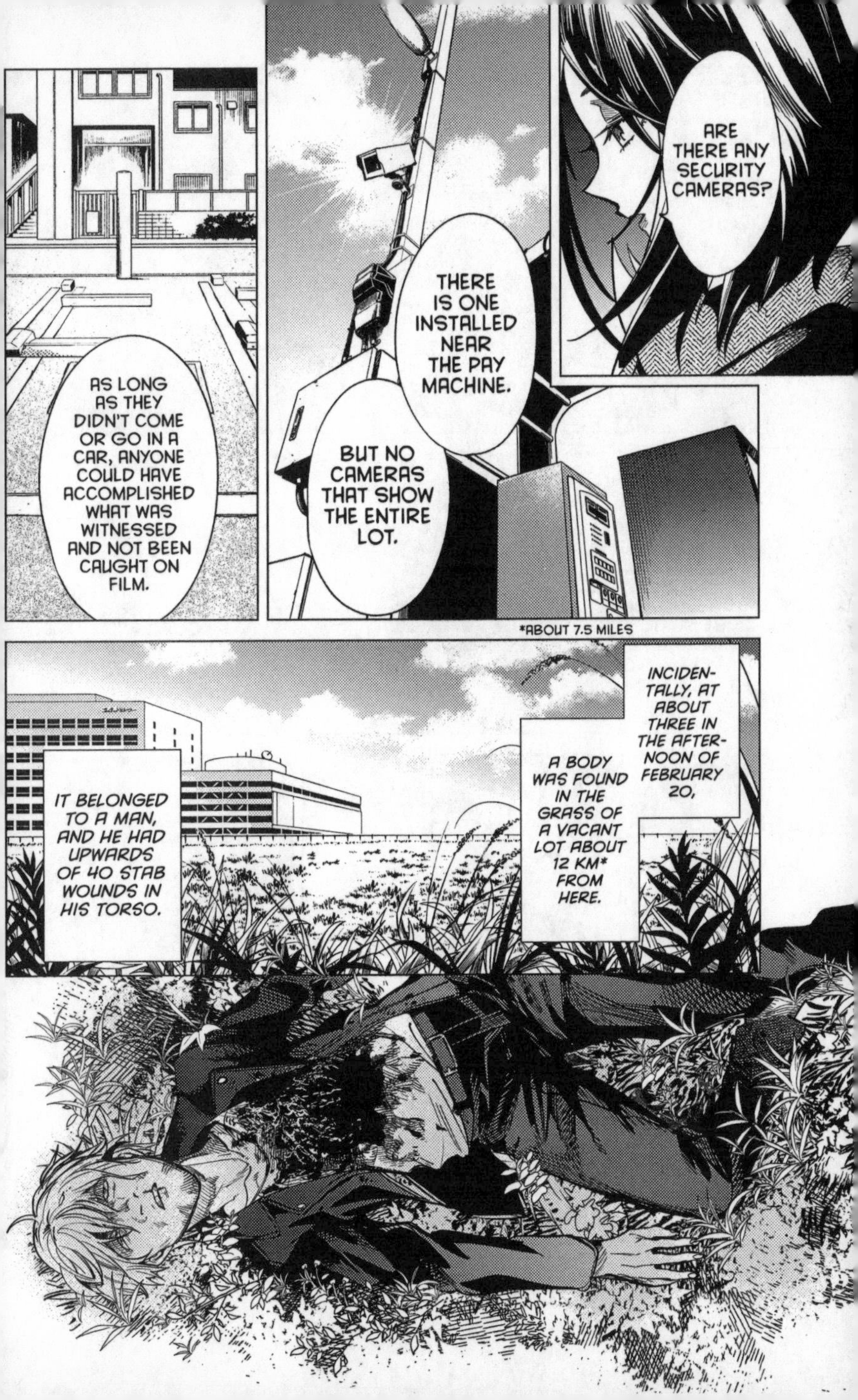
ARE THERE ANY SECURITY CAMERAS?
THERE IS ONE INSTALLED NEAR THE PAY MACHINE.
BUT NO CAMERAS THAT SHOW THE ENTIRE LOT.
AS LONG AS THEY DIDN'T COME OR GO IN A CAR, ANYONE COULD HAVE ACCOMPLISHED WHAT WAS WITNESSED AND NOT BEEN CAUGHT ON FILM.
INCIDENTALLY, AT ABOUT THREE IN THE AFTERNOON OF FEBRUARY 20,
A BODY WAS FOUND IN THE GRASS OF A VACANT LOT ABOUT 12 KM* FROM HERE.
IT BELONGED TO A MAN, AND HE HAD UPWARDS OF 40 STAB WOUNDS IN HIS TORSO.

*ABOUT 7.5 MILES

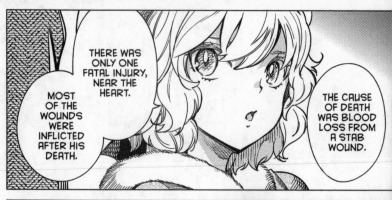

THE CAUSE OF DEATH WAS BLOOD LOSS FROM A STAB WOUND.
THERE WAS ONLY ONE FATAL INJURY, NEAR THE HEART.
MOST OF THE WOUNDS WERE INFLICTED AFTER HIS DEATH.
SO THE KILLER MUST HAVE DUMPED THE BODY IN THAT VACANT LOT AFTER CARRYING IT AWAY FROM HERE.
IT WAS IN THE NEWS. THE MAN WHO WITNESSED THE STABBING HAD AMPLE OPPORTUNITY TO HEAR ABOUT IT.
WHAT ABOUT BLOOD SPAT-TER?
THERE WAS ALMOST NO BLOOD LEFT AT THE SCENE.
AFTER THE KILLER LEFT,
THE SUNE-KOSURI DID FIND A FAINT STAIN.
BUT YOU WOULDN'T IDENTIFY IT AS BLOOD UNLESS YOU WERE LOOKING FOR IT.

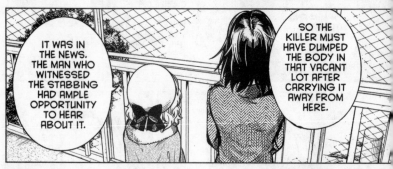

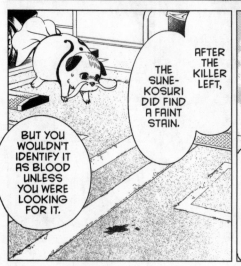

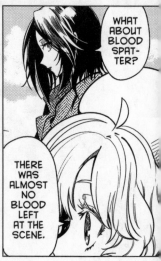

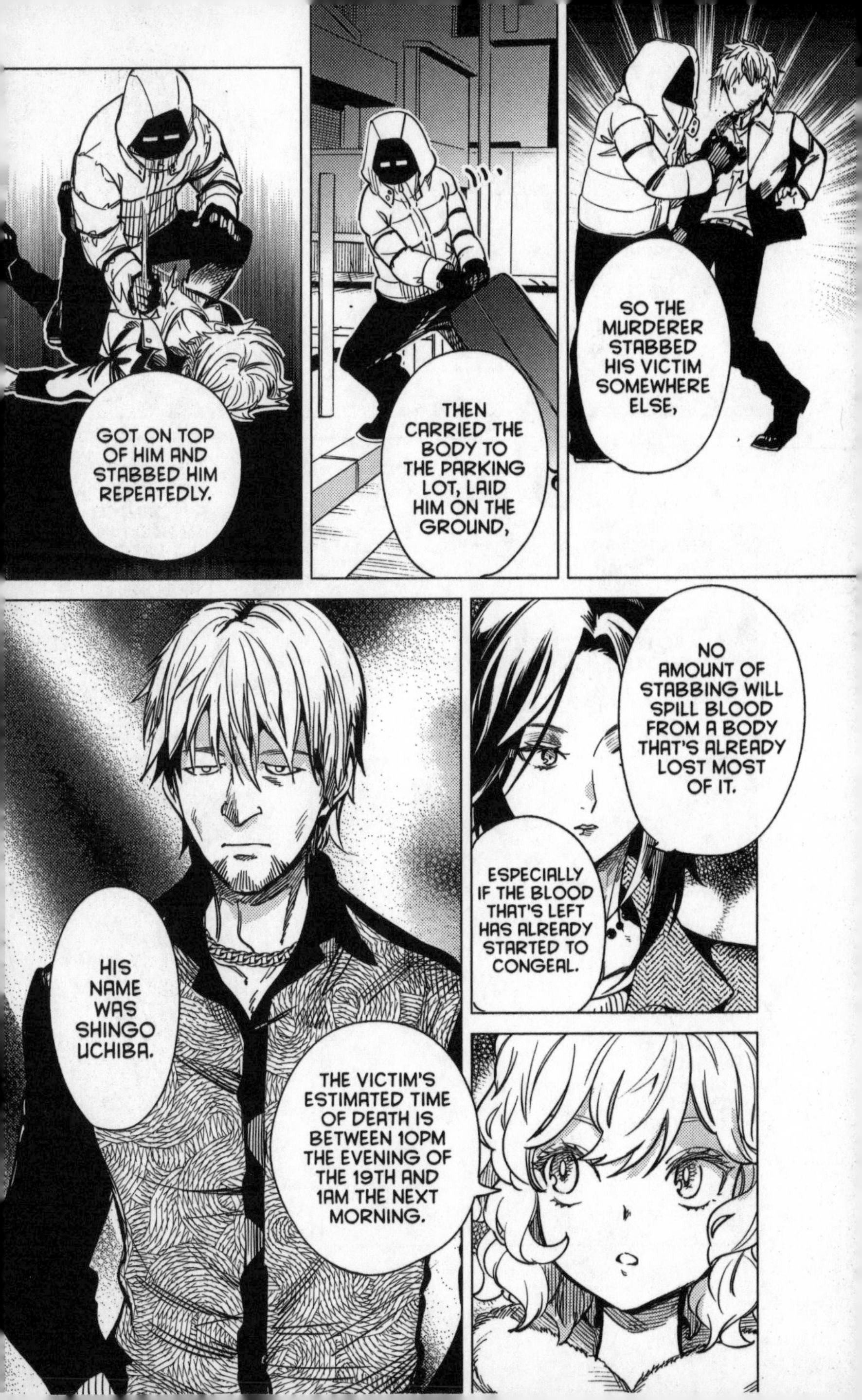
SO THE MURDERER STABBED HIS VICTIM SOMEWHERE ELSE,
THEN CARRIED THE BODY TO THE PARKING LOT, LAID HIM ON THE GROUND,
GOT ON TOP OF HIM AND STABBED HIM REPEATEDLY.
NO AMOUNT OF STABBING WILL SPILL BLOOD FROM A BODY THAT'S ALREADY LOST MOST OF IT.
ESPECIALLY IF THE BLOOD THAT'S LEFT HAS ALREADY STARTED TO CONGEAL.
HIS NAME WAS SHINGO UCHIBA.
THE VICTIM'S ESTIMATED TIME OF DEATH IS BETWEEN 10PM THE EVENING OF THE 19TH AND 1AM THE NEXT MORNING.

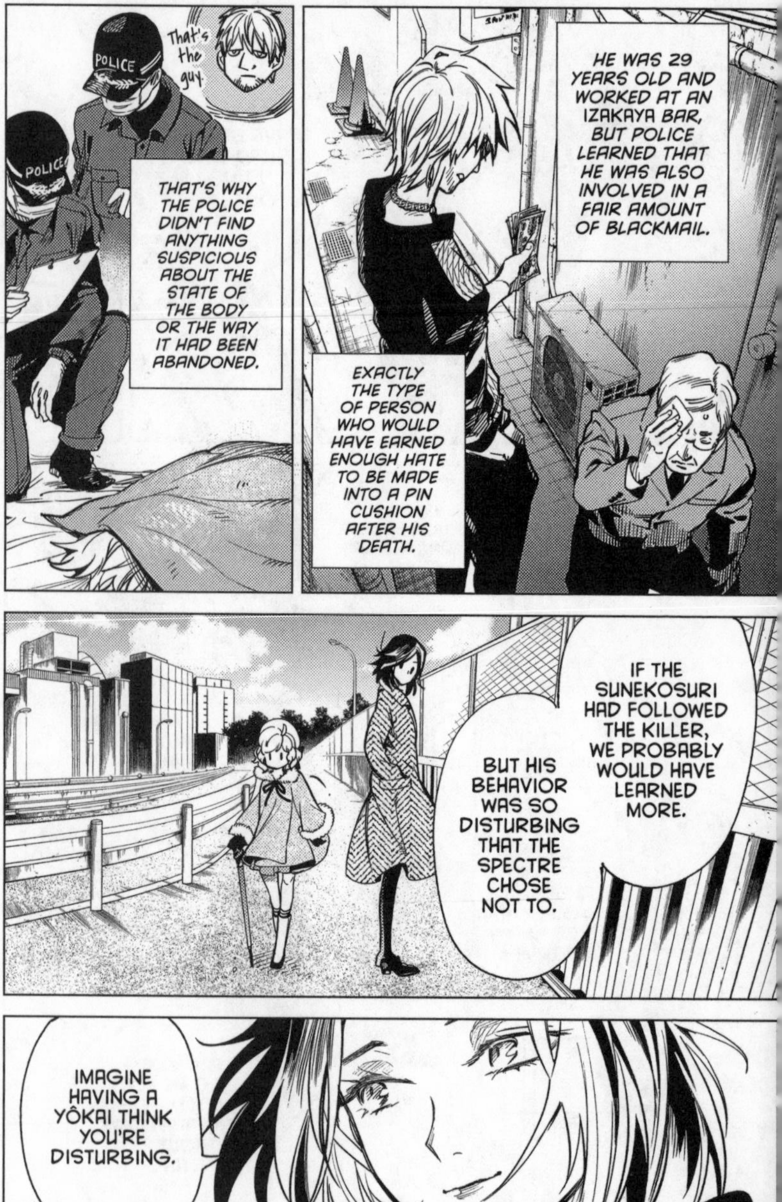
HE WAS 29 YEARS OLD AND WORKED AT AN IZAKAYA BAR, BUT POLICE LEARNED THAT HE WAS ALSO INVOLVED IN A FAIR AMOUNT OF BLACKMAIL.
EXACTLY THE TYPE OF PERSON WHO WOULD HAVE EARNED ENOUGH HATE TO BE MADE INTO A PIN CUSHION AFTER HIS DEATH.
That's the guy.
POLICE
POLICE
THAT'S WHY THE POLICE DIDN'T FIND ANYTHING SUSPICIOUS ABOUT THE STATE OF THE BODY OR THE WAY IT HAD BEEN ABANDONED.
IF THE SUNEKOSURI HAD FOLLOWED THE KILLER, WE PROBABLY WOULD HAVE LEARNED MORE.
BUT HIS BEHAVIOR WAS SO DISTURBING THAT THE SPECTRE CHOSE NOT TO.
IMAGINE HAVING A YÔKAI THINK YOU'RE DISTURBING.

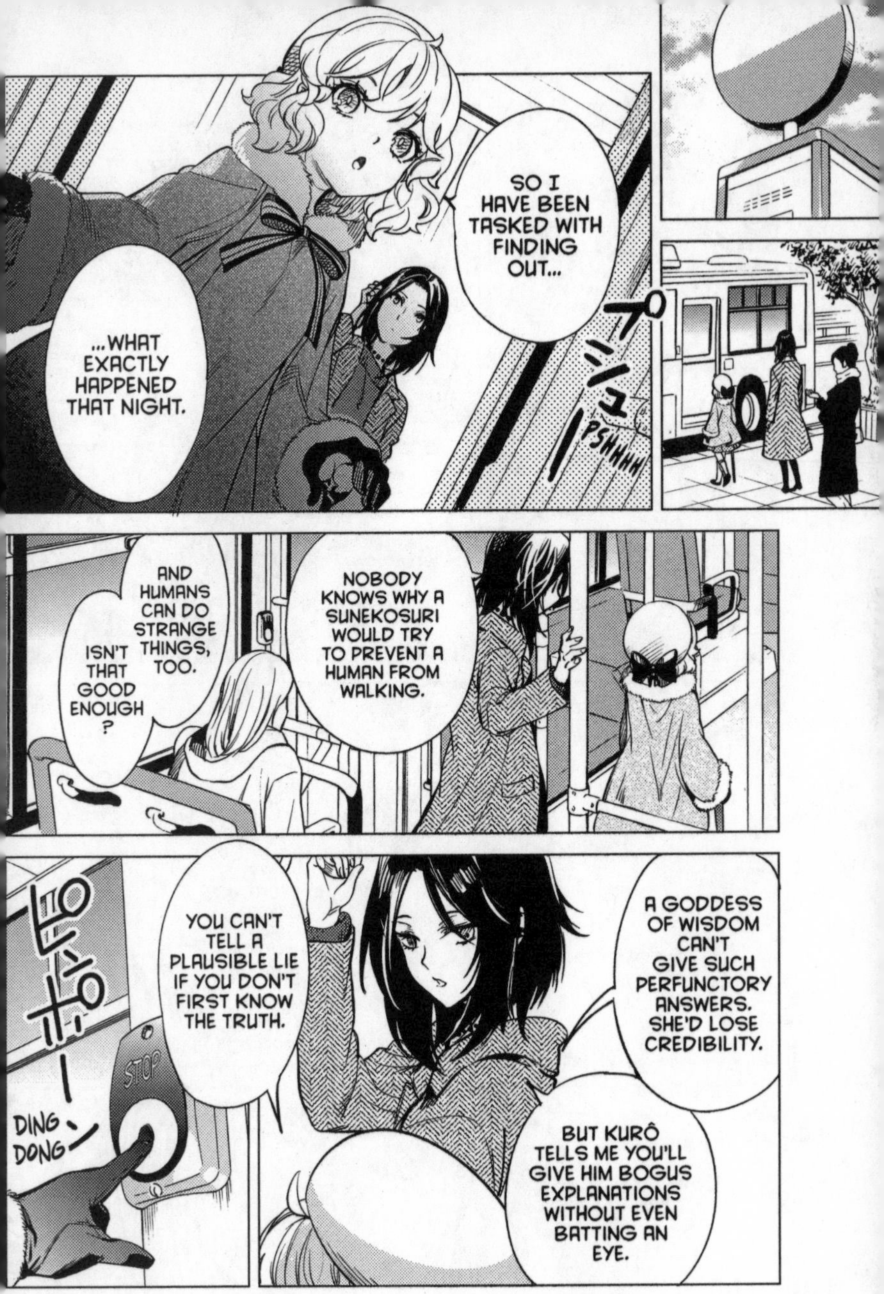
プシュー
PSHHHH
SO I HAVE BEEN TASKED WITH FINDING OUT...
...WHAT EXACTLY HAPPENED THAT NIGHT.
NOBODY KNOWS WHY A SUNEKOSURI WOULD TRY TO PREVENT A HUMAN FROM WALKING.
AND HUMANS CAN DO STRANGE THINGS, TOO.
ISN'T THAT GOOD ENOUGH?
A GODDESS OF WISDOM CAN'T GIVE SUCH PERFUNCTORY ANSWERS. SHE'D LOSE CREDIBILITY.
BUT KURÔ TELLS ME YOU'LL GIVE HIM BOGUS EXPLANATIONS WITHOUT EVEN BATTING AN EYE.
YOU CAN'T TELL A PLAUSIBLE LIE IF YOU DON'T FIRST KNOW THE TRUTH.
ピンポーン
DING DONG
STOP

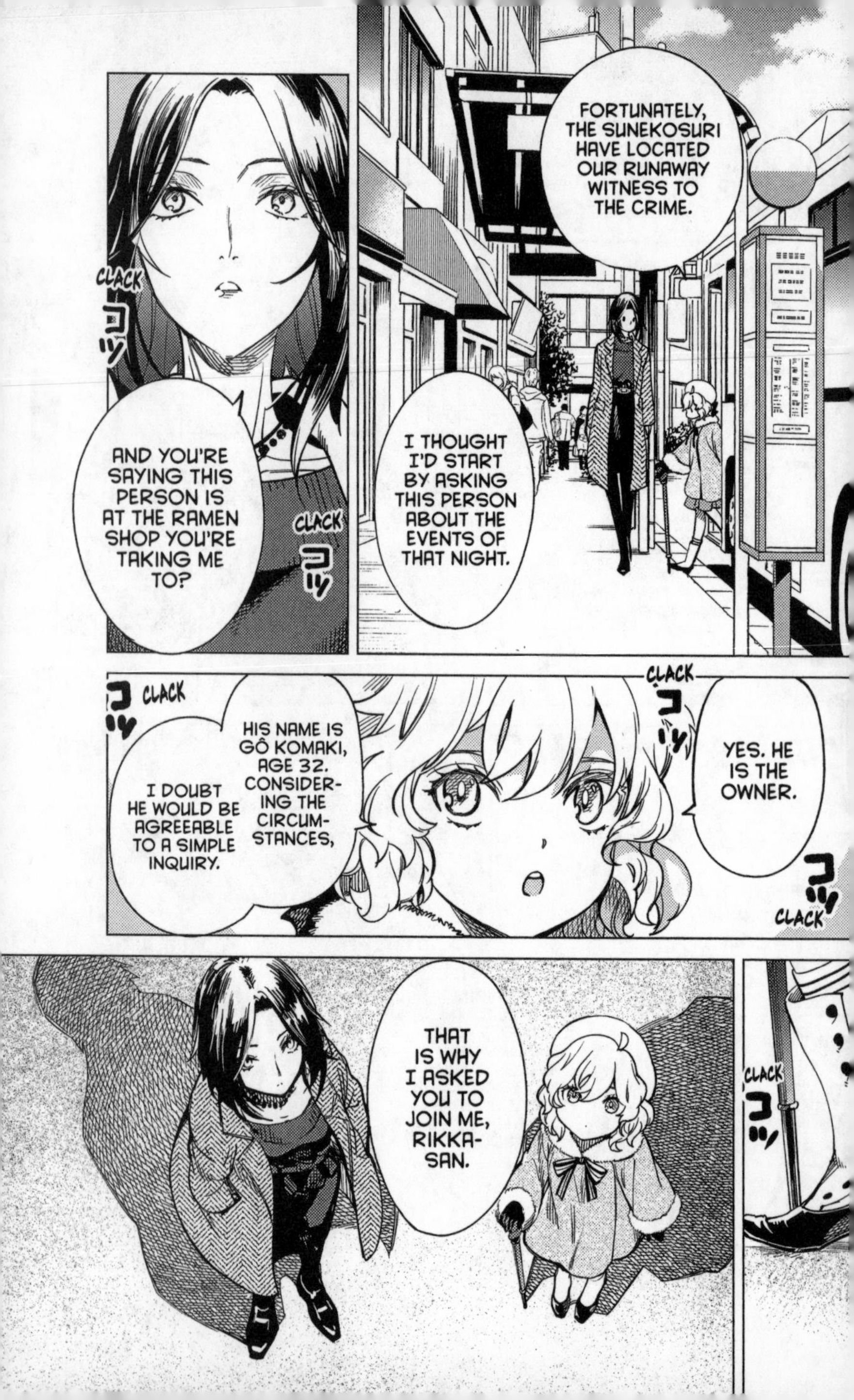
FORTUNATELY, THE SUNEKOSURI HAVE LOCATED OUR RUNAWAY WITNESS TO THE CRIME.
I THOUGHT I'D START BY ASKING THIS PERSON ABOUT THE EVENTS OF THAT NIGHT.
CLACK
コッ
AND YOU'RE SAYING THIS PERSON IS AT THE RAMEN SHOP YOU'RE TAKING ME TO?
CLACK
コッ
CLACK
コッ
YES. HE IS THE OWNER.
コッ
CLACK
HIS NAME IS GÔ KOMAKI, AGE 32. CONSIDER-ING THE CIRCUM-STANCES,
I DOUBT HE WOULD BE AGREEABLE TO A SIMPLE INQUIRY.
コッ
CLACK
CLACK
コッ
THAT IS WHY I ASKED YOU TO JOIN ME, RIKKA-SAN.

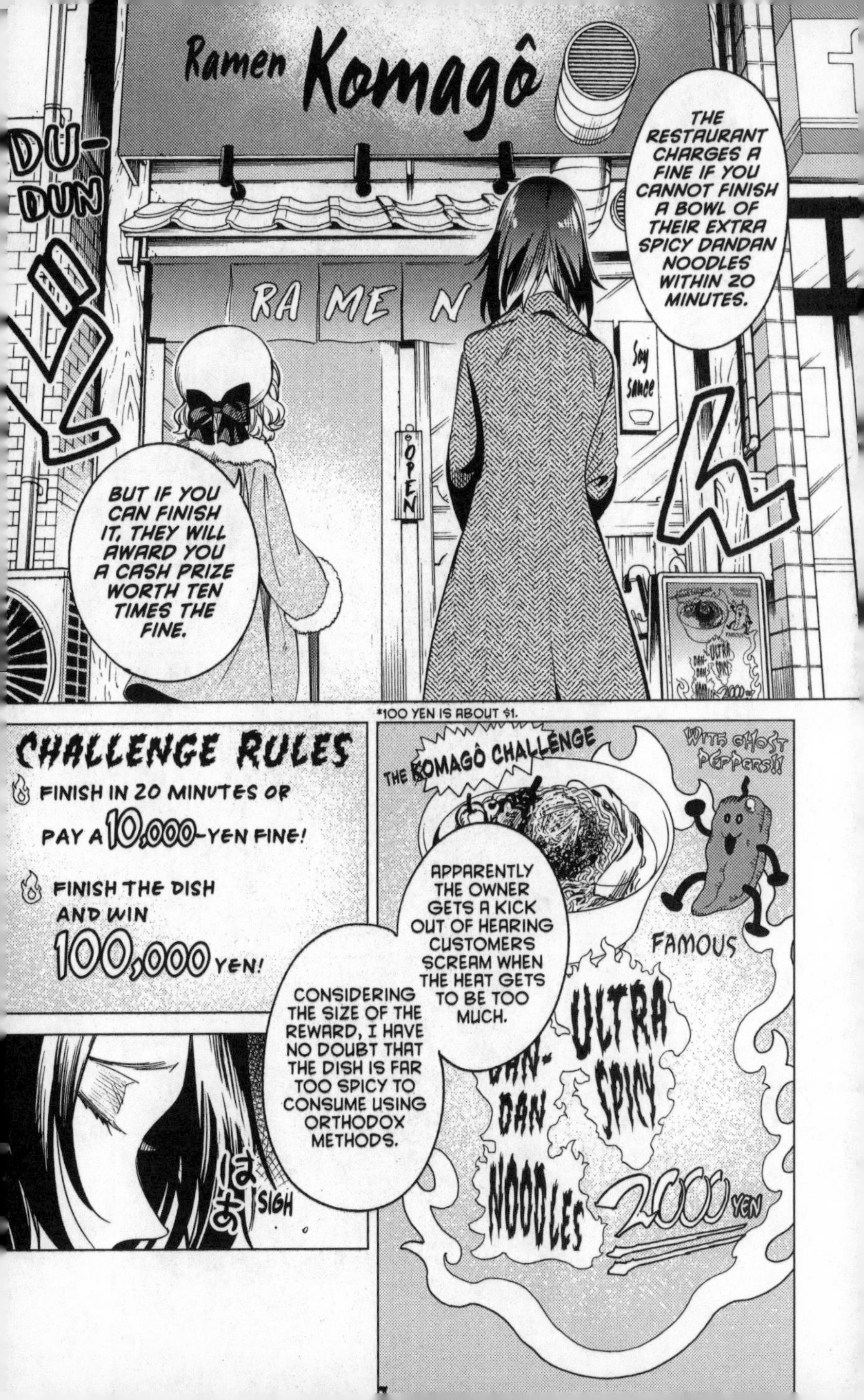
Ramen Komagô
RAMEN
DU-DUN
OPEN
Soy Sauce
THE RESTAURANT CHARGES A FINE IF YOU CANNOT FINISH A BOWL OF THEIR EXTRA SPICY DANDAN NOODLES WITHIN 20 MINUTES.
BUT IF YOU CAN FINISH IT, THEY WILL AWARD YOU A CASH PRIZE WORTH TEN TIMES THE FINE.
THE KOMAGÔ CHALLENGE
WITH GHOST PEPPERS!!
FAMOUS
ULTRA SPICY
DAN-DAN NOODLES
2000 YEN
APPARENTLY THE OWNER GETS A KICK OUT OF HEARING CUSTOMERS SCREAM WHEN THE HEAT GETS TO BE TOO MUCH.
CONSIDERING THE SIZE OF THE REWARD, I HAVE NO DOUBT THAT THE DISH IS FAR TOO SPICY TO CONSUME USING ORTHODOX METHODS.
CHALLENGE RULES
FINISH IN 20 MINUTES OR PAY A 10,000-YEN FINE!
FINISH THE DISH AND WIN 100,000 YEN!
はあ
SIGH

*100 YEN IS ABOUT $1.

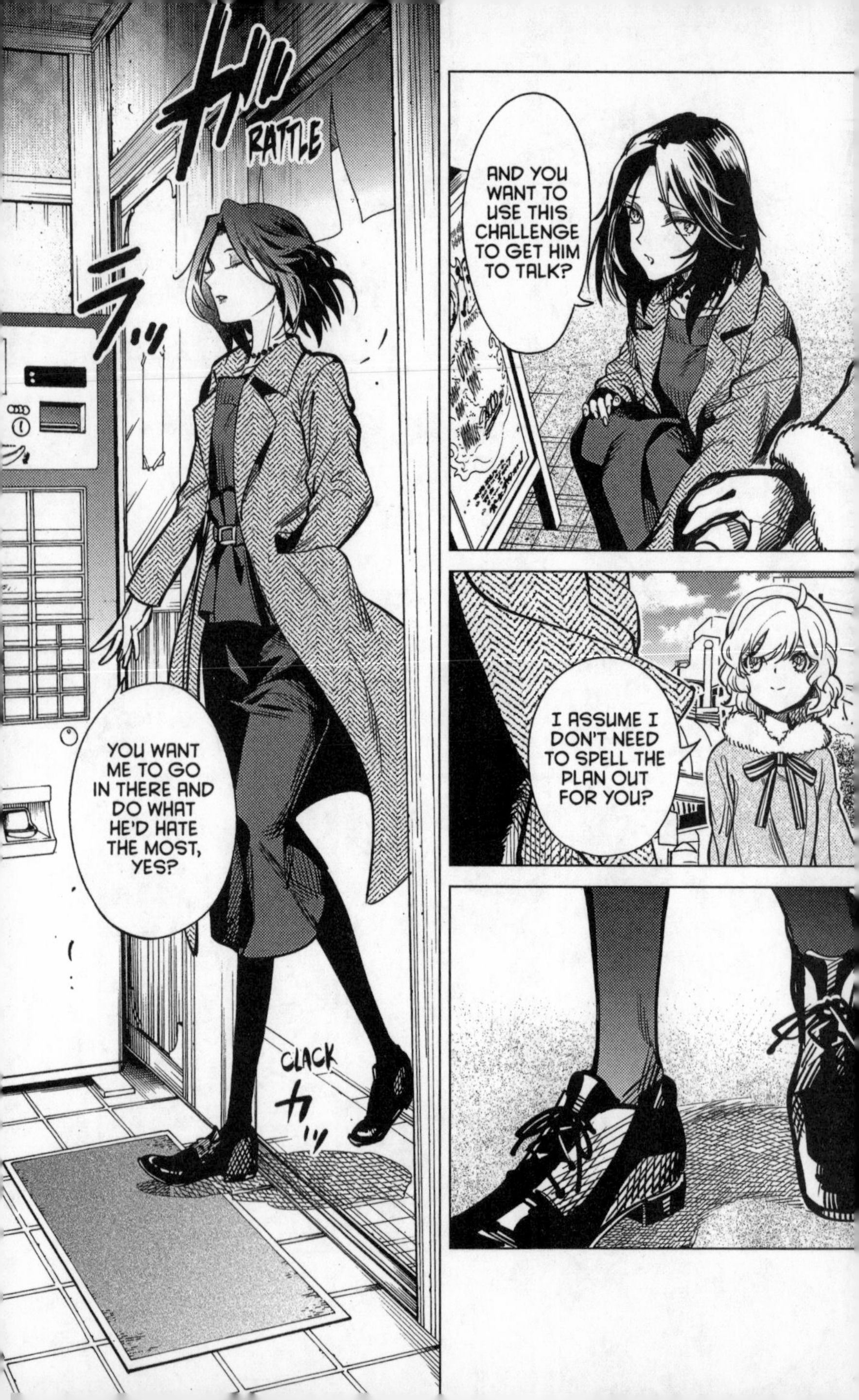
AND YOU WANT TO USE THIS CHALLENGE TO GET HIM TO TALK?
I ASSUME I DON'T NEED TO SPELL THE PLAN OUT FOR YOU?
RATTLE
YOU WANT ME TO GO IN THERE AND DO WHAT HE'D HATE THE MOST, YES?
CLACK

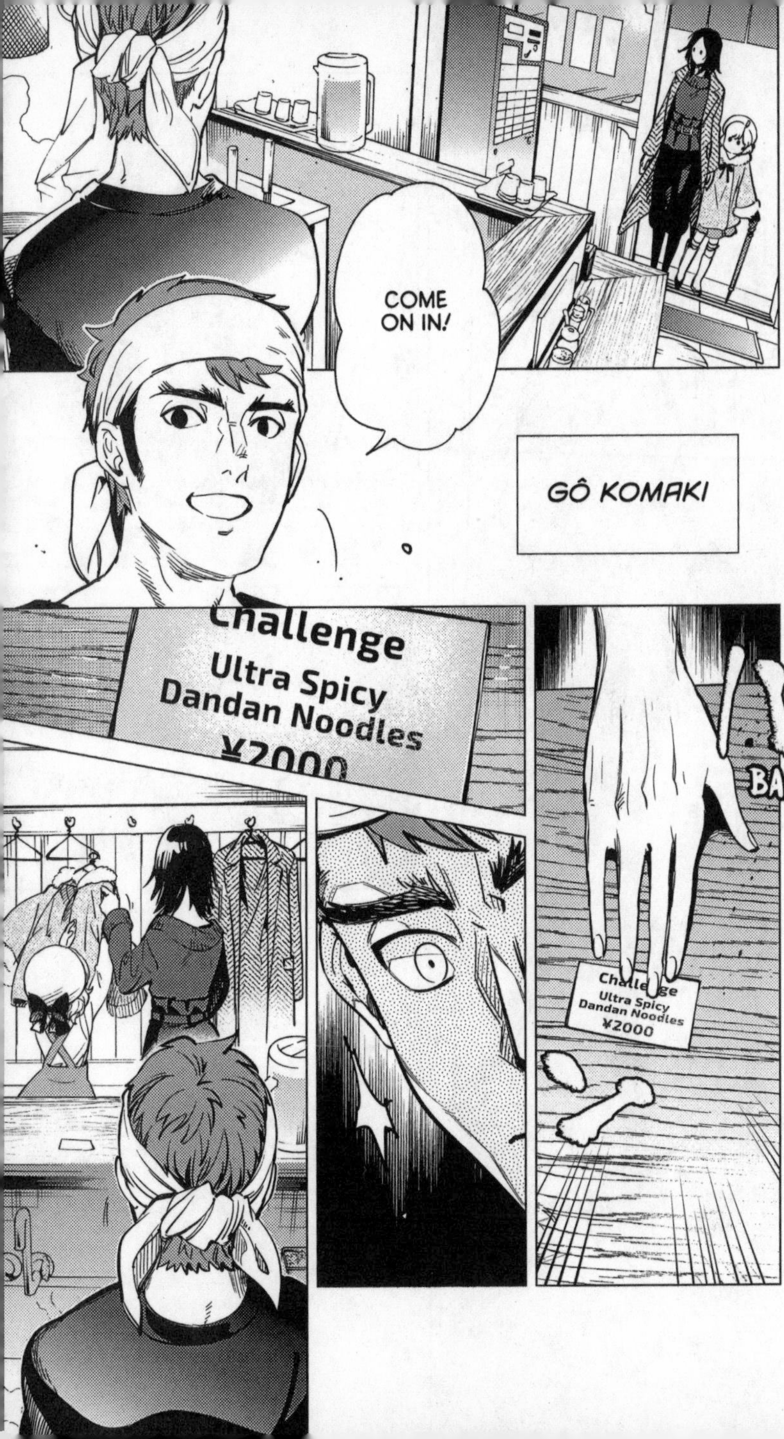
COME ON IN!
GÔ KOMAKI
BAM
Challenge
Ultra Spicy
Dandan Noodles
¥2000
Challenge
Ultra Spicy
Dandan Noodles
¥2000

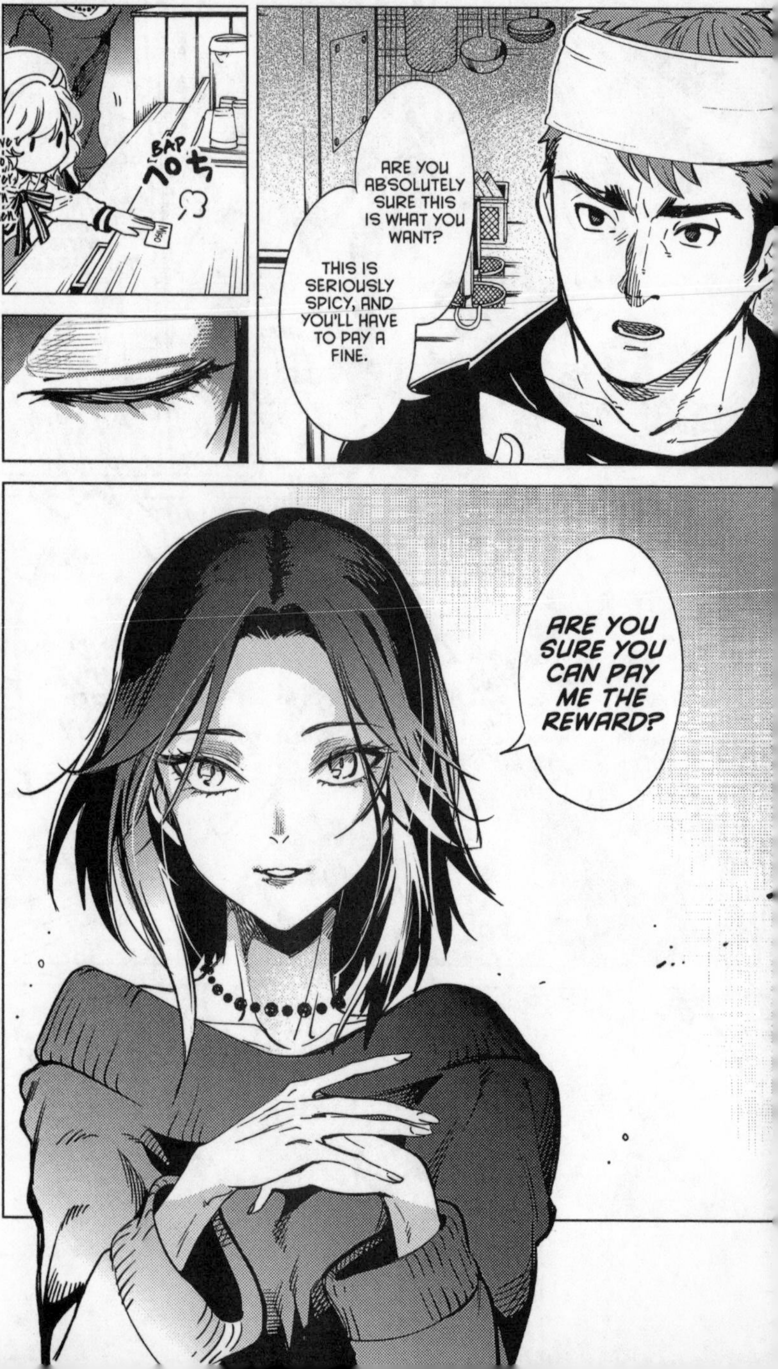
ARE YOU ABSOLUTELY SURE THIS IS WHAT YOU WANT?
THIS IS SERIOUSLY SPICY, AND YOU'LL HAVE TO PAY A FINE.
I'll have miso butter corn ramen.
BAP
MISO
ARE YOU SURE YOU CAN PAY ME THE REWARD?

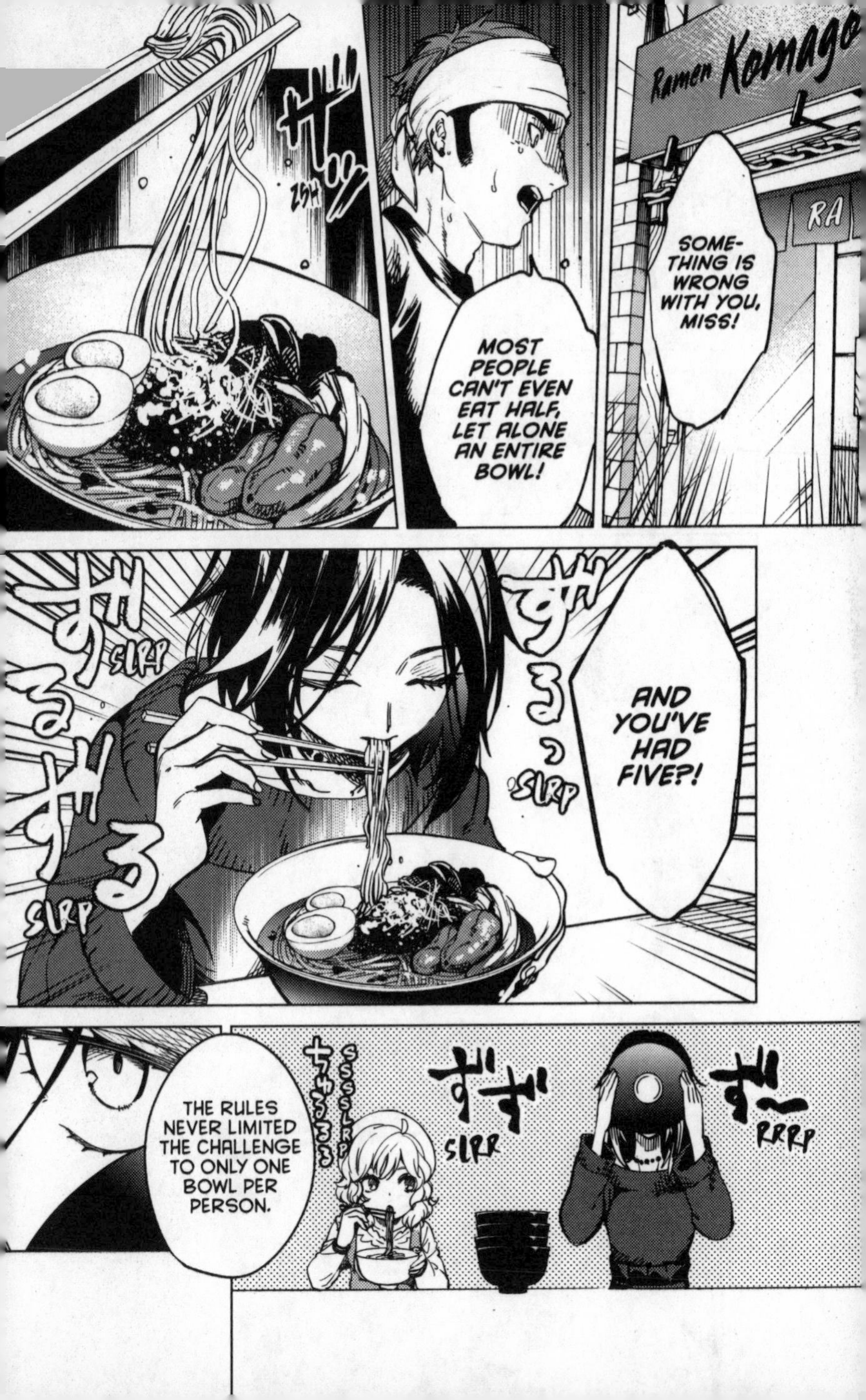
Ramen Kamago
RA
SOMETHING IS WRONG WITH YOU, MISS!
MOST PEOPLE CAN'T EVEN EAT HALF, LET ALONE AN ENTIRE BOWL!
ZSH
AND YOU'VE HAD FIVE?!
ずるっ SLRP
ずるずる SLRP SLRP
ずー RRRP
ずず SLRR
ちゅるるる SSSSLRP
THE RULES NEVER LIMITED THE CHALLENGE TO ONLY ONE BOWL PER PERSON.

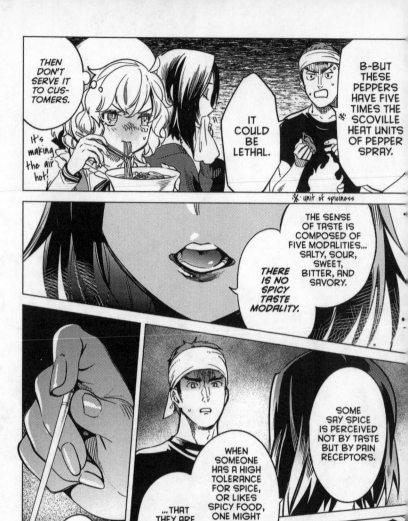

B-BUT THESE PEPPERS HAVE FIVE TIMES THE ※SCOVILLE HEAT UNITS OF PEPPER SPRAY.
IT COULD BE LETHAL.
THEN DON'T SERVE IT TO CUSTOMERS.
It's making the air hot!
※: unit of spiciness
THE SENSE OF TASTE IS COMPOSED OF FIVE MODALITIES... SALTY, SOUR, SWEET, BITTER, AND SAVORY.
THERE IS NO SPICY TASTE MODALITY.
SOME SAY SPICE IS PERCEIVED NOT BY TASTE BUT BY PAIN RECEPTORS.
WHEN SOMEONE HAS A HIGH TOLERANCE FOR SPICE, OR LIKES SPICY FOOD, ONE MIGHT INTERPRET THAT TO MEAN...
...THAT THEY ARE INSENSITIVE TO PAIN, OR THEY ENJOY STRONG STIMULI.
SFF
ERGO...

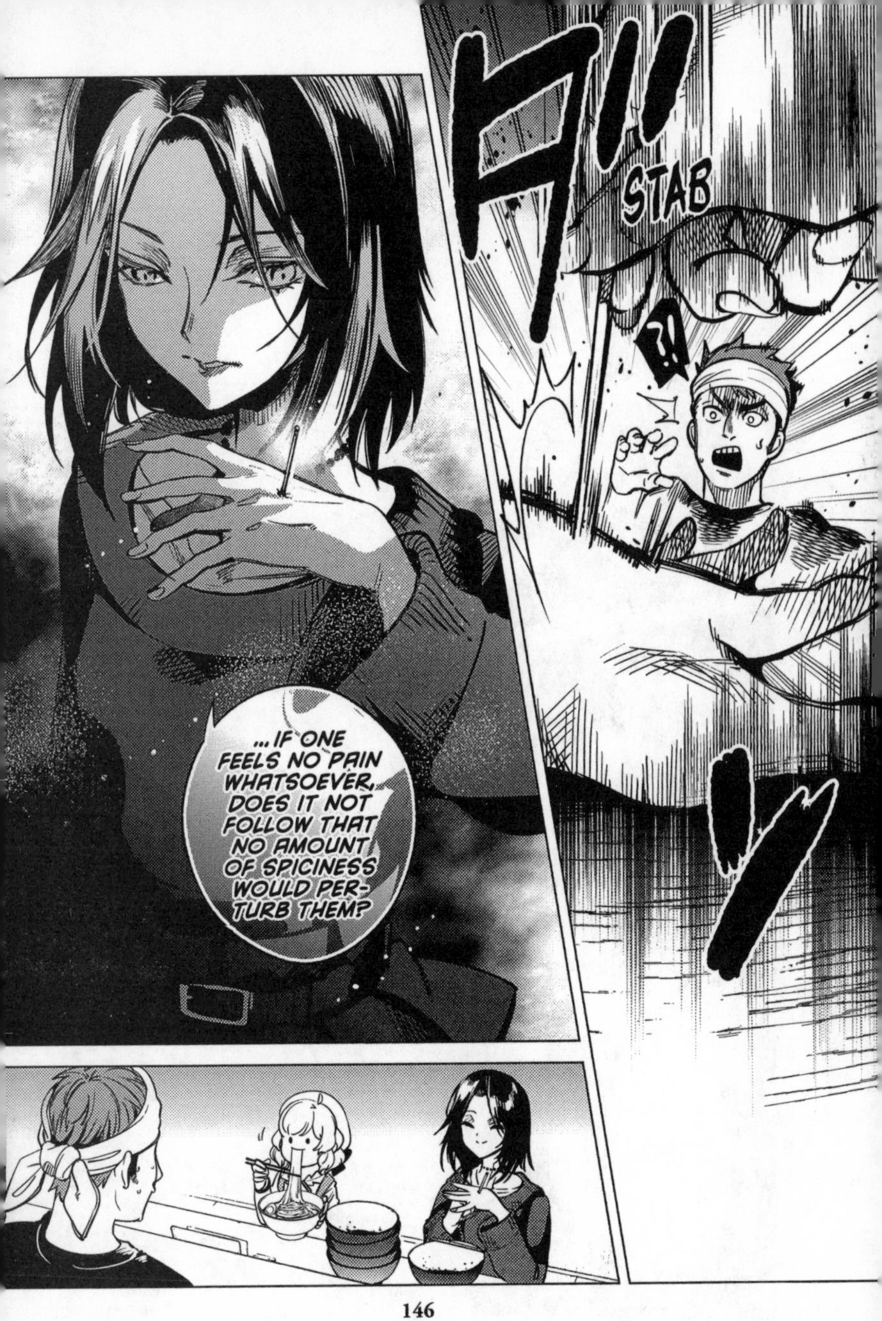
STAB
?!
...IF ONE FEELS NO PAIN WHATSOEVER, DOES IT NOT FOLLOW THAT NO AMOUNT OF SPICINESS WOULD PER-TURB THEM?

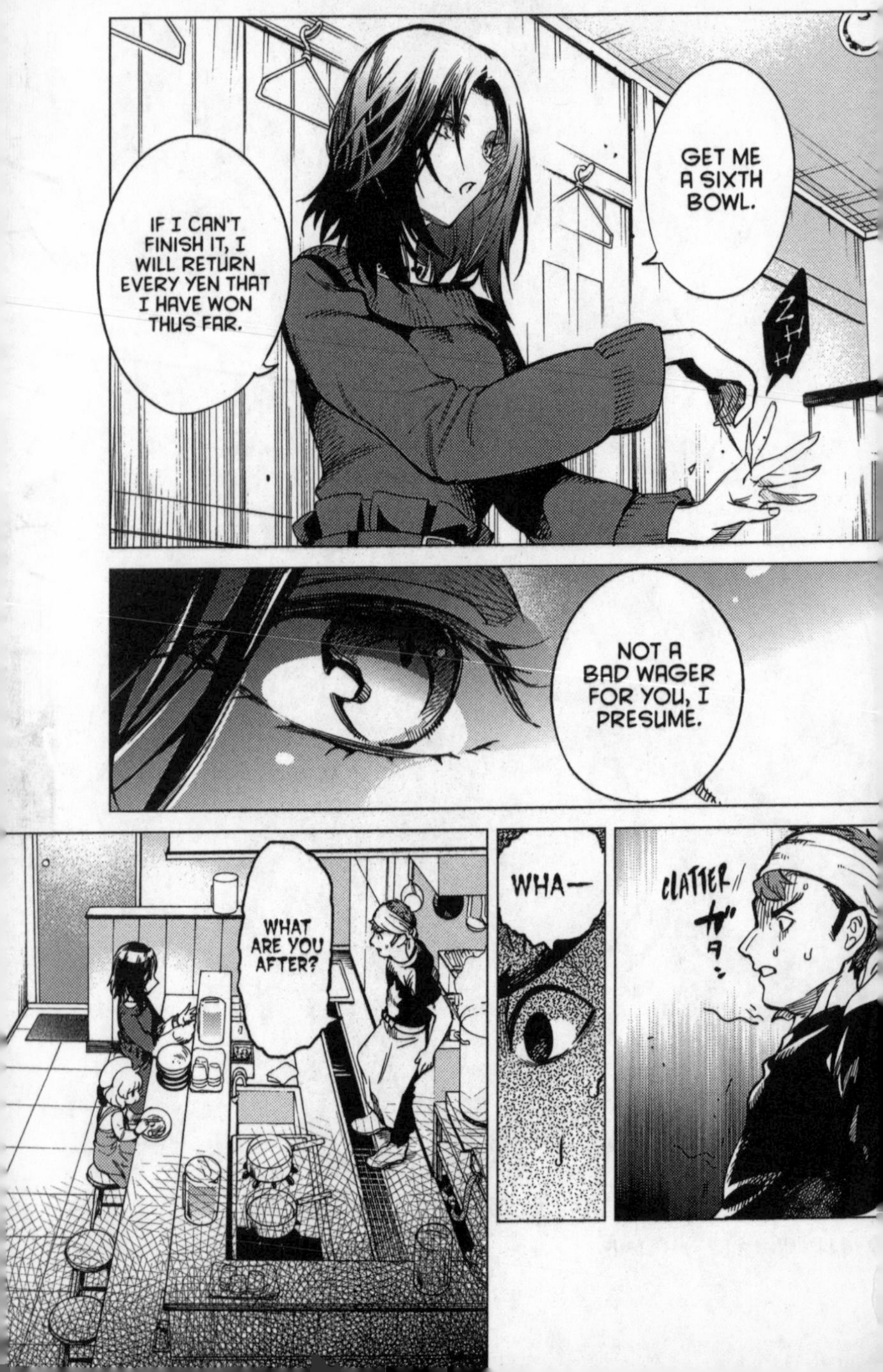
GET ME A SIXTH BOWL.
ZHH
IF I CAN'T FINISH IT, I WILL RETURN EVERY YEN THAT I HAVE WON THUS FAR.
NOT A BAD WAGER FOR YOU, I PRESUME.
CLATTER
ガタ
WHA—
WHAT ARE YOU AFTER?

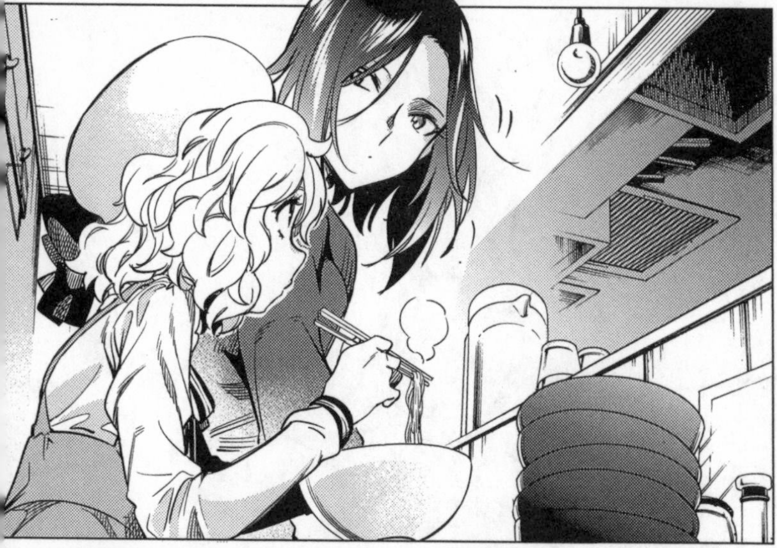

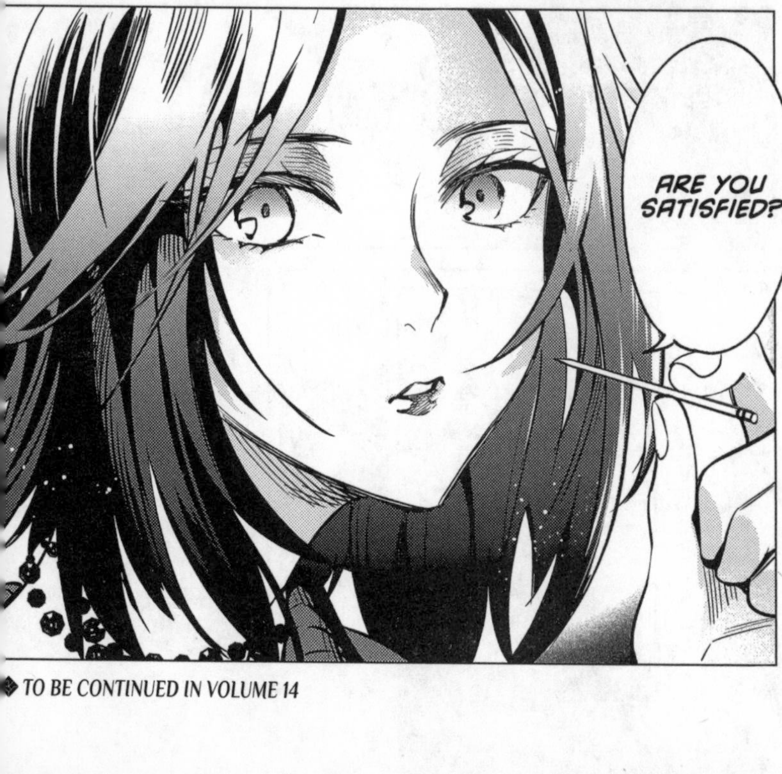
ARE YOU SATISFIED?

TO BE CONTINUED IN VOLUME 14

Kotoko Iwanaga's shins are nuzzled.

NUZZLE
するり

NUZZLE
ぬるり

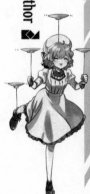

Thoughts on the Line Between Fair and Unfair from the Author

I am the author, Kyo Shirodaira, and this is volume 13. Although it happens in flashback, the woman behind the curtain, Rikka Sakuragawa, steps pretty far into the spotlight.

This is partly because a change in serialization circumstances made a reintroduction necessary, and partly because Iwanaga and Kurô had been handling crimes as a pair for most of the series, and it can be good for the readers and the writer to change things up a bit. This case won't be solved until the next volume, but it all happened in the past, so you can rest assured that nothing too dangerous is going to happen.

Now, the Yuki-Onna's Dilemma case is solved in this volume, but I believe some of you may not be too happy that the killer turned out to be someone who had been mentioned before, but we had no idea what they looked like, or even their name or gender. I imagine that more than a few of you will feel that this is unfair. By my own criteria, given how the story was set up, what I wrote still fits within the boundaries of "fair," but I can also understand thinking that it was unfair. Arguments aside, I absolutely respect the opinion of, "What? The killer was 'Former Employee A'? That's cheating."

There is a very small number of characters in this case, and almost zero named characters that could be considered suspects, and in that situation, someone's presence is felt even if they're only briefly mentioned in a conversation, so there's definitely a chance to suspect them, and the readers will remember them when they are identified as the killer—these are the thoughts that led me personally to determine that this outcome could be fair.

In fact, there are some examples of mysteries, inside and outside Japan, where the killer is a similar type of character. The detective's deduction lays out the profile of the killer, and whether we know their name or not, whether they've been in the story continuously or not, whoever fits the bill is the guilty party, be it a janitor, a taxi driver, or a bartender. Closer to home, I already did it in the Steel Lady Nanase case.

For a more unique example, there's a story where you never even hear the killer's name, but there's someone who actually existed at the time the story took place and they're brought in at the end as the killer. It's like if there were a historical mystery that took place during the Warring States Era, and even though his name had never come up before, it turns out that the killer was Oda Nobunaga. Anyone with a passing knowledge of the Warring States Era would recognize the names of places or servants and know that Nobunaga was around, so it wouldn't be unfair to suddenly throw his name in the story as the killer. But even if the readers could accept Nobunaga as the killer because he's so famous, if it was Oda Nobuhide or Oda Nobutada, the name recognition might be too low to convince them.

Regardless, it's true that these methods can come across as pulling one over on the readers, and if the writer is not careful, they run the risk of reducing the number of mystery fans in the world.

The plan is to give Rikka-san a full comeback in the next volume. I can't put the final showdown off too much longer. That, too, may reduce the number of fans.

Well, I hope to see you again.

Kyo Shirodaira

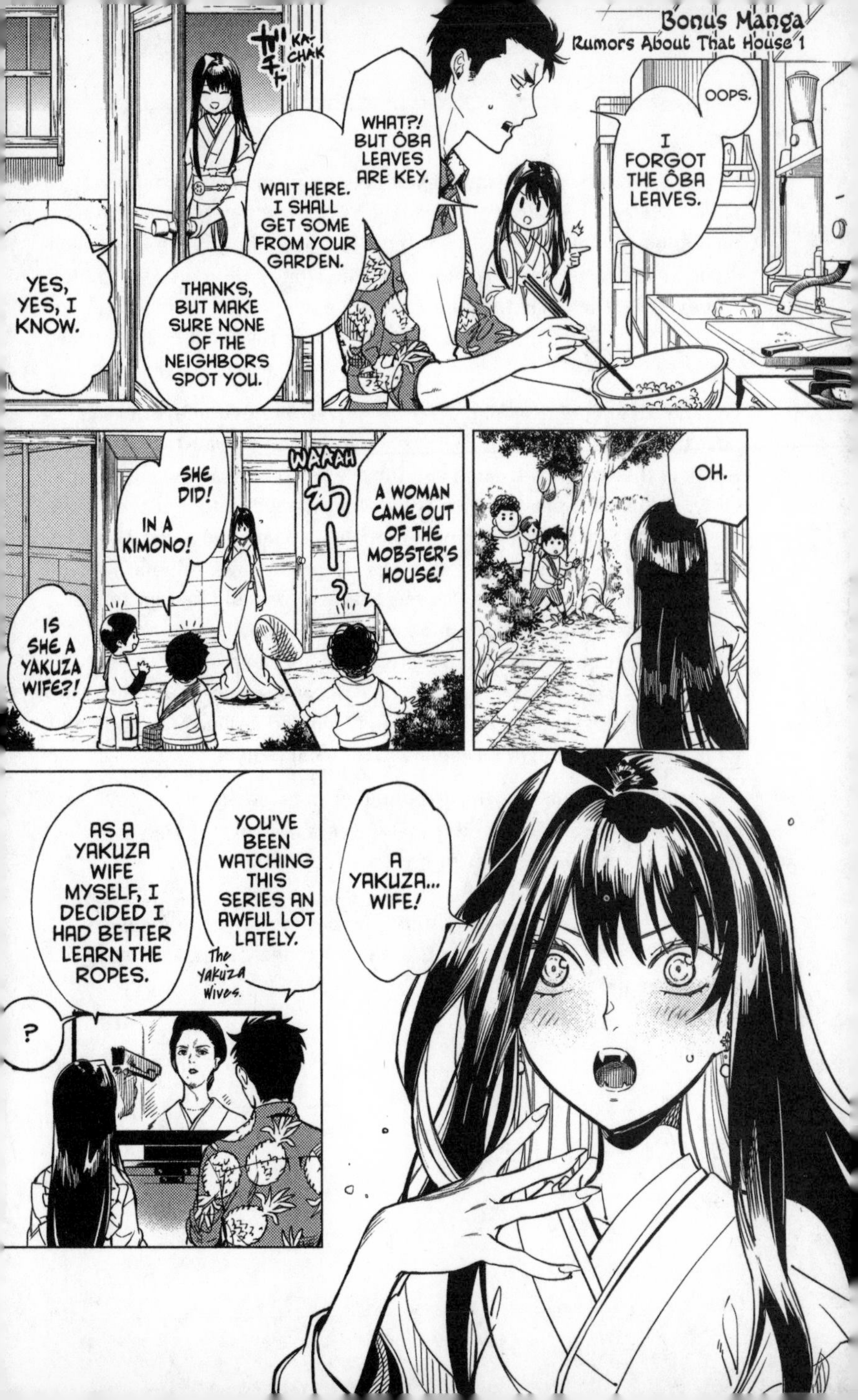
Bonus Manga
Rumors About That House 1
OOPS.
I FORGOT THE ÔBA LEAVES.
WHAT?! BUT ÔBA LEAVES ARE KEY.
WAIT HERE. I SHALL GET SOME FROM YOUR GARDEN.
KA-CHAK
THANKS, BUT MAKE SURE NONE OF THE NEIGHBORS SPOT YOU.
YES, YES, I KNOW.
OH.
WAAAH
A WOMAN CAME OUT OF THE MOBSTER'S HOUSE!
SHE DID!
IN A KIMONO!
IS SHE A YAKUZA WIFE?!
A YAKUZA... WIFE!
YOU'VE BEEN WATCHING THIS SERIES AN AWFUL LOT LATELY.
The Yakuza Wives.
AS A YAKUZA WIFE MYSELF, I DECIDED I HAD BETTER LEARN THE ROPES.
?

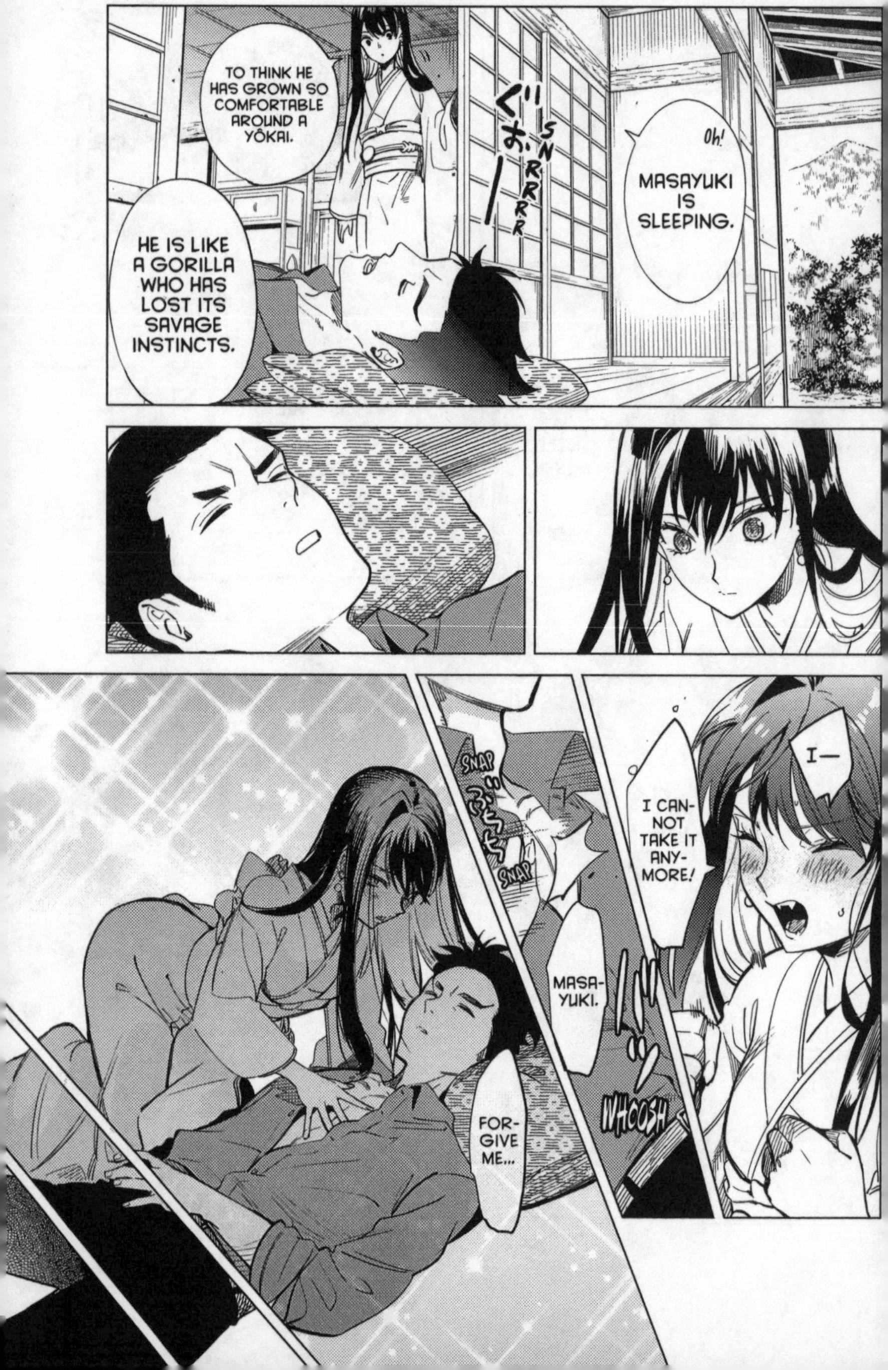
Oh!
MASAYUKI IS SLEEPING.
SNRRRRR
TO THINK HE HAS GROWN SO COMFORTABLE AROUND A YÔKAI.
HE IS LIKE A GORILLA WHO HAS LOST ITS SAVAGE INSTINCTS.
I—
I CAN-NOT TAKE IT ANY-MORE!
WHOOSH
SNAP
SNAP
MASA-YUKI.
FOR-GIVE ME...

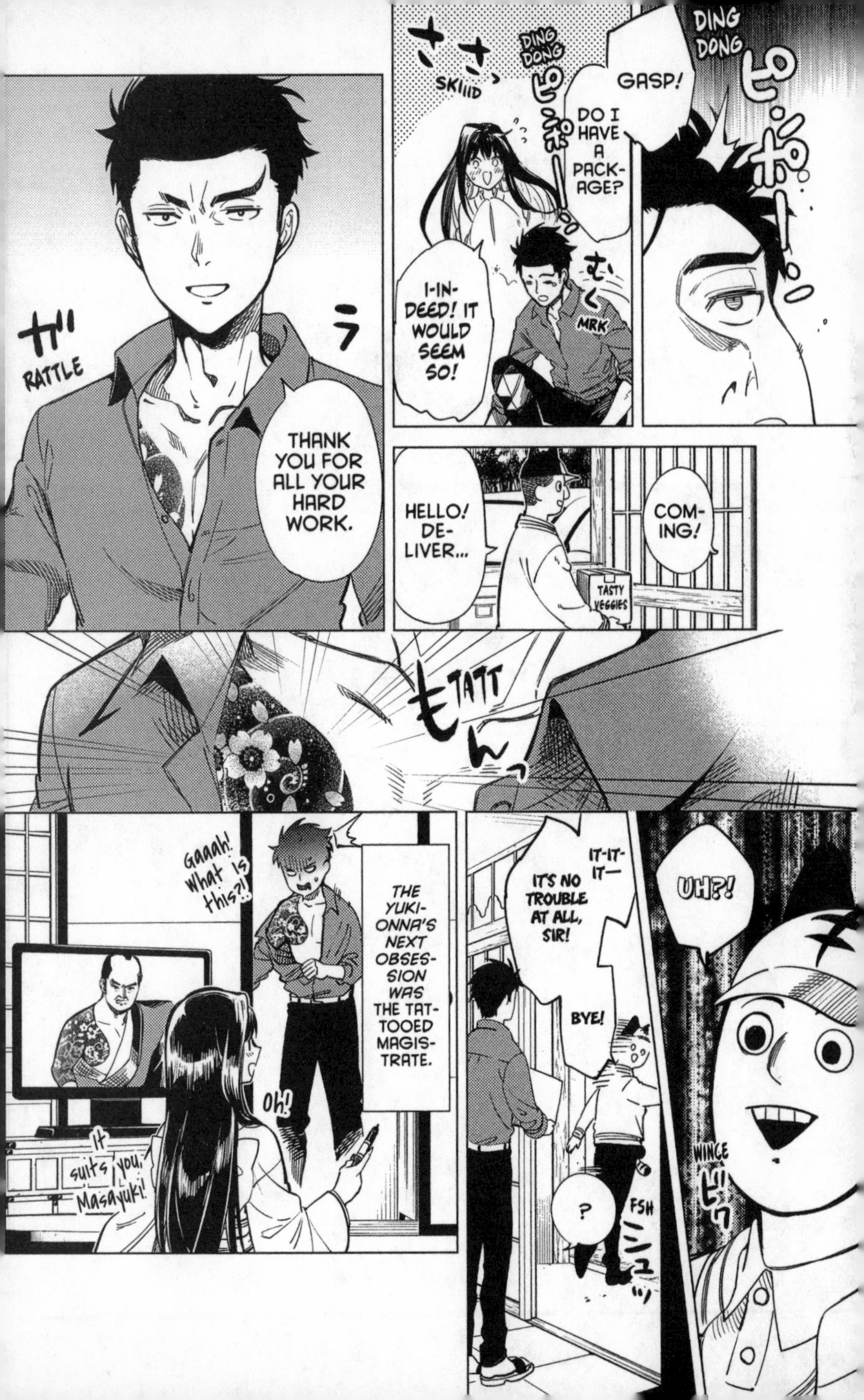

DING DONG
GASP!
DO I HAVE A PACKAGE?
DING DONG
SKIIID
I-INDEED! IT WOULD SEEM SO!
MRK
COMING!
HELLO! DELIVER...
TASTY VEGGIES
THANK YOU FOR ALL YOUR HARD WORK.
RATTLE
TATT
UH?!
WINCE
IT-IT-IT—
IT'S NO TROUBLE AT ALL, SIR!
BYE!
?
FSH
Gaaah! What is this?!
THE YUKI-ONNA'S NEXT OBSESSION WAS THE TATTOOED MAGISTRATE.
Oh!
It suits you, Masayuki!

Rumors About That House 3

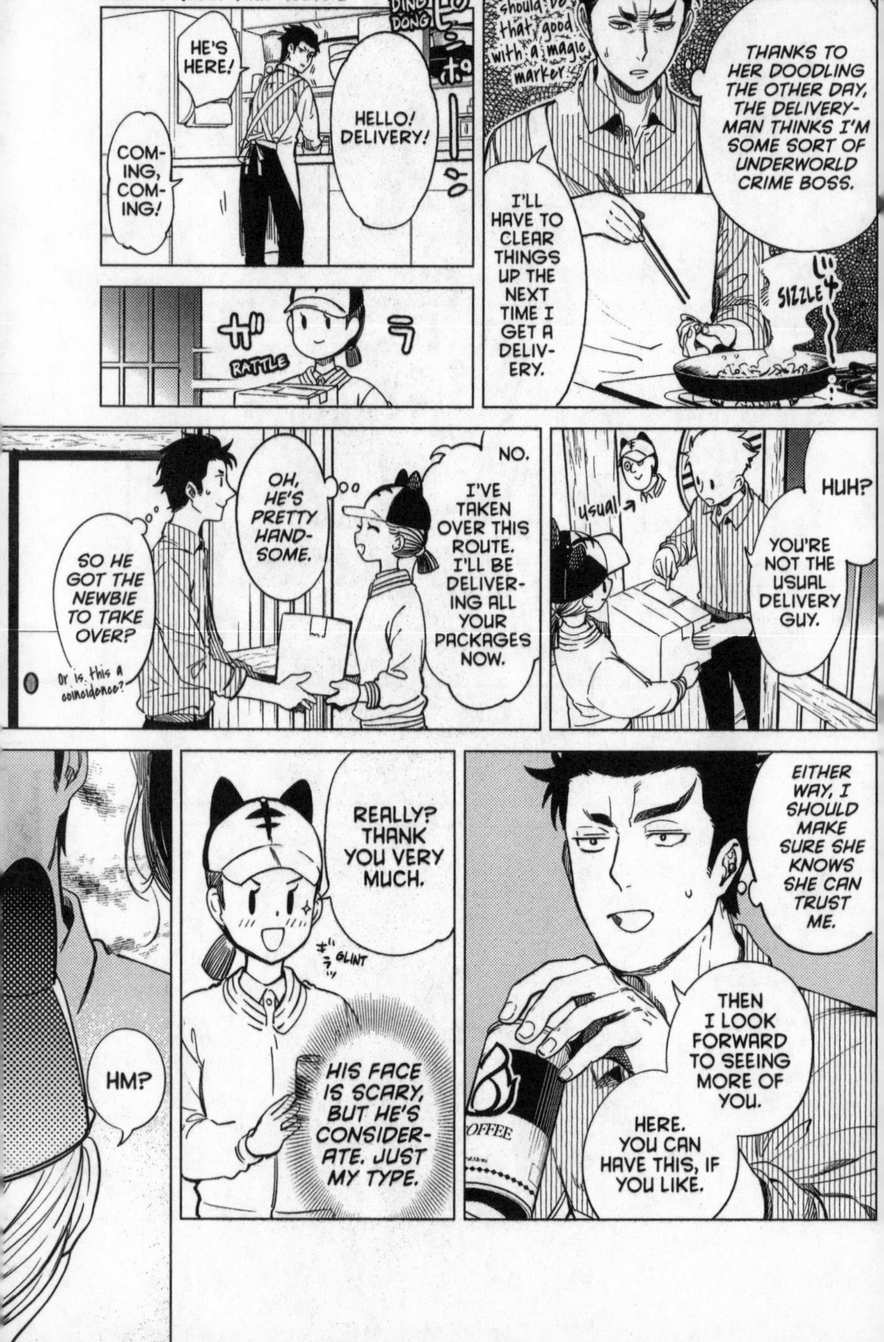
No, one should be that good with a magic marker.
THANKS TO HER DOODLING THE OTHER DAY, THE DELIVERYMAN THINKS I'M SOME SORT OF UNDERWORLD CRIME BOSS.
I'LL HAVE TO CLEAR THINGS UP THE NEXT TIME I GET A DELIVERY.
SIZZLE
DING DONG
HELLO! DELIVERY!
HE'S HERE!
COMING, COMING!
RATTLE
HUH?
YOU'RE NOT THE USUAL DELIVERY GUY.
usual
NO.
I'VE TAKEN OVER THIS ROUTE. I'LL BE DELIVERING ALL YOUR PACKAGES NOW.
OH, HE'S PRETTY HANDSOME.
SO HE GOT THE NEWBIE TO TAKE OVER?
Or is this a coincidence?
EITHER WAY, I SHOULD MAKE SURE SHE KNOWS SHE CAN TRUST ME.
THEN I LOOK FORWARD TO SEEING MORE OF YOU.
HERE. YOU CAN HAVE THIS, IF YOU LIKE.
COFFEE
REALLY? THANK YOU VERY MUCH.
GLINT
HIS FACE IS SCARY, BUT HE'S CONSIDERATE. JUST MY TYPE.
HM?

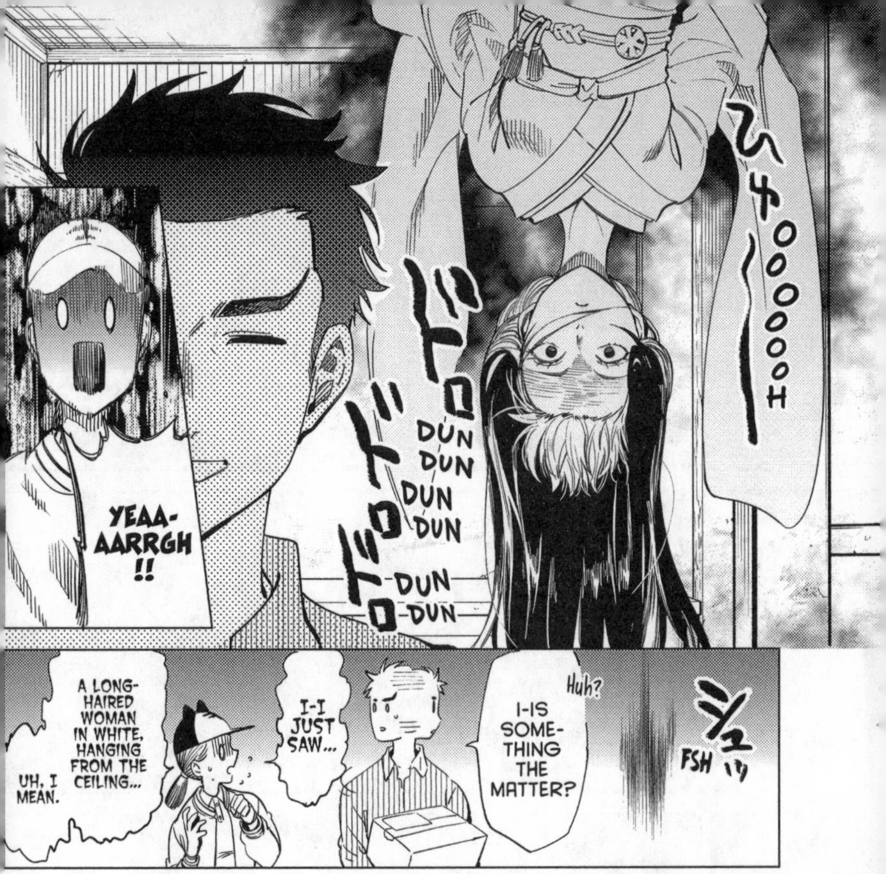
OOOOOOH
DUN DUN DUN DUN DUN DUN
YEAA-AARRGH!!
FSH
Huh?
I-IS SOMETHING THE MATTER?
I-I JUST SAW...
A LONG-HAIRED WOMAN IN WHITE, HANGING FROM THE CEILING...
UH, I MEAN.

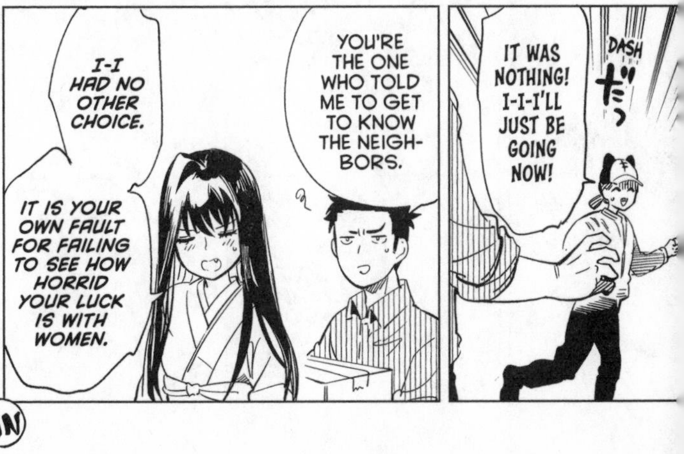
DASH
IT WAS NOTHING! I-I-I'LL JUST BE GOING NOW!
YOU'RE THE ONE WHO TOLD ME TO GET TO KNOW THE NEIGHBORS.
I-I HAD NO OTHER CHOICE.
IT IS YOUR OWN FAULT FOR FAILING TO SEE HOW HORRID YOUR LUCK IS WITH WOMEN.

Thank you for picking up volume 13! I hope you'll read the next one, too.

* Staff *
Asai
Shimameguri
Gomakuro

* Editors *
O-kawa
T-da
(honorifics excluded)

FIN

IN/SPECTRE

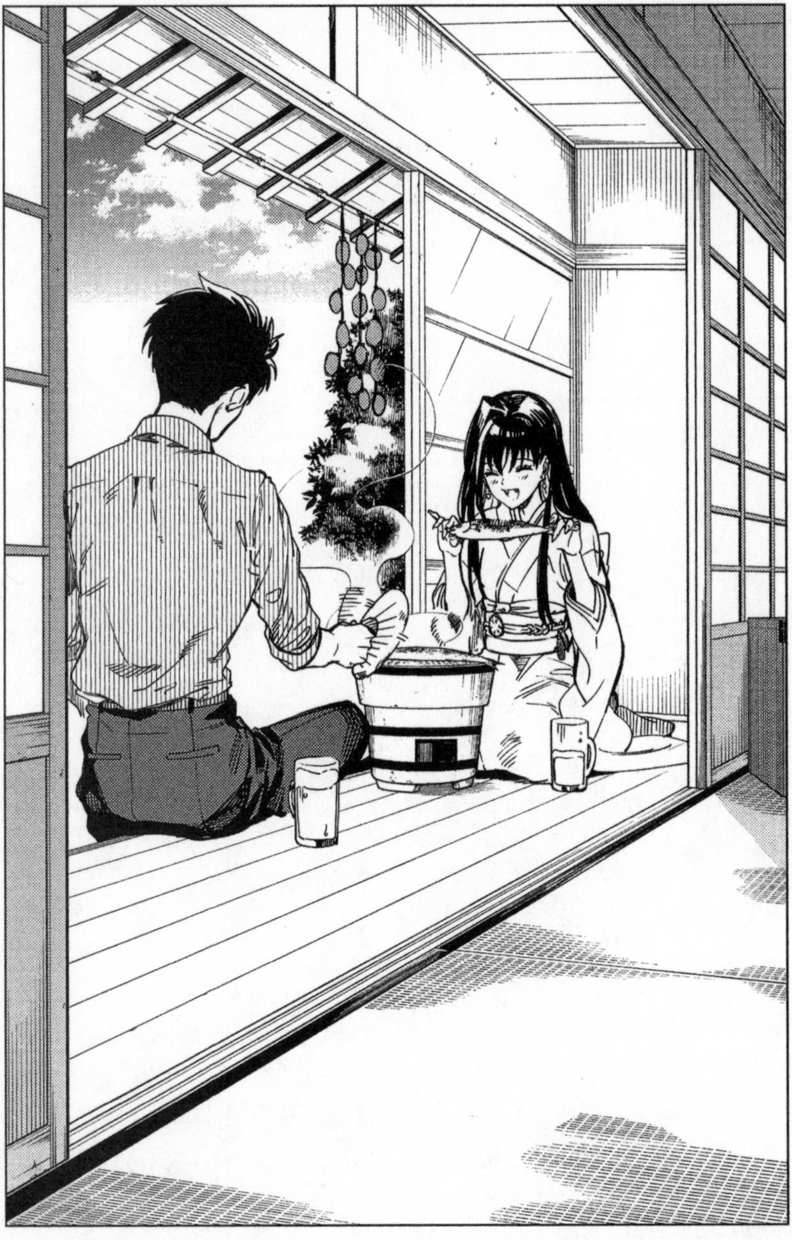

A drawing that has nothing to do with the story.

TRANSLATION NOTES

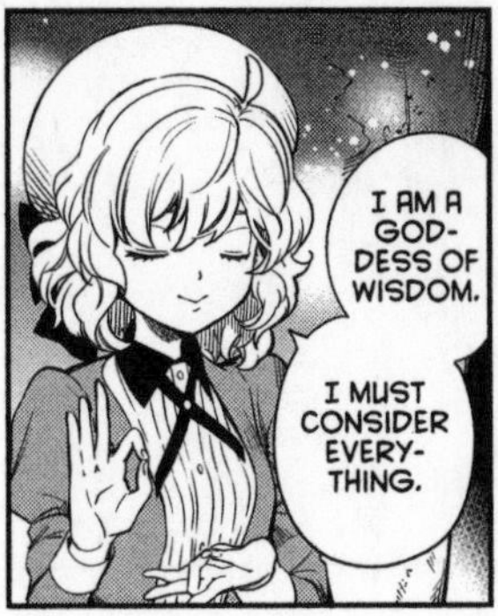
I AM A GOD-DESS OF WISDOM.
I MUST CONSIDER EVERY-THING.

Kotoko's pose, page 55
Perhaps to give more credibility to her claim of divinity, here Kotoko strikes a pose that evokes images of the Buddha. With her right hand, she is forming a mudra (Sanskrit for "symbol" or "sign"). This particular mudra is the Vitarka Mudra, or the teaching mudra. With her left, she may be forming the Sharagamana Mudra, or mudra of protection, which has several variations.

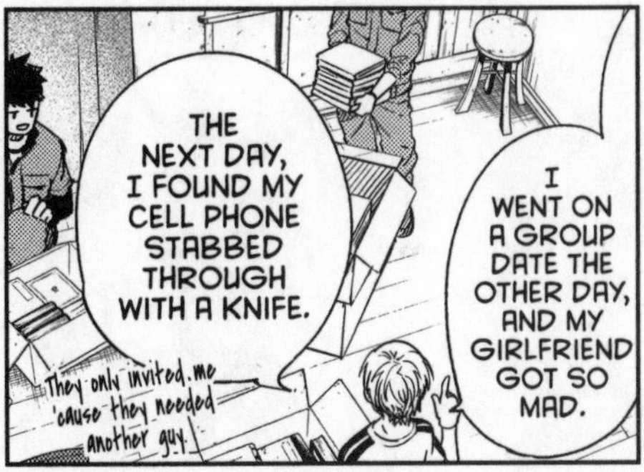
I WENT ON A GROUP DATE THE OTHER DAY, AND MY GIRLFRIEND GOT SO MAD.
THE NEXT DAY, I FOUND MY CELL PHONE STABBED THROUGH WITH A KNIFE.
They only invited me 'cause they needed another guy.

Group date, page 83
Specifically, Ishizaki attended a *gôkon*, which is roughly equivalent to a group date; it's a little get together with equal numbers boys and girls who may or may not have all known each other previously. The idea is for people to pair up and, in the perfect situation, become official couples.

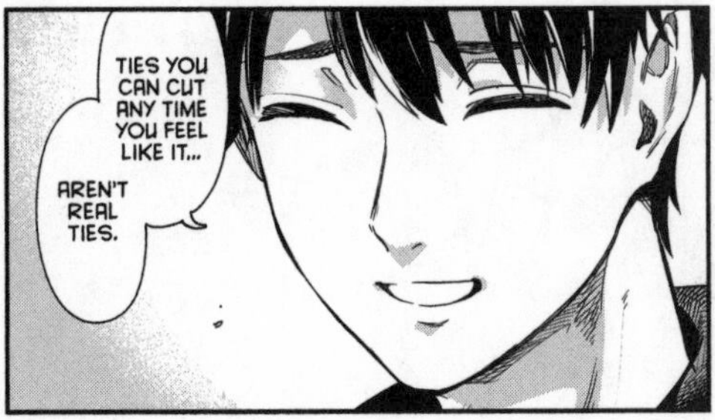
TIES YOU CAN CUT ANY TIME YOU FEEL LIKE IT...
AREN'T REAL TIES.

Cutting ties, page 88
The word "ties" is a translation of the Japanese *en*, which refers to ties, relationships, bonds, etc. The word is also closely connected to "fate," because even seemingly random encounters can have a profound effect on those involved.

***Horumonyaki*, page 91**

Horumonyaki is grilled *horumon*, which is a play on words from the Greek "hormone," meaning "stimulation," and the Japanese (Kansai dialect) *hôrumon*, meaning "discarded goods." It is made from the normally discarded parts of the animal—often beef, but usually pork. This particular *horumonyaki* place is called *Gyû Gyû*, which is onomatopoeia describing things being packed in tightly together. It's also a repetition of the word for "beef."

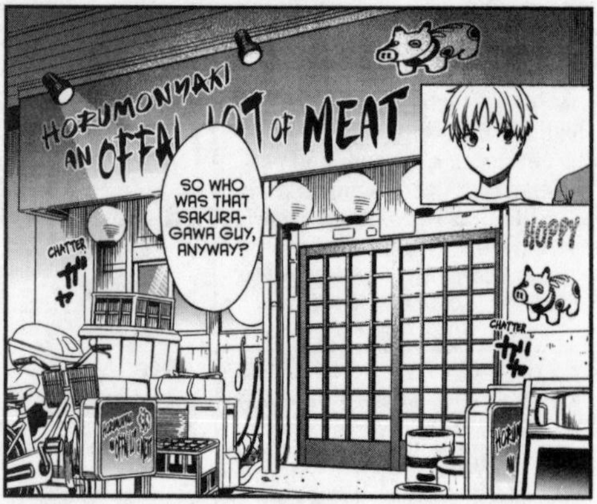
HORUMONYAKI
AN OFFAL LOT OF MEAT
SO WHO WAS THAT SAKURA-GAWA GUY, ANYWAY?
CHATTER
HOPPY
CHATTER

They serve Hoppy, which is a drink that is unique to Tokyo and was made as a substitute for beer, which was considered a luxury back when Hoppy was invented in 1948. It's mostly non-alcoholic, but is intended to be mixed with stronger (and cheaper) spirits.

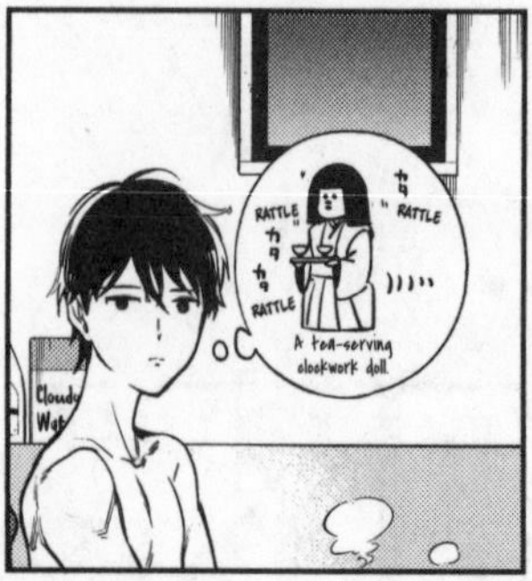
RATTLE
RATTLE
RATTLE
A tea-serving clockwork doll.

Tea-serving clockwork doll, page 102

Kurô compares Kotoko to a *zashiki karakuri ningyô*, which roughly translates to "guest-entertaining clockwork doll." These mechanical dolls were used to entertain guests. The tea-serving variety, imagined here by Kurô, would be set into motion when a teacup was placed on its tray. It would then walk forward to the guest, who would remove the teacup, thereby deactivating it. When the cup is replaced, the doll would turn around and return to the host.

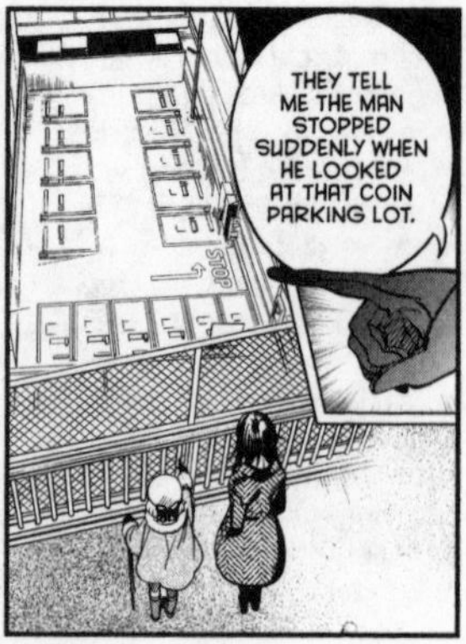
THEY TELL ME THE MAN STOPPED SUDDENLY WHEN HE LOOKED AT THAT COIN PARKING LOT.

Coin parking lot, pate 125

A coin parking lot is a lot where one pays to park in an entirely automated process. After a car is parked in the lot, a metal plate will rise from the parking spot, preventing the car from leaving its spot until the fee is paid at a machine.

Ticket machine, page 142
Many ramen shops in Japan have a ticket machine that resembles a vending machine. It displays all the different ramen options, and the customer can order and pay directly with the machine. When the order has been placed, the machine will give the customer a ticket, which they then hand to one of the restaurant staff.

Challenge
Ultra Spicy
Dandan Noodles
¥2000

YOU'VE BEEN WATCHING THIS SERIES AN AWFUL LOT LATELY.
The Yakuza Wives.
AS A YAKUZA WIFE MYSELF, I DECIDED I HAD BETTER LEARN THE ROPES.
?

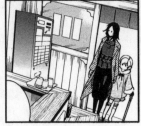

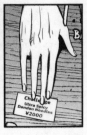

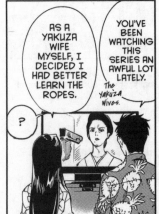

***The Yakuza Wives*, page 152**
The Yakuza Wives is a film series about the wife of a yakuza boss who takes over while her husband serves time in jail.

***The Tattooed Magistrate*, page 154**
The Tattooed Magistrate, or *Tôyama no Kin-san*, is a character based on the historical Tôyama Kagemoto. He appears in many movies and TV series, often working undercover to solve crimes. One of his most distinguishing features is the cherry tree tattooed on his shoulder. However, in Japan, tattoos (especially large tattoos) are commonly associated with organized crime, and sporting one such as seen here could easily cause some misunderstanding.

THE YUKI-ONNA'S NEXT OBSESSION WAS THE TATTOOED MAGISTRATE.
Gaaah! What is this?!
Oh!
It suits you, Masayuki!

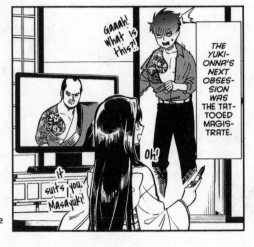

IN/SPECTRE

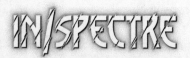

Young characters and steampunk setting, like *Howl's Moving Castle* and *Battle Angel Alita*

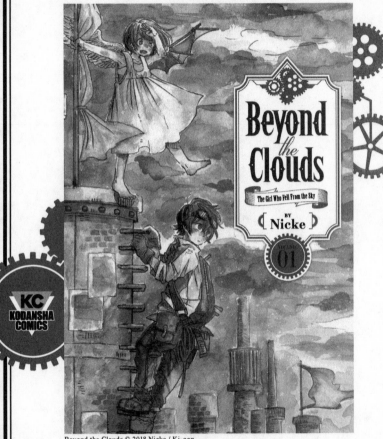

Beyond the Clouds © 2018 Nicke / Ki-oon

A boy with a talent for machines and a mysterious girl whose wings he's fixed will take you beyond the clouds! In the tradition of the high-flying, resonant adventure stories of Studio Ghibli comes a gorgeous tale about the longing of young hearts for adventure and friendship!

PERFECT WORLD

Rie Aruga

A TOUCHING NEW SERIES ABOUT LOVE AND COPING WITH DISABILITY

An office party reunites Tsugumi with her high school crush Itsuki. He's realized his dream of becoming an architect, but along the way, he experienced a spinal injury that put him in a wheelchair. Now Tsugumi's rekindled feelings will butt up against prejudices she never considered — and Itsuki will have to decide if he's ready to let someone into his heart...

"Depicts with great delicacy and courage the difficulties some with disabilities experience getting involved in romantic relationships... Rie Aruga refuses to romanticize, pushing her heroine to face the reality of disability. She invites her readers to the same tasks of empathy, knowledge and recognition."
—Slate.fr

"An important entry [in manga romance]... The emotional core of both plot and characters indicates thoughtfulness... [Aruga's] research is readily apparent in the text and artwork, making this feel like a real story."
—Anime News Network

KC
KODANSHA COMICS

The boys are back, in 400-page hardcovers that are as pretty and badass as they are!

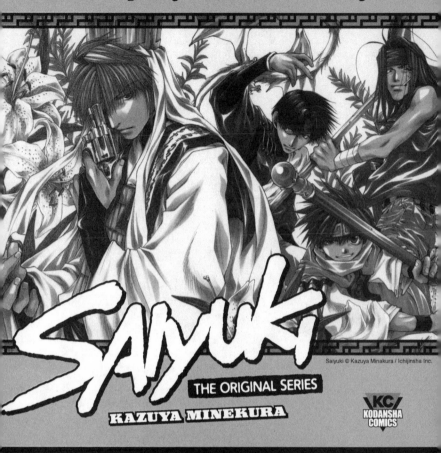

Saiyuki © Kazuya Minakura / Ichijinsha Inc.

SAIYUKI

THE ORIGINAL SERIES

KAZUYA MINEKURA

"AN EDGY COMIC LOOK AT AN ANCIENT CHINESE TALE." —YALSA

Genjo Sanzo is a Buddhist priest in the city of Togenkyo, which is being ravaged by yokai spirits that have fallen out of balance with the natural order. His superiors send him on a journey far to the west to discover why this is happening and how to stop it. His companions are three yokai with human souls. But this is no day trip — the four will encounter many discoveries and horrors on the way.

FEATURES NEW TRANSLATION, COLOR PAGES, AND BEAUTIFUL WRAPAROUND COVER ART!

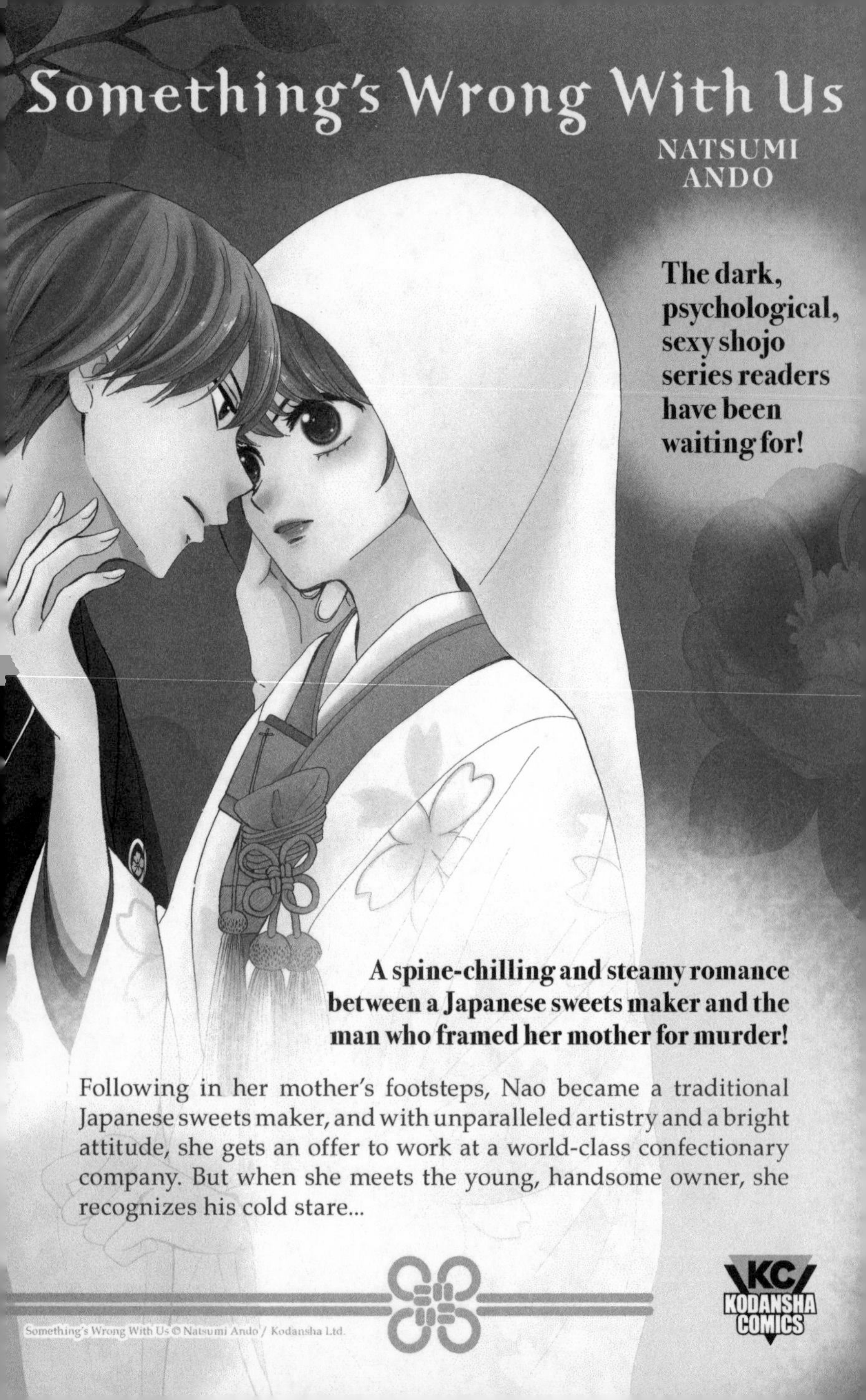
Something's Wrong With Us
NATSUMI ANDO
The dark, psychological, sexy shojo series readers have been waiting for!
A spine-chilling and steamy romance between a Japanese sweets maker and the man who framed her mother for murder!
Following in her mother's footsteps, Nao became a traditional Japanese sweets maker, and with unparalleled artistry and a bright attitude, she gets an offer to work at a world-class confectionary company. But when she meets the young, handsome owner, she recognizes his cold stare...
KC KODANSHA COMICS
Something's Wrong With Us © Natsumi Ando / Kodansha Ltd.

The adorable new odd-couple cat comedy manga from the creator of the beloved *Chi's Sweet Home*, in full color!

Sue & Tai-chan

Konami Kanata

Sue is an aging housecat who's looking forward to living out her life in peace... but her plans change when the mischievous black tomcat Tai-chan enters the picture! Hey! Sue never signed up to be a catsitter! *Sue & Tai-chan* is the latest from the reigning meow-narch of cute kitty comics, Konami Kanata.

THE SWEET SCENT OF LOVE IS IN THE AIR! FOR FANS OF OFFBEAT ROMANCES LIKE *WOTAKOI*

Sweat and Soap © Kintetsu Yamada / Kodansha Ltd.

In an office romance, there's a fine line between sexy and awkward... and that line is where Asako — a woman who sweats copiously — meets Koutarou — a perfume developer who can't get enough of Asako's, er, scent. Don't miss a romcom manga like no other!

Knight of the ICE

Yayoi Ogawa

SKATING THRILLS AND ICY CHILLS WITH THIS NEW TINGLY ROMANCE SERIES!

A rom-com on ice, perfect for fans of *Princess Jellyfish* and *Wotakoi*. Kokoro is the talk of the figure-skating world, winning trophies and hearts. But little do they know... he's actually a huge nerd! From the beloved creator of *You're My Pet* (*Tramps Like Us*).

Chitose is a serious young woman, working for the health magazine *SASSO*. Or at least, she would be, if she wasn't constantly getting distracted by her childhood friend, international figure skating star Kokoro Kijinami! In the public eye and on the ice, Kokoro is a gallant, flawless knight, but behind his glittery costumes and breathtaking spins lies a secret: He's actually a hopelessly romantic otaku, who can only land his quad jumps when Chitose is on hand to recite a spell from his favorite magical girl anime!

KC KODANSHA COMICS

A SMART, NEW ROMANTIC COMEDY FOR FANS OF *SHORTCAKE CAKE* AND *TERRACE HOUSE!*

LIVING ROOM

MATSUNAGA-SAN

Keiko Iwashita

A romance manga starring high school girl Meeko, who learns to live on her own in a boarding house whose living room is home to the odd (but handsome) Matsunaga-san. She begins to adjust to her new life away from her parents, but Meeko soon learns that no matter how far away from home she is, she's still a young girl at heart — especially when she finds herself falling for Matsunaga-san.

SAINT ☆ YOUNG MEN

A LONG AWAITED ARRIVAL IN PREMIUM 2-IN-1 HARDCOVER

After centuries of hard work, Jesus and Buddha take a break from their heavenly duties to relax among the people of Japan, and their adventures in this lighthearted buddy comedy are sure to bring mirth and merriment to all!

"Brilliant…the physical comedy and facial expressions will make you literally LOL."

—Sam Humphries
(host of *DC Daily*;
writer, *Green Lanterns*,
Legendary Star-Lord)

One of CLAMP's biggest hits returns
in this definitive, premium, hardcover
20th anniversary collector's edition!

Poor college student Hideki is down on his luck. All he wants is a good job, a girlfriend, and his very own "persocom"—the latest and greatest in humanoid computer technology. Hideki's luck changes one night when he finds Chi—a persocom thrown out in a pile of trash. But Hideki soon discovers that there's much more to his cute new persocom than meets the eye.

KC
KODANSHA
COMICS

THE WORLD OF CLAMP!

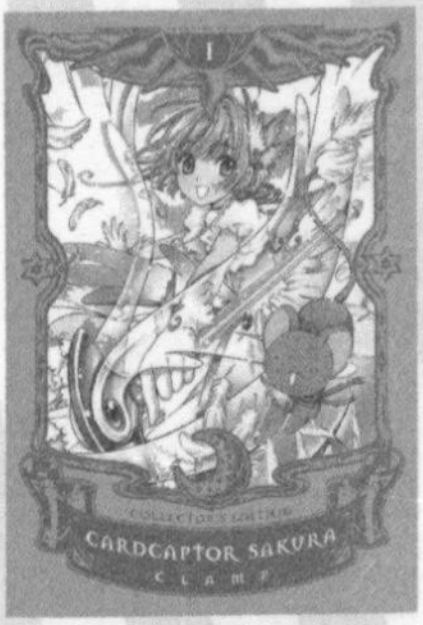
1
CARDCAPTOR SAKURA
CLAMP

Cardcaptor Sakura Collector's Edition

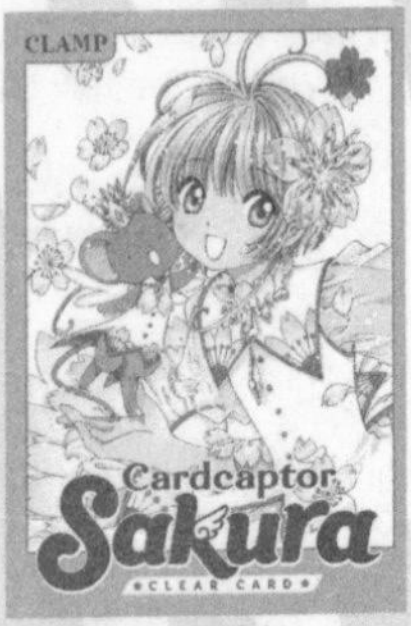
CLAMP
Cardcaptor Sakura
CLEAR CARD

Cardcaptor Sakura: Clear Card

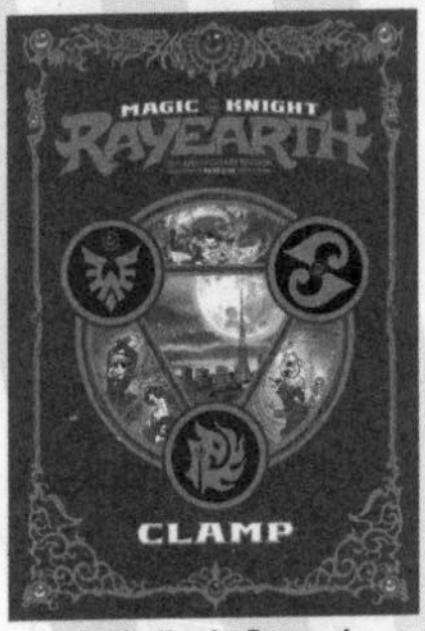
MAGIC KNIGHT
RAYEARTH
CLAMP

Magic Knight Rayearth 25th Anniversary Box Set

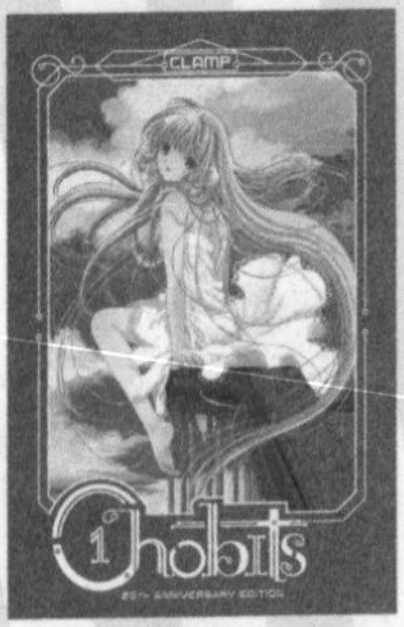
CLAMP
1 Chobits

Chobits

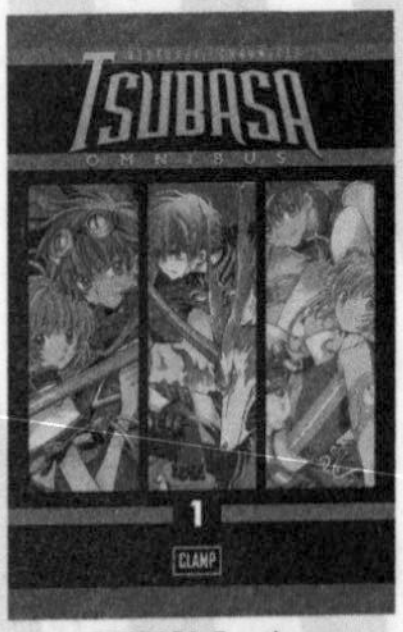
TSUBASA
OMNIBUS
1
CLAMP

TSUBASA Omnibus

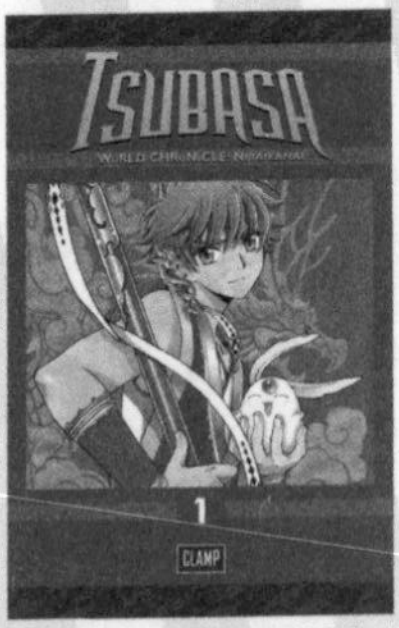
TSUBASA
1
CLAMP

TSUBASA WoRLD CHRoNiCLE

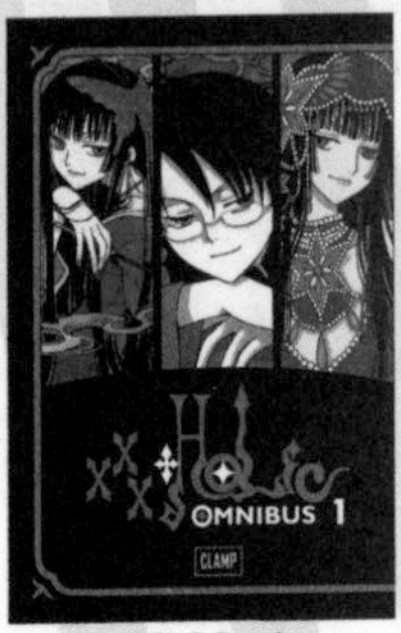
xxxHOLiC
OMNIBUS 1
CLAMP

xxxHOLiC Omnibus

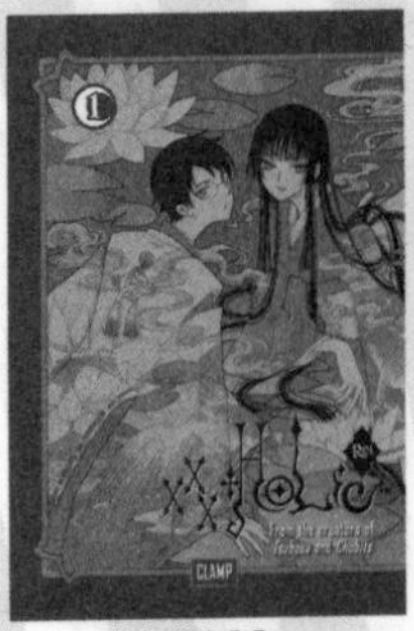
1
xxxHOLiC
CLAMP

xxxHOLiC Rei

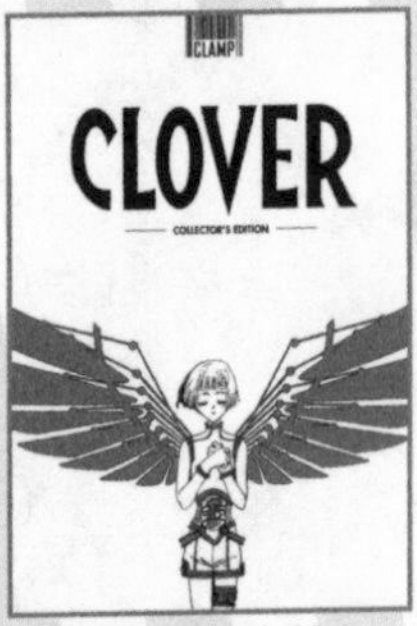
CLAMP
CLOVER
COLLECTOR'S EDITION

CLOVER Collector's Edition

KC KODANSHA COMICS

Kodansha Comics welcomes you to explore the expansive world of CLAMP, the all-female artist collective that has produced some of the most acclaimed manga of the century. Our growing catalog includes icons like *Cardcaptor Sakura* and *Magic Knight Rayearth*, each crafted with CLAMP's one-of-a-kind style and characters!

A Kodansha Comics Trade Paperback Original

In/Spectre 13 copyright © 2020 Kyo Shirodaira/Chashiba Katase
English translation copyright © 2021 Kyo Shirodaira/Chashiba Katase

Published in the United States by Kodansha Comics, an imprint of
Kodansha USA Publishing, LLC, New York.

Publication rights for this English edition arranged through
Kodansha Ltd., Tokyo.

First published in Japan in 2020 by Kodansha Ltd., Tokyo
as Kyokou Suiri, volume 13.

ISBN 978-1-64651-157-0

Original cover design by Takashi Shimoyama and Mami Fukunaga (RedRooster)

Printed in the United States of America.

www.kodanshacomics.com

9 8 7 6 5 4 3 2 1
Translation: Alethea Nibley & Athena Nibley
Lettering: Lys Blakeslee
Editing: Vanessa Tenazas
Kodansha Comics edition cover design by Phil Balsman

Publisher: Kiichiro Sugaw

Director of publishing services: E
Associate director of operations: Step
Publishing services managing editor: Noelle We
Assistant production manager: Emi Lotto, Angela Zurlo